How Parents Deal wit
on the Autism Spectru

STUDIES IN INCLUSIVE EDUCATION
Volume 26

Scope

This series addresses the many different forms of exclusion that occur in schooling across a range of international contexts and considers strategies for increasing the inclusion and success of all students. In many school jurisdictions the most reliable predictors of educational failure include poverty, Aboriginality and disability. Traditionally schools have not been pressed to deal with exclusion and failure. Failing students were blamed for their lack of attainment and were either placed in segregated educational settings or encouraged to leave and enter the unskilled labour market. The crisis in the labor market and the call by parents for the inclusion of their children in their neighborhood school has made visible the failure of schools to include all children.

Drawing from a range of researchers and educators from around the world, Studies in Inclusive Education will demonstrate the ways in which schools contribute to the failure of different student identities on the basis of gender, race, language, sexuality, disability, socio-economic status and geographic isolation. This series differs from existing work in inclusive education by expanding the focus from a narrow consideration of what has been traditionally referred to as special educational needs to understand school failure and exclusion in all its forms. Moreover, the series will consider exclusion and inclusion across all sectors of education: early years, elementary and secondary schooling, and higher education.

How Parents Deal with the Education of Their Child on the Autism Spectrum

The Stories and Research They Don't and Won't Tell You

Jasmine McDonald
Telethon Kids Institute, The University of Western Australia, Perth, Australia

SENSE PUBLISHERS
ROTTERDAM/BOSTON/TAIPEI

A C.I.P. record for this book is available from the Library of Congress.

ISBN: 978-94-6209-780-3 (paperback)
ISBN: 978-94-6209-781-0 (hardback)
ISBN: 978-94-6209-782-7 (e-book)

Published by: Sense Publishers,
P.O. Box 21858,
3001 AW Rotterdam,
The Netherlands
https://www.sensepublishers.com/

Printed on acid-free paper

NIHIL DE NOBIS, SINE NOBIS

(Nothing About Us, Without Us)*

*A slogan used to communicate the idea that no policy should be decided by any representative without the full and direct participation of members of the group(s) affected by that policy.

TABLE OF CONTENTS

FOREWORD

As Jasmine McDonald declares in the opening of this book, *How Parents Deal with the Education of their Child on the Autism Spectrum,* the dramatic increase in the incidence of children with Autism Spectrum Disorders has not been matched by growth and improvement of support for these families. Given the volume and intensity of official declarations on the education rights of people with disabilities from governments, peak international organisations such as the United Nations and the OECD, and education jurisdictions globally, we ought to be able to expect more.

The Disability Standards for Education were foreshadowed in the Disability Discrimination Act (1992) and were enacted in August 2005. The recent *Report on the Review of the Disability Standards for Education 2005 (DEEWR, 2012)* published in June 2012 by the Department for Education, Employment and Workplace Relations highlights serious shortcomings in their implementation across state and territory jurisdictions. That same year the Victorian Equal Opportunity and Human Rights Commission (2012) released *Held Back,* a report based on extensive research it had commissioned to investigate the experiences of children with disabilities in Victorian schools. On the basis of a survey completed and returned by 883 educators, 617 parents and carers and 60 students the researchers reported that the educational experiences of children with disabilities are not consistent, that discrimination exists and that not all children with disabilities are eligible for support to enable them to access the curriculum as is required by the Disability Discrimination Act (1992).

Notwithstanding this evidence of exclusion as an established feature of our education landscape there remains little public acknowledgement of this fact. *The Sydney Morning Herald* (May 15th, 2013) reported on then Prime Minister Julia Gillard choking back tears as she spoke to the final reading of the Bill before parliament to enact the National Disability Insurance Scheme. According to Prime Minister Gillard, " *... there will be no more 'in principle' and no more 'when circumstances permit'. There will be launches not trials, permanent care not temporary help ... there will be no turning back.*" Education policies on inclusive education, taking their lead from disability discrimination legislation, do apply caveats of conditionality. Education for children with disabilities in this country, as is certainly the case elsewhere, remains contingent. Parents and carers are at the mercy of systems that have a highly variable track record when it comes to including students with disabilities.

This book draws on empirical research in Western Australia to demonstrate the reluctance of an education jurisdiction to include the voice of parents of children on the autistic spectrum in decisions about their children's education. This is not an isolated occurrence. We have accepted as an article of faith in education that we are in a partnership with parents to educate their children. Too frequently there is a variance of contract for parents of children with disabilities. *How Parents Deal*

CHAPTER 1

WHO HAS THE RIGHT TO SPEAK?

INTRODUCTION

There has been a worldwide explosion of children being diagnosed on the autism spectrum over the past twenty years (Fombonne, 2009). Recent figures in Australia indicate that at least 1 in a 100 individuals has a confirmed diagnosis of an autism spectrum disorder (ASD) with rates acknowledged to be on the rise (Aspect, 2012; Australian Advisory Board on Autism Spectrum Disorders, 2011; Buckley, 2009, 2012). However, these figures belie the fact that many Australian parents find it difficult to gain an accurate and timely diagnosis for their child that will allow them to gain much needed, funded intervention at the earliest opportunity (McDonald, 2010; Valentine, Rajkovic, Dinning, & Thompson, 2010).

Powerful moral, social justice and political arguments have convinced parents that it is their democratic right to place their children into mainstream educational environments so that their children may eventually take up their rightful place in a mainstream adult life (Oliver, 1990, 1996; Oliver & Barnes, 2010; Slee, 2011). But what is really happening for some of these parents when they try to gain and maintain an appropriate education for their child on the autism spectrum in these mainstream contexts and beyond? What is the educational experience like for these families who are in the midst of this generational change from historical exclusion to inclusion?

Current research indicates that while islands of excellent mainstream inclusive practice do exist (Cologon, 2013; McDonald, 2010; Morewood, Humphrey & Symes, 2011) the educational experience for many students on the autism spectrum can often be one of hostility, inconsistency and unreliability (Harrington, Foster, Rodger & Ashburner, 2013; Cologon, 2013; Humphrey & Lewis, 2008a, 2008b; Humphrey & Symes, 2010; MacDermott, 2008; McDonald, 2010; Roberts, 2013). Without appropriate training in best practice educational methods, these students can present an inordinate educational challenge to both parents and educators alike. To begin with, each student on the autism spectrum has their own unique, idiosyncratic profile with distinctive difficulties found in the common areas of communication, socialization, restricted and repetitive behaviour and sensory processing (American Psychiatric Association, 2013b; Australian Autism Education and Training Consortium (AAETC), 2008a, 2008b). Additionally, these students frequently have problems with theory of mind skills and executive function. They also often experience weak central coherence and motor functioning problems (AAETC, 2008a, 2008b). Such students may also have a number of relative cognitive strengths in the areas of rote memory, visual spatial abilities, compartmentalized learning, preference for routine and rules, intense interests and being logical (AAETC, 2008a, 2008b).

How do parents and educators deal with such complex educational profiles? How do they continue to maximize these students' development over time? What are the barriers that hinder their quest? What are the facilitators that help their quest? To answer these questions, this book provides an in-depth, recent examination of the real life journeys of six families who attempted to gain an appropriate education for their children on the autism spectrum over a five year period in a West Australian metropolitan setting. It provides a 'grass-roots', parental view of the issues involved with their child's diagnosis, early intervention, mainstream schooling, home education and segregated schooling. It also describes the processes and strategies that parents used to overcome some of the difficulties they encountered trying to maximize their children's educational potential in both mainstream and other educational contexts.

Many publications regarding education of students on the autism spectrum are written from the perspective of the educational professional and researcher. Research often concentrates on what is needed to promote the practice of inclusivity in mainstream contexts (Frederickson, Jones and Lang, 2010; Jordan, 2005; Leach and Duffy, 2009; Morewood et al., 2011; Parsons, Guldberg, MacLeod, Jones, Prunty & Balfe, 2011; Ravet, 2011; Roberts, 2013). While these publications are imperative and highly useful, there is relatively little published about the actual experience of education from the perspective of parents of children on the autism spectrum and how such parents deal with this process over time. This publication seeks to address this gap. The book reveals how parents initially broaden their view of 'education' in relation to their unusual children and how such meanings drive their decision making regarding the best ways to maximize their children's ultimate and unique life potential. It also shows how such parents often continually strategize solutions to gain, maintain and create educational fit to maximize their children's educational potential.

The parent voice is featured throughout this publication to explain the often complex processes undertaken by them. This publication has been written in the hope that it will potentially benefit parents who may be struggling to gain and maintain an appropriate education for their child on the autism spectrum in mainstream and other educational contexts. It provides an understanding of the processes undertaken by these parents from pre-diagnosis to the final years of their child's formal schooling and immediately beyond. Parents will be better placed to make informed decisions about the realities of the different educational contexts that potentially exist for their children inclusive of home education and segregated schooling sites (education support schools). The book also shows ways that families have strengthened their overall well-being over the course of the educational journey by gaining appropriate early intervention and timely support for all family members not just the child on the autism spectrum.

Additionally, this publication is potentially of benefit to researchers, policy makers, educators and health professionals who may regularly deal with families who have a child on the autism spectrum. It provides an understanding and explanation of the cumulative effect of the ongoing difficulties such families often face trying to access an appropriate education for their child on the autism spectrum over time. The book will provide professionals with a deeper and more realistic understanding of the collective pressures these families often endure over many years. It also explains why it is important that appropriate and timely support be gained for not only the child on the autism spectrum but other family members at the earliest opportunity to ensure the overall well-being and stability of the family across time.

While the stories captured are taken from a recent Western Australian (WA) context, current research indicates these issues have broad relevance for parents and professionals in most developed Western nations who regularly deal with the education of children on the autism spectrum (Eldar, Talmor & Wolf-Zukerman, 2010; Humphrey & Lewis, 2008a, 2008b; Humphrey & Symes, 2010; Lynch & Irvine, 2009; MacDermott, 2008; McDonald, 2010; McDonald & Lopes, 2012; Parsons et al., 2011; Ravet, 2011).

WHO HAS THE RIGHT TO SPEAK?

Common sense would dictate that parents of children on the autism spectrum should have the fundamental right to speak and be heard about their own child's educational welfare but research informs us that their views are often discounted. Many parents have historically been seen as peripheral to their child's education and in some cases they have been viewed as obstacles or even adversaries (Hardman, Drew, & Egan, 1995; Turnbull & Turnbull, 2001). It has been found that less than optimal levels of cooperation can often emerge between parents and the education system and this can affect the overall efficacy of service delivery and eventual well-being of those being served (Lake & Billingsley, 2000). Much of the research conducted has examined parent-professional interaction from the perspective of the education community with limited studies being undertaken from the parent perspective (Stoner, Bock, Thompson, Angell, Heyl, & Crowley, 2005). Limited research from a parental perspective has identified such issues as: difficulty obtaining services, inadequate service delivery, and lack of collaboration as key parental concerns (Dunlap, Robbins, & Darrow, 1994; Kohler, 1999, MacDermott, 2008; McDonald, 2010).

Research has also found that the process of educators engaging with parents of children on the autism spectrum is an integral component towards the achievement of teacher-parent efficacy in the 'inclusive' classroom (Ferraro, 2008). An Australian review of early intervention ASD research has further shown the importance of parents by stating that parents "play a critical role in supporting their children's learning" (Roberts & Prior, 2006, p. 74). Research also indicates that parents can often drive the decision making process and regularly take a primary role in delivering intervention (Feinberg & Vacca, 2000; Lord & McGee, 2001; Roberts

& Prior, 2006). This allows all key stakeholders to be part of the decision-making process and often leads to improved learning outcomes for the child on the autism spectrum (Roberts & Prior, 2006). Interaction with parents also helps the education team to more easily transition a child from one education environment to another; identify the child's strengths and interests; to develop student-centred plans and provides joint problem solving opportunities when difficulties arise (AAETC, 2008a, 2008b; Stoner, Angell, House & Bock, 2007).

For these reasons and over many years, regular schools in Australia have been encouraged to engage parents in active communications, however, such interactions do not typically occur as state policy directives require (Stanley, Beamish, & Bryer, 2005, MacDermott, 2008; McDonald, 2010). Given that many parents of children on the autism spectrum spend many years researching their child's circumstances (MacDermott, 2008; McDonald, 2010; Stoner et al., 2005), they often feel justified in their expectation that they will be included in discussions and decision-making regarding their child's specific educational situation. The importance of this element is further confirmed in Western Australian research by MacDermott (2008) who investigated the views of 92 local families who had school-aged children with a suspected or confirmed ASD. MacDermott (2008) found:

> One of the 'loudest' points to come out of this study's findings was the need by families to be heard and for their experiences, expertise and opinions to be accepted as important and equal in the care and development of their children … It is essential that the professionals and service providers working with families listen, hear what is being said, and engage with parents in a respectful and collaborative process to not only maximize the day-to-day functioning of these families and their children but also to enable them to thrive and weave their unique voices into the fabric of their surrounding communities (pp. 7-8).

Unfortunately, Australia does not presently have an equivalent to the U.S. 1997 amendment to the Individuals with Disabilities Education Act (IDEA), which mandates that parents of children with disabilities have the legal right to be involved in all aspects of their children's education. On this point, MacDermott (2008) states that:

> families / carers need to be recognized as having unique and specific information regarding their child's strengths, challenges and learning styles and provided with opportunities to be ongoing collaborative partners in designing and implementing intervention / educational programs (p. 9).

The positive value of parental involvement in the educative process cannot be understated or underestimated and is supported throughout the research literature but engagement with parents is often lacking throughout schooling communities (Ferraro, 2008; MacDermott, 2008; McDonald, 2010; Stoner & Angell, 2006; Stoner et al., 2005). This is the case even though parents are a constant in the lives of their children on the autism spectrum and as such have the ability to provide a rich, on-going account of what works best for their offspring when engaging with education professionals (Ferraro, 2008; O'Brien & Daggett, 2006). Not surprisingly, it has been found that parental involvement, parent-efficacy and satisfaction with the education process of children on the autism spectrum is closely related to the cognitive, behavioural and social development of their children (Ferraro, 2008). However, this parental involvement needs to be part of a collaborative process with school-wide commitment among parents, educators, students, community, and policy makers towards long-term outcomes (Ferraro, 2008).

However this collaborative process is often not easy to establish or maintain. Research by Stoner et al. (2005) revealed that over time parents' trust in recognized experts often diminishes while parents' trust in their own instincts is reinforced. Stoner et al. (2005) explain how:

> The struggle for a diagnosis initiated a pattern of persistent behaviour, and a sense of distrust (in the parents) with medical professionals, which continued and influenced parent interactions with education professionals (pp. 41- 42).

Parents of children on the autism spectrum often need to take on a variety of roles when interacting with their child's school and such interactions are mediated by trust. Stoner and Angell (2006) indicate that:

> Parent participants, especially mothers, consistently engaged in four roles: (a) negotiator, (b) monitor, (c) supporter, and (d) advocate. In addition, the degree of perceived parental trust in education professionals affected the extent of their engagement in the roles of negotiator, monitor and supporter. The data also indicated that parents' education monitoring was mediated by the trust the parents placed in the education professionals (p. 177).

Research shows that most mothers adopt an enhanced advocacy role for their child on the autism spectrum and in some cases demonstrate an activist role and extend their efforts towards campaigning for change outside of their own families (Ryan & Cole, 2009). It is within this space that this book is written. As a fellow parent of an adult son on the autism spectrum, I have felt for some time that the voices of parents and other family members have not been heard loudly or considered seriously enough by the external world especially in the area of education. This began my journey into further study and research which has now culminated in the publication of this book.

WHY WRITE THIS BOOK?

When considering the reasons for undertaking the present publication, I recalled one tragic Australian case which illustrates the sometimes, extreme pressures associated with parenting a child on the autism spectrum. In 2003, a desperate Australian mother suffocated her ten-year old son who was diagnosed with severe autism and then attempted suicide. After her son's death, a news article commented that she had despaired about her son's future and that her existence had grown unbearable

(Lamont, 2004, June 1). At the same time as caring for her child 24 hours a day, she was losing countless battles trying to gain better services and more specialist support for her son. Her marriage was ending and her father had died only a few weeks before. In her misery and confusion, she believed her son could not cope without her. The New South Wales Deputy State Coroner cited depression and lack of appropriate services as the main reasons for her despair. He cautioned that unless services improved for families with disabled children, especially those children on the autism spectrum, there was a strong possibility that this tragedy could happen again (Cummings, 2006, October 14).

I remember relating closely to this tragic case because of my own family's situation. Discrimination, lack of understanding and support had permeated my own family's life since the birth of my son on the spectrum and I knew how excruciatingly difficult life could be at different points in time. At the beginning of my journey with my son I would have appreciated greatly an understanding of the ways other parents negotiated the lengthy, often inordinately difficult, education process of their child on the autism spectrum. However, such information was not readily available some twenty years ago. For some time, there has been a call for disability research to give more consideration to the 'authentic voices' of those in the field inclusive of parents, disabled students and their advocates (Simpson, 2005; Slee, 1996). This call is embedded in the understanding that:

> discourses are about what can be said and thought, but also about who can speak, when, where and with what authority (Ball, 1994, p. 21).

With a teaching background in secondary, tertiary and home education and experience educating my own son on the autism spectrum over two decades, I felt well-placed to 'speak' and do research investigating how parents deal with the education of their child on the autism spectrum over time. I also knew that there were an ever-increasing number of families who had a family member diagnosed on the autism spectrum who may need such parental insight regarding the educational journey. I was cognizant that all of these families would eventually need to navigate an acceptable educational pathway for their children in order to maximize their child's progress.

Surprisingly, my background as an educator had not greatly prepared me for the significant difficulties that lay ahead when parenting and teaching my son. In response, I embarked on a search for appropriate ways to maximize his progress in order to help not only him, but the rest of my family as well. I reasoned that if he gained skill and became more independent it would make things much easier for us all. This eventually led me down a pathway to further study.

In my studies I came across research that confirmed that the impact on families who have a child on the autism spectrum could be extremely high where parents were more likely to experience serious psychological distress than parents of children with other developmental disabilities (Benson & Karlof, 2009; Bromley, Hare, Davidson, & Emerson, 2004; Sanders & Morgan, 1997; Sivberg, 2002). Early research had also indicated that this stress could be potentially reduced over time in inverse proportion to the success of the education of the child on the autism spectrum (Robbins, Dunlap, & Plienis, 1991). This had been borne out in my own family's experiences. We found that as our son gradually gained skill in negotiating the world and became more independent our own stress levels reduced slowly but significantly over time. It became obvious that an appropriate and effective education for our son was a key factor in the survival of all members of our family.

I had also witnessed similar, gradual improvements in the lives of other families in the autism community who had access to appropriate and timely educational intervention for their child on the autism spectrum. I had noted that the eventual progress of such children was not only determined by the amount and quality of evidence-based intervention that parents were able to gain for their child, but factors such as support, family resources, severity and complexity of impairment also seemed to be important. Sadly, I had also seen how some parents were unable to put in the time, energy and targeted intervention necessary to maximize their child's progress because of lack of appropriate support and services and the complexity of their family's circumstances. These children often became more difficult to deal with as they grew in physical maturity. Without appropriate intervention, the stress experienced by such families often increased over time with sometimes devastating results for all family members.

The complexity inherent in writing a book about how parents deal with the education of their child on the autism spectrum over time was daunting. For a start, the nature of the disorder is highly idiosyncratic and each child manifests their autism differently. This makes educating individuals on the autism spectrum a very difficult task for both parents and professionals alike. I had experienced and witnessed how we, as parents, often struggled to ensure that our child's needs were being reliably met over the course of their educational journey. For some time research has indicated that there was no single best-suited and universally effective educational method for all children on the autism spectrum over time (National Research Council, 2001; Parsons et al., 2011). The best programs are those that incorporate a variety of objectively verified practices and are designed to address and support the needs of individual students, the professionals and families with whom they are linked (National Research Council, 2001; Olley, 1999; Parsons et al. 2011; Simpson, 2005, 2007; Simpson & LaCava, 2007).

This placed us all, parents and professionals alike, in very demanding circumstances regarding adoption of appropriate and effective educational practices for individual children on the autism spectrum. Consequently, there has been a longstanding tradition by some parents of children on the autism spectrum of accepting educational and supplementary strategies that sometimes lack efficacy and proven utility (Francis, 2005; Gresham, Beebe-Frankenberger, & MacMillan, 1999; Heflin & Simpson, 1998). As parents, we have not had access to educational research of specific profiles of students on the autism spectrum which meets rigorous peer review and has a history of yielding positive results (Simpson, 2004) especially in the latter years of schooling (Parsons et al., 2011). The difficulty is that there are only limited samples of students on the autism spectrum with similar characteristics because of the highly idiosyncratic nature and progress of the disorder (Parsons et al., 2011; Simpson, 2005).

Additionally, there appears to be no apparent correlation among the severity of difficulty experienced by individuals on the spectrum in one area of their profile to that experienced in another area. This variability and lack of apparent correlation among areas of difficulty is only now being investigated and understood through recent research (Happe, 2009).

I have also witnessed how some children on the autism spectrum have a superior skill or hyper-focus in one or more areas that can be used to improve their educational, recreational and career prospects (Grandin & Duffy, 2004; Howlin, 2009; Sonne, 2009a, 2009b). Research is only now beginning to provide understandings of the many different ways autism can present itself in an individual with superior splinter skills sometimes being part of the profile (Grandin & Duffy, 2004; Sonne, 2009a). In line with this, there has been a call by some in the autism community to change our understanding of Autism Spectrum Disorders (ASDs) to include the notion of "diff-ability", focusing on difference rather than impairment (Lawson, 2009). Some parents and individuals on the spectrum have also called for autism to be viewed as a 'condition' rather than a deficit, disorder or disability (Lawson, 2009).

Recent research confirms that adults on the autism spectrum are significantly disadvantaged regarding employment, social relationships, physical and mental health and quality of life (Aspect, 2012; Howlin & Moss, 2012). There is an urgent call for more to be done to understand the trajectories of development over the lifespan of an individual on the autism spectrum, from childhood through to the adult years, to determine what factors influence prognosis to ensure a better future (Howlin & Moss, 2012). In a preliminary way this publication seeks to answer such a call.

THE VOICES OF PARENTS

I have therefore done research and subsequently written this book highlighting the parent voice in response to these calls to help unravel some of the complexity associated with the education process of children on the spectrum over time. For it is my belief that if we are all more knowledgeable about the education process from the outset we can make better, informed decisions and thereby give our children on the spectrum and the rest of the family the best chance to maximize their emotional well-being and life potential.

To capture the voices of parents currently in the field I investigated the educational experiences of six diverse families who all had children diagnosed on the autism spectrum over a five year period from 2005 to 2010 in a metropolitan West Australian context (McDonald, 2010). As is recommended in such qualitative, grounded theory studies, diversity of family profile was built into the mix of families chosen to be included in the study. Constant comparative (Charmaz, 2000) and autoethnographic (Ellis, 2009) research methodologies were chosen and used to compare different parents' views, situations, actions, accounts, experiences and documentation. This allowed a number of diverse parent voices to be heard and their situations to be investigated over an extended period of time. The seven children in the six families had various diagnoses on the autism spectrum resulting in assorted, idiosyncratic profiles. All were male reflecting the disproportionate numbers of males diagnosed on the autism spectrum as compared to their female counterparts (University of California, 2009). The basis for data collection was semi-structured interviews, participant observation, informal interviews and documentary data sources consistent with the interpretivist qualitative research tradition. Data analysis occurred concurrently with data collection and incorporated open coding, focused coding and member checking that led to generation and confirmation of propositions of a constructivist grounded theory (Charmaz, 2006).

I was interested in capturing the similarities and differences of each family's individual educational trajectories and what processes they undertook to deal with their diverse situations. The ages of the children involved in the study ranged from 4 to 16 years of age at the beginning of the study. By the end of the study the youngest child was 9 and the eldest was 21 years of age. This incorporated investigating and following these families and their children through diagnosis, early intervention, primary, secondary and tertiary education incorporating mainstream (public and private), segregated (public), home education and work contexts.

The background of the families involved in the study included Italian, Greek, Indian, Australian and Irish heritages. All families in the study nominated the mother as the driving force behind the education process and as such she became the main source of information gained for the study. The geographic location of the families was varied across the Perth metropolitan area.

Perth is the capital and largest city of the Australian state of Western Australia. It is the fourth most populous city in Australia, with an estimated population of 1.9 million. The families in the study came from low to upper middle class socio-economic backgrounds, with parents' educational background ranging from secondary schooling to post-graduate education. Two of the families were single parent families. The families chosen all had other children apart from their child or children on the autism spectrum. As research attests, many of these other children also had complex educational issues of their own which further complicated the task for these parents (Bailey, Palferman, Heavey & Le Couteur, 1998). Pseudonyms have been used throughout this book and information used has been de-identified to protect the identity of these families.

CURRENT RESEARCH ON INCLUSION

There has been an increasing development of inclusive practice regarding accommodation of students on the autism spectrum over the past two decades

(Frederickson et al., 2010; Jordan, 2005; Laluvein, J. 2010; Leach and Duffy, 2009; Lynch & Irvine, 2009; Morewood et al., 2011; Ravet, 2011). For the purposes of this publication, the elusive notion of 'inclusion' refers to:

> A unified system of public education that incorporates all children and youths as active, fully participating members of the school community; that views diversity as the norm; and that ensures a high-quality education for each student by providing meaningful curriculum, effective teaching, and necessary supports for each student (Lynch & Irvine, 2009, p.286).

This increase in the development of inclusive practice has been in response to powerful moral, social justice and political arguments that have for some time asserted that positive attitudes towards individuals with disabilities are developed when children with disabilities and their typically developing peers interact at school and these attitudes are sustained in adult life (Cologon, 2013; Oliver, 1996; Fuchs and Fuchs, 1994). Further to this, there is an increasing imperative that schools be an agent of change, provide an education in democracy and be a model for social improvement (Slee, 2011).

However, research has also shown that students with intellectual disabilities, including those on the autism spectrum, often cannot access reliable and consistent mainstream inclusive practice that maximizes their progress over time (Cologon, 2013; Crosby, 1998; Ford, 2007; Forlin, Keen & Barrett, 2008; Humphrey & Lewis, 2008a, 2008b; Humphrey & Symes, 2010; MacDermott, 2008; McDonald, 2010; Shaddock, 2005; Shaddock, Smyth King and Giorcelli, 2007; Wing, 2007). Concerns have been raised about the lack of appropriate, individualized attention and support available, the high attrition rates and the inordinate degree of bullying experienced by students on the autism spectrum in mainstream settings (Attwood, 2007; Harrington et al., 2013; Heinrichs, 2003; Humphrey & Lewis, 2008b; Humphrey & Symes, 2010; Lynch & Irvine, 2009; MacDermott, 2008; McDonald, 2010; Roberts, 2013; Rosendorff, 2007). Additionally, such students often experience social isolation, anxiety and sensory difficulties in mainstream settings where their need for routine and predictability is often at odds with the chaotic, noisy happenings of mainstream school life, especially at the high school level (Humphrey & Lewis, 2008a; Symes and Humphrey, 2010; Wing, 2007).

Among children with disabilities, students on the autism spectrum have been reported to have some of the most complex profiles to deal with in mainstream settings (Leach and Duffy, 2009). Research has also found that those who parent such children, especially mothers, are potentially at greater risk for mental health problems than any other parent group who have a child with a disability (Allen, Bowles, & Weber, 2013; Benson and Karloff, 2009; Tehee, Honan and Hevey, 2009). In response to these difficulties, some parents have been compelled to seek other educational pathways, such as segregated schooling sites and home schooling for their children on the autism spectrum (Attwood, 2007; Kidd and Kaczmarek, 2010; McDonald, 2010; McDonald & Lopes, 2012).

AN INTEGRATED SYNTHESIS OF SIX FAMILIES' JOURNEYS

To help the reader understand the essence of the central process adopted by the six families investigated and reported in this publication, I adopt Strauss & Corbin's (1998) suggestion of writing an integrated storyline that explicates both the central idea, and the other concepts and categories that relate to it. Following this, a diagrammatic representation of the full theory is included showing the four stages of the grounded theory (McDonald, 2010). Full development of the theory and its associated diagrammatic representation is provided in later chapters to follow:

Before their child is born, parents imagine a wonderful future and ideal scenarios often abound in their minds. When their child finally arrives and is significantly different from their dream vision, parents struggle to match their internal, idealized scenario with the reality of parenting such a child. After experiencing often, inordinate difficulties with their child's behaviour, parents feel increasingly worried about their child. The atypical behaviour of the child continually sets off alarm bells in their minds. Parents recognize early in their children's lives that the external world will not necessarily welcome, accommodate or be supportive of such different children. In response to this, parents set about gaining an appropriate education for their unusual child to help maximize their progress and increase their independence and skill levels in all areas.

Within the family, the child frequently becomes the centre of attention because of the inordinate difficulties associated with their behaviour. The lives of others in the family often become subsumed under the demanding needs of this unusual child. Sometimes, parents are able to register almost from the beginning that there is something very different about the development of their child in relation to other children. In contrast to this, some parents do not notice any significant differences until sometime later when their child loses previously held skills and regresses into their own world. Still other parents notice worrying differences but interpret them as a positive sign of the child being of superior intellect, and are encouraged by others to believe that they are raising a little genius. Parents often feel driven to share their fears about their child with trusted and qualified others. Unfortunately, they are often told their worries are unjustified and mainly based on their own parental inexperience.

As difficulties persist, most parents feel compelled to research their situation through various informal and formal sources. Through researching, parents gradually gain more awareness and trust in their own estimation of the unfolding situation; however, this is often juxtaposed against variable negative feelings regarding the difficulties of everyday life and the possible future consequences of a diagnosis of an autism spectrum disorder. After researching their situation for some time, parents often seek an accurate diagnosis in earnest for their child. Parents initially expect that a diagnosis will lead them to appropriate early intervention and, eventually, suitable schooling in order to improve the difficult situation experienced by both the child and their family. However, some parents question whether such a diagnosis will be advantageous to their child's overall life chances because it has the potential to be a double-edged sword. Some parents fear that while there may be successful intervention with a diagnosis there could also be the prospect of lifelong stigmatization.

When parents continue with the process of seeking a diagnosis, they are often met with a punishing diagnostic process. The diagnostic process is a very difficult time to endure where family emotions run extremely high and misdiagnoses are common. Many parents experience a long-winded pathway toward an eventual diagnosis of an autism spectrum disorder. Some parents feel relief with a diagnosis because they finally understand what they are dealing with. With diagnosis, parents realize they are only just beginning to battle a situation that could be potentially life-long. Parents receive little formal emotional support during this time even though it is one of the most stressful and lonely times in these parents' lives. Parents assess the value and accuracy of a diagnosis against their own experience with their child, their research into the area and the potential intervention benefits gained by such a diagnosis. Parents experience different time trajectories when seeking a formal diagnosis depending upon the conditions operating in their lives and the complexity of their child's profile. The length of time that it takes for parents to believe that there is something atypical about their child's development and to then gain an accurate diagnosis has a direct bearing on when effective, early intervention can be undertaken.

From their perspective, parents define 'early intervention' as including many different types of therapies, educational or otherwise, delivered as early as possible and assessed by them to be useful in their quest to help their child learn and improve in all areas of development. For most parents, intervention does not just occur during the distinct time phase before formal schooling starts but often continues in the form of supplementary programs alongside the child's regular schooling over many years.

Parents often feel like they are waging the war of their lives trying to gain appropriate and effective services to maximize the potential of their children on the autism spectrum. Some parents store hope in the belief that with the right type and intensity of intervention they will be able to cure their child of their autism. As time goes on, parents gradually realize they will have to become increasingly self-reliant and continually strategize solutions to secure the most appropriate educational interventions for their individual child. The resources of the family, both financial and otherwise, often determine the type and intensity of early intervention eventually available to their child on the autism spectrum.

Parents in the most vulnerable of circumstances have to settle for early intervention services only available through the government system. This lack of family resources also affects the length of time taken to gain an accurate diagnosis. These vulnerable parents can only use the most accessible, least intensive of the government-funded services because their reduced circumstances do not allow other options to be investigated or funded.

By contrast, a second set of less vulnerable parents feel compelled to improvise their own early intervention programs based on their own research because there is little appropriate, specific ASD intervention on offer to their child at the time. They employ maverick intervention strategies and implement individualized, home-based programs based on their child's profile so that intervention can occur at the earliest possible opportunity.

Yet, a third set of parents find themselves able to choose from early intervention programs based on best practice ASD intervention both through the private and public system. However these parents experience particular difficulties in terms of prohibitive cost, availability of staff and the on-going quality and intensity of these programs. These parents discover that home-based early intervention is heavily reliant upon family and financial circumstances supporting the high demands of the program and this often places increased pressure on the families involved with them. By contrast, parents involved in government-funded best practice school-based early intervention programs find that it delivers a high standard of intervention with consistency and quality built into the program. It reduces the financial strain and also provides some much needed respite for their family. However, parents find that places in such programs are often limited and parents often compete with one another to secure a place for their child.

All three early intervention pathways experienced by parents result in particular difficulties that are combated by the creation of various parent-devised strategies. Some of the difficulties experienced by parents are time-period specific and give rise to use of a particular strategy. However, once learned, parents often use a particular strategy repeatedly in order to combat difficulties at other times in the educational journey of their child on the autism spectrum.

During the time of early intervention parents learn that an appropriate education that targets both the strengths and difficulties of their child on the autism spectrum is the best way to help their child progress during their formal schooling years. Through research and discussion with other families, parents develop a starting belief that placing their child into a mainstream formal schooling environment will give their child the best chance to take their rightful place in preparation for a mainstream adult life. Therefore, parents initially try to gain a place for their child in a mainstream schooling situation. Parents broaden their understanding of education for their child on the autism spectrum to include both mainstream curriculum requirements and supplementary programs to address the idiosyncratic nature of their child's profile. This process is undertaken with the hope of maximizing the development and future independence of their child.

Parents gradually realize that the education of their child on the autism spectrum will be much more expensive, time-intensive and arduous than what is required for their neurotypical peers. Some parents also have the accompanying belief that a successful education for their child on the autism spectrum will eventually decrease the pressure on the rest of the family over the course of their child's life.

After early intervention, parents often desperately chase a mainstream schooling placement where their child will be welcomed for enrolment and where appropriate educational expertise and commitment to their child will be found. Parents are very reluctant to place their child into a school where they and their child feel unwelcome because they fear the on-going negative treatment their child may receive in such an environment. At enrolment, parents feel that their children are often perceived by schools to be burdensome and to place more pressure on staff and other students. Additionally, they feel their children are often seen by schools as students who need extra resources and are therefore much less desirable when such support is not readily available. Parents find that some schools reject their child outright or demand specific diagnoses and external financial support in the form of aide time before they will accept their child for enrolment even though such actions are potentially against the spirit and letter of Australian disability discrimination laws. Parents combat this discrimination by use of many creative strategies but such strategies place even more pressure on the fragile lives of such families.

When parents eventually gain a place for their child on the autism spectrum at a mainstream school, they experience a process of variable involvement with the school depending upon the school's notion of 'inclusive' practice. Parents find that mainstream schools have many different understandings of 'inclusion' and this affects the type and intensity of inclusive teaching practice undertaken by staff over time. Parents are often forced to continually negotiate and advocate an acceptable educational pathway for their child on the autism spectrum. Parents' involvement with the school is variable according to the success or otherwise of the inclusive culture and practice operating at the school. Parents progressively recognize the fragile and fluid nature of inclusive practice operating in their child's schooling context that can increase or decrease educational fit at any time for their child on the autism spectrum.

Some parents describe situations where a final crisis point is reached for their child on the autism spectrum in some mainstream schooling contexts. This occurs after numerous traumatic incidents have occurred where the child either refuses to attend school or is excluded, suspended or expelled from school. Parents indicate that without a firm commitment by staff, especially the administration, to appropriate inclusive practice, allocation of resources and specific evidence-based staff training to deal with students on the autism spectrum, the situation often rapidly deteriorates into one where the student is blamed for any difficulties that arise. Most parents believe that the difficulties that occur with their child are directly precipitated by a lack of appropriate inclusive practice operating in the schooling context over time.

By contrast, some parents reveal how they can sometimes find exemplary inclusive mainstream school contexts that provide appropriate educational fit for their child on the autism spectrum. Parents indicate that the key element found in these mainstream schooling environments is the unwavering devotion of the staff, including the principal, toward the emotional, social and academic welfare of the child on the autism spectrum and their family. Parents also nominate as important the welcome they receive at enrolment and the self-awareness shown by the staff regarding their own skill level (or lack thereof) when dealing with a child on the autism spectrum. Parents claim that this awareness allows parents and qualified others the opportunity to be part of a team (a community of practice) and provide appropriate, evidence-based support to staff regarding inclusivity and the individual educational requirements of the student on the autism spectrum. Parents find that when key educators behind the inclusive culture leave the school, the situation can rapidly deteriorate for their child on the autism spectrum.

Through experience, parents gradually learn that mainstream school environments can have very different cultures and commitments to inclusive practice that directly affects their ability to continually and reliably provide an appropriate education for their child on the autism spectrum over time. In response to this fragility of educational experience, parents often choose to supplement their child's formal schooling with a multitude of interventions to ensure that they maximize the educational progress and emotional well-being of their child irrespective of their mainstream experience. The quality and quantity of supplementing, however, is directly affected by the individual circumstances of each family.

At its best, the school is able to work with the family to incorporate and utilize these supplementary programs within the child's educational program at school to maximize their development. When a family's resources are limited, supplementing is reduced to what is provided through the government-subsidized system. Parents find such services are often lacking in appropriate individualization, intensity and quality of service provision. Parents also find that when they supplement their child's education they undertake yet another responsibility associated with maximizing the educational progress of their child and this adds to the already burdensome nature of their lives.

When parents continually struggle to maintain an appropriate inclusive mainstream schooling context they often reach a crisis point with their child's schooling. At this time some parents feel compelled to remove their child altogether from mainstream schooling to preserve the mental health of their child and the rest of the family. Some parents choose to home educate their child on the autism spectrum. Parents find that home education dramatically increases the educational fit for their child and generally reduces stress on the whole family. Parents indicate they are able to create individualized education plans organized to target their child's specific profile without the need to negotiate an external schooling context. Parents specify on-going negative socialization (bullying), insufficient academic progress and the failure of schools to understand their child's academic and social profile or the nature of their disability as reasons for their decision to home educate their child. Parents make use of both informal and formal external home education services and often adopt maverick strategies to improvise their own educational programs depending upon the parent's background, experience, confidence, the age of their child, finances and the nature of the educational programs that their child may need. Parents receive little financial support for the home education of their child which translates to yet another financial burden that is borne by such families.

Alternatively, when some parents experience a continual lack of educational fit or a crisis point for their child on the autism spectrum in a formal mainstream schooling context they opt to place their child into a segregated education support school contextually designed for children with disabilities. Parents find that such schools in WA are generally only available to children on the autism spectrum who have an accompanying intellectual disability (IQ of approximately 70 or below). Some parents are frustrated to find that other states in Australia have education support schools for children on the autism spectrum on offer irrespective of a child's IQ status.

Parents inculcated in the notion of 'inclusion' sometimes find it hard to reconcile their decision to segregate their child to an education support school with their quest to help their child eventually take up their rightful place in the external mainstream world. However, parents gradually accept that they must place their child in an educational environment where their child can experience the most reliable educational fit and maintain their mental health in order to realize their greatest educational and emotional progress. Parents note that some of the best aspects of inclusive practice experienced in mainstream schools are utilized in some of these segregated school sites.

In the final years of the formal schooling process, parents' thoughts turn to seeking appropriate future educational, employment and recreational pathways for their child. This influences their educational decisions sending parents' minds down many future planning tracks. Previous experiences warn parents that seeking, finding, creating and maintaining an appropriate fit for their child on the autism spectrum in the adult mainstream world will be an on-going and potentially difficult quest. While parents have gradually learned multiple coping strategies over time that help them seek, gain, maintain and create an appropriate educational fit for their child on the autism spectrum, they have also become acutely aware of the discrimination and difficulties their older child potentially faces in the external world. Parents find that they can not just rely on external services to support their child's transition process into the adult world. Parents have to, once again, advocate on behalf of their child and often become the driving force behind any successful transitions to the adult world that need to occur.

As the schooling process progresses, some parents begin to shift their thinking from mainly focusing upon maximizing the educational potential of their child on the autism spectrum to one that incorporates the quality of life and mental health experienced by all members of the family. Some parents realize earlier than others, that unless the family can survive intact over time the chances of maintaining the best quality of life for their child on the autism spectrum over their entire lifetime will be diminished. Some parents redress this imbalance of attention afforded their child on the autism spectrum by gradually reducing their own involvement and importing more external support and respite. Other parents redress the imbalance by reaping the benefits of their child's increased competence and independence gained during their formal schooling years. By contrast, still others are limited in their ability to redress the constant imbalance in their lives because of their reduced circumstances and the lack of progress achieved by their child on the autism spectrum. In all circumstances, improved funding and autism specific, support services implemented early are nominated as imperative to help families survive and maintain a healthy life balance for all family members throughout the life journey of the child on the autism spectrum.

DIAGRAM OF THE PROCESS

For ease of understanding, the following diagram provides a generalized representation of the process undertaken by the families involved in the study. It is inclusive of four stages and shows the types of movement possible throughout these four stages. The strands of 'increasing awareness and confidence' and 'variable negative feelings' are presented as distinct; however, in the application of this model these entities are typically integrated. The battle metaphors (*Beginning Battle, Waging War*) used to name two of the stages were taken directly from the parents' own words when they described the difficulties they encountered when dealing with their child's educational journeys. The constructivist grounded theory method (Charmaz, 2006) used to conduct the study (McDonald, 2010) delineated in this publication encourages use of such 'in vivo' codes where these codes "serve as symbolic markers of participants' speech and meanings" (Charmaz, 2006, p. 55).

In the study (McDonald, 2010), *seeking progressive fit* emerged as the overriding basic social process that permeated the lives of these parents when dealing with the education of their child on the autism spectrum. This notion of 'lack of fit' between a school's established mainstream practices and some of its students, disabled or otherwise, has been raised previously in discourse on inclusive practice (Ainscow, Booth & Dyson, 2006, p.304; Laluvein, 2010, p.42).

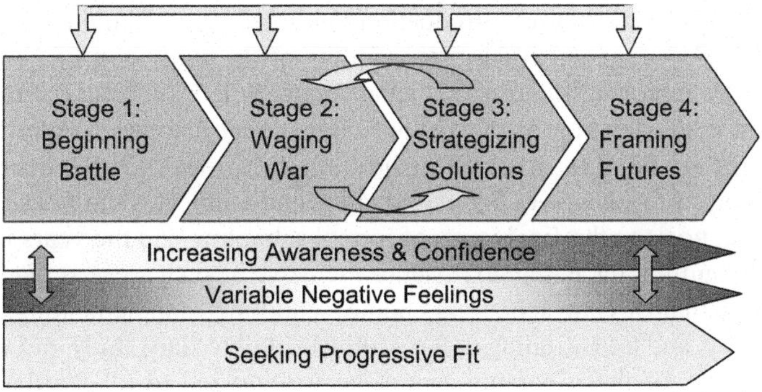

A key finding of the study (McDonald, 2010) was that parents struggled to seek, gain, maintain and create educational fit for their child on the autism spectrum in order to maximize their child's educational potential and progress. The four iterative stages involved in the process were identified as:

1. Beginning Battle – the stage where parents struggle to find an appropriate diagnosis.
2. Waging War – the stage where parents fight to seek, gain, maintain and create educational fit.
3. Strategizing Solutions – the stage where parents strategize solutions to remedy the constant difficulties associated with education.
4. Framing Futures – the stage where parents frame futures and begin redressing life imbalance.

It should be noted that the iterative movement between Stages 2 and 3 has the greatest level of interaction where parents continually strategized solutions to remedy the constant difficulties associated with educating their child on the autism spectrum.

The study also found that parents' direction and speed of movement through the various stages was mediated by the following intervening conditions:

a. the attitude and background of the parents,
b. the level of support and accommodation available,
c. the educational progress of the child over time,
d. the timing and type of engagement with the educational context,
e. the advancing age of the person on the autism spectrum and their parents.

As these parents gradually cycled through the stages they were imbued with an increasing awareness and confidence regarding how to deal more effectively with the individualised education of their child on the autism spectrum. However, the educational journey also created variable negative feelings in the parents as they progressively realised the enormity of the difficulties they often faced throughout the educational journey of their child on the autism spectrum.

CONCLUSION

This chapter has given a brief introduction to the reasoning behind this publication. Chapter 2 provides a contextual understanding of the study and Chapter 3 offers a brief literature review of the research area. Chapters 4, 5, 6, 7 and 8 provide a deep, synthesized understanding of the various educational pathways undertaken by the parents in the six families involved in the study (McDonald, 2010) over a five year period. It gives precedence to the parent voice and explicates the parent experience from pre-diagnosis to the final years of formal schooling and the years immediately beyond. It examines the parent experience inclusive of such areas as diagnosis, early intervention, mainstream schooling, home schooling, supplementing, segregated schooling sites and transitioning to the adult world of tertiary study and work. While the experiences of these parents cannot be generalized to all families who may educate their children on the spectrum, it is hoped that their stories will resonate and be instructive for other parents and help to inform and fortify them during their own difficult educational decision making. The final chapter of the book gives an overview of the parent experience with suggestions for future research and recommendations for policy and practice.

CHAPTER 2

CONTEXTUAL UNDERSTANDINGS

This chapter is broken into three major sections and gives a brief contextual background to this publication locating it appropriately in both time and place. Section one, The International Context, gives a brief history of the international trends regarding the education of students with disabilities. Section two, The Australian Context, gives a short outline of how the Australian educational context has responded to such trends. Finally, in section three, The West Australian (WA) Context, there is a more concentrated examination of the WA context in relation to Diagnosis, Prevalence, Early Intervention, General Disability Educational Provision and specific ASD Educational Provision.

THE INTERNATIONAL CONTEXT

Historically, the international movement toward inclusive educational practices for disabled students has been a gradual one. For some time, the notion of 'inclusion' has been seen as a problematic term because of its overuse and its lack of understanding in everyday discourse (Skidmore, 2004, p. ix). The term 'inclusion' is primarily used to describe situations where a disabled child's education is "embedded within the normative educative pathways within the classroom and the school" (Uditsky, 1993, p. 88). More recently the term 'inclusion' has incorporated the notion that schools should view 'diversity as the norm' as evidenced by the definition of 'inclusion' included in the introduction to this publication (Lynch and Irvine, 2009, p.286). Research over time informs us that because we live in a time of generational educational change for students with disabilities there can often be a divide experienced between the rhetoric and reality of inclusive practice (Cologon, 2013; Kavale & Forness, 2000, Oliver & Barnes, 2010).

There has been an interaction of differing factors spanning several decades, in various Western countries that has influenced the range of educational options now on offer to students with disabilities within Australia. Significant international influences on Australia's movement toward 'inclusive' practice can be found in binding and non-binding international conventions, disability legislation of both the United States of America (USA) and the United Kingdom (UK) and the deconstruction of traditional notions of 'disability' by leading voices in the disability movement over time (Oliver, 1990, 1996; Oliver & Barnes, 2010, Slee, 2011).

One significant international influence on Australia's movement toward inclusive practice has been the binding and non-binding international conventions by the United Nations. Through a rights-based approach, UNESCO has promoted inclusive education policies, programmes and practices to ensure equal education opportunities for persons with disabilities. Various conventions have confirmed the rights of disabled students to be educated in mainstream schools. The United Nations (UN) Convention on the Rights of the Child (1989) decreed that all children with disabilities should have the right to an education that would allow their fullest possible social integration and individual development. The UN Standard Rules on the Equalisation of Opportunities (1993) reaffirmed that the education of students with special needs should be an integral part of education systems (Shaddock et al., 2007). The influential Salamanca Statement (United Nations Scientific & Cultural Organisation (UNESCO, 1994) further proclaimed that schools should accommodate all children including those with a disability (Shaddock et al., 2007). The Dakar Framework for Action (2000) (UNESCO, 2000) restated an international commitment to education for all children in 'inclusive', educational environments. This has since been strengthened by the UNESCO (2004) Changing teaching practices: Using curriculum differentiation to respond to students' diversity (UNESCO, 2004) agreement and Article 24 of the UN Convention on the Rights of Persons with Disabilities (2006). Since the Salamanca Statement (UNESCO, 1994) Australia has adopted a similar approach to the international movement towards greater inclusion (Forlin et al., 2008). However, the majority of jurisdictions in Australia retain a continuum of placement options for students with disabilities (Forlin et al., 2008; Pearce & Forlin, 2005).

Another significant influence upon Australian inclusivity has been the movement toward inclusive education in the USA. This influence had its roots in the American civil rights movements of the 50s and 60s. This movement focused attention on race-related educational segregation, gained impetus and started to exert international influence during this time (Shaddock et al., 2007). This led educators, parents of disabled children and the disabled themselves to question the legitimacy, ethics and cost effectiveness of segregated educational placements of students with disabilities (Barnes, 1996; Forlin, 2004; Shaddock et al., 2007). Specific legislation in the USA in the form of the Education for All Handicapped Children Act in 1975 mandated that there should be free and appropriate public education (FAPE) for all disabled children between the ages of 3 and 21. In 1990, this Act was amended and re-authorised under the Individuals with Disabilities Education Act (IDEA) (Shaddock et al., 2007). Further re-authorizations in 1997 and 2004 (Disabilities Education Improvement Act of 2004) required school staff to continually monitor and evaluate the student's progress by developing an Individualised Education Plan (IEP) at least once a year (Shore & Rastelli, 2006). Parents were also given the legal right to be involved in all aspects of their child's education (Stoner & Angell, 2006). Parents were also entitled to an Individualised Family Service Plan (IFSP) for pre-schoolers at risk, which took into account the strengths and needs of parents (Shore & Rastelli, 2006).

Disabled students were also afforded the right to be educated with their peers in the least restrictive environment possible (Myles, Swanson, Holverstott, & Duncan,

2007). Students with behavioural difficulties were also entitled under the Act to a functional behavioural assessment to determine the most appropriate intervention to change such behaviour (Myles et al., 2007). Parents were able to request an extended school year for their child if the child needed help in the summer break to maintain his or her progress (Shore & Rastelli, 2006). Prior to the implementation of IDEA individuals with disabilities often did not attend school or were placed in segregated special education settings without access to the general education curriculum or their non-disabled peers (Myles et al., 2007). Over the past 25 years, IDEA has ensured significant progress has been made in the development and implementation of special education programs and services for students with disabilities in the USA (Shaddock et al., 2007). However, on-going concerns have been expressed regarding the dissonance between the rhetoric and reality of 'inclusive' practice as it operates in different educational contexts irrespective of legislation (Kavale & Forness, 2000). This has led to an increase in litigation by some US parents who wish to ensure that an appropriate, supported mainstream education is available to their child on the autism spectrum (Yell, Katsiyannis, Drasgow, & Herbst, 2003).

The UK experienced the emergence of a similar climate of social reform that resulted in a comprehensive national review of educational provision for individuals with disabilities. This culminated in the Warnock Report (1978) which outlined recommendations and was subsequently used as a basis for legislation. As a consequence of the report, the Education Reform Act (1988) legislated that every child, disabled or otherwise, should have access to the national curriculum (Shaddock et al., 2007). Subsequent to this was the implementation of the 1995 British Disabilities Discrimination Act (DDA) which legislated that all schools should allow admission of disabled students and provide facilities to allow these students to access an appropriate education (Shaddock et al., 2007). This was followed by the Special Education Needs and Disability Act of 2001 which legislated that children with special needs should be educated in mainstream schools (Shaddock et al., 2007). More recently, there has been the implementation of the UK Autism Act 2009. This Act makes specific provision about the needs of adults who have autism. It is the first ever disability-specific legislation to be passed in the United Kingdom (National Autistic Society, 2014).

One UK initiative, the Index for Inclusion (Booth, Ainscow, Black-Hawkins, Vaughan, & Shaw, 2000), initially devised and implemented in the UK, has been trialled in Australian schools (Deppeler & Harvey, 2004; Forlin, 2004; Jenkins, 2005). This instrument allows schools to identify and address issues surrounding inclusivity (Forlin, 2004; Jenkins, 2005) and has been used in both government and private West Australian rural and metropolitan schools in both primary and secondary sectors.

Underpinning the evolving nature of the international conventions and legislation in both the UK and USA has been a deconstruction of traditional notions of 'disability' by international disability scholars. Skidmore (2004) asserts that there are three major paradigms which currently permeate modern discourse on disability.

These incorporate the psycho-medical, sociological and organizational models of disability. The psycho-medical paradigm traditionally focuses on assessment and treatment of deficits in the individual and operates at the micro level. This theoretical model conceptualizes "special needs as arising from deficits in the neurological or psychological make-up of the child, analogous to an illness or medical condition" (Skidmore, 1996, p. 34). 'Disability' is seen as an individualized paradigm where a disabled child's 'misfit' with mainstream education is due, in the main, to the disabled child's deficits and provides the rationale for 'special education'.

By contrast, the sociological model, asserts that there are "structural inequalities in education at the macro level" (Shaddock et al., 2007, p. 13). There is a clear distinction in this model between 'impairment' and 'disability'. Whereas 'impairment' refers to a mental or physical deficit, the term 'disabled' is used to describe the environmental, social and political relations of disability (Ainscow, 1993, 1995; Fulcher, 1993; Oliver, 1990, 1996; Slee, 1996). While some students are deemed to have 'special needs' the onus seems to fall upon the student to 'fit' the system and not the reverse. This "individualistic gaze" is explained by Ainscow (1993) as "an approach to naming and framing the problems experienced by pupils and teachers which takes little or no notice of the wider environmental, social and political contexts in which they occur" (p. 206). It is the contention by a number of leading voices that it is the system itself which 'disables' because it fails to 'enable' many children with different educational needs to be successful in mainstream education (Ainscow, 1993; Fulcher, 1993; Oliver, 1990, 1996; Slee, 2011).

Related to the social model is the construct of the organizational model which occurs at the meso or institutional level which argues that "learning difficulties arise from deficiencies in the way schools are currently organized" (Skidmore, 2004, p. 10). In recent times this organizational paradigm has come to "assume a position of dominance in the field" (Skidmore, 2004, p. 7). The solution to such organizational deficiences is to restructure schools where a:

> … properly implemented policy of school restructuring will produce a system of schooling which is better adapted to meeting the educational needs of all pupils, and which will therefore eliminate or reduce to a minimum the problem of students who fail to fulfil their learning potential in the formal education system (Skidmore, 2004, p. 7).

The 'inclusive' school would therefore, adapt and respond to the diversity found in the student population and no group would require a so-called 'special' form of educational provision (Skidmore, 2004).

Each model draws on a distinctive theoretical framework, operates with its own implied epistemology and level of focus, posits a different model of causation and proposes a correspondingly different form of intervention (Skidmore, 2004). There are limitations inherent in each paradigm. Skidmore (2004) asserts that trying to reduce 'disability' into any one of the three paradigms is potentially reductionist and does not account for the complexity inherent in the nature of disability.

Skidmore (2004) explains reductionism as "the tendency to explain an intrinsically complex phenomenon in terms of a single, unidirectional model of causation, and (concomitantly) to propose a single form of intervention as a complete and adequate solution to the problem" (p. 11). It may be as Skidmore (2004) suggests that "learning difficulties are conceptualized as the product of factors located within the individual, or society at large, *or* the school, but the possibility or interaction between factors operating at different levels of analysis" should not be "overlooked" (p. 11).

Disability is increasingly being reconstructed as natural to the human condition with the understanding that most people will experience some form of disability (indirectly or directly) at some stage in their lives (Shaddock et al., 2007). According to Shaddock et al. (2007), the practical implication of this is that "if disability comes to be seen as *unexceptional* then all mainstream services, including education will 'naturally' be required to take responsibility for a more diverse clientele" (p. 15). This sentiment has been echoed in the research literature on 'inclusive' education and best practice for children with an ASD where there has been a similar call to use a more unified model of education where all children will receive the educational support they require (Lynch & Irvine, 2009) as a matter of basic human rights (Nussbaum, 2009). Shaddock et al. (2007) further suggests that the way forward may be "to pay more attention to the everyday effects on a person's life of disability and impairment" (p. 16). This framework "draws attention to what is happening, and what can be done, at the level of the *body*, the *person* and the *society* and emphasizes the person's access, or lack of it, to activity and participation" (Shaddock et al., 2007, p. 16).

More recently, in specific relation to students on the autism spectrum, there has been a questioning of dominant and seemingly contradictory perspectives – the rights-based and needs-based perspectives – where an integrative inclusionist position is tentatively explored as a bridge between such polarising perspectives and where the needs of the individual student more rightly drive educational decision making (Ravet, 2011).

THE AUSTRALIAN CONTEXT

Australia is presently involved in the process of creating and disseminating a national curriculum (ACARA, 2013) and until it is fully implemented its six states and two territories are individually responsible for the provision of primary and secondary school education. The major responsibility for 'special education' was devolved to the states and territories with the Commonwealth retaining limited power (Forlin & Forlin, 1998). Historically, there were limited educational opportunities for children with disabilities in Australia prior to the Second World War. Following this time, federal, state and territory governments enacted legislation to ensure that all students of differing ages and abilities received an education. To illustrate, the *Western Australian Education Act* (1928) was amended in 1952 to make education of children with disabilities compulsory (Chalmers, 1998). Responsibility for educating these children was originally given to the health departments of different states and territories. However, by the 1970s this responsibility shifted to the education departments of those states and territories (Jenkinson, 2001). During this time, segregated 'special education' institutions were established and were seen as the most cost-effective method of delivering intensive educational programs to children with disabilties (Jenkinson, 2001).

In line with the international disability movement, segregation of disabled students was eventually challenged in Australia by parents, educators and researchers who voiced concerns about excluding students with disabilities from their non-disabled peers (Ashman & Elkins, 2005). In response to this, the Schools Commission in Australia in 1975 recommended a system of 'integration' and by the 1980s this was endorsed by education systems throughout Australia (Ashman & Elkins, 2005). Despite this, there was little 'integration' evident and most students with disabilities still received their education in locations that excluded them from regular classrooms (Dempsey, Foreman, & Jenkinson, 2002).

Like its international partners, Australia has supported a strong philosophical movement over the last two decades toward greater inclusion of students with special needs into regular school communities (Forlin, 2004). Inclusion has been supported at a federal level within Australia by the enactment of both the *Disability Discrimination Act* (DDA) (Commonwealth of Australia, 1992) and the *Disability Standards for Education* (Commonwealth of Australia, 2005). The DDA has been revised several times and requires that educational institutions in Australia be free from discrimination on the grounds of disability in terms of admission, access or harassment (Commonwealth of Australia, 2006). The DDA has been seen as mainly providing direction for individuals who have experienced discrimination and does not have the far reaching human rights protection of the USA *Bill of Rights* (Lindsay, 2004). The DDA does not prevent discrimination from taking place but rather deals with it after the discrimination has occurred. The alleged victim of discrimination must therefore take his or her case to the Human Rights Equal Opportunity Commission (HREOC). The HREOC does not have the power to enforce decisions resulting from its hearings and when conciliation has not been successful, the complainant has the right to take their case to the Federal Court (Jones & Basser Marks, 1999). The DDA has several exemptions for institutions with the most contentious being the exemption of 'unjustifiable hardship'. This potentially allows any educational institution to avoid a finding of unlawful discrimination if it can prove an 'unjustifiable hardship' would be imposed on their institution if it complied with the DDA (Commonwealth of Australia, 2006; Waldeck & Guthrie, 2004).

Following on from the DDA (Commonwealth of Australia, 1992) has been the formulation of the *Disability Standards for Education* (Commonwealth of Australia, 2005) which explains sections of the DDA that pertain to education (O'Reilly & Smith, 2008). These *Standards* have the same legal status as the DDA and encompass the following five areas where disabled students are entitled to support and accommodations: enrolment; participation; curriculum development, accreditation and delivery; student support services; harassment and victimization. According to the *Standards (Commonwealth of Australia, 2005)*, disabled students have the same right to services and facilities as anyone else and education providers have an obligation to make 'reasonable adjustments' (O'Reilly & Smith, 2008). The term 'reasonable adjustments' is understood to mean "an adjustment is a measure or action taken to assist a student with disability to participate in education and training on the same basis as other students" (O'Reilly & Smith, 2008, p. 146). Accommodations and support are subject to an educational institution receiving formal documentation regarding a students' disability and their resultant requirements. An institution is only required to provide what is considered to be 'reasonable' under the circumstances and decisions do not necessitate consultation with all stakeholders. In line with the DDA (Commonwealth of Australia, 1992) the *Disability Standards for Education* (Commonwealth of Australia, 2005) also has exemptions inclusive of the difficulties associated with the 'unjustifiable hardship' exemption. A recent review on the *Standards*, *Report on the Review of the Disability Standards for Education 2005 (DEEWR, 2012)* has found serious shortcomings in its implementation across both state and territory jurisdictions.

Despite their limitations, both the DDA (Commonwealth of Australia, 1992) and the *Disability Standards for Education* (Commonwealth of Australia, 2005) have been credited with exerting a major influence on education providers in Australia (Shaddock et al., 2007). Modification of education policies to comply with the DDA and *Disability Standards for Education* has occurred in state and territory education departments throughout Australia and substantial funding has occurred to support these changes. However, while individual policies exist the responsibility to implement these policies still rests with each individual education provider. Most states and territories continue to provide an array of education options including segregated special schools, education support centres and special education classes within regular schools, however, there are an increasing number of students with special needs being catered for in regular classrooms (Ashman & Elkins, 2005; Forlin, 2004).

More recent Australian research indicates that despite the legislation and resultant state and territory policies, Australian teachers in regular classrooms indicate that they tend to incorporate "accommodations that can be made for the whole class, that are efficient of teacher time and effort and that do not involve major changes to class organization or substantial individualization" (Shaddock et al., 2007, p. xiv). This aligns with comprehensive international research which shows that "many teachers worldwide say they do not have the time or resources to make adaptations for students with significant individual needs and these concerns have been expressed for many years" (Shaddock et al., 2007, p. xiii). Hence, while students with disabilities may have increased rights regarding access and enrolment in regular schools and classrooms, issues have now arisen regarding the quality and outcomes of the education they receive in such environments (Cologon, 2013; Kavale & Forness, 2000; MacDermott, 2008; McDonald, 2010; Ravet, 2011; Shaddock et al., 2007; Ypinazar & Pagliano, 2004,).

This is borne out in recent extensive research (Victorian Equal Opportunity and Human Rights Commission, 2012) conducted in Victorian schools which surveyed 883 educators, 617 parents and carers and 60 students and found that the educational experiences of children with disabilities was not consistent, that discrimination still exists and that not all children with disabilities are eligible for support to enable them to access the curriculum as is required by the Disability Discrimination Act (1992). Further to this, preliminary results from a Queensland study investigating how nine students on the autism spectrum and their parents experience participation in mainstream school over time has found that seven of the nine students experienced frequent, disrupted mainstream participation for most of their schooling years (Harrington et al., 2013). The study recommended more support for transitions; finding a student champion at school; greater collaboration among school staff, students on the spectrum and their parents; and, provision of a continuum of education options being made available to families (Harrington et al., 2013).

In response to the education difficulties experienced by families who have a child on the autism spectrum, specific government support has been undertaken. From 2008 the Australian Government committed funds to provide a *Helping Children with Autism* (HCWA) support package (The Hon Bill Shorten MP, personal communication, 7 May, 2008). The package seeks to provide earlier and more accurate diagnosis of children with an ASD, increased access to early intervention programmes, and further support services for educators and parents/carers of children with an ASD (O'Reilly & Smith, 2008).

Further to this in 2014, under the Australian Education Act, 2013, the federal government has begun a funding loading formula for school students with disability which applies to eligible students with disabilities whether they attend a government or non-government school (The Hon Christopher Pyne MP, personal communication, 2014). The loading is set at 186 per cent of the base per-student Schooling Resource Standard (SRS) amount which is $9271 for primary students and $12,193 for secondary school students. Students with disabilities in segregated school sites are eligible for an extra loading of 223 percent in recognition of the more complex needs of these students (The Hon Christopher Pyne MP, personal communication, 2014). Additionally, under their More Support for Students with Disabilities (MSSD) initiative, the government is providing $300 million over the 2012–2014 school years to build capacity of Australian schools and teachers in educating students with disability, contributing to improved student learning experiences, educational outcomes and transitions to further education or work under their MSSD initiative (The Hon Christopher Pyne MP, personal communication, 2014). Unfortunately, the latest 2014 federal Budget indicates that these school funding commitments may be scrapped from 2017–18 (Gonski et al., 2011; Australian Government, 2014).

It is important to note that home educators in Australia are presently not eligible to access the same funding provided to schools for their children with disabilities even though it could be argued that they are often compelled to provide an appropriate education for their children with disabilities when there has been a repeated failure by formal schooling contexts to do so.

THE WEST AUSTRALIAN (WA) CONTEXT

Diagnosis

Education of individuals with disabilities in WA has followed the same linear pattern set by other states in Australia and countries in the Western world (O'Donoghue, 1998). The pattern has been initially exclusion (1830s to 1920s), through to segregation and integration (1930s to 1960s) and finally to limited inclusion (1970s to the present) (O'Donoghue, 1998). For students with a suspected ASD to gain funded services in WA they must seek a diagnosis. All states in Australia have different assessment and diagnostic practices for a diagnosis to be made. To receive government funding in WA for early intervention and educational support, parents must firstly seek a diagnosis of an ASD. Prior to 2013, the Diagnostic and Statistical Manual-IV-TR (DSM-IV-TR), was used in Western Australia to identify a set of Pervasive Developmental Disorders (PDDs) that were considered "autism spectrum disorders" (ASDs). These included: Autistic Disorder, Asperger's Disorder, and Pervasive Developmental Disorder Not Otherwise Specified (PDD-NOS).

According to the DSM-IV-TR, PDDs were "characterized by severe and pervasive impairment in several areas of development: reciprocal social interaction skills, communication skills, or the presence of stereotyped behaviour, interests, and activities" (American Psychiatric Association, 2000, p. 69). The DSM-IV has been under revision for 14 years and a new edition, the DSM 5, has recently been released in 2013. Significant changes to the criteria and categories of ASDs have occurred in the new edition.

One of the most significant changes is that the separate diagnostic labels of Autistic Disorder, Asperger's Disorder, and PDD-NOS have been replaced by one umbrella term "Autism Spectrum Disorder" (DEEWR, 2013). Diagnosis has also been reduced from considering three to two domains. The domains of social interaction and communication have been collapsed into one domain with the accompanying domain of restricted interests/repetitive behaviour being preserved as the other domain (DEEWR, 2013). Under the domain of restricted interests/ repetitive behaviour there is now recognition of the sensory difficulties experienced by many on the autism spectrum. Further distinctions have also been made according to three severity levels, from level 1 (requiring support) to Level 3 (requiring very substantial support) (DEEWR, 2013).

Concerns have been raised regarding how these changes might impact individuals on the spectrum. One of the biggest concerns is that some individuals who are higher functioning will no longer meet the stricter diagnostic criteria and will therefore have difficulties accessing relevant support services, even though these individuals may have the greatest chance of making a substantial contribution to the community if appropriate intervention and support is provided. Questions have been raised about what will happen to people currently diagnosed with Asperger's Disorder or PDD-NOS. Furthermore, there is uncertainty regarding how state educational services and insurance companies will adopt these changes (Matson, Hattier, & Williams, 2012; Gibbs, Aldridge, Chandler, Witzlsperger, & Smith, 2012; McPartland, Reichow, & Volkmar, 2012)

In response to these concerns, a recently released statement by the American Psychiatric Association (APA) titled, *DSM-5 Autism Spectrum Disorder Fact Sheet,* indicated that:

> The DSM-5 criteria were tested in real-life clinical settings as part of DSM-5 field trials, and analysis from that testing indicated that there will be no significant changes in the prevalence of the disorder. More recently, the largest and most up-to-date study, published by Huerta, et al, in the October 2012 issue of American Journal of Psychiatry, provided the most comprehensive assessment of the DSM-5 criteria for ASD based on symptom extraction from previously collected data. The study found that DSM-5 criteria identified 91 percent of children with clinical DSM-IV PDD diagnoses, suggesting that most children with DSM-IV PDD diagnoses will retain their diagnosis of ASD using the new criteria. Several other studies, using various methodologies, have been inconsistent in their findings. (American Psychiatric Association, 2013a)

However, such assurances will need to be borne out in further studies undertaken over the next few years.

Presently, the West Australian Disability Services Commission (DSC) applies internationally recognized standards for diagnosis (Lewis, 2009). Primary government diagnostic and assessment agencies (State Child Development Centre, DSC Individual and Family Support Autism Team) and private practitioners/organizations are currently able to make ASD diagnoses (Lewis, 2009). The *Diagnostic and Statistical Manual of Mental Disorders,* fourth edition, text revision (DSM-IV-TR) (American Psychiatric Association, 2000) has been the most commonly used basis for diagnosis of children with a PDD (Lewis, 2009). However, this will change with the recent release of the DSM 5 (American Psychiatric Association, 2013b).

To gain a diagnosis, parents or carers generally seek a referral from medical and allied health practitioners, school psychologists and/or other educators in both government and private sectors (MacDermott et al., 2007). The Disability Services Commission (DSC), Health Department and private practitioners are then able to receive the referral and organize an assessment (MacDermott et al., 2007). Diagnosis of children currently usually involves a multi-disciplinary team made up of a paediatrician, psychologist and speech pathologist conducted either privately or through the health or disability sectors (Palm Consulting Group, 2005). However, when needed, a psychiatrist, social worker and occupational therapist may also be involved (MacDermott et al., 2007). The multi-disciplinary team responsible for the diagnosis then makes intervention referrals and recommendations. The client is then referred to DSC for eligibility for level and type of services determination (MacDermott et al., 2007).

Diagnosis through the government system and private practitioners has often been a protracted experience in WA. WA has however, a relatively high standard of practice regarding the difficult task of diagnosis. There is a WA Autism Diagnosticians' Forum (http://www.waadf.org.au/) that meets quarterly to discuss international standards, processes, and clinical issues in assessment and diagnosis of ASDs. This forum includes clinicians across the disciplines of speech pathology, paediatrics, psychiatry, social work, psychology and research who are working in the government and non-government sectors. From 2008 the federal Helping Children With Autism (HCWA) package has provided some extra funding for diagnosis and development of a treatment plan for children under the age of 13 years.

Prevalence

WA presently has an established ASD diagnostic register, the *WA Register for Autism Spectrum Disorders* (Glasson et al., 2006). The register is prospective and has been collecting information since 1999 on: the number and ages of people diagnosed; the severity of disability; shared biological, psychiatric and developmental features; and group changes over time (Glasson et al., 2006). It serves as a primary resource to researchers, clinicians and service providers to assist with their knowledge of ASDs in WA (Glasson et al., 2006). WA is an ideal location to manage a register because of its geographic isolation and centrally distributed population (Glasson et al., 2006). The register has application in both research and planning for services. Over the past two decades the number of new diagnoses per year has increased nearly 20 fold (Glasson et al., 2006). This increase in identified children with an ASD has been similarly observed internationally (MacDermott et al., 2007). Some reports indicate that approximately 300 WA children are diagnosed with an ASD each year (Painter, 2009). A recent study comparing prevalence statistics for Denmark and Western Australia found that ASD prevalence rates were higher in Denmark (68.5 per 10,000 children) compared with Western Australia (51.0 per 10,000 children), while the diagnosis of childhood autism was more prevalent in Western Australia (39.3 per 10,000 children) compared with Denmark (21.8 per 10,000 children) (Parner, Thorsen, Dixon, deKlerk, Leonard, Nassar, Bourke, Bower & Glasson, 2011).

Early Intervention

After diagnosis, the Disability Services Commission (DSC) eligibility determination team provides the family with a letter informing them of what government-funded early intervention (EI) services their child is eligible. The family then chooses which EI provider they wish to receive services from and wait lists vary at each centre (Lewis, 2009; Painter, 2009; Therapy Focus, 2012). Parents who want to use government funding for EI may choose from accredited Autism early intervention providers who offer a choice of ASD early intervention models (Lewis, 2009). They may also choose to use other organizations that have contracts with DSC to provide EI services for children with disabilities (Lewis, 2009). Parents may also choose private organizations/professionals where families may purchase services.

Unfortunately, some government-funded EI services that are on offer do not necessarily provide the type or intensity of intervention recommended in best practice programs (Roberts & Prior, 2006) at the earliest possible time and wait lists are common (Painter, 2009). Funding for one of the most efficacious interventions based on long term research (Roberts & Prior, 2006) is presently still under-funded, although some extra money has become available through the federal Helping Children with Autism (HCWA) package. The package provides all children aged six and under who are diagnosed with an ASD and are not yet school-age to gain funding of up to $12 000 (up to $6 000 per financial year) to assist with the financial cost of accessing EI services. This funding is not dependent upon whether the child with an ASD has an accompanying intellectual disability. Parents access this funding through an Autism Advisor located at the Autism Association of WA.

This figure unfortunately falls far short of providing appropriate funding for the intensity of EI recommended by a government review (Roberts & Prior, 2006) which investigated current research regarding the most effective models of EI for children with an ASD. The recommended model of intervention is based on Applied Behaviour Analysis / Discrete Trial Training (ABA/DTT) methods and recommends that EI "be extensive and intensive" and be conducted "a minimum of 20 hours a week over two or more years" as early as possible in order for young children to make major gains (Prior & Roberts, 2006, p. 3). Government funding for this model is still inadequate and does not cover the hours per week of recommended intervention needed in best practice models.

WA also presently has EI transition to school programs conducted by the West Australian Department of Education (DoE) to teach essential skills to children with an ASD or Global Developmental Delay/Special Needs for eventual transition into mainstream (Lewis, 2009). These programs are conducted over the kindergarten and pre-primary years and are generally based on the principles of ABA incorporating DTT (Lewis, 2009). The programs were initially set up in response to research and parent input outlined in the report commissioned by Department of Education and Training, *Models of Educational Service Provision for Students with Autsim Spectrum Disorder within Government Mainstream Schooling* (Crosby, 1998). The report indicated that parents wanted a government funded, best practice EI program specifically using ABA/DTT that would allow their children to gain skills to cope more successfully with eventual mainstream schooling (Crosby, 1998).

General Disability Educational Provision

Each Australian state or territory is required to ensure that federal legislation regarding schooling for children with special needs is appropriately embedded within their individual Acts and policies (Forlin, 2004). Various educational reports (Andrews, Elkins, Berry, & Burge, 1979; Beazley, 1984; Shean, 1993) undertaken in WA have increasingly supported the principle of integration. These reports and subsequent legislation and policy documents have led to improvements in service provision towards placement of students with disabilities in regular schools, whenever possible (Education Department of Western Australia, 1993, 1998, 1999; Forlin, 2004).

WA school-age children are currently educated in a variety of settings ranging from one-teacher schools in remote rural locations to large senior high schools (both public and private) in metropolitan locations with student populations of 2,000 or more. The system is similar to those operating in other Western nations in that WA has generally well trained teachers, modern school facilities and educational resources, and highly developed curricula. Students with general disabilities constitute 3-4% of the total student population in WA government schools with the majority attending local schools with differing provision of resources, services and supports (Department of Education and Training, 2004; Forlin, 2004). A continuum of placement options still exists in WA and range from segregated Education Support Schools, Education Support Centres (separate schools on shared sites with regular schools), Education Support Units (classes within regular schools), to full inclusion in regular schools. Presently, students with disabilities in WA may experience a range of segregated, integrated, inclusive or home education settings (Forlin et al., 2008; O'Donoghue, 1998; O'Donoghue & Chalmers, 2000; Kidd & Kaczmarek, 2010; McDonald, 2010; McDonald & Lopes, 2012; Reilly, 2007; Wills & Jackson, 2000).

With regard to the majority of students with an intellectual disability in WA, these students are most often enrolled in an Education Support Unit, Education Support Centre or Education Support School (Forlin, 2005; Forlin et al., 2008). Initiatives by the WA Department of Education regarding providing 'inclusive' practice in mainstream schools have included a comprehensive review of educational services for students with disabilities in the form of the 2004 *Pathways to the Future* (Department of Education and Training, 2004). The report outlines the seven principles of 'inclusive' education adopted in the review: (1) all students have the right to enrol, access and participate in schooling which meets their individual needs; (2) all levels of the system value diversity and operate within an 'inclusive' framework; (3) a range of effective and appropriate adjustments is provided to ensure access, participation and achievement; (4) adjustments are provided on a needs basis and are equitably resourced; (5) the system supports the development of pedagogy to meet individual student needs; (6) the range of coordinated programs and services provided are flexible and delivered according to student needs; and (7) services are provided and supported by collaborative models and partnerships (Department of Education and Training, 2004). More recently, the Australian Curriculum, Assessment and Reporting Authority (ACARA) has provided guidance to WA schools on how to appropriately accommodate student diversity in the Australian Curriculum (inclusive of students with a disability, gifted and talented students and students for whom English is an additional language or dialect) (ACARA, 2013).

Additionally in 2014, a change to WA school funding is to occur (Bickers, 2014, July 20). A new stream-lined funding model is to be introduced where early intervention and student-centred funding is to be given precedence. The funding changes are based on the results on a 2012 review of WA school funding which recommended that schools be funded on student numbers with additional money to help children with special needs/disabilities. Presently, WA has a current budget of $4.6billion in 2014-15 of which 83.7% comes from the State Government. How such funding decisions will impact on the inclusivity of WA schools in relation to students on the autism spectrum is yet to be determined.

The Australasian Curriculum Assessment and Certification Authorities (ACACA) has also developed Guidelines for Assessment Quality and Equity (1995) and confirmed the right of students of 'difference' to alternative assessments and accommodations (Toner, 2009). All Australian states and territories education departments have now given students with disabilities the right to request accommodations during assessments. Potential accommodations include: separate settings, extra time, alternative presentation and response modes (Toner, 2009). Disabled students need to justify their reasons for requiring accommodations substantiated by expert opinion to prove that they are not seeking an unfair advantage (Cumming, 2006).

International research of students with general disabilities has shown a gradual increase in the number of students with disabilities entering universities, with the biggest increase being students with 'invisible disabilities' (Wolf, 2001). In Australia, this increase has been due to the overall improvement of educational provision of the disabled and the Federal government's formal recognition of people with disabilities as a designated equity group entitled to accommodations in tertiary study (Cooper, 2003). University policies introduced in response to the 1992 Disability Discrimination Act (Commonwealth of Australia, 1992) affirmed the responsibility of the tertiary sector to provide necessary accommodation for disabled students to realize their potential in higher education (Toner, 2009). The number of disabled students attending Australian universities doubled between 1996 and 2006 (Carrick Institute for Learning and Teaching in Higher Education, 2006). In 2006, an original policy *Guidelines Relating to Students with a Disability* (Australian Vice-Chancellors' Committee, 1996) was upgraded and revised to comply with the *Disability Standards for Education (2005)* (Commonwealth of Australia, 2005). It covered three key areas: Policy and Administration; Teaching and Learning; and Campus Life. The *Guidelines* also obliged all universities to have a Disability Action Plan, which is lodged with Universities Australia. A website (www.cats.edu.au), *Creating Accessible Teaching and Support* (CATS) is available to university staff to assist them in meeting the requirements of the Guidelines and their institution's individual policies (Toner, 2009).

Most tertiary institutions in WA have mandatory policies to support students with disabilities. There has been a significant increase in students with 'invisible disabilities' seeking accommodations in the WA tertiary sector (Toner, 2009), although the real number of disabled students needing accommodation is probably under-reported (James, Baldwin, Coates, Krause, & McInnis, 2004). Research has indicated that some students with 'invisible' disabilities at tertiary level fear perceived reactions to their disability and therefore do not declare their disabled status (Patwell & Herzog, 2000; Smith, English, & Vasek, 2002; Wade, 2003). When tertiary students do register their disability to receive accommodation they must furnish documentation to prove their disabled status and an agreed 'management plan' is then discussed, approved and distributed to those concerned. Disability officers in WA tertiary institutions have no control over lecturers' teaching methods and can only make recommendations regarding appropriate accommodation regarding individual students' needs (Toner, 2009). At this stage, the WA tertiary sector provides support when it is requested by individual disabled students. Flexible methods of course delivery are sometimes on offer to benefit all students who potentially have learning differences. There is a growing need by the tertiary sector to proactively promote universal teaching design in all teaching staff to cater for individual student differences (Garguilo & Metcalf, 2013; Toner, 2009).

Educational Provision for Students on the Autism Spectrum

Presently, WA students on the autism spectrum can be found in mainstream schools, schools with Education Support Units, Education Support Schools/Centres and in home schooling environments. They may be enrolled in a WA Department of Education (DoE) school, a Catholic Education Office of Western Australia (CEOWA) school or an Association of Independent Schools of Western Australia (AISWA) school. All of these schools have varying autism educational provision. DoE provides services for students with disabilities, including those on the autism spectrum, through their Socio-Psycho Education Resources (SPER), Schools Plus (SP) and School of Special Educational Needs: Disability (SSEND) programs. CEOWA provides a Special Learning Needs Team who help schools respond to the special needs and talents of students who experience significant difficulties with learning; support the inclusion of students with disabilities in appropriate educational settings; and promote exemplary pedagogical practices for students with special learning needs (MacDermott et al., 2007). AISWA employs a small number of Inclusive Education Consultants who are available to give advice aimed at supporting their students with a range of learning difficulties and disabilities. The consultants provide a range of collaborative services for parents and teachers within and across member schools (MacDermott et al., 2007; Therapy Focus; 2012).

From the commencement of school-age, the major educational service provision for children on the autism spectrum rests with the DoE. A 1998 report, *Models of Educational Service Provision for students with an ASD within Government Mainstream Schooling* (Crosby, 1998), sought information about existing practices so that policy and a range of educational options could be developed to cater for the varying needs of students on the autism spectrum in WA government schools.

Results indicated that in order to meet the needs of a wide range of students on the autism spectrum in a variety of mainstream schools a flexible approach to the delivery of educational services was essential. A range of issues were identified that impact on the ability of the Department of Education to develop and implement effective models of service delivery for students on the autism spectrum. No single approach completely addressed all the issues as many of the solutions had a degree of incompatibility with solutions to other issues (Crosby, 1998).

In relation to specific educational service provision for students with an ASD in WA, the WA government has indicated commitment to providing evidence based, flexible and responsive support to students on the autism spectrum in public schools (Banks, 2005). Their nominated aim is to provide a quality lifelong learning environment in which everyone will have the opportunity to reach their learning and skills potential and contribute to society (MacDermott et al., 2007). In relation to this, *Schools Plus* (SP) (Department of Education and Training, 2006) was developed by DoE as a model of informed practice to match the educational needs of students to supplementary resourcing for schools. SP allows schools to plan, implement and review appropriate educational programs on the basis of educational need and provides supplementary resources to schools that have eligible students. A diagnosis on the autism spectrum qualifies as one of the 8 groups identified by SP as an eligible condition. This is determined on a case-by-case basis and the student must require significant levels of on-going adjustments that are beyond the school's current level of resourcing to access SP support (MacDermott et al., 2007).

The DoE School of Special Educational Needs: Disability (SSEND) also provides support to government school students on the autism spectrum. SSEND provides state-wide support for students with disabilities and learning difficulties via dedicated teams inclusive of the Autism Education Service Team (Therapy Focus, 2012). The team is comprised of a Team Coordinator and Visiting Teachers for students on the autism spectrum (MacDermott et al., 2007). The team allocates members according to particular districts' needs and the team meets on a regular basis to discuss student, school and district based issues and needs (MacDermott et al., 2007).

DoE was the only state education department to be one of the four members of the national Australian Autism Education & Training Consortium (AAETC) responsible for the formulation and implementation of the *Helping Children with Autism* (HCWA) package being undertaken across Australia (AAETC, 2008a; 2008b). This innovative package provided nationwide professional development for teachers and other school staff in both metropolitan and country areas to support school students with an ASD. Workshops and information (including an ASD website) for both parents and carers of preschool and school-aged children on the autism spectrum in both city and rural areas are also being provided through the HCWA initiative. An interim evaluation (AAETC, 2009) of the positive partnerships component of the HCWA support package indicated that participants in the professional development program "reported statistically significant increases in five areas: attitudes, knowledge, skills, inclusive teaching and collaboration and partnerships" (AAETC,

2009, p. 1). It is also reported that "participant evaluation data from the parent/carer workshops and information sessions indicates statistically significant increases in knowledge of educational environments, knowledge of parenting and partnerships" (AAETC, 2009, p. 2). Based on its success, the program has been extended past its 2012 end date and is presently still operating across Australia.

Unlike some states in Australia, WA does not have any purpose-built primary or high schools for students on the autism spectrum or appropriate support for home educators of these students. There has been a strong call by parent groups over many years in WA for a specific school for students on the autism spectrum to be established and more appropriate home education support and funding to be provided so that all education options may be available to families when mainstream education options are no longer viable (See Parliamentary Submission in Appendix A).

Presently, in response to on-going difficulties experienced by adolescent students on the autism spectrum, there have been a small number of specific DoE Secondary Autism Extension Units set up at the mainstream high school level. These units have been specifically designed for students with an ASD in Years 8, 9 and 10 with the intention of being responsive and flexible to the individual needs of such students. Each unit presently caters for a small number of students with increased staffing. The Units provide a different model of service delivery to high school students on the autism spectrum who are experiencing significant difficulties in a high school setting and are at risk of disengagement and alienation. They have limited intake numbers and as such entry can be competitive between students/families (McDonald, 2010).

The students in the Units have access to both a mainstream and a home-room environment within the school. Staff involved in the Units have specialist training and are given support by the DoE Autism Intervention Team. The educational program undertaken is flexible and is determined by the students' individual needs. The learning program uses such evidence-based practices as transitional programming, structured environments, specific teaching strategies, computer technologies, visual tools and documented education plans. The program also offers students with an ASD the opportunity to explore their special interests. The Units have not yet been independently evaluated (McDonald, 2010). However, the WA Department of Education is presently conducting a review of public high school options in the Fremantle area where the South Fremantle Autism Extension Unit is located. It remains to be seen what the results will be from such a review and if these results will be released to the community.

At the university level, courses available to teachers in WA are presently ad-hoc in their content regarding 'inclusivity' and may or may not have much specific instruction on supporting or accommodating students on the autism spectrum. To combat this, the DoE Autism Education Service has been offering a semester-long accredited unit of instruction on supporting students with ASDs in the mainstream classroom. Not all faculties in the WA tertiary sector have the inclination, time or the requisite funding to include such courses in their pre-service teaching programs even though such instruction has widespread application for the increasingly diverse population regular mainstream teachers must now accommodate and support in their 'inclusive' classroom (McDonald, 2010).

In terms of specific investigation of the current state of students on the autism spectrum at the tertiary level, only a small amount of research has been done. Recent Australian research indicates that while many on the autism spectrum may not have an intellectual disability they may still have significant learning support needs in tertiary settings. A recent Australian study of 300 adults with a diagnosis of high functioning autism or Asperger's syndrome from every Australian state and territory found that more than 80% had commenced or completed a tertiary qualification (Aspect, 2012). However, adults in the study reported that they had experienced significant struggles to reach their full potential in education. Almost half the respondents reported they received no or insufficient additional support for their learning needs and many felt their teachers failed to understand their needs and treated them unfairly as a result. Approximately one quarter of adults on the spectrum reported having commenced a course of study only to abandon it before completion (Aspect, 2012).

A small number of tertiary education disability officers who were also interviewed for the study identified:

> … difficulties in verbal comprehension, planning and organisation, social awareness, and group work as key challenges for adult students with ASD. They perceived a lack of awareness and understanding of ASD among tertiary educators (Aspect, 2012, p.13).

More recently a pilot peer-to-peer specialist mentoring program has been set up at Curtin University in WA specifically providing support for students on the autism spectrum. This Curtin Specialist Mentoring Program (CSMP) has recently gained Cooperative Research Centre (CRC) funding to have the program replicated and evaluated at the University of WA. The results will eventually be available to other tertiary institutions on the CRC website (www.autismcrc.com.au).

CONCLUSION

This chapter has provided a brief description of pertinent aspects of the context of the study. It identified the differing factors that have influenced, over several decades in various Western countries, the range of educational options now on offer to students with disabilities within Australia and WA. The chapter also provided a more specific investigation of the WA context inclusive of the following areas: ASD prevalence, diagnosis, early intervention, general disability educational provision and educational provision for students on the autism spectrum. The following chapter will provide a brief review of the research literature and is approached with the intention of providing a general overview of relevant areas of research that informed the study (McDonald, 2010) explained in this publication.

CHAPTER 3

WHAT DOES THE RESEARCH TELL US?

While the research field regarding educating a child on the autism spectrum has grown exponentially, parents often find it difficult to navigate their best course of action in relation to educating their individual child because all children on the autism spectrum have their own unique, idiosyncratic profile and progress. It is increasingly evident that there is no single best-suited and universally effective educational method for all children on the autism spectrum over time. Research has found that the best programs are those that incorporate a variety of objectively verified practices and are designed to address and support the needs of individual students and the professionals and families with whom they are linked (National Research Council, 2001; Olley, 1999; Parsons et al., 2011; Simpson, 2005, 2007; Simpson, de Boer-Ott, & Smith-Myles, 2003). In relation to how parents deal with this situation over time there has been limited research undertaken. The study (McDonald, 2010) reported in this publication seeks to address this gap in the research.

Treatment of the research literature in this chapter has been approached with the intention of providing a brief general overview of pertinent, relevant areas. This chapter examines the research literature in five main sections: History; Prevalence; Aetiology; Social Impact/Coping; and Education. The final section on Education is given a more concentrated treatment due to its particular relevance to the focus of this investigation. Education is further broken into the following six sub-sections: Evidence Based Practice; Early Intervention; Formal schooling; Post-Secondary Education; Australian & WA General Disability Educational Provision Research; WA Autism Educational Provision Research and Home Schooling.

HISTORY

The term 'autism' has its origins in the Greek word 'autos' meaning 'self'. According to the prominent UK psychiatrist and autism spectrum researcher, Lorna Wing (Wing, 1976), this term was originally used by Swiss psychiatrist, Eugene Bleuler, nearly a century ago to describe individuals who seemed to escape from reality into the isolation of schizophrenia. In terms of education of such people, the earliest cited case is that of the so-called 'Wild Boy of Aveyron'. In the early 1800s a French physician named Jean Marc Itard attempted to educate a young 'wild' boy, Victor, who was found living alone in a forest. The child exhibited many behaviours often associated with autism, such as rocking back and forth, perseverating on an object, an indifference to people and a fear of loud noises. Itard took the child to Paris and attempted to educate the boy in such areas as communication and social skills

(Itard, 1962). Itard had hopes of curing the child because he assumed that the child's problems stemmed only from his lack of human contact. However, even though he was able to teach the child to read and follow simple directions, the child was never able to fully relate to others and continued to have limited language skills (Itard, 1962). Historically, Itard has been credited as being one of the pioneers of autism education (Frith, 1989).

In more recent times, two physicians on different continents noted similar unique behaviours in two different sets of children. In 1943, in his ground breaking paper, *Autistic Disturbance of Affective Contact* (Kanner, 1943), Leo Kanner, a U.S. researcher at Johns Hopkins University, described eleven children in his study as having "inborn autistic disturbances of affective contact" (p. 50). Coincidentally in 1944, the Austrian physician, Hans Asperger, studying a similar group of four children in Austria, published his results in his research paper, *Autistic psychopathy in childhood* (Asperger, 1991 / 1944). Unfortunately, his contribution was not widely recognized until some 40 years later when Lorna Wing coined the term 'Asperger's Syndrome' to describe the high-functioning children she was studying at the time (Wing, 1981).

In his study, Kanner (1973) described the children's behaviour as "characterized by extreme aloneness and preoccupation with the preservation of sameness" (p. 100). Kanner indicated that these children displayed: an inability to relate to others; a failure to assume an anticipatory posture; an excellent rote memory; delayed echolalia; literalness; an all-powerful need for being left undisturbed; monotonously repetitious noises and motions; a limitation in the variety of spontaneous activity; good general appearance; and cognitive potential (AAETC, 2008a). Kanner postulated that the cause of this behaviour could be both environmental and biological. He noted that many of the children's parents seemed cold, detached and obsessive. He called for research into the biological, psychological, and social aspects of autism. Unfortunately, these observations led to "the development of the notion that Autism was caused by cold, unfeeling parents" (AAETC, 2008a, p. 5). This was the beginning of parents being seen as the possible cause of their child's autism. Unfortunately, this led to decades of research investigating the legitimacy of such a proposition and the persecution of parents who had a child with autism during this time.

In a similar vein, Hans Asperger observed that the children in his study lacked appropriate social maturity and reasoning (Asperger, 1991 / 1944). There was seemingly a gap between the children's emotional maturity and their intellectual abilities. They showed impairments in verbal and non-verbal communication and had preoccupations with specific areas of interest. Some of the children also had learning and social difficulties at school. They showed a need for more self-help and organizational skills and had coordination difficulties. Asperger also described how these children were often extremely sensitive to sounds, aromas, textures and touch (Attwood, 2007). Asperger has been credited with the idea that autism occurs on a continuum where some children in his study showed superficially normal language development and IQ (Attwood, 2007). Importantly, Asperger did not view these children as having a mental illness but rather a personality disorder and hypothesized that "the condition was probably due to genetic or neurological, rather than psychological or environmental, factors" (Attwood, 2007, p. 13). According to Attwood (2007), "it is apparent that he *(Asperger)* considered autistic personality disorder as part of a natural continuum of abilities that merges into the normal range" (p. 13). Over three decades, Asperger observed that the personality disorder was life-long and stable and that the specific talents of these children could be utilized to gain successful employment and in some cases, develop life-long relationships (Attwood, 2007).

The 1950s and early 60s saw the rise of parent attribution theories whereby early severe stress was seen as a possible cause of a child's autism. This early stress was either supposedly caused by a separation between the parent and child at a critical stage of ego development or where there had been early trauma such as a family tragedy or discord (Cantwell & Baker, 1984). In particular, an Austrian Jewish psychologist and concentration camp survivor, Bruno Bettleheim, furthered Kanner's original assertion that parents could be to blame for their children's autism in his best known work, *The Empty Fortress: Infantile Autism and the Birth of the Self* (Bettelheim, 1967). He theorized that 'refrigerator mothers' were somehow responsible for their child's difficulties (Bettelheim, 1967). Professionals viewed such 'refrigerator parents' as responsible for their children withdrawing into their own world. Treatment sometimes consisted of psychotherapy for parents and play therapy for the children and often the child was removed from the home and placed into an institution (Schopler, 1971; Schopler & Mesibov, 1984; Schreibman, 1988). Bettleheim's work has since been discredited because of a profound lack of empirically-based evidence (AAETC, 2008a). Bernard Rimland, a psychologist and parent of a child on the autism spectrum, successfully challenged such notions in his 1964 paper, *Infantile Autism: The syndrome and its implication for a neural theory of behaviour*, by asserting that autism was a biological disorder with a neurological aetiology (AAETC, 2008a).

Some researchers also studied parent-child communication and interaction patterns as possible causes of autism (Cantwell & Baker, 1984). However, the results of these studies were varied and while earlier studies (Goldfarb, Levy, & Meyers, 1972; Goldfarb, Goldfarb, & Scholl, 1966) indicated that mothers displayed inadequate communication patterns with their children, methodological flaws discounted the accuracy of these results (Cox, Rutter, Newman, & Bartak, 1975; Howlin, Cantwell, Marchant, Berger, & Rutter, 1973). Later studies (Cantwell & Baker, 1977; Cantwell, Baker, & Rutter, 1979) did not find any differences in the communications of such mothers and their children with autism from the norm. Similarly, there was also research (Cantwell & Baker, 1984) into the idea that parents of children with autism exhibited a personality disorder prior to having their child, thus contributing to their child's difficulties. The results of some of these studies revealed that while fathers and mothers (Dor-Shav & Horowitz, 1984; Wolff, Naraan, & Moyes, 1988) did show some differences their results were far from conclusive. One of the major problems cited with such research was how do researchers determine "whether parents of children with Autism exhibit differing personality characteristics prior to having autistic children or whether these characteristics appear as a result of parenting autistic children" (Ewart, 2002, p. 20).

During the 1970s and 80s, there was a shift away from parent attribution theories to studies which hypothesized that there was a biological basis of autism (Cantwell & Baker, 1984; Schopler, 1994). There was also research evidence emerging through family and twin studies which indicated that this biological disorder had genetic roots (Le Couteur et al., 1996; Rutter, 2005a). Behaviourist techniques also began to gain favour and replace psychoanalytic practices in terms of treatment for autism (Schopler & Mesibov, 1986; Schreibman, 1988). Parents were no longer seen as the possible cause of their child's autism but were now enlisted to become co-therapists in their child's treatment. Often such interventions consisted of at-home, intensive, and individualised behavioural treatment programs conducted over a number of years (Lovaas, 1987; Schopler & Mesibov, 1986; Schreibman, 1988).

Wing and Gould (1979) have been credited with identifying the 'triad of impairments' which was the early diagnostic criteria for autism, namely, severe impairments of social interaction, language abnormalities, and repetitive stereotyped behaviours. In 1988, Wing described the notion of an autistic 'continuum' but revised this in 1996 by replacing it with the term 'spectrum' (Wing, 1988, 1996). The reasoning being that the disorder was overlapping in nature with variation on its dimensions rather than occurring as a linear continuum (Wing, 1996). During the early 1980s Wing also "became increasingly aware that the descriptions of Leo Kanner that formed the basis of our understanding and diagnosis of autism in America and Britain did not accurately describe some of the children and adults within her considerable clinical and research experience" (Attwood, 2007, p. 35). In response to this, Wing wrote a research paper in 1981 (Wing, 1981) which indicated that the profile of abilities of 34 children and adults in her study showed a greater resemblance to the descriptions of Asperger (Asperger, 1991 / 1944) than those put forward by Kanner (Kanner, 1943). This paper eventually led to the new diagnostic category of Asperger's Syndrome/Disorder being included within the autism spectrum of both the *International Classification of Diseases* (ICD-10) in 1993, and the *Diagnostic and Statistical Manual of Mental Disorders* (DSM-IV) in 1994 (Attwood, 2007).

The diagnostic categories of autism have broadened over time. In 1980, the category of 'autism' replaced the category of 'early infantile autism' in the *Diagnostic and Statistical Manual of Mental Disorders* (DSM-III) (American Psychiatric Association, 1980; Simpson & LaCava, 2007). 'Pervasive Developmental Disorder-Not Otherwise Specified' (PDD-NOS) was added to the revised DSM-III (American Psychiatric Association, 1980) in 1987 to describe individuals who had some but not all characteristics of autism (Simpson & LaCava, 2007). By 1994 the categories of 'Childhood Disintegrative Disorder', 'Rett's Disorder' and 'Asperger's Disorder' had all been added under the umbrella classification of 'Pervasive Developmental Disorders' (PDDs) in the DSM-IV (American Psychiatric Association, 1994; Simpson & LaCava, 2007). This broadening of the diagnostic criteria has been touted as one of the major reasons for the dramatic increase in the number of individuals diagnosed with an ASD or PDD over the last twenty-five years (Fombonne, 2009; Rutter, 2005c). Environmental causes and greater public awareness of the disorder have also been raised as possible reasons for the increase (Fombonne, 2003, 2009; Kirby, 2005; MacDermott et al., 2007).

As previously discussed in Chapter Two (Diagnosis Section), the DSM-IV has been under revision and a new edition, the DSM 5, has been recently released in 2013. Significant changes to the criteria and categories of ASDs have occurred in the new edition. It remains to be seen how such changes will impact individuals on the spectrum and their families.

PREVALENCE

Prevalence is understood to be "a measure of the number of cases of a disorder in a defined population at a particular point in time" (MacDermott et al., 2007, p. 6). The number of children diagnosed with autism spectrum disorders continues to grow in Australia. Based on Centrelink Carer Allowance data, Buckley (2012) has recently indicated that the national average autism prevalence in school age children exceeded 1.4% (1 in 62.5) by June 2012.

However, the rate of prevalence of ASDs has been and continues to be controversial (Myles et al., 2007). There is no single and reliable test to confirm an autism spectrum disorder (ASD) and diagnosis is presently made through mainly behavioural observations and other subjectively related methods. These methods of diagnosis are therefore based on the individual clinical judgments of professionals that can sometimes produce differences of opinion regarding a specific diagnosis (Baird, Cass, & Slonims, 2003; Coo et al., 2008; Mandell, Ittenback, Levy, & Pinto-Martin, 2007; Simpson & LaCava, 2007). In relation to this, there has been a call in Australia for more accurate, early universal screening of ASDs within Australia (Dissanayake, 2009). Since 2007 in the USA there has been a 'Two screens by Two years' guideline where very young children are routinely screened for an ASD by their paediatrician twice before they reach two years of age (Duby & Plauche Johnson, 2009).

Prevalence rates for all forms of ASD's worldwide have seemingly risen dramatically since the mid-1960s (Fombonne, 2009). Such increases have, most often, been attributed to a refinement of the conceptualization of autism, a corresponding broadening of diagnostic criteria and improved methods of case finding and ascertainment (Fombonne, 2003, 2009; Fombonne, Zakarian, Bennett, Meng, & McLean-Heywood, 2006; MacDermott et al., 2007; Rutter, 2005c; Simpson & LaCava, 2007). Many other theories associated with possible environmental causes (Kirby, 2005; McCarthy, 2009; Wakefield et al., 1998) are also now apparent in mainstream discourse. Along with this, intervention services have progressively become more available under the different diagnostic categories of ASDs and specific ASD diagnoses have been sought by parents to access such services (Simpson & LaCava, 2007). However, a 'true' rise in the rate of ASDs has not been firmly excluded (Fombonne, 2009; Rutter, 2005c).

Accuracy of the prevalence rate of all ASDs is also questionable given that Attwood (2007) estimates that "we are currently detecting and diagnosing about 50 per cent of children who have Asperger's syndrome" because they are "able to camouflage their difficulties and avoid detection, or a clinician fails to see Asperger's syndrome and focuses on another diagnosis" (p. 46). To further complicate the situation in the future, prevalence will continue to be affected by the different diagnostic criteria used to generate prevalence data. In relation to this, the recently released fifth edition of the Diagnostic and Statistical Manual (American Psychiatric Association, 2013b) has changed some diagnostic criteria and made substantial revision of others. This will, in turn, probably affect the prevalence rate of those diagnosed with an ASD over time (Matson, Hattier, & Williams, 2012; Gibbs, Aldridge, Chandler, Witzlsperger, & Smith, 2012; McPartland, Reichow, & Volkmar, 2012).

AETIOLOGY

Presently, ASDs have no established common cause or aetiology (Myles et al., 2007; O'Reilly & Smith, 2008; Rutter, 2005a). While many theories exist to explain the enigma of autism no one common cause has yet been able to explain the wide expression of phenotype which occurs across the spectrum of the disorder (Rutter, 2005a). It may be that there is an interplay between a number of causes which may make discovery of a specific aetiology very difficult if not impossible (Rutter, 2005a). Alternatively, it may be there are different causes for different expressions of the disorder (O'Reilly & Smith, 2008).

There have been many and varied investigations into this area over the last twenty-five years because of the seeming explosion of prevalence of the disorder. Some parent groups have been convinced that while genetics play a part there has been an environmental insult, which has triggered their child's autism (Kirby, 2005; McCarthy, 2009). This situation is further complicated by the problem that it may be that there is a convenient correlation occurring rather than a causal link being established (Shore & Rastelli, 2006). Researchers have found it difficult to determine whether an issue has caused the autism or is one of the results of the child having autism in the first place (Shore & Rastelli, 2006). Presented below are some of the main theories regarding the elusive aetiology of autism apparent in current discourse.

Genetic liability undoubtedly plays a part in the reason why a child may have an ASD (Rutter, 2005a, 2005b). Twin studies have shown that there is a 60% concordance rate of ASD in monozygotic twin pairs and this reduces to a 5% concordance in dizygotic pairs (Rutter, 2005a). Heritability for ASD is approximately 90% and this figure is one of the highest among all multifactorial child psychiatric disorders (Rutter, 2005a). To further complicate matters for parents, families with one affected child have a 45 times greater recurrence risk of siblings also being affected by an ASD than would occur in the general population (Jamain, Betaneur, Giros, Leboyer, & Bourgeron, 2003). According to Rutter (2005a):

> Putting together the twin and family findings, the figures indicate that it is likely that there are somewhere between 3 and 12 susceptibility genes for Autism that act synergistically. The reason why most siblings do not have ASD, despite the high heritability, is that they have only some of the relevant genes (p. 232).

Along with any ASD diagnosis there is also a 25% greater susceptibility of comorbidity with another psychiatric disorder and/or medical condition (Gillberg & Billstedt, 2000). Autism is over represented amongst males with a male to female ratio of 4.3:1 (Fombonne, 2003; American Psychiatric Association, 2000).

The single gene condition of tuberous sclerosis has had an established association with ASD and is found in approximately 1-3% of cases of ASD (Harrison & Bolton, 1997; Smalley, 1998). The Fragile X anomaly has also been shown to occur in about 2-3% of individuals with an ASD (Rutter, 2005a). However, there is still no exact mode of inheritance indicating how genes and traits are passed from parent to child with an ASD. According to Rutter (2005a), even if susceptibility genes for ASDs could be found it is unlikely that this discovery would be of much practical utility in terms of either screening or diagnosis.

Over the years, research into the physiology and workings of the brain has also been another area of promising research. An abnormality in brain size, structure and functioning is generally accepted as what may cause or be a by-product of an ASD in some children (Courchesne et al., 2001; Kemper & Bauman, 1993; Shore & Rastelli, 2006). One significant study indicated that there was atypical head circumference in 59% of children with an ASD who were measured at birth and between the ages of 6 and 14 months (Courchesne, Carper, & Akshoomoff, 2003). This finding suggests that increased head growth in infancy could be a possible early symptom or risk marker for an ASD (Myles et al., 2007). However, it has also been found that this increase in size changes over time for different age groups of individuals with an ASD where early overgrowth is followed by a premature arrest of growth (Courchesne, 2004). This research potentially links with other research which suggests that there may be an overgrowth of nerve connections occurring in the brains of individuals with an ASD at an early stage of development which may cause the brain to become overwhelmed with neurotransmitter signals (Shore & Rastelli, 2006).

Some researchers theorize that an ASD is a disorder of brain circuit dysfunction. Studies have indicated that the fusiform gyrus, located in the temporal lobe of the cerebrum, has lower activation levels than the normal population and this interferes with processing faces and social cognition (Pierce, Muller, Ambrose, Allen, & Courchesne, 2001; Sasson, 2006). Other researchers however, have speculated that the brain processing of individuals with an ASD may be organized or react differently (Just, Cherkassky, Keller, & Minshew, 2004). It has been found that while individuals with an ASD may have intact cortical brain cells important for thought, language, and reasoning, they may be less efficient in the way these cells communicate with each other because of differences in myelin production which insulates brain cell connections (Herbert, Ziegler, Deutsch et al., 2005; Herbert, Ziegler, Makris et al., 2004).

Some neuroimaging researchers investigating individuals with an ASD have also discovered impairment in a network of brain regions located in the medial frontal cortex associated with understanding the mental state of others or 'theory of mind' (Castelli, Frith, Happe, & Frith, 2002; Happe et al., 1996; Nieiminen-von Wendt et al., 2003). Other neuroimaging researchers investigating high functioning individuals with an ASD have found that there is reduced activity in the dorsolateral prefrontal regions of the brain during working memory tasks which may explain difficulties with executive function (Koshino et al., 2005; Luna et al., 2002). Neuroimaging researchers have also examined patterns of intellectual strength or 'savant skills'. One study has found that individuals with an ASD showed greater activity in the ventral occipitotemporal regions of the brain than did controls when undertaking central coherence tasks (Ring et al., 1999). While these areas of research are gradually increasing our understanding regarding differences inherent in the brains of individuals with an ASD it does not provide anything conclusive regarding a specific, common aetiology.

Environment is one of the most contentious areas implicated as a possible cause of ASDs. One of the most controversial theories put forward, often by parent groups, has been that some environmental trigger or triggers in conjunction with a genetic predisposition has caused a generation of children to be disproportionately affected by ASDs (Kirby, 2005; Myles et al., 2007). There has also been speculation that the severity of the disability depends on the number of genes affected in an individual and the type of environmental insult that has occurred (Myles et al., 2007).

Heavy metals, such as mercury, have been implicated especially in the immunization schedule of the US (Kirby, 2005). It has been suggested that the spike in the reported cases of ASDs has coincided with a doubling of the number of childhood vaccines given to children from 1988 onward (Kirby, 2005). The theory is that some of these vaccines contained a preservative called thimerosal, which is made up of 49.6% mercury, and the cumulative effect of successive immunizations in a susceptible portion of the population has resulted in an 'epidemic' of children with an ASD (Kirby, 2005). In 2004 the US Institute of Medicine issued a report indicating that the bulk of the evidence favoured rejection of a causal relationship between thimerosal and autism (Institute of Medicine - Committee on Immunization Safety, 2004). The bulk of evidence against the thimerosal theory was from large-scale population studies (Madsen et al., 2003; Stehr-Green et al., 2003) comparing United States ASD prevalence and incidence rates with rates from other countries that had removed thimerosal totally from their immunization schedule (Kirby, 2005).

> factors contributing to their ongoing and changing challenges and successes. It is incumbent on service providers to recognize and value these differences and respond accordingly (p. 7).

Both formal (professional service providers) and informal (other ASD parents, family etc.) sources are cited as potential avenues of knowledge and support. However, the use of these avenues is complicated by the need for families "to develop unique skills for parenting their child with ASD, skills that are often totally unfamiliar within their personal experience, or even that of their social networks" (MacDermott, 2008, p. 8). Also, other immediate and extended family members often need their own support and "it is not possible, therefore, to plan effectively to meet the needs of the child with ASD without also taking into account the needs of their whole family system" (MacDermott, 2008, p. 8).

Another general grounded theory study examining how parents cope with their physically and/or intellectually disabled children indicates that:

> To cope, the family uses its existing resources and strategies. These coping strategies are defined as the active processes and behaviours that the family actually try to employ to help to manage, adapt to or deal with a stressful situation. Coping entails constantly changing cognitive and behavioural efforts to manage specific external and/or internal demands that are appraised as taxing the family's resources .... The aim of familial coping procedures is to maintain or restore the balance between the demands and resources ... The family can do this by reducing the number or intensity of the demands applied to it ... It can also strengthen its existing resources ... may also involve a cognitive appraisal aiming to alter the meanings applied to the situation (Taanila, Syrjala, Kokkonen, & Jarvelin, 2002, p. 74).

Other general studies on family coping and disability (Berry & Hardman, 1998) also indicate that success in coping is a long-term process that is linked to a gradual accumulation of skills by family members over time and often a changed perspective on their situation.

The use of both problem focused and emotion focused coping strategies by parents of children with an ASD was also borne out by Gray (1994, 2006) in an Australian longitudinal research project that examined specifically how parents of children with an ASD coped over a ten-year period. Gray's (1994) initial study, at the beginning of a ten year period, indicated that most parents used a variety of coping strategies with the most common being the use of service agencies, family support, social withdrawal, religion, normalisation, individualism and activism. Gray's (2006) follow-up study indicated that:

> Coping strategies changed from the time of the initial study, as fewer parents coped through reliance on service providers, family support, social withdrawal and individualism and relatively more parents coped through their religious faith and other emotion-focused strategies. The results tentatively support

> previous research on coping that indicates that aging is linked to the use of more emotion-focused coping strategies (p. 970).

Such changes in the belief systems of parents of children with an ASD over time have also been documented by King et al. (2005) who found that "although parents may grapple with lost dreams, over time positive adaptations can occur in the form of changed world views concerning life and disability, and an appreciation of the positive contributions made by children to family members and society as a whole" (p. 353).

EDUCATION

The social impact research indicates that parents who have a child with an ASD are potentially a very vulnerable group who are at greater risk for mental health problems than other parent groups who have a child with a disability (Benson & Karlof, 2009; Singer, 2006; Tehee et al., 2009). The general welfare of the family potentially underpins their ability to deal effectively with all aspects of their lives, including the education of their child with an ASD. Overall, research investigating the effect of having a child with an ASD in the family has revealed variation in levels of distress among parents which has been explained by such factors as differences in child characteristics and protective parent resources such as social support (Hastings, 2008). The research also indicates that appropriate and targeted informal and formal support can improve the outcomes for many of these families (Benson & Karlof, 2009; Ewart, 2002; Hastings & Brown, 2002; MacDermott, 2008). One key area, which has been nominated as a potential source of both stress and support, is that of education (MacDermott, 2008; Trudgeon & Carr, 2007).

In the Western Australian study investigating the thoughts, feelings, experience, needs and wants of 92 families parenting school-aged children who have a suspected or confirmed ASD, MacDermott, (2008) indicates the importance of education for parents when she writes, "Of all the issues that families must address during their child's school-aged years, their relationship with the educational system that their child participates in is of primary importance" (p. 84). Past research has shown that the stress experienced by mothers has potentially an inverse relationship with the educational progress of their child with an ASD (Robbins et al., 1991). Hence, one potential avenue of reducing stress in families who have a child with an ASD is to access a successful, evidence-based education program consistently over time which maximizes the progress of their child with an ASD. However, according to West Australian research (Crosby, 1998; Forlin, 2004; Forlin et al., 2008; Jenkins, 2005; MacDermott, 2008; Wills & Jackson, 2000) and Australian research (Ford, 2007; Roberts & Prior, 2006; Shaddock et al., 2007) the ability of WA parents to reliably gain such an education for their child with an ASD over time is potentially problematic because of the inconsistent inclusive landscape they must continually traverse.

Evidenced-Based Practice

Research investigating the cognitive characteristics of individuals on the autism spectrum is ever increasing. It is commonly agreed that there are a triad of impairments in students on the autism spectrum involving difficulties in the areas of communication, socialization and rigid/repetitive behaviours (AAETC, 2008b). More recently with the publication of the latest Diagnostic and Statistical Manual (DSM-5) (Department of Education, Employment and Workplace Relations, 2013), there has been recognition that there is also often sensory dysfunction in such individuals. Beyond these impairments, there are more cognitive characteristics to consider and these involve deficits in 'theory of mind' skills, difficulties with executive function, weak central coherence, sensory processing difficulties and motor functioning problems (AAETC, 2008b; Ministry of Health, 2008). Students on the autism spectrum may also have a number of relative cognitive strengths in the areas of rote memory, visual spatial abilities, compartmentalized learning, preference for routine and rules, intense interests and being logical (AAETC, 2008b).

The degree to which an individual on the autism spectrum is variously affected in these areas of functioning produces an idiosyncratic profile that should be assessed and appropriately addressed through any education program undertaken by both parents and professionals (AAETC, 2008b). It is increasingly evident that there is no single best-suited and universally effective educational method for all children on the autism spectrum over time. As previously noted research has found that the best programs are those that incorporate a variety of objectively verified practices and are designed to address and support the needs of individual students and the professionals and families with whom they are linked (National Research Council, 2001; Olley, 1999; Parsons et al., 2011; Simpson, 2005, 2007; Simpson et al., 2003).

A research review of ten years of research conducted by Iovannone et al.(2003) that investigated effective educational practices for students on the autism spectrum revealed six best practice core elements that have empirical support and should be included in any educational program:

a. individualized supports and services for students and families,
b. systematic instruction,
c. comprehensible/structured learning environments,
d. specialized curriculum content,
e. functional approach to problem behavior, and
f. family involvement (p. 150)

The need to individually tailor educational programs for students on the autism spectrum places parents and professionals in very demanding circumstances regarding adoption of appropriate and effective educational practices concerning their individual child. Consequently, there is a long-standing tradition by parents of children on the autism spectrum of accepting educational methods and strategies that sometimes lack efficacy and proven utility (Gresham et al., 1999; Heflin & Simpson,

1998; Simpson, 2004, 2005). Families often do not have access to educational research of specific students which meets rigorous peer review and has a history of yielding positive results over time (Simpson, LaCava, & Graner, 2004). The difficulty is that there are only limited samples of students with similar characteristics and needs because of the highly idiosyncratic nature and progress of the condition (Simpson, 2005). In addition to this, Prior and Roberts (2006) indicate that while there is comprehensive early intervention research available there is limited research regarding what types of intervention are best for improving long term learning and adaptive functioning into adolescence and adulthood.

Early Intervention

There is an ever-growing body of research regarding the most efficacious educational interventions for students on the autism spectrum. This is especially so in the early intervention stages of education (Roberts & Prior, 2006). Comprehensive early intervention research shows that early, intensive, behavioural and psycho-educational intervention can sometimes dramatically improve the often bleak prognosis given to children diagnosed on the autism spectrum. The last 20 years of research has revealed that evidenced based, early intervention (EI) can have a significant positive impact on the educational progress of the child on the autism spectrum (Birnbrauer & Leach, 1993; Francis, 2005; Green, 1996; Howard, Sparkman, Cohen, Green, & Stanislaw, 2005; Jordan, 2004; Lovaas, 1987; Magiati, Charman, & Howlin, 2007; McEachin, Smith, & Lovaas, 1993; Roberts & Prior, 2006).

One of the most efficacious, evidence-based early intervention methods is the Applied Behaviour Analysis / Discrete Trial Traning (ABA/DTT) method which recommends up to 40 hours per week of one-on-one intervention in some best practice models (Birnbrauer & Leach, 1993; Francis, 2005; Howard et al., 2005; Lovaas, 1987, 2003; McEachin et al., 1993; Palm Consulting Group, 2005; Roberts & Prior, 2006; Smith, Wynn, & Lovaas, 1996). Research indicates that: early intervention is time-critical; and that it should be conducted as early as possible over a number of years; be intensive; be generalized over as many environments as possible; be initially one-on-one; and be based on behavioural and psycho-educational principles (Birnbrauer & Leach, 1993; Francis, 2005; Green, 1996; Howard et al., 2005; Howlin & Rutter, 1987; Lovaas, 1987; Magiati et al., 2007; McEachin et al., 1993; Roberts & Prior, 2006; Smith & Lovaas, 1998; Smith, 1996; Lovaas, 2003; Eccleston, 2005; Myles, 2005).

An study commissioned by the Australian Government Department of Health and Ageing to review the research to identify the most effective models of practice in early intervention for children with an ASD, confirmed that current recommended best practice is as follows:

> The most systematic evidence available has come from evaluations of intensive behaviour intervention programs, such as The Lovaas program which uses

> Applied Behaviour Analysis (ABA) including Discrete Trial Training. These evaluations have shown improved learning and behavioural development in a significant proportion of children. However, these methods do not suit all children and families, and strict conditions of timing, intensity, and quality of therapist training influence the success of these methods. Other programs have so far not provided sufficient evidence of short or long term improvement to qualify for unreserved support.... To be successful EI needs to be extensive and intensive. A minimum of 20 hours a week over two or more years is essential for young children to make major gains (Prior & Roberts, 2006, p. 3).

Prior and Roberts (2006) list the following key common elements as necessary for effective early intervention:

- An Autism specific curriculum content focusing on attention, compliance, imitation, language, and social skills.
- Highly supportive teaching environments which deal with the need for predictability and routine, and with challenging behaviour, obsessions, and ritual behaviours.
- Support for children in their transition from the preschool classroom.
- Support for family members including partnership with professionals involved in treatments (p. 3).

Any program should also account for individual variation in both the child with an ASD and their family, in terms of their relative strengths and needs, with the understanding that "no one program will suit all children with Autism and their families" (Prior & Roberts, 2006, p. 3). According to Roberts and Prior (2006), parents also need current accurate information about treatment options and "emotional support, advice, and training in working with their children" during diagnosis and beyond (p. 74).

Given the intensity of recommended, best practice, behavioural interventions it is not surprising that many parents find the funding of such programs problematic. In a US study investigating financial issues associated with having a child with an ASD, Sharpe and Baker (2007) indicated that "many survey respondents forfeited future financial security and even experienced bankruptcy to provide needed therapy for a child with Autism" (p. 247).

In another study investigating the economic costs of Autistic Disorder and Asperger's Disorder in Australia, it was found that ASD has a total overall annual cost of between $4.5 and $7.2 billion per annum (Synergies Economic Consulting Pty Ltd, 2007). It is reported that "This equates to an average *incremental* cost of approximately $56,000 per person with ASD (this is not the total expenditure – it represents the costs over and above other costs that would normally be incurred by people without ASD)" (Synergies Economic Consulting Pty Ltd, 2007, p. 13). The report indicates that these figures are underestimates and do not include the cost of implementing intensive early intervention programs. They only reflect costs associated with general and mental healthcare; social services; education; employment; informal care; and the impact on well-being (Synergies Economic Consulting Pty Ltd, 2007).

Along with problems associated with cost, Roberts and Prior (2006) indicate there is often a lack of appropriately trained consultants that has sometimes compelled parents to conduct their own home-based intensive behavioural programs with only intermittent support from professionals (Johnson & Hastings, 2002). Research (Bibby, Eikeseth, Martin, Mudford, & Reeves, 2002; Mudford, Martin, Eikeseth, & Bibby, 2001) indicates that it is unlikely that home-based, intensive behavioural programs will result in the same gains as those clamed in the original Lovaas (1987) study without appropriate support. In a study examining the facilitating factors and barriers to the implementation of home based intensive behavioural intervention programs, it was found that having a supportive committed team, financial resources, and the support of family and friends were the most frequently cited facilitating factors (Johnson & Hastings, 2002). Most frequently cited barriers to parents running successful home based programs were difficulties recruiting experienced, trained staff, funding, and personal/family resource constraints. The most frequently cited barrier and facilitating factor was the quality of the program team (Johnson & Hastings, 2002).

Further to this, another study explored the range of impacts on families who were running early, intensive, behavioural intervention programs for their children with an ASD and found that the programs had mixed impacts – "specific sources of anxiety and stress on families through the programmes' demands were accompanied by significant sources of support provided through the programmes' benefits" (Trudgeon & Carr, 2007, p. 294).

Additionally, Roberts and Prior (2006) point out that there are considerations and limitations regarding the intensive, early intervention, behavioural research. There are potential issues regarding the quality of expertise, training and supervision required to maintain the treatment integrity of an intensive behavioural intervention (home-based or otherwise) (Mudford et al., 2001; Smith, 1993). There is also no conclusive evidence about the optimal intensity of early behavioural programs. Roberts and Prior (2006) indicate that "a number of researchers (Anderson, Dipietero, Edwards, & Christian, 1987; Sheinkopf & Siegal, 1998; Smith, Groen, & Wynn, 2000) have suggested that the smaller gains made by the participants in their studies compared to the original group in the Lovaas study (1987) were a result of fewer hours of treatment per week" (p. 49). However, other research by Sallows and Graupner (2005) found little difference in treatment outcomes between children who received slightly more intensive clinic-directed behavioural intervention versus children who received slightly less intensive parent-directed therapy. By contrast, another comprehensive study found that increasing treatment hours within an early, intensive, behavioral intervention program resulted in greater efficiency in new skill acquisition and this effect was the strongest in younger children within the study (Granpeesheh, Dixon, Tarbox, Kaplan, & Wilke, 2009).

Questions have been raised about whether the use of contingent aversives in the original Lovaas (1987) study could account for the success of the Lovaas style intensive behavioural program over others (Lovaas, 1987; McEachin et al., 1993). More recent research by Sallows and Grapner (2005) has indicated that current Lovaas style intensive behaviour programs no longer use contingent aversives and have been found to be as effective for some children with autism. There have been some claims made that intensive, behavioural programs can help some children achieve 'normal functioning' over time (Lovaas, 1987; McEachin et al., 1993). However, such claims have been questioned regarding the magnitude of the reported changes (Mesibov, 1993).

Formal Schooling

Historically, students with an ASD were often segregated from their neurotypical peers and placed in separate schooling or separate classrooms within mainstream schools. In Western countries, there has been an increasing trend toward the 'inclusion' of such students in mainstream classrooms as part of an international emancipatory, democratic movement to include the disabled in regular classrooms and mainstream life. Some educators have expressed misgivings about 'inclusive' education for disabled students in mainstream settings when the necessary ingredients are missing or inadequate (Kavale & Forness, 2000). Kavale & Forness (2000) write that:

> Inclusion appears to be not something that simply happens, but rather something that requires careful thought and preparation. The focus must not simply be on access to general education, but rather the assurance that when inclusion is deemed appropriate, it is implemented with proper attitudes, accommodations, and adaptations in place (p. 287).

The efficacy of 'inclusion' for all students with an ASD into mainstream classrooms at all stages of their education has also been questioned over time. Research has found that some students with an ASD can benefit from mainstream, partly or fully segregated programs depending upon their individual profile, development and the educational context they must negotiate with or without support (Jordan, 2005; Myles & Adreon, 2001; National Research Council, 2001; Parsons et al., 2011; Shaddock, 2003, 2005; Simpson, 1995, 2004, 2005). Research by Mesibov and Shea (1996) who reviewed the outcomes of full 'inclusion' for students on the autism spectrum found that these students often benefited less than other students with other types of disabilities.

Some studies (Howlin, 1998; Kasari, Freeman, Bauminger, & Marvin, 1999; Moreno, Aguilera, & Saldana, 2008) have found that parents of children on the autism spectrum are more likely to endorse schooling where teachers have specialised training and the educational program focuses on the specific needs of students on the autism spectrum. Moreover, some parents of children on the autism spectrum in mainstream settings have been found to be less satisfied with their child's schooling than their parental counterparts in education support schools (Moreno et al., 2008). In terms of mainstream inclusion of students on the autism spectrum, Moreno et al. (2008) conclude "that it is not the inclusive process itself that parents are concerned with, but the risks of insufficient provision that sometimes accompany it" (p. 172). Roberts and Prior (2006) drawing on the work of Shaddock (2003) indicate that "it may be preferable to put focus on providing students with appropriate education to meet their needs rather than assuming that inclusion in a regular classroom is the optimum placement for all students with Autism at all stages of their education" (p. 86).

Taking into consideration the earlier research of Dawson and Osterling (1997), Howlin (1997), Marcus, Garfinkle, and Wolery (2001), and Rogers (1998) who have comprehensively reviewed international educational programs for children on the autism spectrum, Roberts and Prior (2006) provide a composite list and explanation of the common key elements of effective educational interventions. While these intervention recommendations have relevance for early educational intervention, some of them also have application in the range of educational settings available to students with an ASD in the later formal schooling years. Roberts and Prior (2006) indicate that while the philosophical approaches may differ in some of the programs, the common key elements are as follows:

1. Appropriate Skill Domains Addressed in Curriculum Content – Successful programs often contain five basic skill domains: Ability to attend to elements of the environment; ability to imitate others; ability to comprehend and use language; ability to play appropriately with toys; and, ability to socially interact with others.
2. Highly Supportive Teaching Environments and Generalization Strategies – Successful programs teach core skills in highly supportive teaching environments and these skills are then systematically generalized to more complex, natural environments.
3. Supporting the Need for Predictability and Routine – Successful programs provide information in a highly predictable manner to help children with an ASD become more socially responsive and attentive.
4. A Functional Approach to Challenging Behaviour – Successful programs focus on the prevention of problem behaviour by means of increasing the child's interest and motivation, structuring the environment and increasing positive reinforcement for appropriate behaviour. Should problem behaviour persist, the behaviour is then analysed to determine the function of that behaviour for the child. The environment is then adapted in specific ways to avoid triggers and reinforcers for that problem behaviour and appropriate behaviour is taught to give the child an alternative, more acceptable behaviour.
5. Transition Support – Successful programs recognize that transition to school is a time when children with an ASD need a great deal of support. Effective programs actively teach school skills to enable the child to be as independent as possible. Programs frequently take an active role in finding school placements that will

best suit the child with an ASD and then actively integrate the child into the new setting.
6. Family Involvement – Successful programs recognize that parents are a critical component in early intervention for children with an ASD. Most programs support parents to choose the type and intensity of their involvement in their child's program. Effective programs are sensitive to the stresses encountered by families of children with an ASD and provide parent groups and other types of emotional support.

In addition to these common key elements, Roberts and Prior (2006) suggest further important strategies or methods not utilized by all models of intervention but recommended by a significant number of the reviewers:

1. Use of Visual Supports – the provision of augmentative communication methods is a characteristic of many programs reviewed.
2. Sufficient Intensity – a minimum of 15 hours per week of early intervention treatment should occur and the concept of 'intensity' is complex where meaningful engagement by the child with an ASD is seen as the key factor of a program's success.
3. Multi-Disciplinary Collaborative Approach – Children with an ASD require a multi-disciplinary approach to assessment and service provision. The team is likely to include speech pathologists, physiotherapists, teachers, psychologists and parents.
4. Inclusion of Peers – Many successful programs include typically developing peers.
5. Emphasis on Independent Functioning – Many successful programs emphasize child independence, initiative and choice making.
6. Addressing Obsessions and Rituals – A good program will recognize the importance of obsessions and rituals as possible underlying causes of many problem behaviours. However, these behaviours may have a positive function for the child in regulating anxiety and may act as a powerful source of motivation and reward.

Roberts and Prior (2006) also indicate that because of individual variation between children on the autism spectrum and their families, programs should be "appropriately adapted to the child's pattern of strengths and weaknesses and take account of family circumstances" (p. 83). Key interrelated aspects of any educational program for students on the autism spectrum should consider type of placement, teaching methods employed and the curriculum (Roberts & Prior, 2006; Roberts, 2004).

Few models and procedures exist regarding facilitation of placement and maintenance of students on the autism spectrum in mainstream classrooms (Roberts & Prior, 2006). As a result, teachers often feel unsupported and have no option but to design their own 'inclusion' programs in the absence of clear guidelines (Roberts & Prior, 2006; Simpson et al., 2003). Two 'inclusion' models suggested for use by

Roberts and Prior (2006) are by Rose et al. (2003) and Simpson et al. (2003). The Rose et al. (2003) 'inclusion' program lists the core elements of educational practice in any instructional program for students on the autism spectrum that have empirical support, as the following:

- environmental and curricular modifications, general education classroom support and instructional methods including systematic instruction
- specialized curriculum content
- individualised supports and services for students and families
- comprehensible/structured learning environments
- functional approach to problem behaviour
- family involvement/home-school collaboration
- attitudinal and social support
- coordinated team commitment
- recurrent evaluation of inclusion procedures.

Simpson et al. (2003) similarly list core elements of their Autism Spectrum Disorder Inclusion Collaboration model which have empirical support as the following:

- availability of appropriately trained support personnel
- access to collaborative problem-solving relationships
- availability of para-educators (teachers' aides)
- reduced class size
- adequate teacher planning time
- availability of paraprofessional (teachers'aide) and teacher in-service training
- a positive school climate
- the development of social skills for the student with Autism in inclusive settings
- shared responsibility by general and special educators and regular school community ownership of the included student(s) with Autism.

There are an ever increasing number of promising educational resources becoming available to educators and parents of children on the spectrum that incorporate aspects of these models (Larkey, 2005; Tullemans & Larkey, 2005, 2008). One such resource is a comprehensive autism planning system (CAPS) devised to help educational staff optimize a student's daily program in a way that incorporates needed supports across the school day (Henry & Myles, 2007). This planning system gives parents and their education team the how, what, when and where of intervention needs.

The limited amount of research which has been conducted into the education of students on the autism spectrum in high school environments has shown that the most salient features of the student's autism are accentuated during adolescence and this can lead to serious academic and social problems (Adreon & Stella, 2001; Myles & Adreon, 2001). In terms of the Australian high school context, Shaddock et al. (2007) indicates that secondary schools experience both external and internal pressures on their use of 'inclusive' practice in relation to students with disabilities. Shaddock et al. (2007) states:

> Ainscow (2005) refers to external factors such as competition between schools and parental choice while Pearce and Forlin (2005) list internal impediments to inclusion that include the structure of some high schools, their organizational practices and the reliance of some teachers on traditional "stand and deliver" teaching and where the emphases seem to be more on subjects and departments than on students and pedagogy (p. 43).

In relation to high school students on the autism spectrum in an Australian context, Shaddock (2005) indicates that a variety of high school inclusion models presently exist in the Australian context with varying success. These range from a 'home room' model to individual placement models. Shaddock (2005) concludes that "perhaps it is not the setting, but what goes on in the setting, that is the crucial variable" (Shaddock, 2005, p. 33).

Further to this discussion, it is recommended that the core elements of effective teaching of students on the autism spectrum should be appropriately adapted to the age of the individual student (Marks et al., 2003; Ministry of Health, 2008). In a comprehensive New Zealand Autism Spectrum Disorder Guideline (2008) core elements were expanded to include application in both the 7-12 and the 13-20 year age bracket (Ministry of Health, 2008). To illustrate, under the core element of 'individualised supports and services' there were recommendations as to how to incorporate the child's preferences and special interests in relation to the two different age groups. In the younger primary years, it was recommended that educators "include the student's preferences and special interests into the learning objectives for teaching in almost any curriculum area" (Ministry of Health, 2008, p. 294); whereas, in the latter high school years, the actual content becomes more prescribed and more difficult to adapt. Therefore, teachers should:

- give students options, such as courses within their interest studies by correspondence.
- consider flexible ways for students to demonstrate their knowledge.
- work with students to give them the social understanding to be able to interpret the achievement criteria (Ministry of Health, 2008, p. 294).

In Mesibov and Shea's (1996) review of the research literature on full 'inclusion' of students with autism it was shown that full 'inclusion' often discourages the development of specialized approaches while the unique characteristics of students with autism make some level of specialization essential. More recent research indicates that a more successful 'integrative' position on inclusion can be achieved if there is an established culture of acceptance and accommodation of diversity within the school; where decisions are made in the best interests of the individual student and where specialization is incorporated where and when needed (Frederickson et al., 2010; Jordan, 2005; Leach and Duffy, 2009; Morewood et al., 2011; Ravet, 2011).

Post-Secondary Education

Limited research has been conducted into the post-secondary circumstances of students with an ASD (Powell, 2003). In terms of students with general learning difficulties and/or psychiatric disorders, tertiary study has been found to be challenging. Depression and anxiety have been commonly reported concerns (Arthur, 1998). The more complex demands of university life often result in exacerbating the student's learning, oral communication and social interaction difficulties (Westby, 2000). Such students often show a lack of understanding of their own learning needs, lack self-advocacy skills and often feel uncomfortable about disclosing their conditions because of possible stigmatization; all of which interfere with their ability to seek support (Patwell & Herzog, 2000; Smith et al., 2002).

In terms of older students with an ASD, research (Kim, Szatmari, Bryson, Streiner, & Wilson, 2000; Tantam, 2000) has shown that the effects of an ASD can be greatest in adolescence and young adulthood where individuals with an ASD must negotiate such areas as completing school, finding work, developing a social network, contributing to a household and participating in a community (Jennes-Coussens, Magill-Evans, & Koning, 2006). It is during this transition time that individuals with an ASD can suffer more seriously from problems of anxiety and depression (Kim et al., 2000). Preliminary research into support services for students with an ASD in higher education indicates that there are an increasing number of individuals with an ASD entering tertiary education (Smith, 2007). While some limited support is available through student services, it is often generic in nature and not ASD specific or tailored to the individual needs of the student.

The research also highlights the need for ASD specific education to help faculty members understand how best to succeed with a student with an ASD (Smith, 2007). There is also a call by Smith (2007) for greater consultation, communication and feedback between faculty members and the student with an ASD to ensure that their specific learning needs are being met over time.

Recent studies indicate that the majority of individuals with an ASD have milder forms of the disorder (VanBergeijk, Klin, & Volkmar, 2008; VanBergeijk & Shrayermman, 2005). Hence, there are potentially many individuals with an ASD who will be intellectually capable of a university level education in the future. According to VanBergeijk et al. (2008), these individuals have the potential to become independent contributing members of society with appropriate and specifically tailored interventions. Such interventions include well-planned transitions from high school to a tertiary environment. There should also be an examination by parents of the 'goodness of fit' between the student and the prospective tertiary institution (VanBergeijk et al., 2008). This should incorporate examination of "the size of the university, the size of the typical classes and the receptiveness of the institution to the students with a variety of disabilities" (VanBergeijk et al., 2008, p. 1368).

Support services at tertiary level should also be expanded to allow effective intervention into potential areas of difficulty for students with an ASD. The areas of difficulty may include communication, social and independent living skills and executive functioning (VanBergeijk et al., 2008). Other recent research, investigating the postsecondary educational aspirations of high-functioning adolescents with an ASD and their parents, has shown that both groups have clear postsecondary goals but have significant concerns about the readiness of postsecondary institutions to meet the specific needs of a student with an ASD (Camarena & Sarigiani, 2009).

A recent international review of studies that investigated the prognosis, outcomes, or effective interventions for adults with ASDs has shown that many individuals with an ASD are significantly disadvantaged regarding employment, social relationships, physical and mental health, and quality of life (Howlin & Moss, 2012). Support to facilitate this population's inclusion into mainstream society has been lacking with little research done into ways to develop more effective intervention programs for these adults (Howlin & Moss, 2012).

One recent Australian survey (Autism Spectrum Australia (Aspect), 2012) investigating the experiences, aspirations and needs of 300 adults with Asperger's Disorder (AD) and high functioning autism (HFA) from every state and territory in Australia confirmed that, despite this group's aptitude for study, they experience significant struggles to reach their full potential in education. More than 80 percent of the 300 respondents with an ASD in the survey had commenced or completed a tertiary qualification. Of this group, almost three-quarters identified as needing support to help them study. Almost half of the 300 respondents reported that they received no, or insufficient, additional support for their learning needs during their time in education.

In the same survey, tertiary educational disability officers reported that this group of students experienced difficulties in verbal comprehension, planning, organisation, social awareness and group work. These officers also perceived a lack of awareness and understanding of autism among tertiary educators (Aspect, 2012). Over two-thirds of parents surveyed stated that in their experience, educators in Australia were not well-informed about ASDs. Approximately half of the parents surveyed were of the view that their child had not performed to his or her full potential while in education. The same survey found that in contrast to an Australian national employment rate of 95%, just 54 % of adults with Asperger's Disorder and HFA (excluding those in full time education) had a paid job at the time of completing the survey.

Research has also shown that such individuals often experience high secondary school dropout rates, low rates of post-secondary education, poor post compulsory school integration and reduced independent living and community participation outcomes (Attwood, 2007; Howlin & Moss, 2012). If not supported appropriately, these students face an increased risk of anxiety, depression and other mental health problems (Attwood, 2007, Howlin & Moss, 2012). They are a particularly vulnerable group of potential tertiary students whose success will depend on the quality of inclusiveness and accommodation that they experience in an educational environment (Leach & Duffey, 2009). Promising programs at the tertiary level are very gradually becoming more available with support in the areas of transition, accommodation, online resources, diagnosis, specialist mentoring, staff awareness training, universal design for learning, careers advice and work experience with the student voice often being given increased importance to ensure that programs remain of greatest, practical benefit to this population of students (Hastwell, Harding, Baron Cohen and Martin, 2012; Hastwell, Harding, Martin & Baron-Cohen, 2013; Wolf, Brown & Bork, 2009).

Australian & WA Disability Educational Provision Research

Historically, research has delivered a disappointing report card regarding how students with disabilities are accommodated in the Australian and West Australian context. A large Australian national research project was undertaken in 2007 and investigated ways to improve the learning outcomes of students with disabilities in the early, middle and post compulsory years of Australian schooling (Shaddock et al., 2007). The project conducted a research review of some 400 references and found that "many teachers worldwide say they do not have the time or resources to make adaptations for students with significant individual needs and these concerns have been expressed for many years" (Shaddock et al., 2007, p. xiii). Moreover, in terms of what adaptations teachers do make for students with disabilities in their classroom, 294 mainstream Australian teachers randomly selected from all states and education sectors indicated that they tend to incorporate "accommodations that can be made for the whole class, that are efficient of teacher time and effort and that do not involve major changes to class organization or substantial individualization" (Shaddock et al., 2007, p. xiv).

This echoes the previous results of an earlier UNESCO-based assessment (Wills & Jackson, 2000) that delivered a disappointing report card regarding 'inclusive' practice in WA. Wills and Jackson (2000) indicate that by contrast with Vermont in the USA, which provides a best practice benchmark of 74% regarding 'inclusion' of children with an intellectual disability, WA presents very poorly:

> Totalling all of the children with an intellectual disability on the WA inclusion project and adding the children in remote and rural areas to the number of exemplary examples where children are included due to positive principals and teachers, from the available figures it is apparent that the figures in WA are still below 10% (p. 28).

The project evaluated physical, social and curricular 'inclusion' and found some progress in the areas of physical and social 'inclusion' but curricular 'inclusion' showed limited progress and was the area most in need of improvement. Both teachers and their aides indicated that poor training and lack of resources left them feeling ill-prepared for students with disabilities in their mainstream classrooms. Inclusion at the curricular level was found to be "reserved for students who are academically able to keep up with the curriculum in an unaltered state and who present teachers with only minor difficulties with access or behaviour" (Wills & Jackson, 2000, p. 27). While "islands of excellent practice" were noted such 'excellence' was not commonplace in the WA education system (Wills & Jackson, 2000, p. 25).

Further to this, West Australian researchers, O'Donoghue and Chalmers (2000) who investigated how country WA teachers managed their work in 'inclusive' classrooms, found that only three of the eleven participating teachers showed selective adaptation in all three areas of classroom organization, teaching methods and curriculum content. This would tentatively indicate that the 'inclusion' experience for disabled children will be different for individual children dependent upon a specific teacher's response to 'inclusion' and its practices. The grounded theory study's conclusion reiterated the finding that "teachers tend not to make radical changes to their existing teaching practices in response to having a student with a severe or profound intellectual disability as a member of their class" (O'Donoghue & Chalmers, 2000, p. 902).

Forlin (1995) who investigated the attitudes and beliefs of educators toward inclusion in 38 Western Australian schools, also found that "educators were not overly accepting of inclusion, and that acceptance levels tend to decline with teacher experience, and with an increase in the severity of a child's disability" (p. 212). More recent research by Forlin et al. (2008) confirms that regular WA teachers find the behaviour of the child with an intellectual disability the issue of most concern for them in their mainstream classroom with a secondary major concern being their own professional competence to deal with such students.

Similarly, Ford, (2007) who investigated South Australian teacher perceptions of students with disabilities and significant behavioural challenges, found that if appropriate expertise was not available for these types of students serious consequences could sometimes follow:

> ... without effective support, students who exhibit such behaviours may be at risk of (a) being suspended or expelled from school, (b) being transferred to more restrictive or segregated placements, (c) receiving intrusive and punitive interventions, (d) being placed on restrictive medications, and (e) experiencing inadequate, socially isolating and stigmatizing post-school outcomes (p. 110).

Ford's (2007) research also indicated that teachers felt they were insufficiently prepared or supported to work successfully with students with significant behavioural challenges and expressed the need for comprehensive, regular, and on-going professional development activities that were aligned with their needs and those of their students.

Additionally, a pilot project was initially conducted by the Education Department of WA to identify the implications of placing students with intellectual disabilities in their local regular school (Chadbourne, 1997). This review indicated that the leadership of the principal was seen as most critical to the success of the 'inclusion' programme (Chadbourne, 1997). Throughout 2001, another major review, the

Review of Educational Services for Students with Disabilities in Government Schools, was undertaken by the Department of Education and Training to investigate service provision for students with disabilities in WA (Forlin, 2004). Two key recommendations from this review were: the need to develop and implement a system-wide leadership program to provide the foundation for supporting an 'inclusive' education system; and, the need to establish a comprehensive staff development process to be implemented across all schools and districts in WA to promote 'inclusive' educational practices within school communities (Forlin, 2004). In response to these recommendations, Forlin (2004) suggested a trial of an established process, the *Index for Inclusion* (Booth et al., 2000), to assess how 'inclusive' WA schools were and suggest ways that they could become more 'inclusive'. Forlin's (2004) multisite case study indicated that "dissemination of the *Index for Inclusion* without a clearly developed professional development process to ensure its use is likely to be given little more than token acknowledgment by schools" (p. 201).

As part of the Inclusive Education Project initiated by the WA Department of Education and Training (DET) Centre for Inclusive Schooling, there was an internal review into the appropriateness of the *Index for Inclusion* tool to assist WA schools to develop, implement and sustain more inclusive school cultures, policies and practices. The review indicated that participating primary schools and education support centres were demonstrating significant improvement in their 'inclusivity'. However, all four participating secondary schools involved in the project were experiencing impediments to the progress of 'inclusion'. This prompted a further study that investigated the barriers and facilitators to building 'inclusive' secondary government schools in a West Australian context (Jenkins, 2005). Jenkins (2005) study found that the factors of "leadership, organizational development, workforce development, curriculum, development of partnerships and resource allocation" accounted for variations among the four secondary schools (p. 3). These critical features either sustained or diminished the 'inclusive' capacity of a secondary school community (Jenkins, 2005). Jenkins (2005) recommended that there needed to be additional structural and functional support from all levels of the government secondary education system to improve 'inclusion' in WA secondary schools.

West Australian independent schools' responses to students with disabilities and learning difficulties have also been investigated. The information was derived from questionnaires from 98 WA independent schools and interviews with 51 of their principals (Jenkins, 2002). The questionnaire responses indicated that all types of independent schools were making educational provision for students with special educational needs. According to Jenkins (2002), these schools were "developing more inclusive models of educational provision to respond to increasing enrolments of children with special needs and writing new school policies related to the functional aspects of managing student learning and participation" (p. iv).

Accordingly, new staffing positions were created; building modifications occurred and efforts were made to prepare staff and students for the 'inclusion' of students with special needs. The costs associated with this type of provision were only partially covered by the Commonwealth funding allocated per student with disabilities at that time. Therefore, school budgetary allocations subsidized the educational provision required at significant cost to both schools and parents. Principals identified nine driving forces associated with current and future educational provision for students with disabilities and learning difficulties: equity of funding; new sectoral strategies; school-wide policy development and effective leadership; positive attitude change; informed, equitable enrolment policies and practices; workforce development; educational program design and implementation; teamwork; and, contemporary dilemmas of schooling. The report concluded that the 'inclusion' of students with disabilities and learning difficulties has had a profound impact on the West Australian independent school sector "with many schools making noteworthy progress towards genuine inclusive education in spite of significant inequities of funding between government and nongovernmental sectors" (Jenkins, 2002, p. viii).

From the research, it would seem that disabled students' experiences of mainstream education in WA is likely to be variable and dependent upon the different commitments, understandings and resourcing of 'inclusive' education that permeate the system. According to the research presently available, secondary schooling is a much less reliable context than primary in relation to provision of 'inclusive' practice for students with disabilities in WA (Jenkins, 2005).

WA Autism Educational Provision Research

Historically, a limited amount of research has been undertaken to investigate the situation for parents trying to access an appropriate, evidence-based education for their child with an ASD in a West Australian context. A 1998 report, *Models of Educational Service Provision for students with an ASD within Government Mainstream Schooling* (Crosby, 1998), commissioned by the Department of Education and Training (DET), sought information about existing practices so that policy and a range of educational options could be developed to cater for the varying needs of students with an ASD in WA government schools. However, most of the information gathered was from primary school and limited home schooling sites with only one parental response gained from a high school context. Results indicated that in order to meet the needs of a wide range of students with an ASD in a variety of mainstream schools a flexible approach to the delivery of educational services was essential (Crosby, 1998).

Parents indicated they were concerned about: the lack of clear guidelines for schools to follow upon enrolling students with an ASD; the lack of clear consultation with parents about their own child's needs; the lack of appropriate training of aides, teachers and school staff; the lack of expertise, continuity and coordination of support services; the lack of teacher aide time; the lack of social skills programs in the curriculum; and the infrequent, inefficient use of case conferences devising Individualized Education Plans (IEPs) (Crosby, 1998). Parents also described where, on occasion, the 'inclusive' situation was working well with the common feature being the establishment of good communication between all parties and a willingness to work together to achieve outcomes (Crosby, 1998).

In another WA study investigating the needs of 21 families of adolescents with an ASD in metropolitan and regional WA it was found that there were a number of significant parent perceived gaps in the availability and accessibility of services (Takahashi, 2005). The parents in the study were a more stressed population in comparison to parents of typical adolescents (Takahashi, 2005). Overall, the parents were not satisfied with current level of support services for their children with an ASD. While a proportion of parents reported being satisfied with their child's current educational provision, location was a factor that affected parental satisfaction (Takahashi, 2005). In relation to this, it was found that parents in the metropolitan areas, who had lower functioning children, were more able to attend special education units or schools where specialized care and curriculum were offered. Parents of higher functioning children in the metropolitan area were also more able to attend a chosen mainstream school affording parents more choices and input regarding their child's needs. This contrasted with the experiences of those families who had an adolescent with an ASD in regional areas who did not have the same range of choices available (Takahashi, 2005).

In another more recent study investigating the needs of 92 WA families who currently have school-aged children with a suspected or confirmed ASD, MacDermott (2008) found the following regarding the relationship many parents currently have with the WA education system:

> Unfortunately, this relationship is frequently characterized by frustration, confusion and conflict, and is described by some families as encountering a "systemic brick wall". Parents routinely feel alienated and excluded from the very environment in which their child spends a majority of each weekday. In addition, they feel that their specific and unique knowledge of their child's strengths, needs and challenges are dismissed as unimportant and irrelevant within the school setting. Too often, this results in compromised learning for the child; unnecessary conflict and wasted opportunities for collaboration between the parents and school staff, at the expense of both parties; and increased stress for both the child and their whole family, further adding to the daily challenge of living with ASD (p. 84).

Further to this, MacDermott (2008) concluded that:

> In order to ensure that all appropriate school based supports are available to the student, parents and staff need to be able to work effectively together. Parents need easy access to information about the full range of school support options available within their specific educational setting and the eligibility and access requirements for each of those options. It is unacceptable that families often find out information coincidentally through conversation with service providers or other families. School based staff need to be as, if not more, knowledgeable

> than parents about these varied options and how they work, as well as proactive in making appropriate service based recommendations. School staff also need to willingly engage with families, and view them as knowledgeable partners in the process, so that they can work together to achieve an optimal educational experience for the student. Parents did not indicate that they expected school based or other educational staff to be able to overcome all the challenges faced by their children, rather they were looking for educators to engage with them in a "spirit of generosity" which would then enable all stakeholders to work together effectively and with mutual regard and appreciation (p. 85).

The limited amount of research investigating ASD educational provision in a West Australian context tentatively indicates that the use of evidence-based 'inclusive' practice by educational practitioners is presently unreliable and variable across the different educational settings available (Crosby, 1998; MacDermott, 2008; McDonald, 2010, McDonald & Lopes, 2012; Takahashi, 2005). Takahashi (2005) calls for future research to investigate different cohorts of WA children on the autism spectrum on a long-term basis and "to assess for functioning at different stages of development with comparisons of the effectiveness and utility of different intervention services available" (p. 46).

Home Schooling

Parents have been increasingly turning to home schooling as an alternative teaching approach for their children in an attempt to increase control over and attend to the individual educational needs of their child (Arora, 2006; Parsons & Lewis, 2010). This increase has been observed in the US, the UK and Australia (Arora, 2006; Kidd & Kaczmarek, 2010; Reilly, 2007). Home education is now legally recognized in every state of Australia (Arora, 2006; Reilly, 2007).

Research indicates that the background of families who choose to home school is varied with respect to their economic status, educational background and their prior professional experience (Arora, 2006). It has for some time been known that home educated students generally academically outperform their regular classroom peers (Medlin, 2000; Ray, 1997; Thomas, 1998); and, that there are positive social and emotional benefits in relation to students who are home educated (Barratt-Peacock, 1997; Thomas, 1998). These benefits are inclusive of home educated students with special needs where it has been found that such students can experience greater academic success than their peers with similar disabilities who attend public schools (Blok, 2004; Duvall et al., 1997).

Research has shown that parents home educate their children with intellectual disabilities and special needs because they are concerned about the ongoing negative socialization (including bullying), insufficient academic progress and a failure by schools to understand their child's academic and social profile or the nature of their disability (Arora, 2006; Parsons & Lewis, 2010; Reilly, 2007). Parents often reach a "crisis point" (Reilly, 2007, p.181) or experience certain negative "push" factors (Parsons & Lewis, 2010, p.76) during their child's formal schooling at which time they feel compelled to home school their children.

Parents generally undertake home education of their children with disabilities with limited funding and the mother often becomes the primary teacher (Ensign, 2000; Parsons & Lewis, 2010; Reilly, 2007). Additionally, parents create support for their home education situation by researching and seeking help from external agencies, especially parent home education networks (Ensign, 2000; Parsons & Lewis 2010; Reilly, 2007). Further to this, Reilly (2007) found that WA parents who home educate their children with intellectual disabilities do so through a process of 'progressive modification'. The three stages involved in this process were identified as:

1. the stage of drawing upon readily-available resources
2. the stage of drawing upon support networks in a systematic fashion
3. the stage of proceeding with confidence on the basis of having a set of principles for establishing a workable pattern of home schooling individualized for each circumstance (Reilly, 2007).

It has been found that parents who home educate their children with intellectual disabilities generally work on a one-to-one basis with their child and eventually, through 'trial and error' individualize instruction according to their child's abilities, interests, social needs and pace of learning (Ensign, 2000; Reilly, 2007). This individualization and flexible approach often results in improved social and academic progress of their child with special needs and disabilities (Parsons & Lewis, 2010; Reilly, 2007).

Consistent with other research on home educating students with disabilities (Duffey, 2002; Parsons & Lewis, 2010; Reilly, 2007), a recent study, that investigated the perspectives of ten mothers who home educated their children with an ASD in a metropolitan WA context, found that the children experienced improvements in terms of their academic learning and psychological well-being through use of individualized tuition, modified teaching strategies and flexibility (Kidd & Kaczmarek, 2010). Congruent with other research on the difficulties associated with educating students with an ASD in mainstream settings (Humphrey & Lewis, 2008a, 2008b; Humphrey & Symes, 2010; MacDermott, 2008; Shaddock, 2005; Wing, 2007), these mothers reported that the regular school environment was a "considerable source of anxiety for their child" (Kidd & Kaczmarek, 2010, p.270).

Additionally, these mothers reported that they decided to home educate because of difficulties with mainstream school resources (specialized staff and individual instruction), and the school's inability to meet the child's unique educational needs (Kidd & Kaczmarek, 2010). The mothers also indicated that the stress experienced by the child in school had a flow-on effect on them and the rest of the family (Kidd & Kaczmarek, 2010). By contrast, when these mothers home educated their children with an ASD they reported a relative decline in their stress and greater family cohesion (Kidd & Kaczmarek, 2010).

However, while some mothers in the study felt a sense of empowerment through their role as home educator, others had feelings of resentment because of the forced nature of their role and voiced a need for considerably more educational, social, financial support and respite (Kidd & Kaczmarek, 2010). These same needs have been similarly expressed in previous research on parents who home educate their children with disabilities (Parsons & Lewis, 2010; Reilly, 2007).

Even though there has been some development in the body of research literature investigating aspects of home education (Arora, 2006), there has been limited research investigating the home education of students with an intellectual disability (Arora 2006; Parsons & Lewis 2010; Reilly 2007) and in particular, those students with an ASD (Kidd and Kaczmarek 2010; McDonald, 2010; McDonald & Lopes, 2012). However, useful publications are beginning to emerge that provide specific support to parents who wish to home school their child on the autism spectrum (Schetter & Lighthall, 2009).

CONCLUSION

The chapter provided a brief review of the research literature and was approached with the intention of providing a general overview of relevant areas of research that informed the study (McDonald, 2010) explained in this publication. The following five chapters capture a deep, synthesized understanding and explanation of the process undertaken by parents in the six families involved in the study by examining their recent, real-life journeys attempting to educate their children on the autism spectrum over a five year period. It examines the parent experience of diagnosis, early intervention, mainstream schooling, home schooling, supplementing, segregated schooling sites, transitioning to the adult world of tertiary study / work and redressing the imbalance in families' lives.

CHAPTER 4

STAGE ONE – BEGINNING BATTLE

This and subsequent chapters develop a theory generated from the central research question 'How do parents deal with the education of their children on the autism spectrum over time?' The study (McDonald, 2010) investigated how West Australian parents (mainly mothers) in six families dealt with the education of their child on the autism spectrum over a five year period. Throughout the following chapters, the key processes, concepts, stages, sub-stages, categories and sub-categories are italicized and sometimes bracketed for ease of understanding by the reader.

To recap, the theory generated from an analysis of the data gathered is that parents deal with the education of their child with an ASD over time by conducting the core social process of *seeking progressive fit* and that in doing so they potentially move through four stages. The four stages of the social process are designated as follows:

1. *Beginning Battle* – the stage where parents struggle to find an appropriate diagnosis.
2. *Waging War* – the stage where parents fight to seek, gain, maintain and create educational fit.
3. *Strategizing Solutions* – the stage where parents strategize solutions to remedy the constant difficulties associated with education.
4. *Framing Futures* – the stage where parents frame futures and begin redressing life imbalance.

The social process generated can best be described as "a series of evolving sequences of action/interaction that occur over time and space, changing or sometimes remaining the same in response to the situation or context" (Strauss & Corbin, 1998, p. 46).

The four stages, while sequential, are also at times indistinct and iterative, where parents may experience two sub-stages at once or revisit a stage depending upon the conditions operating in their lives at the time. For example, a parent may have their child diagnosed with one disorder in Stage One (*Beginning Battle*) but this may subsequently only reveal part of the picture for their child. They will then be compelled, once again, to have their child reassessed at a later time in order that a more accurate picture may be gained and more appropriate intervention services sought. This may then involve an iterative movement by the parents from Stage Two (*Waging War*) back to Stage One (*Beginning Battle*) where a more accurate diagnosis will again be sought.

The movement between Stages Two (*Waging War*) and Three (*Strategizing Solutions*) has the greatest level of interaction for parents. Parents move through a series of feedback loops where they continually strategize solutions to remedy the often constant, overwhelming difficulties associated with educating their child with an ASD. For example, parents may have difficulty locating a mainstream school that will accept their child with an ASD for enrolment (Stage Two – *Waging War*). They will then have to work out ways to overcome such a difficult situation (Stage Three – *Strategizing Solutions*). When they finally locate a school that will agree to enrol and welcome their child, they may then be confronted with how this child will be treated educationally when they are placed in such a school (Stage Two – *Waging War*). Once again, the parent, often in combination with the school, must help resolve this situation (Stage Three – *Strategizing Solutions*). This cyclical pattern repeats itself throughout the education process.

Parents' direction and speed of movement through the various stages is mediated by the following intervening conditions:

a. the attitude and background of the parents,
b. the level of support and accommodation available,
c. the educational progress of the child over time,
d. the timing and type of engagement with the educational context, and
e. the advancing age of the person on the autism spectrum and their parents.

As a parent gradually cycles through the stages they are imbued with an *increasing awareness and confidence* regarding how to deal with the individualised education of their child with an ASD. However, the educational journey also creates *variable negative feelings* in the parents as they progressively realise the enormity of the difficulties they often face trying to *seek, gain, maintain* and *create educational fit* for their child with an ASD over time. This tension operates throughout the educational journey where parents are continually *seeking progressive fit* for their child with an ASD. The basic social process of *seeking progressive fit* is present throughout all stages of the education process and its intensity waxes and wanes according to the conditional matrix (Strauss & Corbin, 1990) operating in the parents' lives at the time. The notion of a 'conditional matrix' incorporates the "complex web of interrelated conditions, actions/interaction, and consequences that pertain to a given phenomenon" (Strauss & Corbin, 1990, p. 161).

This chapter presents a detailed exposition of Stage One (*Beginning Battle)*. For ease of understanding the following diagram illustrates an expansion of the full theory of *seeking progressive fit*. It encompasses all the different pathways undertaken by the families during their educational journeys over the five year period. It is inclusive of diagnosis, early intervention, mainstream education, segregated school sites, home education, supplementing, transitioning and redressing the imbalance in families' lives.

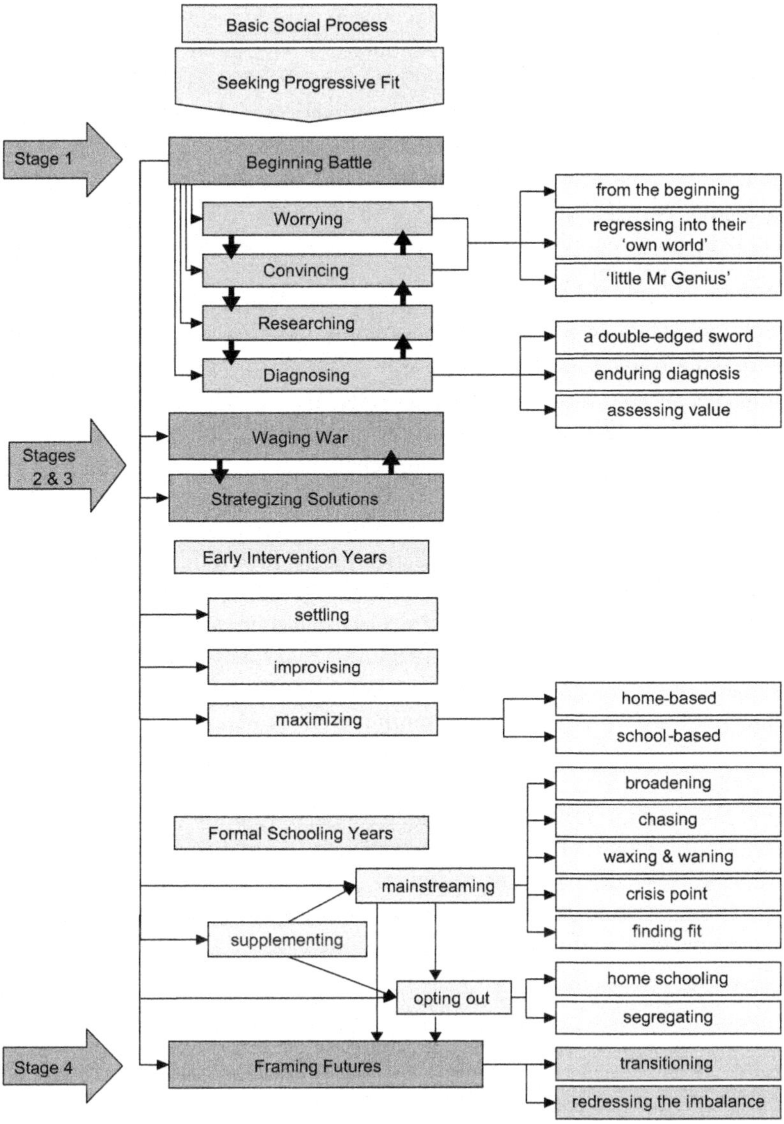

STAGE ONE – BEGINNING BATTLE: AN OVERVIEW

The length of time that it takes for parents to believe in their own estimation that there is something wrong with their child's development and to then gain an accurate diagnosis often has a direct bearing on when effective, early intervention can be gained. Research has revealed that evidence based, early intervention (EI) can have a significant, positive impact on the educational progress of the child on the autism spectrum (Birnbrauer & Leach, 1993; Francis, 2005; Green, 1996; Howard et al., 2005; Lovaas, 1987; Magiati et al., 2007; McEachin et al., 1993; Roberts & Prior, 2006). This research indicates that early intervention is time-critical and the skills learned should be generalized over as many environments as possible in the life of the child on the autism spectrum. Hence, it is important to track differences in parents' trajectories of awareness as such awareness has a major impact on a parents' ability to gain effective, educational intervention for their child with a potential ASD at the earliest opportunity.

Parents in the study indicated that after experiencing inordinate difficulties with their child as compared to other children they felt increasingly worried about what could be wrong with their child. The child often became the centre of attention in the family because of their difficult and unusual behaviour. Parents attempted to gain help for their situation by trying to convince others of their child's differences but were often told by significant others that their worries were unjustified. As difficulties persisted, most parents felt compelled to research the situation for themselves through various sources and then to seek out a possible diagnosis in earnest for their child. They expected that this would lead to appropriate intervention and eventually, suitable schooling in order to improve the difficult situation experienced by the whole family. Through engagement with the system on offer, parents began to develop an awareness that their situation was potentially far more difficult to negotiate than they first imagined. Parents began to realize over time that they were only just beginning to battle with a situation that could be potentially life-long. Throughout this first stage, parents constantly wondered and worried about how their child on the autism spectrum would find acceptance within their own family and the external world at large. In relation to this, parents had to overcome continually their own internal struggle in order to deal with the external battles that were occurring on many fronts.

Four sub-stages were generated from the first stage, *Beginning Battle*, in relation to how parents deal with the education of their child with an ASD over time. The following section elaborates on the first *(worrying)* and second *(convincing)* sub-stages of Stage One (*Beginning Battle*) that often occur concurrently. At the first sub-stage (*worrying)*, parents feel increasingly worried about the difficulties associated with trying to parent their child as compared to other children. This leads them to the second sub-stage (*convincing)*, where they try to convince significant others of their child's differences. When such concerns are often dismissed by trusted others, parents are compelled to move into the third sub-stage (*researching*), where they research the situation for themselves. The final section of this chapter explains the fourth sub-stage (*diagnosing)* where parents seek a diagnosis in earnest because the situation with the child becomes increasingly difficult and, with diagnosis, parents assume that targeted effective help for their situation will be forthcoming.

Sub-stages One and Two: Worrying and Convincing

Before their child is born, parents often imagine a wonderful future for their offspring and ideal scenarios abound in their minds. When the child finally arrives and is very different from their dream vision, parents struggle to 'fit' their internal, idealized scenario with the reality of parenting such a child. Parents have an expectation about parenting that is often based on previous experiences with other children and information that is available in the public domain. When these expectations are continually unmet, parents worry (*worrying*) and try to convince (*convincing*) others of their inordinate difficulties with their child in order to gain help and support for their situation.

Three categories of parent experience were identifiable in the first and second sub-stages of *worrying* and *convincing.* Sometimes, parents were able to register almost *from the beginning* (category one) that there was something very different about the development of their child in relation to others. In contrast to this, some parents did not notice any difference in their child in relation to others until some time later when their child lost previously held skills and seemed to be *regressing into their 'own world'* (category two). Still other parents noticed worrying differences but interpreted it as a positive sign of the child being of superior intellect and were encouraged by others to believe that they may be raising a *'little Mr. Genius'* (category three). All three scenarios eventually lead to *worrying* by the parents who, over time, recognized the growing difficulties associated with parenting their child with a potential ASD. They felt compelled throughout this first sub-stage to share their fears with trusted and qualified others and tried to convince them (*convincing)* of their child's inordinate difficulties as a preliminary way of trying to gain help for their situation.

The background and experience of the parents and the response of significant others determined the level of confidence which parents gained in their own estimation of what was happening for their child. These three different scenarios affected the time taken for parents to believe in their own estimation that a serious problem existed and to gain effective help. The parents in the first category (*from the beginning*) experienced the quickest trajectory of awareness and movement through the sub-stages. The second fastest movement was experienced by parents in the second category (*regressing into their 'own world')* and the longest passage was generally experienced by parents in the third category (*'little Mr. Genius*'). Parents in all three categories experienced ambivalence to a lesser or greater degree regarding the appropriateness of the development of their child. Each of the three categories of parent experience at the sub-stages of *worrying* and *convincing* are considered below.

Category One: from the beginning. The first category of parent experience at the sub-stages of *worrying* and *convincing* is termed *from the beginning*. Parents in this category report that behaviour exhibited by their children almost *from the beginning* indicated a very measured difference between their child and their child's peers and/or siblings. From autobiographical accounts (Maurice, 1993; Stehli, 1991) and the accounts of all parents in the present study, it is evident that, in all three categories of experience of sub-stages one and two (*worrying* and *convincing*), the child's behaviour can have a wide range of expression. The young child may exhibit a disturbing, disinterest in the world or alternatively, they may present with an idiosyncratic mix of excessive crying, communication difficulties, sensory sensitivities, rigidity, repetitive behaviour, self-stimulation, self-injurious behaviour and many more worrying signs. Such behaviour often results in the child gaining the most attention in the family. According to descriptions by all parents in this study, these children show an individual, idiosyncratic profile of behaviour that makes assessment and comparison of their child's situation difficult; hence, parents often need to confirm their suspicions with others.

Two different mothers, one from an autobiographical account and another from the present study, exemplify the two ends of the spectrum of *worrying* behaviour that can sometimes be witnessed by parents:

> By the time she was a month old, I was absolutely certain of it. Her eyes were still completely unfocused, and she wouldn't grab my finger, something Dotsie had done almost immediately, something babies did instinctively and automatically. I tried to chalk everything up to her pre-maturity, thinking she'd catch up, but I was afraid she was retarded, and was baffled by how she didn't seem to care whether or not she was held, fussed over, sung to, or cooed at. She acted detached, as if she lived in her own world, as content as a goldfish (Stehli, 1991, p. 14).

> The main language Jack had was screaming. He would scream from the time he got up to the time he went to bed. The only thing that would calm him down was driving. So, I guess that is the way that I found my way around Perth because I must have gone through every little back street in and out of suburbs. I used to just drive and he wouldn't always sleep. He would just sit and look out the window. He would just be happy and if it meant that I could get an hour's peace it was worth it.

Most parents in the study indicated that they were often highly stressed when trying to deal with the continual, inordinate demands placed upon them by their child with a potential and eventually diagnosed ASD. Most often, the child's behaviour required an inordinate amount of attention and time from parents to address such behaviour. However, the parent experience represented in this first category (*from the beginning*) revealed that these parents were able to register much more quickly than other parents the strong possibility of an ASD because they were able to compare the child in question with an older child who already had an ASD diagnosis. This served to increase the confidence of these parents in their own assessment of the situation.

To illustrate, one parent in the study had her second son diagnosed with an ASD when the child had only just turned two even though significant, qualified others were 'unsure' whether to diagnose him at such a young age. The mother of the two boys concerned commented about this situation in the following way:

> But, I guess knowing what I knew from Chris (*first son diagnosed with an ASD*) I investigated it for Jack (*second son*). I think that is why they were unsure to diagnose him as such because he had only just turned two. He was much younger when he was first diagnosed. But, I just knew that there were things, the talking especially, as soon as I thought that, I thought ok, they are quite different the boys but there were similarities.

The former experiences of this parent with her first child with an ASD increased her level of confidence and served to accelerate her movement along the trajectory of awareness needed to continue through to diagnosis and to eventually receive more timely help for her situation.

To summarize, parents in this first category of experience register, almost *from the beginning,* their child is not developing appropriately. The parent's awareness and confidence is heightened by their former experience with an older child with an ASD. This heightened awareness and confidence of the parent allows them to be more strident in their attempts to convince others (*convincing*) about their concerns and to move much more quickly to the fourth sub-stage of *diagnosing.*

Category two: regressing into their 'own world'. The second category of parent experience in the sub-stages of *worrying* and *convincing* is *regressing into their 'own world'*. This occurs when the child seems to be developing normally and then after some time the parents notice that the child is losing skills in many areas and is *regressing into their 'own world'*. Three sets of parents in this category indicated in the following comments that their experience included an obvious regression in their child:

> Adam (*son with an ASD*) was developing quite normally until his second birthday and that's when things started to slide downhill. He regressed, the words that he had begun to say, he would get angry if we would try to get him to say something. He didn't want us to sing to him anymore, it was like this blanket of frustration just fell over him and he was a completely different child.

> He stopped attending at all like a big blackness came over him. He no longer wanted to relate to us. He was just in his own world. He was almost depressed, if he wasn't screaming and crying, he was just very serious and by himself. He stopped talking and just virtually went into his own world which didn't involve us anymore.

> It wasn't until I went into hospital to have Jack (*second son*) and Chris (*first son with an ASD*) would have been about eighteen months. I came back after about eight days and just felt that he was quite different after that. I thought

> that he was very withdrawn, he didn't seem to have so much acknowledgement or affection for me. In fact, it was like he didn't know that I had been away or anything. It was very different to before I went away.

Parents in this group report that these children were often their first-born or were the first of a different gender to be born in their family. According to these parents, this circumstance served to reduce their awareness and confidence that the difficulties they were experiencing with their child were above those associated with normal parenting.

Similar to the first category of experience (*from the beginning*), when parents tried to convince (*convincing*) trusted and qualified others of their difficulties their concerns were dismissed. In one case, a parent of two older girls and a younger son with a suspected ASD said the following about this situation, "I was continually being told by my friend it was because he was a boy, that girls develop quicker, and I had only experienced the girls". Another parent in the study had a similar response from family members as evidenced below:

> So, I started to worry then and I would talk to other people like my sisters and sisters-in-law. Mine were the youngest at the time, so I figured I am new at this sort of thing. I just wanted to know if they found the same thing. They all said, 'Don't worry, he'll talk when he is ready'.

These situations served to reduce the parent's ability to move along the trajectory of awareness needed to access meaningful help for their child in the shortest period of time possible. It also served to indicate the lack of knowledge apparent in the general community regarding the possible spectrum of diverse behaviour sometimes associated with an ASD.

Some parents in this group also indicated that this *regressing into their 'own world'* occurred just before or together with a marked physical deterioration of their child. This situation served to increase the state of *worrying* experienced as evidenced by the following comments by two different sets of parents:

> Soon after the birth of Jill (*younger sister*), Kim's (*son with a suspected ASD*) health deteriorated and he had his first serious asthma attack. He was taken to the children's hospital where he was diagnosed as asthmatic. It was very traumatic for all concerned because his language development was so limited he could not understand at all what was happening.

> And at that stage, also prior to the regression, he had two lots of severe gastroenteritis and had been very sick with them and got the next lot and from that point on suffered a lot of diarrhoea. And his regression was almost like a follow on of how children are when they are sick. How they get a bit withdrawn and quiet and his regression seemed like that, as well as the depression which came over him. We wondered whether he could have had Chronic Fatigue Syndrome or something like that because he seemed to sort of have very little energy as well. He seemed to lose a lot of muscle tone and all those sorts of things.

So while parents became increasingly worried about the regression in their child's behavioural and sometimes, physical state, they found it difficult to move past the *worrying* sub-stage. Efforts to have their worries taken seriously by trusted and qualified others were often met with comments that their concerns were based on inexperience. This, in turn, reduced their confidence in their assessment of their own situation, which then delayed their movement along the trajectory of awareness needed to seek a diagnosis in order to gain timely educational intervention for their child.

In summary, parents in this second category of experience notice their child *regressing into their 'own world'* after a period of normal development. Parents' confidence in assessing their own situation is reduced when they try to convince trusted and experienced others of their concerns and are then charged with inexperience. Parents continue to feel worried as their child's behaviour and health problems persist and often escalate. This compels them to continue in their movement from the sub-stages of *worrying* and *convincing* to the next sub-stage of *researching*, which finally allows them to proceed seriously to the next sub-stage of *diagnosing*.

Category three: 'little Mr. Genius'. The final category of parent experience in the sub-stages of *worrying* and *convincing* is *'little Mr. Genius'*. This category includes parents who initially think they are raising a *'little Mr. Genius'* but very gradually become aware that other parts of the child's development are an increasing cause for concern. This period of misconception can last a relatively long time, sometimes years, as compared to the awareness shown by parents in the other two previous categories. Children in this category differ from the other two categories in that they generally have seemingly good language skills from a comparatively young or developmentally normal age, even though aspects of their behaviour are an increasing cause for parental concern.

These children are often later diagnosed with Asperger's Disorder which is notoriously difficult to diagnose early (Attwood, 1998, 2007; Myles, 2005) because the seemingly advanced or normal language development masks other behavioural difficulties in the minds of the parents and others. Reports indicate that the average age for diagnosis of Asperger's Disorder is between eight and eleven years of age (Attwood, 2007; Eisenmajer et al., 1996; Howlin & Asgharian, 1999). It is also estimated that only fifty per cent of children who have Asperger's syndrome are currently being detected and diagnosed (Attwood, 2007, p. 46). One parent representing this category of experience describes below how confusing the profile of such children can be:

> But he was so precocious and so bright and such a good talker. And you know how some of them talk like little professors when they are little. And you know even at age five he had such an amazing general knowledge because he just watched TV and it would all go into the video, computer brain and just stay there. He would just regurgitate it. He would know about astronomy and things that he watched on TV and books that I read to him. And people thought that he was little Mr. Genius happening.

According to this parent, the period of misconception in this category was elongated by two factors. The first factor was the successful progression of an older sibling who displayed similar early behavioural traits to the child with a potential ASD, but then dealt relatively successfully with mainstream schooling. This 'red herring' was described by the parent in the following words:

> It was completely normal development as far as that goes, the eye contact and playing peek-a-boo games and waving bye, bye. Yes, so I didn't really notice anything until he (*son with a potential ASD*) was doing some 'flopping'. We call it in the family 'flopping', because my elder daughter had already started 'flopping'. I didn't know what it was. But when the second child came along and started doing it I realized that something was going on. It was not just the eccentricity of the first one. I just thought that she was just eccentric, because she had everything else. She was a very precocious speaker, she spoke almost fluently at eighteen months and started talking at sixteen months. She was very engaging with people.

Hence, while this parent was cognizant of 'eccentric' behaviour in both children, concern about the younger child's development was ameliorated by the relatively successful passage of the older sibling through early life events and eventual mainstream schooling.

The second factor which elongated the period of misconception was the reaction of significant others who discounted the ever growing concerns that this mother had about her child's behaviour. These ever growing concerns included such worrying behaviours as rigidity, obsession with time and topics, self-stimulatory behaviours, toe walking, excessive tantrums, sensitivity to light and sound, and in later years, dysgraphia. To illustrate, this parent commented about her child's excessive rigidity in the following way:

> Yes, and then he would start with the routine thing, things had to be done according to a routine. He would get very upset if the routine changed to the extent where I had to put a blackboard in his room and write down what would happen right through the day. I couldn't change things then without major tantrums happening. 'No, no, no, you said this, we are going to do this', and he had to wear a watch from age five onwards so that he could …'We're doing this at eleven o'clock'.

When this parent voiced her concerns about her son's behaviour to a trusted teacher she was told that her worries were more to do with the sometimes, precocious nature of intellectual ability rather than any notion of accompanying 'impairment'. This is evidenced below:

> He (*son with a suspected ASD*) went to (*school's name*) with a very, very, well-known and respected pre-primary teacher. I knew then that he was different. I actually said to her that I think Paul is autistic. And she said to me, 'Don't

> be ridiculous … Paul could not possibly be autistic he is much too bright'. I thought that was good to know because I did not want an autistic son. And then she let on about things that he was doing at pre-primary. About how they had to separate him from other children, sometimes put him in a room on his own.

Understandably, this scenario then set up the parent to discount her own concerns in favour of the opinion of a highly regarded professional who was outlining a far, more desirable explanation for her child's differences. It also fortified other family members' belief that there was a limited amount to be concerned about regarding this child's development. Therefore, this parent's awareness and confidence in her own estimation of the situation was decreased. In this case, it delayed the process of *diagnosing* by years and dramatically reduced the parent's ability to gain help for her child and the rest of the family at the earliest possible time.

It is important to note that even when this parent met this particular teacher some years later and revealed her son's diagnosis there was still disbelief on the part of the very experienced 'professional' as evidenced below:

> And when I caught up with her (*pre-primary teacher*) at the shops once when Paul (*son with an ASD*) was 8 or 9 … I told her that Paul had been diagnosed with Asperger's Disorder and she just looked vaguely away into the distance. I guess they didn't know, to her autism was someone who sat in the corner and rocked and banged. It wasn't someone who could tell you about all the planets at age five.

Hence, resistance to a possible diagnosis of an ASD by some professionals can remain high especially when dealing with children who are eventually diagnosed with Asperger's Disorder. According to this parent, much of her earlier difficulty could be attributed to the fact that trusted professionals just "didn't know" about Asperger's Disorder or the autism spectrum.

Parents in this category of experience also indicated that this resistance to a possible diagnosis of an ASD by trusted professionals also put in train a much more difficult trajectory of acceptance by the parents themselves as well as other family members when a diagnosis was finally made. As will be discussed in sub-stage four (*diagnosing*) some family members find it difficult to give up the idea that there is a possible *'little Mr. Genius'* in the family versus the stigma associated with a family member being diagnosed with an ASD. It is significant to note that the parent represented in this category of experience made comment that such difficulty with acceptance of diagnosis placed even more pressure on the family's fragile circumstances and significantly contributed to the breakdown of her marriage.

In summary, parents in this third category (*'little Mr. Genius')* feel worried and try to convince others over a substantially, longer period about the seemingly, contradictory nature of their child's development. On the one hand, there is evidence that they are raising a *'little Mr. Genius'*, while on the other hand, there is increasing concern about the child's unusual behaviour. This situation eventually forces parents to continue in their movement from the sub-stages of *worrying* and *convincing* to the next sub-stage of *researching* so that a diagnosis can finally be made and hopefully appropriate support and intervention gained.

Sub-stage Three: Researching

In all three categories of the previous two sub-stages (*worrying* and *convincing)* parents seek to explain their situation to significant others in order to substantiate the concerns that they have about their child's development in the hope of gaining appropriate help. Their own confidence and parenting experience and the response of significant others influences the time that it takes to move through the first two sub-stages. Parents seek to remedy their own ambivalence about their child's development in this third sub-stage by *researching*. The success of this strategy serves to reduce the time taken to move to the next sub-stage of *diagnosing*. When parents experience concern about their child's behaviour but have those concerns dismissed by significant others they often choose to research (*researching)* the situation for themselves. This strategy improves their awareness about their child's and their family's situation and at the same time serves to increase the parent's self-reliance, awareness and confidence (*increasing awareness and confidence*). Unfortunately, this strategy also has the unintended effect of increasing parents' alarm *(variable negative feelings)* regarding the implications of the possible lifelong situation they and their family may have to face.

Sources used by parents in this study ranged from television programs to detailed library research where parents attempted to investigate and confirm their suspicions about their child's *worrying* development. The type and amount of research parents were able to do was directly related to the conditional matrix (Strauss & Corbin, 1990) operating in parents' lives at the time. Therefore, if a parent had other small children and had limited external support, they were less likely to have the time or opportunity to research their situation. To illustrate, one mother in the study commented:

> If only I knew it (*knowledge about autism*) then, but I didn't know. I felt I was reading as much as I could. I should have read more but you can always say I should have done this, I should have done that. I had a four year old, a three year old and a six month old, and I was on my own a lot. I think we had only just moved into a place because that took a while because we were renting.

This same parent indicated that she eventually saw a great similarity between herself and a character of a mother portrayed in a TV medical drama that alerted her to a possible ASD diagnosis for her son:

> I had seen 'GP', and I don't normally watch TV, but I was constantly having videos put on. But I happened to watch this one episode and there was a child with autism and just how the mother discovered that, that was what was wrong with him. And it wasn't so much the child's behaviour that rang true with me

> it was hers because she was really frustrated because he wasn't coming when she was calling him. So I saw a lot of similarities between her and me. With that in mind when I went to see this paediatrician, I said to him I think Chris (*eldest son*) has autism and can you refer me to someone in Perth because I am going to follow it up.

In this case, the parent used such information to gain enough confidence to request a referral from her paediatrician that moved her to seek a formal diagnosis for her son.

Another parent in this study found that the process of *researching* proved to be a lengthy, necessary but frustrating path because other possible diagnoses were initially put forward to explain her child's behaviour. In this case, the parent had an initial diagnosis of Attention Deficit Disorder (ADD) given to her son but questioned its accuracy given her own research regarding this condition:

> So, then I started getting the phone calls and I had to come to a meeting with the psychologist and the school-teacher. The psychologist never mentioned autism, they talked about ADD, he doesn't comply he must have ADD. So, I read up on ADD and I realized that he didn't have that.

Sometime later, this same parent continued her own research regarding a possible diagnosis for her son and found, by chance, a book on autism, which she felt, fitted her son's profile far more accurately:

> And then, I was cataloguing the books in the library and this book came in called 'Autism' by Uta Frith. Gee, I know what autism is, what is Asperger's Syndrome? So I opened up the book and started reading and the light bulbs just went ping, ping, ping. I read the twenty three or so case histories and I thought this one is like Paul (*son*).

This parent was able to use research to initially discount and then support possible diagnoses for her son. The research also served to heighten this parent's confidence in her own estimation of the situation (*increasing awareness and confidence*) and hastened the movement toward gaining a formal and more appropriate diagnosis for her son. It is significant to note that this parent had a tertiary qualification and specific employment that allowed her greater access to appropriate resources. In other words, her conditional matrix affected positively her ability to help her own situation and allowed her to move more quickly along a trajectory needed to gain an accurate diagnosis.

During the *researching* process, parents may also unintentionally come across other information about what life will potentially be like with a child on the autism spectrum. This can add to the parent's already worried state and while they may feel some relief that they have a possible diagnosis for their child the ramifications of such a diagnosis can often also bring about an increase in their overall concern (*variable negative feelings*). This is exemplified in the response of one of the parents in the study:

> The phone call to the autism group did not initially turn out well. A recorded message was my first contact with the group. The tape outlined the behaviour associated with autism. It also gave a very bleak prognosis of what the future held for people with autism. The tape outlined how many people with autism were often intellectually disabled and most likely had to be institutionalized later in life. If I wasn't frightened enough before I had rung the group I was now completely terrified that my child may be one of the people who would eventually have to be institutionalized. One part of me wanted to find out as quickly as possible what could be done, while another part of me did not want to consider what the future would hold for a child like our son if he was found to be Autistic.

So while parents seek to confirm their own suspicions about their child's situation they inadvertently learn about lifelong difficulties that may accompany having a child on the autism spectrum.

To summarize, parents in this study use the strategy of *researching* to check their own suspicions regarding what could be a possible explanation for their child's difficult behaviour. Parents' ability to research their own situation is affected by the conditional matrix operating at the time in their own lives. This research is often necessary because parents find that their concerns are often being dismissed by significant and qualified others, including professionals. Unfortunately, when *researching* a possible diagnosis for their child they also find other disturbing information that serves to increase their overall worry about their situation. Parents hope that by seeking an accurate diagnosis they will be able to gain much needed help for their situation.

Sub-stage Four: Diagnosing

Once parents have gained enough confidence in their assessment of their own situation regarding their child's unusual development through seeking confirmation *(convincing)* in others and *researching* the situation themselves they often move to the fourth sub-stage of *diagnosing*. Before they seek a diagnosis, some parents question whether such a diagnosis will be advantageous to their child's overall life chances because such a diagnosis has the potential to be *a double-edged sword* (category one). Parents report that while there may be successful intervention with a diagnosis there is also the prospect of lifelong stigmatization with a formal diagnosis of an ASD.

When parents continue with the sub-stage of *diagnosing* they are often met with a punishing diagnostic process. The diagnostic process is a very difficult time to endure where family emotions often run extremely high. Parents can wait months, sometimes years, to gain an accurate diagnosis if they must use the overloaded state system. Certain diagnoses preclude access to particular intervention services hence the nature of the diagnosis becomes paramount in the minds of some informed parents and professionals. Parents assess the value of the diagnosis against their own experience with the child; their own research into the area; and the potential intervention benefits to be gained with such a diagnosis.

Some parents and family members have difficulty in accepting the diagnosis especially if their original estimation of the child included the notion that the child was in the 'genius' range. If they feel the diagnosis is not accurate parents may revisit the system a number of times in order to gain a more appropriate diagnosis and intervention. However, during this potentially, long-winded process, parents register that even more valuable time is passing when their child could be potentially helped and this adds to the burden of their already stressed lives.

Category one: A double-edged sword. The first category of parent experience at the sub-stage of *diagnosing* is termed *a double-edged sword.* It is termed such because some of the parents in the study were mindful that *diagnosing* could be *a double-edged sword* for their child. They were concerned that the labeling of their child with an ASD was something that could potentially stigmatize their child and reduce their child's life chances in the eyes of others. Some parents in the study had absorbed the autobiographical accounts of others (Maurice, 1993; Maurice, Green, & Luce, 1996; Stehli, 1991) who had achieved a relative 'cure' through various means including intensive, evidence-based, educational early intervention with their child. This hope served to delay some parents' movement toward a formal diagnosis and was a source of both internal and external conflict. This is evidenced in an account of one of the older parents in the study who entered the system at an earlier time when specialized intervention for a child with an ASD was not as readily available at the end of the diagnostic process:

> The paediatrician also suggested that we may like to have Kim (*son with a suspected ASD*) formally diagnosed with autism, the idea being that if services and funds were eventually offered for children with autism we could access them. I instinctively rejected this idea even though an easier life in the short term may have resulted from it. At the time, I felt very strongly that if we did insist on a formal diagnosis the label would be with our son for the rest of his life. It would never leave him and may give others the right to reject him out of hand. We had already seen how the medical profession viewed the prognosis of children with autism. I could not in all conscience purposefully seek a label that might limit Kim's life's chances from the age of four. This was one of the worst arguments that I had ever had with my partner.

Another parent in the study also expressed the difficulties associated with labeling and potentially stigmatizing her child:

> I was only comfortable a long way down the track, come Year 6 or 7, that I was happy to let people know that my son had autism. I told the school that I was very much wanting it to be done on a need-to-know basis. I didn't want him to be labelled and have the stigma associated with that. I was hoping he

> would have improvements and then outlive the label. I just didn't want people forming judgments of him so I very much felt the information was personal and it didn't need to be blabbed everywhere. It is amazing when you mention the word 'autism' all sorts of people recoil quite a bit and don't hold much hope for your child's future and they don't want to get overly involved in it.

Another younger parent accessing the system somewhat later than the previous two parents also expressed similar concern about the stigmatization associated with labelling her child with an ASD diagnosis. However, this parent's acceptance of the need for the label was greater because it held the hope of access to a greater level of ASD specific intervention:

> Well, having this label on your child in my opinion can have its downfalls as well. If you have a child and you say that the child has autism or the child next to him, who may have autism, but you have said they have a speech impairment, it just makes a huge difference, there is a stigma attached to that label. I did take that into consideration as well. I hated the word 'autism' for a long time and I still do. I hate using it.

However, this same parent also commented that she was grateful to have had her child diagnosed early because of the ever-increasing waiting lists in the public system:

> Oh yes, if I hadn't done it (*had her son diagnosed with an ASD*), if I hadn't have acted when I did I would have been on a massive waiting list because a few months after that the funding changed and that really mucked things up a bit as far as a waiting list goes – they were huge. I wouldn't have got in. I knew a lot of people that I had met that were going through what I went through were on a six month waiting list. And you have not got six months to wait and it can make a huge difference.

This mother, like other parents in the study, was aware of the ever-changing nature of disability funding and how this could seriously affect a parent's ability to access much needed services. She also reflected all parents' preoccupation in the study with the passing of time in relation to the lack of development being shown by her son in comparison to his peers. The hope of gaining intervention which targeted the individual profile of her child with an ASD served to overcome some of the unease this younger parent felt about the stigmatization associated with gaining a diagnosis of an ASD.

To summarize, parents in this category of experience register that diagnosis can be *a double-edged sword*. On the one hand, there is hope that diagnosis will bring much needed, timely help to not only the child experiencing difficulty but also to the rest of the family. On the other hand, there is the realization by some parents that the diagnosis itself can stigmatize the child and reduce their worth in the eyes of significant others over their lifetime.

Category two: Enduring diagnosis. The second category of parent experience at the sub-stage of *diagnosing* is termed *enduring diagnosis.* Parents in the study indicated that the diagnostic process was one of the most difficult periods of their lives, both difficult to navigate, endure and accept. Most parents also experienced ambivalence about their situation while *enduring diagnosis*. While parents wanted to gain an accurate diagnosis so that they could more fully understand their child and gain targeted help for them, parents also knew that once a diagnosis of an ASD was made the lifelong consequences of what that diagnosis could mean for both the child and the rest of the family would become inescapable. In the case of a child being diagnosed with an ASD this could mean a bleak prognosis, including the need for life-long care or eventual institutionalization, depending upon the severity of the child's difficulties.

For most of the parents in the study, eventual diagnosis of an ASD involved a multi-disciplinary team made up of a paediatrician, psychologist and speech pathologist. The assessment was conducted either privately or through the health or disability sectors depending upon the financial situation of the family. According to the parents, formal requests by them to have their child diagnosed could take as long as 24 months in the state system depending upon the age of the child. Parents indicated that the waiting for an accurate diagnosis, the actual assessment of the child and the resulting diagnosis were causes of great stress for them. To illustrate, one parent in the study described the traumatic time that she and her child endured when she went to see a private psychologist as part of the diagnostic process in the following way:

> That was like … if I'd had half a bottle of vodka on the way home I would have drunk it. She (*the psychologist*) was so strict with him. He had tantrum, after tantrum, after tantrum and she had a beautiful dog. It was a St. Bernard, a big sloppy thing, and Paul (*son with a suspected ASD*) just wanted to just lie on it and play with it. She had a cuckoo clock upstairs and it cuckooed every fifteen minutes and he wanted to go and see it and she wouldn't let him. And he had a tantrum every time it cuckooed and she wouldn't let him see it. I think she just wanted to see the worst aspects of his behaviour. It was dreadful, she made him do this IQ test and he kept wandering around. I thought she is never going to find out what his IQ is.

And after such a harrowing assessment session this same parent described her response to the news that her child had been diagnosed with Asperger's Disorder:

> And I was just shell shocked, I could have been a World War One victim, because I knew that Asperger's Disorder and autism … there's no cure. That it is a life-long, non-curable disability. And that is what you have just been told your child has got. He is not just bright and eccentric, he is actually never going to be better. So, I was totally gobsmacked.

Similarly, a fellow parent in the study also described her and her partner's devastated response to an upgraded diagnosis from receptive/expressive language disorder to one of Autistic Disorder in the following way:

> Straight after the assessment, we walked from the building with the occupational therapist leading the way. She could plainly see that my partner and I were very distraught and overwhelmed. We had come with the intention of gaining help and had been hit by what we perceived at the time as a bombshell. If Kim (*son*) was autistic then any hope we had for him could virtually be a waste of time. By the time we left the hospital grounds my partner and I were in a sea of panic and despair. We walked through the hospital grief stricken as though we had just lost our son even though he was still physically with us.

This response was typical of the difficulties and pain experienced by parents throughout the diagnostic process. Parents indicated that there was little follow-up after the diagnosis to ensure their emotional welfare even though research indicates this is one of the most stressful times in parents' lives (Gray, 2002b, 2006). At this time, some parents' thoughts were not only trying to process the diagnosis but they were also trying to understand what the prognosis would mean for both the child with an ASD and the rest of their family as evidenced below:

> I began to have strange and disturbing thoughts. I was very worried about the life that lay before my daughter with a brother who would, in all probability, have to be institutionalized. I became convinced that it would be better for my partner and our daughter to leave Kim (*son with a suspected ASD*) and myself. My partner could then at least try to give her a life of relative acceptance. Why ruin four lives when two could be saved? Logical madness is the only way to describe my thoughts at this time. At my most desperate times, I had thoughts of suicide. Somehow, my mind was trying to solve a situation which did not have a solution.

While most parents experienced distress at the diagnosis, they also experienced frustration that it had often taken too much time to gain an accurate diagnosis. Some parents also expressed relief that they could finally understand the reasons for their child's different behaviour. There was an expectation in parents that assessments and diagnoses would lead to timely, appropriate intervention but, drawing on this same parent again to illustrate, this was often not the case:

> As a parent, I found assessment sessions very traumatic. There was always the fear beforehand about what Kim's (*son with a suspected ASD*) behaviour would be like during testing, given his usual lack of compliance, and what the tests would eventually reveal about his difficulties. We had been to enough assessment sessions to know that many of them were about diagnosing the problems without offering any functional help or effective remediation. We could only hope this speech pathologist would make the whole trauma worth our son's while and draw some remediation plan to address his difficulties.

Hence, while parents experienced successive, often traumatic, assessments there was a growing awareness in them that the assessments would not necessarily lead to timely, appropriate or specific intervention for their child. This increased the stress already borne by these parents and their families.

Added to this stress was the differential acceptance of the diagnosis by some family members. This is evidenced in both the research literature (Ewart, 2002; Gray, 1998; Moses, 1987; Perryman, 2005) and in the parent experience represented in category three (*'little Mr. Genius'*) of sub-stages one and two (*worrying* and *convincing*). It has been found that some family members and professionals have trouble accepting the diagnosis especially if it sits in direct contrast to previously held views of the child's life potential. To illustrate, one of the parents revealed the following about her husband's response to a potential diagnosis of Asperger's Disorder:

> (*Paediatrician's name*) gave me the card for the Asperger's support group. He didn't say to me that he had Asperger's Disorder because Paul (*son with a suspected ASD*) had to see a psychologist and he had to see a speech pathologist. We had to get a triad of people and he had to get a formal diagnosis, but he gave me the card. I said to my husband, 'I think I will ring this lady up'. And he said, 'You don't know, he hasn't got that'. And I said, 'Well, we got given the card for the support group', but he said, 'But he didn't say he had Asperger's Syndrome'. And I said, 'They don't give you the card for the support group unless that is what they have got'. He said, 'No, no, we did not get told that he had that'. He was living in the great river in Egypt after that … King of Denial. I don't know, I think he just dealt with it in a different way. He just closes down. He is emotionally quite a closed person. I am a bit more volatile and out there. But he never wanted to talk about it.

Hence, parents must not only deal with their own individual response to the diagnosis but they sometimes must navigate their way through the different series of responses to the diagnosis by family members and others. This is borne out again by the further comments of this same parent below:

> I had them (*her three children*) 24/7 and my mother was very angry with me because according to her it was my fault my husband had left home. And also, by that stage it was my fault that Paul (*son with an ASD*) was autistic because of the way that I had brought him up. So, she withdrew her services to the family. I was very punished. I was a very bad mother.

Research has revealed that this 'denial' of the diagnosis is another source of continued stress for some parents and can sometimes have long term negative consequences in terms of the sort of relationship which is experienced with significant others who find it difficult to accept that the child has an ASD (Gray, 1998, 2002b). This can impact negatively on the ability of a parent to gain targeted educational help for their child, especially if the family breaks down, because different family members may have variable acceptance of the diagnosis. Research has also revealed that some family members may have potentially similar or other cognitive differences (Bailey, Palferman, Heavey, & Le Couteur, 1998; Briskman & Happe, 2001; Scheeren &

Stauder, 2008) or shadow syndromes (Ratey & Johnson, 1997) themselves which may add to the difficulties associated with accepting the diagnosis.

In summary, parents in this category of experience find that to gain a diagnosis they must endure a punishing diagnostic process which most often involves waiting lists, especially in the public system. Parents find both the assessment process and the gaining of the diagnosis one of the most stressful times of their lives. Parents carry with them the hope that with diagnosis they will be able to maximize the progress of their child by gaining much needed intervention services. This hope is juxtaposed alongside the depressing prognosis often given to children diagnosed with an ASD. Both the assessment process and the differential acceptance of the diagnosis by family members and others can sometimes lead to further difficulties and this, once again, places even more pressure on parents' already stressed and complicated lives.

Category three: assessing value. The third category of parent experience at the sub-stage of *diagnosing* is termed *assessing value.* Parents in this category of experience indicated that they had difficulty assessing the eventual value of diagnosis. In the first instance, actually gaining an accurate diagnosis for their child's situation was seen as problematic for nearly all of the participants. This is borne out in current research which indicates that despite increasing evidence that an ASD can be accurately identified in very young children (Baird et al., 2003; Charman et al., 2005; Lord et al., 2006; Nixon, 2008) diagnosis is often delayed until children are of school-age (Attwood, 2007; Howlin & Moore, 1997; Mandell, Novak, & Zubritsky, 2005). Some researchers have suggested that the similarity of features of autism with other disorders can often lead to misdiagnosis (Mandell et al., 2007; Noterdaeme, Amorosa, Mildenberger, Sitter, & Minow, 2001; Ohta, Nagai, Hara, & Sasaki, 1987). The spectrum of behaviour associated with an ASD can present a very confusing profile to both parents and professionals alike. Therefore, many misdiagnoses precede the eventual diagnosis of an ASD and this has proven to be a source of great frustration to many parents who need an accurate diagnosis to gain targeted, effective, evidence-based services for their child.

To combat this, in 2007, the American Academy of Pediatrics took the step of recommending that all pediatricians screen for ASD's with a core developmental checklist when children reach the age of 18 months and again at 24 months (O'Hanlon & Firestone, 2007, November 14). Current research also indicates that autism can often be detected accurately before twelve months of age (Clifford & Dissanayake, 2008; Donovan, 2008, 20 May; Nixon, 2008; O'Hanlon & Firestone, 2007, November 14). There has been a recent and urgent call in Australia to create a similar developmental surveillance approach where infants are monitored regularly throughout their first two years for the development of early social attention and communication behaviours by primary health care professionals (Dissanayake, 2009).

Participants in this study had other primary diagnoses initially given to their children including: Attention Deficit Hyperactivity Disorder (ADHD), Receptive/

Expressive Language Disorder, Conductive Deafness, Dyspraxia, Dysgraphia, Global Developmental Delay and so on. One parent explained this difficulty in the following way:

> They were arguing between PDD (*Pervasive Developmental Disorder*), that was one of them, they said it could have been severe Dyspraxia. And when I looked back to see what the symptoms of severe Dyspraxia were they were very similar, they overlap.

While these other diagnoses may have revealed part of the picture for parents, they often did not carry enough evidence to sustain them as a primary diagnosis for the child over time. Hence, parents often took a meandering, sometimes iterative pathway toward an eventual diagnosis of an ASD. This served to lengthen the time needed to access appropriate intervention and increased the stress and frustration felt by the parents. Some parents continued to use the strategy of *researching* throughout the diagnostic process and beyond when they felt that the situation outlined by others did not seem accurate or complete in relation to their own experience with their child. This strategy reinforced parents' growing understanding that there was a need to be self-reliant and resourceful in order to overcome difficulties in relation to their child with an ASD.

Parents in the study explained how some professionals seemed reluctant to diagnose a child with autism because of the prognosis associated with such a diagnosis. One parent in the study commented about this difficulty in the following way:

> … he *(son)* wasn't at that stage diagnosed properly with autism, he was diagnosed with Pervasive Developmental Disorder Not Otherwise Specified because I was able to show what he had been like previously. The doctor at the time who was on the panel did say to me he was very reluctant to put a label like autism on a child like Bill (*son*).

By contrast, other professionals were keen to gain a particular diagnosis of an ASD for a child so that specific intervention services and funds could be gained through the government system for that child. Sometimes there was significant disagreement between professionals about the relative accuracy of the diagnosis. One of the younger mothers in the study explained her frustration with diagnosis in the following way:

> I found it so frustrating that in the end I didn't care if they came back and told me that he didn't have a leg, just let us get the help for what is wrong with him. I think they were so desperate to put a label on him, like he had to be in a category somewhere. That was the worst part about the diagnosis because I had the psych. saying to me … to this day I am still scarred by this because I have to wonder about what the priorities are … the psych. said to me, 'No, no, no, push for autism, push for autism because you are going to have so many more benefits'. Well, what are we really focusing on here, are you looking at

> this child or the money side of things, the benefits? There aren't huge benefits anyway which I know now. And then I would have the speech therapist saying, 'No, no, no, I don't agree with the diagnosis of autism at this stage'. I just thought between the three of them, the psych., the speechie and paediatrician there wasn't a conclusive agreement on what they thought this label was and in the end everyone just signed it – the papers to say it is autism – just shaking their heads saying, 'Yes', 'No', 'Yes', 'No'. In the end, I didn't care because I was just so frustrated and it was delaying ... because I had to have a label before I started therapy.

Even amongst the professionals dealing with diagnosing children with autism there were alternative perspectives evident regarding the benefits and drawbacks of a specific diagnosis. This ambivalence mirrored the internal conflict experienced by many of the parents who were also unsure of the relative merits of specific diagnoses. Only one of the parents in the study was able to have her child diagnosed accurately in the first instance, and that was the parent who already had an older child previously diagnosed with Autistic Disorder. The remaining parents in the study had many other possible diagnoses given to their child before an eventual appropriate diagnosis of autism was made. This served to increase the stress experienced by these families and delayed any possible appropriate, timely and targeted early intervention that could occur.

Through *researching* parents learned that certain diagnoses allowed access to different types and levels of intervention. Sometimes, parents sought or omitted certain diagnoses so that they could access particular educational services for their children. This situation is evidenced by some of the older parents in this study who sought a place for their children at the government-funded Language Development Centres (LDCs). According to these parents, these centres provided early intervention focusing on specific language instruction in relatively small groups and students had access to both teaching and speech therapy staff. Students could attend these centres for a number of their earlier primary years and were mainstreamed later into their local school when they were deemed ready.

However, parents in the study found that gaining selection into one of these centres was particularly difficult because there was great competition for the small number of places available. Professionals warned parents of this and parents tried to shape their applications to maximize their child's chances of selection. If a parent already had a number of private differential diagnoses given to their child they could choose to present whichever diagnosis would give them the best chance of selection in their application. Professionals warned parents that children who presented with more than purely 'language' difficulties would have greater difficulty gaining selection. Therefore, some parents in this study chose to exclude certain diagnostic information from their applications that would preclude their child's selection into an LDC.

Parents learned over time that certain interventions were only on offer to students who would supposedly gain the most from the intervention. This, according to parents, often translated to those students who were the least difficult to deal with. In the case of the LDCs this precluded students who were seen to have both behavioural as well as language difficulties even though it could be argued these students would gain just as much, if not more, than students whose difficulties were purely language-based. This pattern of 'cherry picking' of students for specialist programs was known by both professionals and parents alike and served to make the process of diagnosis even more harrowing, frustrating and difficult. One parent in the study described her experience with this situation as follows:

> She (*Education Department psychologist*) seemed very experienced and kind in her dealings with me. She acknowledged that Kim (*son with a suspected ASD*) was having difficulty with the behavioural and social side of pre-primary life and also suggested the Language School as an option. I told her that we were already exploring this option privately with the appropriate testing in train. She suggested that she could arrange for one of the Language School staff to visit the pre-primary. A Language School staff member apparently visited an ex-student weekly at the primary school anyway and may not mind visiting Kim's class at the same time. I was very apprehensive about this idea given that my son's behaviour at the pre-primary was somewhat unreliable. He would have presented more reliably cooperative at his private kindergarten placement where he was a valued member of the group. I reluctantly agreed to allow the visit knowing that if Kim was not cooperative on that day his chances of being accepted into the Language School would be minimal. I had already been warned that the Language school did not take children whose problems were seen as more behavioural than language based. They could afford to be selective from their point of view given the oversupply of candidates.

Another parent in the study also commented about this same situation in the following way:

> Right from when speech therapy first started, we were told that they were really great centres (*Language Development Centres*) and they didn't take kids with autism but being as Bill's (*son*) autism was so linked to language and I guess at the beginning he didn't regress as far as he eventually did, then Bill's speech therapist felt that it would be a very beneficial place for him to go and that he would probably settle in reasonably well and that the fact that he had autism that you didn't need to mention it. It may become apparent to them but it wouldn't and certainly shouldn't be too much of a problem for them. So, I was very keen on this. I was aware there were very small classes and limited places and a lot of applications which seemed really wrong to me. I felt if all these children had the need then more positions should be made rather than include just some lucky ones. It seemed a bit like the Nazis and the gas chamber – here you are, you can have the future, you can't.

Some parents in the study became increasingly aware of the unfair competitiveness they faced *(Waging War)* in order to access appropriate educational intervention for their child and the strategies *(Strategizing Solutions)* that had to be employed to give their child the best chance of success. Such tactics, as manipulating the diagnosis to receive educational services, often made parents feel uncomfortable about the very injustice of their situation and this increased their inner turmoil and stress.

Parents experienced different time trajectories when seeking a formal diagnosis of an ASD for their child which determined the value of gaining a specific diagnosis. The earliest that any of the children in this study was formally diagnosed was at the age of two years. This child belonged to a family who already had another older child previously diagnosed with autism as evidenced in the category *from the beginning*. With their experience of the first child, this family were already alerted to the need for a timely and accurate diagnosis so that intervention could occur at the earliest possible time. By contrast, another family in the study waited until their child was fifteen years of age before a formal diagnosis of an ASD was made. This child belonged to a family who had been given multiple, differential diagnoses for their child's difficulties. The parents initially chose to accept a less serious diagnosis for their child's difficulties in his earlier years because his educational needs were being met in a particularly 'inclusive', private primary schooling environment where specific labeling to gain services was not needed. The school also allowed the parents to bring in their own privately funded intervention team so that successive, individualized education plans could be put in place for the child over the course of the child's primary education.

This experience contrasted sharply with what the parents found was on offer in the high school sector. The child, by then an adolescent, attended two separate high schools in both the private and public system but eventually had to leave both schools because of the bullying he received in both contexts. In response to this, the parents sought the option of home schooling through the government's Schools of Isolated and Distance Education (SIDE) but a formal diagnosis was needed to access such a state schooling service. Hence, both families' circumstances determined the length of time taken to gain a formal diagnosis of an ASD for their child and what services were on offer at the completion of such a diagnosis.

In summary, most parents in this category of experience found that they endured an iterative pathway toward an eventual diagnosis of an ASD. There was often some question in the minds of the parents regarding the accuracy and value of the diagnosis of an ASD. This served to both frustrate and elongate the process of eventual diagnosis. There was also a growing understanding in parents that alternative diagnoses allowed access to different types and levels of intervention services. Parents and professionals sometimes tried to manipulate the diagnosis to gain access to the most appropriate educational intervention available for the child. Over the four sub-stages of *Beginning Battle,* parents found that the external context often did not have proper processes in place to diagnose quickly and accurately children with an ASD in order that they may access appropriate early intervention in the timeliest manner possible.

CHAPTER 5

STAGES TWO AND THREE – THE EARLY INTERVENTION YEARS

The following four chapters explain the experiences of parents in the study from the time of early intervention (EI) to the latter stages of the formal schooling process and immediately beyond. During these times parents move through a series of feedback loops in order to strategize solutions to progressively increase overall 'fit' *(seeking progressive fit)* for their child on the autism spectrum both within their family and the external context. Some of the difficulties experienced by parents give rise to use of a particular strategy. However, once learned, parents often re-use a particular strategy repeatedly in order to combat other similar difficulties at other times in the educational journey of their child. For example, some parents initially used the strategy of *researching* in response to difficulties associated with diagnosis. This same strategy, having been learned in Stage One, was subsequently used by some parents over the educational lifetime of the child in order to combat their own and others' ignorance regarding many autism issues.

According to parents in the study, EI education generally includes many different types of therapies delivered relatively early and deemed to be useful by parents in their quest to help their child learn and improve in all areas of development. These included psychological interventions, speech therapy, occupational therapy, physiotherapy, social skills programs, specific academic programs, drug therapies and so on. In the words of three sets of parents, there is often little difference between 'therapy' and 'education' as evidenced below:

> In the sense that both are concerned with increasing the ability of the individual to gain skill in negotiating the world, 'therapy' and 'education' are very similar. The external 'therapy' has served to maximize the educational progress of our son in many different areas. In the early years there was little, if any, difference between the two. In terms of some forms of early intervention the two occur simultaneously. For example, occupational therapy seeks to improve gross and fine movement but also improves handwriting and comprehension.

> I suppose it is all about learning. Therapy is about how a person can get the best effect out of their body or their senses then it might be educational. If a therapy is about dropping medication then I suppose it is not directly educational, though it may be an educational enabler.

> And so therapy is a supplementation to school, but I think that therapy is just as capable of offering your child education as education is just as capable of

> offering your child therapy. A school should be able to offer whatever is needed and therapy should be able to offer whatever is needed. They are really one and the same. It is just the fact that education takes place in a school environment and that's a compulsory thing whereas therapy is something that you choose to do.

Programs used by parents in this study ranged from those that were evidence-based to others that were highly experimental. The resources of the family, both financial and otherwise, often determined the choice, quality and intensity of EI undertaken for the child. Parents indicated that the division between EI and schooling was blurred and was not necessarily a distinct time phase just inserted before formal schooling occurs. For most families supplementary interventions occurred alongside the formal schooling experience over many years. Parents found that EI offered by government-funded agencies occurred prior to and during the kindergarten and pre-primary years and this intervention reduced substantially when the child entered Grade One. However, when parents could afford it, they often chose to pay privately for intervention services to not only precede but also to supplement the formal schooling program of their child over as many years as they felt it beneficial.

By the time parents in the study had finally had their child diagnosed on the spectrum they had begun to realize that the task of educating their child would not be an easy one. They had already experienced the difficult and often meandering, pathway associated with gaining an appropriate and accurate diagnosis. For most parents this had involved a process of *researching* the situation in order to reduce the time taken to receive an accurate diagnosis and to, hopefully, access much needed, appropriate intervention services. With diagnosis, most parents assumed they would receive ASD specific, evidence-based, educational intervention services that would have the greatest chance to improve the progress of their child and thereby improve the overall welfare of their family. However, by contrast, parents often found a disappointing situation regarding the early intervention services that were on offer. Parents found that services could be: subject to waiting lists, highly competitive, expensive, oversubscribed, not necessarily evidence-based, lacking in appropriate intensity, not individually tailored, varying in quality and with entry practices that were sometimes discriminatory. Policy and funding decisions of individual state and federal governments also affected the type and intensity of early intervention on offer and this ground was shifting continuously for families.

Three categories of parent experience emerged in the study when parents tried to access EI for their child. These categories were based on the different pathways traversed by parents and were most often determined by the degree of vulnerability of parents' personal circumstances and the time-period when they tried to access services. The three categories of experience that emerged were as follows: category one – *settling*, category two – *improvising* and category three – *maximizing*. Parents in the first category, *settling*, were the most vulnerable and had to settle for what EI services were on offer through the government system. These parents initially used the most accessible, least intensive of the government-funded services because their circumstances did not allow many other options to be researched or funded by them. This lack of personal and family resources also affected the length of time taken to gain an accurate diagnosis. These parents, like the other parents in the study, gradually realized that publicly funded services were often inadequate and fell short of making much difference in their child's development but they were often powerless to change their situation. Out of sheer necessity but over a longer period than other parents in the study, these parents did learn to become more assertive and strategic in order to advocate on behalf of their child's needs. However, often years had passed in the lives of their children before appropriate services were gained and parents in this category were regretful regarding the valuable time wasted during their child's earlier years.

Another category of parent experience, *improvising*, includes a set of parents whose children were often difficult to diagnose and these parents subsequently devised their own EI programs. These families had the oldest children in the study and entered the system at the earliest time and therefore had the least amount of choice regarding appropriate EI for their child on the autism spectrum. They often employed maverick intervention strategies and implemented individualized, home-based programs so that intervention could occur at the earliest possible opportunity. Parents in this category realized that they could not just rely on either the government or private system to provide an accurate or timely diagnosis and the EI that their individual child would need. They set about *improvising* their own purpose-built intervention packages tailored to the individual needs of their child irrespective of their diagnosis. This option however, was heavily reliant upon family circumstances, both personal and financial, supporting such a situation and served to, once again, make the child on the autism spectrum the major focus of attention in the family unit.

A third category of parent experience, *maximizing*, emerged where parents chose to maximize their options by using evidence-based intervention on offer both through the private and public system. This group chose to research their situation and base the majority of their EI plan on evidence-based, educational best practice for children on the autism spectrum. Their research generally revealed that best practice intervention for children on the autism spectrum traditionally involved early, intensive, one-on-one, behavioural and psycho-educational intervention over a number of years. These parents found that such intensive intervention was on offer both privately and publicly. However, parents who were able to access these best practice EI options still experienced difficulties that needed to be addressed by them. The two sub-categories (*home-based* and *school-based)* explain the two different experiences of these parents. Both these two options relied heavily upon family circumstances supporting the demands of the EI situation chosen and parents had to continue to be strategic to ensure that their child's development was maximized.

For ease of understanding the following diagram illustrates an expansion of Stages Two and Three (*Waging War and Strategizing Solutions*) in relation to parent experience of the EI years:

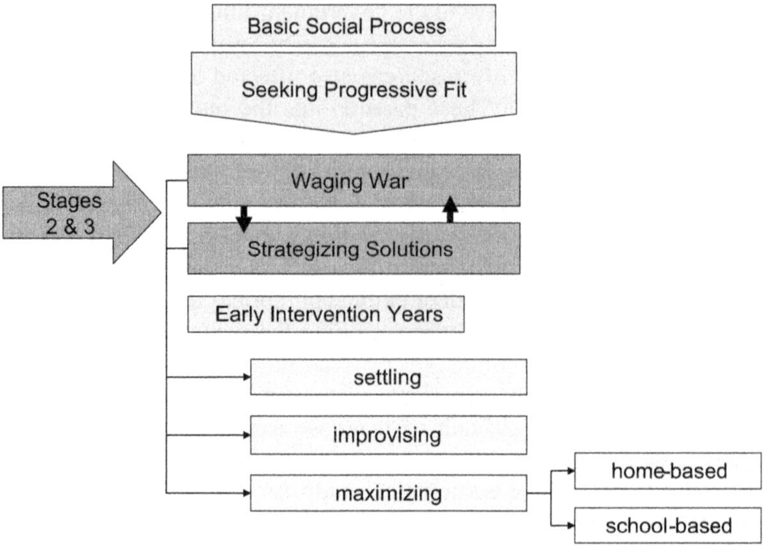

In summary, the process of accessing and using EI was determined by the conditional matrix operating in the lives of the parents at the time. Three categories of parent experience (*settling, improvising* and *maximizing)* emerged during the EI phase of education. All categories revealed difficulty in the lives of the parents trying to seek or create appropriate EI for their child on the autism spectrum. Parents developed a host of strategies to combat these difficulties to ensure the greatest development in their child on the autism spectrum. However, this constant need to strategize solutions added even more pressure to the already stressed lives of these families.

CATEGORY ONE: SETTLING

One parent in the study emerged as a representative of this category of experience, *settling*. Unfortunately, this parent was in the onerous position of having to settle for EI services that were only on offer through the government-funded system because of her complex single-parent family circumstances. The difficulty of gaining in-depth access to such vulnerable families in order to capture their situation has been previously documented in the research literature on coping strategies of families who have a child on the autism spectrum (Higgins et al., 2005).

This present investigation also found that the parent represented in this category of experience had the most difficulty participating in the study because of the fragility of her demanding circumstances and appointments for interview had to be rescheduled often. This affected the mother's ability to investigate and improve her own child's situation in the areas of diagnosis, EI and eventual schooling. This lack of family resources, especially financial, translated into the mother needing to run the family business and being unable to afford private diagnostic or EI services other than what government-funded agencies provided.

In the initial instance, this mother reported that she took her child to the State Child Health Nurse because she was very concerned about the delays in her son's development as compared to the development shown by her older two daughters at similar ages. The nurse at the State Child Development Centre referred her for more testing which occurred many months later. The parent concerned commented about this delay in the following way:

> I initiated all of this… how long it had taken to get to see them, six, seven months down the track before you go down the track before you go through everything ... and then by the time they do their testing and it comes back, and because we had the lunch bar at the time.

In response to the testing, her son was initially diagnosed with Global Developmental Delay and was termed 'vulnerable' until he turned five. In response to this diagnosis, government agencies then offered a small of amount of therapy as described by the parent below:

> I went to therapy over in East Perth, Lord Street, a big therapy centre over there. And he (*son*) got involved in things like SPOT which was speech, physiotherapy, occupational therapy and there would be groups of us. We would have individual sessions but not like what you get for early intervention for autism. They would only be once a week, like a Tuesday afternoon.

It was not until a couple of years later when this parent was at crisis point caring for her child and supporting her other two daughters, that she went in desperation to her local family doctor for emergency help. With the advocacy of her family doctor, this mother was then able to access a far more appropriate diagnosis and level of intervention at the State Child Development Centre to help address her son's needs as evidenced by her words below:

> I'd had a gutful and I went to my old family GP and he was gobsmacked at what I was being left to deal with, with Bob (*son*). So he got onto the State Child Development Centre and the social worker and they had a big meeting without me. (*Name of paediatrician*) was head of the Child Abuse Unit at Princess Margaret as well, well he was back then. He wanted to know immediately and wanted something done. So all of a sudden people were making appointments for Bob because he couldn't believe that Bob had not been referred to anybody and not been referred for a diagnosis and he just went straight to the top and I was given an appointment with *(name of paediatrician*).

It was not until her son was nearly five and in pre-primary that this mother was able to access a much greater level of appropriate, ASD specific EI through the government system for him.

As time went on, like other parents in the study, this parent progressively became more assertive about her son's situation. To increase the EI options available to her son this parent decided to elongate the time her son spent in the pre-primary years against the advice given by her son's school. She understood that access to the type of government-funded ASD specific, EI services she was finally receiving would finish when her child began formal schooling in Year One. This mother purposefully insisted that her son repeat his pre-primary year. This then enabled her son to continue accessing a much greater level of ASD specific intervention for one more year as described in her words below:

> Then when the autism diagnosis came in I then started getting increased therapy … and it took a bit of fighting on behalf of (*name of school*) they don't like to keep a child back. Once Bob (*son*) went into Year One he was going to speech with (*name of state-funded intervention service provider*) and I felt the benefit of him repeating pre-primary and me still picking him up at lunchtime and him having speech, OT and physiotherapy at home far outweighed his academic needs. I said to (*name of primary school principal*), 'Well no, I don't see the benefit if he can get all of this therapy now that he has been diagnosed that is what I want'. So Bob did not do full time pre-primary until the second year of pre-primary in the last term.

Like other parents in the study, this parent gradually learned that to gain desired services she had to become much more assertive and strategic regarding her son's situation and not rely solely on the expertise of others deemed to have more experience than herself in these areas. This is evidenced in her words below:

> And this is where people like me, this is not a woe begone thing, but this is part of what we are here for, if you don't have the funds to go private and get the help then you do struggle. You have to actually become difficult.

This parent recognized, somewhat later than the other parents in the study, that the personal qualities of assertiveness or being 'difficult' were necessary when trying to gain the best of services, EI or otherwise, for her child. This was also the beginning of this parent developing more independence and confidence when advocating on behalf of her own situation. However, this parent's situation precluded her from having as much time or opportunity to research her situation as other parents in the study. It also precluded her being able to afford private diagnostic services and EI therapies that were available to other families represented in the other two categories of experience in this study. While this particular parent did not have the opportunity to research broadly her situation, she intuitively knew that the timing of early intervention was very important to her son's development. She also understood that the delay in accessing appropriate, early intervention had affected her son's ability to maximize his gains from the ASD specific intervention given. Parents in all three categories of EI experience similarly sensed valuable time passing both intuitively and through their understandings of the EI research.

To summarize, the parent represented in the category of experience of *settling* began her journey with her child in the most vulnerable of situations. She did not have the time or the personal resources to investigate broadly or gain the most accurate or timely diagnosis or appropriate EI at the earliest time. However, this parent did become more assertive over time in order to advocate on behalf of her child's needs. Like the other parents in the study, she also gradually developed more independence and confidence in her ability to increase the educational options available to her child.

CATEGORY TWO: IMPROVISING

Two families involved in the study emerged as a representatives of this category of experience, *improvising*. The children in these two families were the oldest in the cohort of children in the study and entered the system at the earliest time. Like the parent in the previous category, both families in this category had difficulty gaining an accurate ASD diagnosis for their child. This led these parents to research, gain and create intervention strategies to directly target the individual profile of their child mainly on their own. When their children were very young there were limited ASD specific EI options on offer through either the government or private system. Once again, the conditional matrix the parents found themselves within determined their courses of action over time.

In the case of the two families in this category, it is important to note that the mothers had university-educated backgrounds. They were therefore in positions of relative strength as compared to other participants in this study regarding the perceived possible courses of action available to them. Both mothers were aware that this background afforded them a greater strength and confidence to employ maverick EI strategies outside of those offered by the generic government or private system. As evidenced in their comments below, both mothers seemed to be aware of this strength and their ability to use it to help their child with a potential ASD:

> If you have the advantage of having an educated mind and you know that these resources are available to you, that is where my librarian background came in handy too. All you can do is educate yourself as much as possible. Think about your child and his needs, what of all these things that you read is going to work for you and your situation as well as the child.

> I feel having a background in education has somewhat helped me because I have been able to foresee the academic skills that my son would need to be able to cope with mainstream high school and beyond. I have also felt more confident in some educational settings than I would have if I had not been a teacher. I have been able to tap into the latest educational research through the studies that I have undertaken. This has helped me greatly to keep abreast of cutting-edge research in the area.

It is also important to note that these same parents were the ones who eventually took the future step of *home schooling* their children on the autism spectrum. Hence, their personal backgrounds and experience with EI served to fuel their developing independence and confidence regarding accessing or creating their own appropriate and specific education for their child over time. These parents' choice of EI was based upon their ability to have the time and the financial resources to research and devise their own EI strategies.

One of the parents in this category of experience explained that her ability to implement EI for her son was hampered by the difficulty she experienced gaining an accurate, early diagnosis. She initially began with external generic services prior to her son's diagnosis on the autism spectrum but found them to be variable in their ability to target her son's needs.

> The school told me to take him to see (*name of occupational therapist*). Paul (*son*) went to *(name of occupational therapist)* and he had tantrums when she tried to get him to cut out and work on fine motor skills and blocks. She had a gymnasium and she held out and if he did this and this, he could go in the gym and on the trampoline. That sort of worked but then it got to the point where he only wanted to go in the gym. He started to throw things at her and belting her if she wanted him to colour in or do anything crap like that.

Unfortunately, occupational therapy only occurred for her son after formal schooling had begun and after her son had been diagnosed with Dyspraxia prior to his ASD diagnosis. This lack of an accurate diagnosis made the provision of appropriate EI problematic for both sets of parents, the professionals dealing with the child and the child themselves.

This same parent indicated that most strategies associated with EI focused upon ameliorating the individualized deficits of her child. However, after her son's ASD diagnosis was confirmed, this same parent began to see that there were difficulties not only with her child's profile, but also with his surrounding context. She was continually dealing with ignorance regarding her son's behaviour. In response to this, she decided there was a need to educate others about her son's situation in order that the surrounding context would be supportive and accommodating of him. This need to educate others occurred on a number of public and schooling fronts as evidenced in the parent's comments below:

> But I actually did do something … when I found out about Asperger's Disorder I got a one page thing off the net that said what it was and then I photocopied it and put them in my handbag. If he (*son*) ever had a tantrum in a supermarket, on the few occasions that I would take him … he had a beauty down at Target at *(suburb name)* when he was about ten. And of course, you see a nice, normal good looking boy having a tantrum people are going to come up and tell you how you should be raising them. So I just take out my little thing and at the

> bottom I used to write if you have any further questions please ring me. And I actually had a couple of people ring me and apologize. They would say, 'We're really sorry, we didn't know about this and how is Paul?' I would burst into tears on the phone and they would burst into tears at the other end.

Another front where this parent needed to educate others occurred in the common social situation of attending church as explained below:

> In the church that we went to, when he was first diagnosed, I wrote a little article in the Parish newsletter about Asperger's Syndrome and so many people came up to me, 'We didn't know anything about this … that really explains why Paul is the way that he is. We always knew he was different'. And the older ladies would say, 'We thought he was a bit funny but we didn't quite know what it was'. And I said in the article that he liked knock, knock jokes, and at that stage he really thought they were a hoot. People would come up every Sunday with a knock, knock joke for him. And then, a couple of years later, I wrote a follow up about how he was going and so on.

This same strategy of needing to educate others was also utilized when this parent was dealing specifically with the education of her child in his earlier primary years. This situation is explained by the parent below:

> … the diagnosis was there but the knowledge and the experience wasn't. There was good-will but there was no knowledge and no experience. And so no-one really knew what to do with these kids … No one really knew how to write an IEP *(individualized education plan)* for a child with Asperger's. That is what it came down to, I think. At the IEP's there was me, the principal, the teacher and the education department psychologist. At the first IEP the psychologist did not even know what Asperger's was, and it was her first job, and I had to tell her what it was. That was in Year Three. Well I just talked, I just gave mini-lectures on what Asperger's was and what needed to be done, what he could and couldn't tolerate ... how they can get around it. There wasn't really any alternative at that stage.

To combat the lack of knowledge and experience of the surrounding context, this parent continually used the EI strategy of educating others repeatedly. The employment of this strategy served to improve her own and her son's quality of life in both public and educational situations.

The other parents in this category of *improvising* similarly entered the system earlier than other parents in the study and had a late ASD diagnosis given to their child. Their child was not diagnosed officially on the autism spectrum until he was 15 years of age. This child had received differential diagnoses of a Receptive/Expressive Language Disorder and autism at the three to four year old mark but the parents chose to accept the lesser diagnosis of Receptive/Expressive Language Disorder because no specialized ASD services were available at that time.

Recommendations for therapy included speech therapy and a generic EI program. Both therapies proved to be hampered by a general lack of knowledge and experience regarding how to deal successfully with a child with a potential ASD. Like the previous parent, these parents were continually dealing with ignorance on many fronts, including their own, and had to improvise their own EI situation to improve their situation for their son. This general lack of knowledge is evidenced in the words of the mother below:

> It was difficult for the speech therapist to engineer the interaction in ways which would motivate compliance in my son. It must be remembered that these speech therapy sessions were occurring only a few years after the use of the applied behavioural analysis model of behaviour modification had been researched by Ivar Lovaas in 1987. More successful ways of dealing with children, like my son, had not yet filtered through the system at this time. So, we were all left groping in the dark to find ways to keep my son on-task and learning. My husband and I could see that with each passing day that he was getting farther and farther behind the development of his peers.

In response to this situation, this mother explains below how she decided to use the best aspects of the generic programs on offer in order to maximize the development of her son:

> Speech therapy was eventually organized through the state system. Often the sessions were quite torturous for all concerned. The therapist was unsure how to handle my son's behaviour and it became a battle of the wills on a weekly basis. I could see that the sessions offered little for my son but I was desperate to receive any help at all. It did alert me to some wonderful language games which could be borrowed from a toy library for children with special needs. This was probably the most help that I received from this source. I worked regularly and persistently with my son on these games and because of his excellent rote memory he was able to achieve some good success with them.

This parent was able to draw from the speech therapy program those aspects that suited her son's profile and target his deficits more efficiently. This targeting of the individual profile became a growing way of operating for parents in this category and this process was subsequently used when home schooling was eventually undertaken in later years. All parents in the study eventually developed this skill to some degree to ensure that they maximized the progress of their child. The speed and degree of development of this skill was dependent upon a parent's personal awareness and the particulars of the conditional matrix operating in their lives (Strauss & Corbin, 1990).

In their quest to find targeted EI, this second set of parents also accepted a place for their son in an experimental, generic EI program. Unfortunately, as the parent explains below, this option was flawed from the beginning because there were too many diverse children in this group who had other difficulties, both physical and intellectual, which hampered her son's chances of gaining any real targeted help:

> We were to take our son to a school which had a purpose-built early intervention program. We were told there were to be a team of specialists in speech, occupational therapy, physiotherapy and special education who would be able to help our son with his development. As desperate parents we assumed this was something which had been done successfully before. Unfortunately, this was not the case. Even though there was a relatively small ratio of students to the teacher and her aide, there were too many children in the group with very high physical needs. Many of the children were not toilet trained and at least one of the staff members was absent most of the time addressing these needs. Therapists appeared at different times and took the children to other parts of the school for therapy and assessments. Often the children looked distressed and frightened when leaving the class with someone they did not know very well. I did not feel comfortable leaving my son alone in this environment, as he was only three and a half and had very poor communication skills.

This parent assessed the inadequacy of the situation and in response to this decided to bridge the gap herself by becoming her son's aide and thereby, provide the level of support needed for him to gain any progress from the program on offer. She explained this process in the following way:

> It became obvious that it was an experimental situation and that the children were there to see if such a situation could be helpful. I could tell even at this early stage that my son needed one-on-one intervention for learning to take place and he was not going to get it in the early intervention environment provided for him. I organized to stay with my son during these twice-weekly sessions with the idea that he would hopefully, get something out of it.

This requirement by parents to bridge the gap in services also occurred frequently in the experiences of other parents in this study across the education process where appropriate and specific support was not provided for their child and subsequently, had to be provided by them.

After the experience of relative failure of external EI programs, the parents in the second family used the strategy of improvising their own intervention with their son, as explained by the mother below:

> The system was unable to give a clear and successful learning path to children like my son and time ticked away mercilessly in the meantime. As other children were gaining ground daily we knew Kim (*son*) was stagnating, if not regressing. In desperation, my partner and I began to realize the system was to be of limited use in terms of its ability to help our son. We were, to a large extent, on our own. We had given the system enough time and it seemed hooked on assessments and short on actual help in addressing my son's difficulties. It actually freed us to try anything and everything to maximize our son's progress.

Like most parents in the study, these parents felt isolated and increasingly responsible for their child's education because of the lack of appropriate and targeted help available to address their child's individual difficulties. In the following quote, this parent explains how she and her husband intuitively tried to address their son's EI needs by creating and implementing individualized home-based programs:

> We tried a number of different ways to increase the absorption of language by our son. We left nursery rhyme tapes playing over and over again in Kim's room to help with the imprinting of language. We narrated the day's events endlessly so that Kim's world would be covered by functional language. We joined the local toy library and took out as many language-based educational games and puzzles that we could find and insisted that Kim play them with us – no matter what his response. We prompted his responses endlessly until he did them himself. We taught Kim how to read phonemes with the use of home-made flash cards. He was already fascinated with the alphabet and numbers so it did not take long to teach him the phonetic understanding of letters. This is the way he eventually learned to read, he was one of the few people who learned to read before he could talk properly. We used computer programs as much as possible. While in the United States we had purchased a computer and bought as much educational software for it that we could afford.

This experimentation, according to the mother, allowed the parents to work out how to target their son's individual profile by understanding the specifics of his learning style:

> My partner spent many hours on the computer with our son prompting his involvement with these programs. The programs were very effective in gaining Kim's interest. They provided immediate and reliable feedback for his efforts. They were visually very interesting and appealed to him, especially the programs with music, which he seemed especially fond of using. In retrospect, they were a fine model for teaching Kim because they made him feel very secure in his learning environment. The areas of learning were broken into small, sequential steps which he could master after as many attempts as needed; they then progressed onto more difficult levels when mastery of the previous levels was achieved. It also taught him the use of the keyboard which would impact on him positively on his ability to learn to this very day.

The employment of a host of maverick strategies by these parents allowed them to create a specific EI program to target their son's individual learning style. This EI category of parent experience further reveals how the conditions operating in parents' lives can affect their child's progress. In particular, in this category of *improvising,* the attitude and background of the parents, the level of financial support available and the type and intensity of engagement with the educational context all served to improve the educational progress of these children over time. This contrasts directly with the experience of the parent in the category of *settling* who had a much less favourable conditional matrix (Strauss & Corbin, 1990) operating and therefore found it much more difficult to have the time or opportunity to maximize the educational progress of her child on the autism spectrum over time.

In summary, parents in the category of experience of *improvising* sought to provide EI that would 'fit' their child's specific educational needs mainly on their own. These parents used a host of creative strategies to combat the difficulties associated with gaining appropriate EI for their child on the autism spectrum. The nature of the parents' personal backgrounds and the iterative process of interaction between Stages Two (*Waging War*) and Three (*Strategizing Solutions*) allowed these parents to develop certain skills to help their child over time. Like the experience of the parent in the previous category, *settling*, these parents gradually learned to become more independent and confident over time regarding addressing the EI needs of their child. All three categories of *The Early Intervention Years* are somewhat indistinct in that parents often experience similar frustrations and difficulties; however, their individual circumstances determine their level of ability to deal successfully or otherwise with such difficulties.

CATEGORY THREE: MAXIMIZING

Three families in the study (McDonald, 2010) emerged in the category of experience, *maximizing*. These families tried to maximize their EI options by seeking to gain best practice, evidence-based EI for their child on the autism spectrum that would 'fit' their child's educational needs more readily. These families were able to access ASD specific early intervention at a later time-period than were parents in the previous category, *improvising*. All three families were able to approximate best practice EI through use of particular EI service providers. The process of using such services, however, was somewhat problematic and parents had to, once again, strategize to maximize the EI options available to their child on the autism spectrum in this category. The experiences of these parents is explained in sub-category one, *home-based* and sub-category two, *school-based*. The parent of the youngest child in the study was also able to access a newer government funded, ASD-specific, intensive, evidence-based, EI through the public system. This showed that opportunities for families who were seeking best practice EI for their child on the autism spectrum in WA had improved over time. However, even this parent still had considerable trouble finding and gaining entry into this publicly funded EI option and had to work out ways to combat such difficulties as evidenced in sub-category two, *school-based*.

Sub-Category One: Home-Based

Like all parents in the study, the parents in the sub-category of experience, *home-based*, felt a sense of urgency and desperation about their situation as they registered valuable time passing. They found that many of the government EI services on offer were oversubscribed, competitive and had waiting lists and that any government funding for intervention dropped dramatically when their child on the autism spectrum began Year One. One of the parents in this sub-category described the beginning of her EI journey in the following way:

> There was nothing available when we first started looking into in-home therapy. We heard a lot about it. I rang (*an autism association*) and they couldn't offer me anything … a waiting list of eighteen months or something like that. I thought well I have just got my son diagnosed and the first thing that you want to do is help them, and help them learn. Your hopes are that you want them to go to school. I want them to do this and I want them to do that. It is just normal. There was just nothing out there. The only other thing was through the psychologist. The psychologist recommended that I contact this lady which is now (*name of private EI provider*). Then it wasn't funded so that was a privately funded organization.

Parents rapidly realized that if they wanted to maximize their child's progress they would need to investigate what best-practice ASD specific EI options were available. Fortunately, these parents' situations allowed them to have the time and the opportunity to research their situation and base their EI program on evidence-based, educational best practice for children on the autism spectrum. In relation to the process of research influencing early educational intervention decision-making, one of the mothers in this category of experience commented:

> I spoke to other people, but also I got out every book that I could on the topic and then went through all of the references at the back of the books and got the libraries to order me in all those references and just read and read and read. It also is a bit of gut feeling I think about what you can see. It is obvious that if a child isn't able to focus and attend then they need to be doing one-on-one work. Some of it is just pure common sense.

Hence, through a combination of research, speaking to others and common sense, this parent was able to make informed decisions about what best practice early, EI plan would best 'fit' *(seeking progressive fit)* the needs of her son on the autism spectrum. The awareness shown by the parents in this sub-category contrasts with the lack of awareness shown by the parent in Category One, *settling,* who did not have the time or opportunity to understand this process or have the resources to privately supplement her child's early intervention program. This, in turn, increased the vulnerability of her child's educational circumstances and reduced dramatically the mother's ability to maximize her child's educational options in a timely manner.

The parents' research, formal or otherwise, generally revealed that best practice EI for children on the autism spectrum involved the following recommended elements. It should be conducted as early as possible over a number of years, be intensive (up to 40 hours per week), be generalized over as many environments as possible, be one-on-one, and be based on behavioural and psycho-educational principles (Birnbrauer & Leach, 1993; Eccleston, 2005; Francis, 2005; Green, 1996; Howard et al., 2005;

Howlin & Rutter, 1987; Lovaas, 1987, 2003; Magiati et al., 2007; McEachin et al., 1993; Myles, 2005; Roberts & Prior, 2006; Smith, 1996; Smith & Lovaas, 1998). This research translated into an eventual search by parents for an EI program that incorporated the features of both Applied Behavioural Analysis (ABA) and Discrete Trial Training (DTT).

Parents in this sub-category of experience realized through their own research that most of the government-funded services that were on offer did not provide the type or intensity of intervention recommended in best practice programs at the earliest possible time. Parents found that only one private service provider at that time potentially offered the type of EI recommended in best practice programs when these parents were trying to access best practice EI for their child. In this program, parents were expected to use their home as a base for EI therapy and subsidize financially the process themselves in order to approximate the intensity needed in best practice models. Parents in this sub-category of experience who wished to use such private services in its earliest years found that it did not attract any government funding at all. It was only in its latter years that the particular EI service provider became accredited and a small amount of the intervention was then subsidized at government cost.

One of the mothers in this category of experience described the difficulties trying to afford the program in the following way:

> I would try to keep to that regime so if you got at least four hours a day, and that was all that I could really afford. If I could afford more I would have got him more, if we had more money. We didn't have a great deal of money spare at the time. It was very expensive. You have to pay for the program. I did all of my own resources. They told me what they would need and I would just make them up. I figured I could save costs that way. Otherwise, you would have to pay for that as well. There weren't really a great deal of therapists available. Some of them were just charging whatever they wanted. That was about eleven years ago. I think at the time it was $15.00 per hour for a student therapist and $35.00 per hour for the actual woman who wrote the program.

Parents in this sub-category of experience also indicated that if they wished to reclaim any of the cost of this ABA/DTT therapy from their private health insurance providers they were often met with resistance. According to the parents, private health insurance providers often conveniently categorized the therapy as an educational rather than medical intervention even though the program was most often delivered or overseen by psychologists. A parent in this study commented about this situation in the following way:

> Health insurance funds have always been unreliable in their payments toward educational interventions, so as parents we were often forced to cover most of the costs ourselves. We did not have time to fight the system or the government to insist on more funds to help the development of our child – even though these

> funds would eventually serve to reduce the burden on the public purse in future years. It is well known that increasing the competency of a disabled person reduces the amount of support they will need over their life-time. Research has shown, especially in the area of autism, that intensive early educational intervention can dramatically increase the competency level of many disabled individuals.

Hence, parents' already vulnerable situations were exacerbated because funds had to be continually gained to cover the cost of much needed therapies, including the ABA/DTT best practice EI program. Presently in the United States some individual states have laws mandating that insurers cover behavioural therapy and medical costs of children on the autism spectrum (Autism Speaks, 2008, October 19).

Parents in this sub-category of experience also found that there were not only difficulties with the funding of the ABA/DTT program but also with ensuring that the quality of the program delivered remained consistently high. To illustrate, one of the mothers in this sub-category commented upon the difficulties of implementing and maintaining such a *home-based* program:

> Different therapists would come in the morning to the ones in the afternoon. Some would say that they would come and they didn't come. They don't ring or they would ring at the last minute. So I would then fill in the gap. I tried to keep to that schedule. He (*son on the autism spectrum*) had only just turned three, I could see some improvements almost immediately, but it was trying to keep up that regime. That was the hard part. And when people didn't turn up for whatever reason, they were sick or they were on holidays or they didn't even bother to come. They weren't on any sort of contract or anything. They were part of (*name of private EI provider*) at the time and most of them were students.

Like parents in the previous category of *improvising*, this parent also felt the need to bridge the gap for services herself and become involved in the program by providing therapy to her child when therapists failed to show up. She also learned to seek out and maintain the best therapists who came in order to maximize her child's EI options. She commented upon this process below:

> They were all trained by her (*head therapist*) and then I wanted to be trained. You had to pay for that. John (*husband*) never really got involved. I pretty much did all of it. Yes, so once I became more confident I started to do more. And if I knew there was a therapist who was stringing me along and coming whenever she felt like it I would tell her not to come. I sort of narrowed it down to probably about two or three that I could rely on. It was too disruptive. Some of them didn't even bother to ring and tell you they were not coming. They just didn't show up until I rang them to say, 'Aren't you coming today?', 'Oh no, I'm sick'. I would rather have people that I knew were reliable, know their stuff, come in and do their job and go. That is all that I wanted.

One of the youngest parents in this sub-category of experience also made similar comments about the lack of consistency in the quality of delivery of the *home-based* program delivered to her son:

> I had a few problems with (*name of private EI provider*). Just because the consistency was going out the window, and consistency to me was more important than having thirty hours a week of therapy with a lack of consistency there, quality in the programming, you've got to be consistent with the programming. Like with (*name of private EI provider*) I would have three therapists coming through and one would let him get away with one thing, the other wouldn't. It's just not going to work, everyone has got to be on the same page otherwise the therapy is just not going to work for you.

Her response to this was to continue to maximize her son's EI options by seeking a position for her child in the newly formed, Department of Education's (DET) Autism Units to supplement the program already operating. This option was not available to the other parents in this sub-category as this DET option did not exist at the time when their children were at an appropriate age to access such services.

All parents in the study indicated that there had been a re-organization of family priorities in response to their child on the autism spectrum being in the family. Most often, the needs of the child on the autism spectrum regularly took precedence over the needs of the rest of the family. Families experienced an on-going imbalance in the resources taken to address the needs of their child on the autism spectrum as compared to the resources taken to address other family members' needs. However, this inequity became more formalized and legitimized in this sub-category (*home-based*) with the introduction of an intensive, home-based, privately funded best practice EI program. This often translated into a situation where there was a necessary separation of the educational and financial roles of the parents in the family. The mothers in this sub-category had the major responsibility for the education of their child on the autism spectrum; while the fathers supported the family financially in order to subsidize the very high cost of the private EI programs. One of the mothers, who eventually had two of her four children diagnosed on the autism spectrum described how she orchestrated the difficult and expensive EI process with her first son on the autism spectrum below:

> Well for Chris (*first son diagnosed with autism*) I would have a therapist come in the morning for two hours and a therapist in the afternoon for two hours. At the time, I could only really afford three days a week and I did the rest. In between, I did again two hours in the morning and two hours in the afternoon. I fitted it in when Jack (*second son*) was sleeping, if he slept. It was easier when Amelia (*elder sister*) was at school so I didn't have to watch her. She was there till normal time. Chris was being toileted at the same time, that was going on all the time but I would also set aside time where I would take him into a room that I had set up like a therapy room and follow the program as well that they had set out for me.

This mother then went on to describe the increased complexity and expense of the process when her second son was also diagnosed on the autism spectrum and her first daughter was diagnosed with ADHD:

> With all that going on with Amelia (*elder sister being diagnosed with ADHD*) and then Chris (*first son diagnosed on the autism spectrum*) and then Jack (*second son diagnosed on the autism spectrum*) ... because we already had therapists coming out to see Chris we sort of engaged the same therapists to also have time with Jack. There would be days where you would have one coming in the morning for Chris and that meant he couldn't have one in the afternoon because Jack was home that afternoon so you would have something for him or I would have to pick up the vacancies. Still (*name of private EI provider*) wasn't funded then so I had two kids using their services at those rates. It was really expensive (*a lengthy pause*) ... we were still renting.

While the separation of roles between spouses was a logical process with regard to servicing the early intervention needs of the child or children on the autism spectrum, it served to isolate family members from one another. It also placed the majority of educational decision-making responsibility into the hands of the mother who generally dealt with the situation on an on-going basis. This then lead to a situation where the mother became the family 'expert' on the education of the child on the autism spectrum and the needs of the other family members often became subordinate to the needs of the child or children on the autism.

According to the parents in this study, this inequity was exacerbated during the time of EI when the time-critical nature and intensity of the intervention compelled parents, especially mothers, to 'hyper-focus' on the educational needs of the child on the autism spectrum. This 'hyper-focus' has been documented previously in the research literature where mothers of children on the autism spectrum have been found to be over-protective, over-involved and more likely to provide accurate information about their child's disability than others in the family (Ewart, 2002; Konstantareas & Homatidis, 1988; Leighton, 1969; Marshall & Long, 2010).

According to parents in this study, this separation of roles and 'hyper-focus' put extra pressure on all family members, who must either oversee and/or implement the program, finance the program or subjugate their own needs in life to accommodate the demanding needs of the child on the autism spectrum. Previous research investigating the well-being of parents who have a child on the autism spectrum confirms the difficulties associated with this on-going dynamic:

> The results from previous research indicated a high level of emotional distress for many of the parents including depression, anxiety and anger (Gray, 1994; Gray & Holden, 1992). Less frequently, parents reported physical health problems, some of which may have had a stress related component. Career problems were also common with some parents reporting moderate to serious limitations on their careers, and others, particularly mothers, denied

> any opportunity for outside employment due to their child's disability.... Both parents were affected by these difficulties; however, mothers were especially likely to report severe distress ... the degree of difference between the mothers and fathers was striking. There were several possible reasons for the mothers' greater distress including greater involvement in child raising, increased exposure to negative social reactions by outsiders and the absence of employment and an alternative role to being the parent of a child with Autism (Gray, 2002b, pp. 217–218).

Two of the mothers in this sub-category of experience described this hyper-focus and the division of roles in the following ways:

> What I have always tried to do, which can be very tiring, and is tiring for the child involved as well, every waking minute can be an educational moment for them. You really feel the strong pull that you have to make at that as well because you know the time is ticking on so it can be a very big burden for a parent to have to feel that ... very tiring, very overwhelming but you don't really get a choice to accept or reject that. It is just the way that it is.

> And work was his (*referring to husband*) life basically but, the thing was, it was where he felt he was making a contribution. If he was busy working and making the money then that was his way of contributing. I still had to do everything and I am talking about the therapy. In my head I knew how much I had to do. I was one of those sort of people who would never have a day off, because a day off meant that they would get behind. You start thinking like that you know what I mean ... You have to make every moment count. Like 'Look Mum, look at the bird'. 'Oh yes, that is the bird', and then you start making a little therapy session out of it. Instead of just ... it takes over. You begin to think like that about everything, finding the learning outcome out of every little incident.

One of these same mothers also identified her own level of burnout during this type of intensive early intervention where she was hoping for a 'cure':

> ... that first year when I first got into (*name of private EI provider*) when Chris (*son*) was newly diagnosed I made it my mission to save him. I did it for six months and I was absolutely exhausted after that. That was my first little look into the world of burnout because I was absolutely exhausted. I remember I was going to my niece's 21st so I was flying back to Melbourne and I took Amelia *(eldest daughter)* with me and remember thinking that I did not want to go back. I was dreading it.

This reorganization of family priorities comes at a high emotional cost to all family members and parents are often troubled later by the inequitable distribution of time and energy placed into the life of the child on the autism spectrum. One of the mothers in this sub-category of experience commented about this need to redress the previous imbalance with other family members, especially siblings of the child on the autism spectrum, in the following way:

> My second son (*without an ASD*) has homework but he also has a lot of after school activities. And sometimes I think I am now trying to compensate for what he missed out on when he was younger so I let him do everything and anything. I mean activity, constructive things-wise. He is in footy, debating, choir, water polo, all sorts of things which normally you might say they can only do one activity. I think it is a compensatory thing, plus he is a capable boy and I want him to reach his full potential as well.

To further complicate matters, some parents and siblings of the child on the autism spectrum may also have other difficulties that do not gain the attention that would normally be given to address such issues. Unfortunately, families with one child on the autism spectrum have a greater recurrence risk of siblings also being affected by an ASD than would occur in the general population (Jamain et al., 2003). Studies have also shown that parents themselves, especially fathers, may also show milder autistic traits (Briskman & Happe, 2001; Scheeren & Stauder, 2008). A review of studies examining the phenotype of autism in relatives indicates that:

> Relatives are sometimes affected by difficulties that appear conceptually related to autistic behaviors. These range in severity from pervasive developmental disorders to abnormalities in only one area of functioning, and possibly extend to related personality traits (Bailey et al., 1998, p. 369).

Hence, when another family member may need extra attention there may not be the same capacity in the family to do so. This situation places even more pressure on the family, especially the mother, to accommodate and support not only the child or children on the autism spectrum but also others in the family.

This pressure was evident in a situation faced by one of the mothers in this sub-category of experience who eventually had four children diagnosed with difficulties. Two of her children were diagnosed on the autism spectrum, while the other two children were diagnosed with Attention Deficit Hyperactivity Disorder (ADHD). While trying to implement an intensive, EI program with her first son on the autism spectrum she was also aware that her eldest child was experiencing learning difficulties at school. Unfortunately, the lack of time and emotional energy on her part left her unable to be as involved with her daughter's situation as much as she felt necessary. She expressed remorse and regret regarding this situation in her comments below:

> So Amelia (*eldest child*) was having problems so I started investigating that and she was diagnosed with ADHD combined. She was about five or six and we had speech therapy for her. So I was trying to do this with her, thank God she had a really nice teacher that year because I don't think that I gave her any

> sort of emotional support. I don't think that I spent any close cuddly times with her. And I often wonder if that is why she hates me now. You have to wonder. All that was happening, there was this little girl who probably needed me, oh anyway, I am sure it had something to do with it.

Parents report that it can be an overwhelming situation and unless families devise ways to redress the imbalance they can break under the pressure. This same mother explained her situation in the following way:

> I remember even once there was a point in our marriage where we were thinking about separating. I called Disability Services and I said that I needed help. I remember up until that point I was doing everything. It was probably more so after Sid (*fourth child diagnosed with ADHD*) was born because I always felt very 'What am I doing? I have got three kids I can't even manage on my own and now I am having another one'. I did, I had a lot of mixed feelings about it. Things were not going well at John's (*husband*) work, I remember at the time. It didn't mean that he was spending more time at home, that wasn't the case. He was spending a lot of time away from home and things were really getting hot then because we were talking about school and all that sort of stuff. And that then adds another dimension to the whole thing because you don't really know what it is like until you get into it. So we were having problems and I was very close to walking away. I don't think John (*husband*) would ever leave me. I started thinking that I could do this on my own. I don't need him. In fact, I was thinking actually I would be better off because I would get a pension with this, just thinking of those things. I remember that is what I was thinking.

In response to this situation, this parent sought to redress the imbalance in her life by adopting a number of family saving strategies. Initially, this parent used the tactic of seeking external help through the government agency, Disability Services Commission (DSC). This gained the family more funds for respite, cleaning and so on. However, the gaining of such support came only when this parent was at breaking point, no help was offered or monitoring of the family situation occurred before this point as evidenced by this mother's comments below:

> But Disability Services then decided that they would grant us some funds. By then I was still paying for certain therapies and I was still paying. Now I started looking at getting respite and I had to pay for that out of my own money. The house was still a mess but the funds meant that I would get a cleaner. Little things started to happen, not straight away, but the fact that I was able to bring it to their attention and they actually did something. But I had to threaten leaving … I was ready to walk out at that point.

Hence, with the ability to access external support this parent realized that going it alone would not have given the family the best outcome. This realization is evidenced in this mother's following comments:

> I think it would have been 500 times worse (*to be on her own*) I think because having John (*husband)* there was much easier than not having him there. When he was away, I knew that he was away and I coped quite well. But you know when he comes back that you can relax a little bit, relax is too strong a word, you can share the needs that is what I mean. It took us a while to get our relationship back on track as well, but the fact that I was going to be able to get some funds now meant that I could get someone into the house to watch the kids so that we could have time together. Because we did not have any family here or nobody was really coming over then back in those days. No-one really wanted to come over. So we just had each other to rely on. He would always help with the housework and he would always help with the baths and he would do all the hands-on stuff. I was beginning to be really drained of even giving that to anybody. Because I was really finding it hard to do the loving mother stuff. It was just work, work, work, all the time.

With some support, this parent was able to recognize the value of the contribution of her spouse and strengthen the family unit. This seeking of external help through DSC served to redress the imbalance enough to allow this mother to keep her family unit together. However the help was not proactive and was only given to the family when they were at breaking point.

To recap, even though parents in this sub-category of experience had potentially one of the more favourable situations regarding access to best practice EI for their child on the autism spectrum, parents had to once again, overcome many difficulties in order to maximize their options. The experiences of the parents in this sub-category demonstrated, once again, the cyclical and iterative pathway between stages two and three of the theory whereby parents continually devised strategies to combat the educational difficulties they experienced over time with their child on the autism spectrum.

Sub-Category Two: School-Based

Only one family in this study emerged in the sub-category of experience of *school-based* and was able to access best-practice EI programs for their child through both government and private service providers. This family had the most favourable conditions with regard to timing and access to the greatest number of best practice EI options as compared to other participants in the study. They had the youngest child on the autism spectrum in the study and were accessing EI services at the latest time. They were able to not only access the EI services of a private provider where they utilized *home-based* best practice, but were also able to eventually access EI through a new autism unit that offered best practice EI at government cost (*school-based*). The Department of Education and Training (DET) school-based program was offered during the kindergarten and pre-primary years across specific government school sites in the Perth metropolitan area.

One of the initial difficulties that the parent in this sub-category experienced was finding out about the existence of the autism units in the first place. While this parent understood the principles of EI best practice for her child, her knowledge of what was currently available in the Perth metropolitan area was variable because these options changed rapidly over time. This parent commented that she only found out about the autism units by sheer chance as their existence was not widely known at the time as evidenced by her comments below:

> I would tell other parents about (*name of autism unit*) and they would say they had never heard of it. And that's another difficulty that for some reason it is not advertised, it is not very available. I found out about it after a year and a half of Adam (*son on the autism spectrum*) doing therapy with (*name of private EI provider*). One day I was discussing schooling with my case manager and I still had a while before schooling was an issue with Adam. She said, 'Have you thought about schooling?' I said that I'd like to send him to mainstream if possible and I asked her for suggestions. 'Is there one school better than another or what about some of these special schools?' She said, 'Oh no, I'd not send him to a special school, only (*name of autism unit*)'. And that is how I got to know about (*name of autism unit*). Had we not had that conversation I would never have got to know about (*name of autism unit*). It is not written anywhere, it is not advertised anywhere. Unless you are getting intervention or you have friends that know of (*name of autism unit*) there is no way of knowing about this school.

Hence, unless this parent had questioned others in the system she would not have found out about such an option. At that time there was no central or established way of finding about all EI options available to parents of children on the autism spectrum. The autism units potentially provided intervention approximating the type and intensity recommended in best practice models similar to that offered through the other private EI provider but at government cost. Hence, this parent felt angry about the lack of communication between those providing services and those desperate to receive them and decided to combat this by sharing this knowledge continually with other parents:

> … and that's why I was so angry and a lot of other people I knew with (*name of private service provider*) I told them about (*name of autism unit*). 'Have you heard about (*name of autism unit*)?' They said, 'What's (*name of autism unit*)?' I said, 'Talk to your case manager because to get into (*name of autism unit*) you need to go through your case manager. They need to write up a report about your child. You just can't apply if you are not with a provider'.

Since 2008 a yearly *Autism Services Directory* (specific to Western Australia) has been produced by Therapy Focus (a government-funded private service provider) to combat this difficulty in dissemination of current information regarding ASD intervention services. This Directory illustrates the complexity of the decision-making process needed by parents when trying to choose and gain intervention services, educational or otherwise, for their child on the autism spectrum. More recently, an Autism Parents Handbook has also been produced by a parent of a child on the autism spectrum, Heidi Brandis, outlining relevant, current WA information (See Appendix 3 for education services).

A second difficulty commented upon by this parent was that of gaining entry for her child into one of the autism units as there was stiff competition between families for places. This parent recognized that there was only one window of opportunity for her child to gain entry into one of these units and this awareness made her feel desperate about her situation as evidenced in this mother's comments below:

> I just knew that you have one chance, there are no other chances you cannot enter the program later on because there is no program. That is, you've only got the two years and if you miss that boat you will never, ever get an opportunity like that again.

It also prompted her to become single-minded, determined and relentless in her quest to gain her child a place in the new program:

> This might sound very selfish of me but at the end of the day I didn't care as long as my son got in. And it is only now that he has gone through the program that I think, 'It's not fair, the way they do this and that, there has to be more of this and more of that'. But at the same time I was very selfish and I didn't care because all I wanted was to get him through that program.

This attitude was especially evident in this parent's efforts when her child was initially denied a place at the school and she had to go to the top of the decision making chain:

> I remember going to the letter box and opening this letter and I was devastated. Devastated like my entire body was about to collapse. I felt like I was having a heart attack, I couldn't breathe. And I thought, "No, he has to get in, I cannot accept this letter that he is not getting in". So that's when my fight of my life started, I did everything, everything I could possibly do to get him into that program. I went to see a number of members of parliament and I really wasn't getting anywhere. And eventually, through contacts, we got to see the Minister for Education, and it was fantastic. And that's how we got Adam (*son on the autism spectrum*) into (*name of autism unit*). I couldn't believe it. And all that hard work, it was so hard.

Even though this parent did eventually manage to gain a place for her son in the Autism Units, she expressed concern about the difficulty and injustice of the selection process as she felt it favoured certain types of children on the autism spectrum over others.

> I actually asked the teachers, 'How do you choose who comes into the program and who doesn't? And they said to me, 'We wouldn't take a child who you

> have been working on something for months and months and they are not getting it. They are not going to profit from the program.' You see this is where I feel that a program like the (*name of autism unit*) program should be available to anyone irrespective of whether they are verbal or non-verbal – whatever the degree of their disability they should be allowed a chance.

According to this parent the autism units provided a high standard in best practice EI for children on the autism spectrum. One of the main benefits being the consistency and quality of the staff dealing with the child on the autism spectrum:

> I know the quality of education does not exist anywhere else in WA – you will not get it. And you have got these fantastic therapists coming in, high quality therapists, which are hard to find. There is a teacher and two assistants and they have been doing it for years. And I know one of the therapists who taught Adam in the last six months she was originally working with (*name of private EI provider*). She was extremely good, she was very, very good.

Other benefits stemmed from the fact that the therapy took place in a school environment. This allowed her son to have school-based experience in preparation for his transition later to a mainstream schooling situation. It also allowed the mother to have some much needed respite from the on-going demands of her situation. The mother in this sub-category of experience commented about these benefits below:

> They are in a classroom situation and you are not at home. You drop the child off and you leave. Even getting to school, something that we all take for granted, you drop your kids off at school and they say, 'See you Mum', three simple words. Adam had to be taught to do that. Every day, we would walk up to the classroom door and the teachers would get down to eye level with the child, and I would have to get down to eye level. And it would be, 'Look at Mum, see you Mum', 'See you Mum', 'Hang up your bag'. Just those two steps, you would never get that through a (*name of home-based EI*) program because it is not in a school. But yet, when they go to school they are expected to hang up their bag on their hook. They haven't even entered the classroom yet and those two things are just so vital, so important to know what to do.

When comparing the Autism Units to what this parent would have received in a generic mainstream kindergarten environment this parent commented:

> As far as education goes (*name of autism unit*) was just fantastic. It really focused on the areas that my child needed. For example, speech, a huge problem with Adam. If I had sent him to mainstream kindy, for example, and he sat in the sandpit filling up a bucket for an hour and a half – that would have been acceptable because he is playing with the sand and he is quiet. Whereas at (*name of autism unit*) that hour and a half would have been spent really getting in there and focusing on something as simple as 'What is your name?' I mean a lot of other kids at school will know their name and when asked their name

> they answer. Adam had to be taught to answer, 'What is your name?' and that took weeks for that response. And it really prepared him for Year 1.

When interviewed, a representative of the autism units indicated that the improvement of the children at the units had been independently evaluated over time and revealed the following promising results:

> It (*autism units program*) was evaluated by David Leach and that was over a period of time. We started with four pre-primary children and he evaluated them prior to starting. He evaluated at the end of the year and after eighteen months and he did that with the follow-up group as well. He evaluated them before they started and so then over time his results showed that the children made gains of up to three years across all areas and that they were maintained in mainstream.

The parent representing this sub-category of experience, who had the youngest child in the study, had the widest choice of best-practice EI options available to her child on the autism spectrum. Her family's experience indicates that the situation for parents seeking affordable, best practice EI for their child on the autism spectrum has improved somewhat in WA over time, providing parents can gain a place for their children in these government ASD specific school-based EI programs.

In summary, the parent representing this sub-category of experience, who had the youngest child in the study, had the widest choice of best-practice EI options available to her child with an ASD. Like other parents in sub-category one *(home-based),* she found that accessing *home-based* EI through a private provider at the intensity needed was a very expensive and inconsistent exercise. By chance, this mother heard about *school-based* DET Autism Units which provided intensive, government funded, best-practice EI for children on the autism spectrum over a two year period during the kindergarten and preprimary years at government cost. This mother became single-minded, relentless and went to the top in her quest to gain a place for her child with an ASD in one of these *school-based* Autism Units. The mother also indicated that the Units provided a very high standard in best-practice EI for her child over the two years that her child attended the program.

CHAPTER 6

STAGES TWO AND THREE – THE FORMAL SCHOOLING YEARS (MAINSTREAMING)

Three categories of experience emerged when parents were dealing with the education of their child on the autism spectrum during the formal schooling years. The three categories that emerged were as follows: category one (*mainstreaming),* category two (*supplementing)* and category three (*opting out)*. This chapter details the first category (*mainstreaming*) and explains the common mainstream pathway taken initially by all participants in the study. The five sub-categories of experience which emerged from this category (*mainstreaming)* were as follows: sub-category one (*broadening)*, sub-category two (*chasing)*, sub-category three (*waxing and waning),* sub-category four (*crisis point)* and sub-category five (*finding fit)*.

All parents in this study began their first foray into formal schooling by attempting to gain entry into a mainstream primary school for their child on the autism spectrum. They did this because of the widespread belief among parents and professionals that a disabled child should have the same right of choice as their non-disabled peers to experience mainstream education in preparation for a mainstream life. This is exemplified in the following comments made by two of the parents in the study:

> Because one of the things you are inculcated with is that the best outcome for your children is that you put them into a mainstream school so that you can prepare them for a mainstream life in adulthood.

> Inclusion to me is whereby individual programs might be worked out for your child because they are going to need that, but where they are included, where he was just one of the kids and he might have needed some sort of individual work and programming but he was part of the whole community. Inclusion can be part of the school community, part of the local community, part of your social community within your friends and their kids.

All parents in the study initially placed their children into a mainstream school setting where they experienced a variable range of 'inclusive' contexts.

The first sub-category (*broadening)* explains how parents broaden their understanding of education for their child on the autism spectrum to include both mainstream curriculum requirements and supplementary programs to address the individual nature of their child's educational profile. This process is undertaken with the hope of maximizing their child's development and independence. Parents develop an expectation that the education of their child on the autism spectrum will be more intensive, time consuming and arduous than what is required to educate their peers. Parents also have the accompanying belief that a successful education for their neurotypical child will eventually increase their child's independence and competence and decrease the pressure on the rest of the family over the course of that child's education.

The second sub-category (*chasing*) explains how parents must repeatedly chase a mainstream place at an accommodating school because children on the autism spectrum are often not welcomed for enrolment. Parents feel uncomfortable about enrolling their child in a school where they are not wanted because they fear the on-going negative treatment their child and family may receive over time. Schools often recognize the difficulty of the child's educational profile during the enrolment process, especially if parents reveal their child's diagnosis up front. Parents indicate that their children on the autism spectrum are often perceived by schools to place more pressure on staff and other students and to need extra resources. Parents combat this discrimination by use of many different strategies. Parents initiate most of these arduous strategies themselves to combat the potential discrimination faced by their families and this adds to the already burdensome nature of their lives.

The third sub-category (*waxing and waning*) explains the process of variable involvement undertaken by parents when they are trying to negotiate an acceptable educational pathway for their child on the autism spectrum in a mainstream schooling environment. Parents advocate, in a *waxing and waning* fashion, on behalf of their child's needs to ensure that the schooling situation maximizes their child's educational progress over time. Parents recognize the fragile and fluid nature of the mainstream schooling context that can change rapidly and increase or decrease 'fit' *(seeking progressive fit)* for their child at any time. Parents often view principals as key members of the school community who can influence positively or negatively the 'inclusive' process for their child on the autism spectrum.

The fourth sub-category (*crisis point*) explains how some parents are compelled to remove their child on the autism spectrum from a school continuously lacking in 'inclusive' practice. Parents indicate that without a firm commitment by staff to 'inclusion', appropriate resources and specific evidence-based skills to deal with students on the autism spectrum, the situation rapidly deteriorates to a crisis point. This crisis point, is often directly precipitated by a lack of 'inclusive' practice operating in the schooling context. Parents find that they are either instructed by the administration to remove their child from the school; or, they feel compelled to withdraw their child because they are alarmed at the on-going psychological and/or physical harm being experienced by their child in the schooling context. Parents feel duty-bound to seek a school environment that 'fits' their child's specific educational needs so that their child's educational development can be maximized over time.

By contrast, the fifth and final sub-category (*finding fit*) explains how some parents find educational 'fit' in a mainstream environment. The paramount element is an unwavering devotion shown by staff toward the child on the autism spectrum. Other elements deemed important by parents include: the type of welcome they and their child receive upon enrolment; establishment of an equal and trusting partnership with staff; self-awareness of staff regarding their ASD expertise (or lack thereof); student-centred decision making and having a key member on staff to promote evidence-based 'inclusion'. Such elements ensured that irrespective of difficulties faced, parents and staff could bring in expertise and work as a team to creatively solve problems as they arose. This ensured that the maximum educational progress was achieved by the child and the 'inclusive' expertise of the staff was continually developing and improving.

The following diagram illustrates an expansion of Stages Two and Three (*Waging War* and *Strategizing Solutions)* in relation to the parent experience during the formal schooling years. The diagram shows all three categories of parent experience *(mainstreaming, supplementing, opting out)* during the formal schooling years. The third category *(opting out)* indicates the pathway taken by some parents in the study who chose to opt out of mainstream schooling in the forms of *home schooling* and *segregating* during the formal schooling years. Stage Four, *Framing Futures*, is the end stage in the basic social process of *seeking progressive fit* and incorporates the two sub-stages of *transitioning* and *redressing the imbalance.* These two final sub-stages straddle both the formal schooling years and those years immediately beyond.

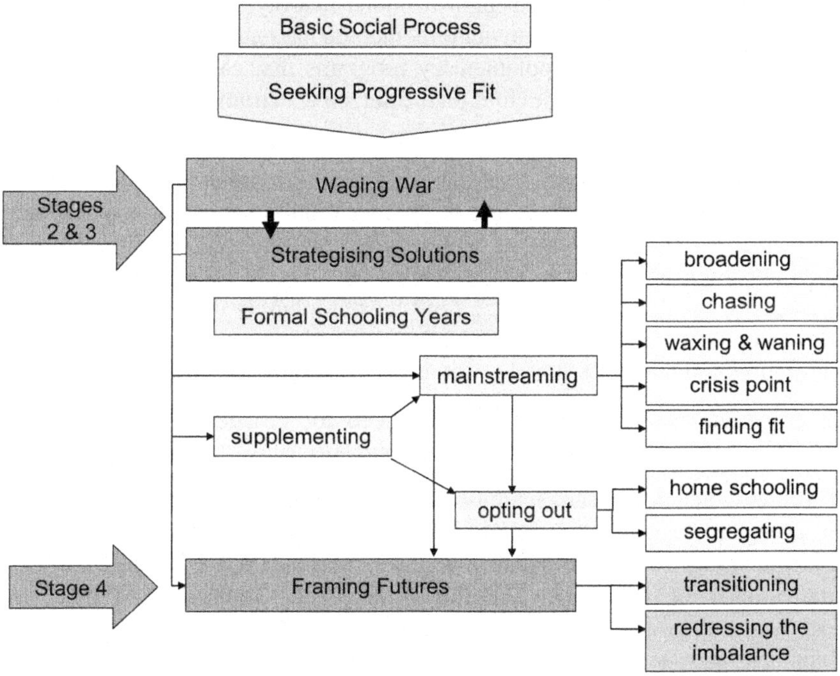

CATEGORY ONE: MAINSTREAMING

Five sub-categories of parent experience emerged from category one (*mainstreaming*). They are explained below in sub-category one (*broadening*), sub-category two (*chasing*), sub-category three (*waxing and waning*), sub-category four (*crisis point*) and sub-category five (*finding fit*).

Sub-Category One: Broadening

By the time, formal schooling is looming on the horizon parents have registered through their previous experiences of diagnosing and early intervention that the quest of trying to *seek, gain* and *maintain educational fit* for their child on the autism spectrum will not be an easy one. This is borne out in research by Stoner et al. (2005) who found that:

> The struggle for a diagnosis initiated a pattern of persistent behavior, and a sense of distrust (*in the parents*) with medical professionals, which continued and influenced parent interactions with education professionals (pp. 41-42).

Parents understand that education for the child on the autism spectrum will have to be somewhat different to that sought for other neurotypical children. Notions of education broaden *(broadening)* to not only include the regular curriculum at school but also encompass many supplementary programs that can address the specific difficulties experienced by their child on the autism spectrum. One parent explained this in the following way:

> I guess education is not only a school setting, but I do think the school setting is the big basis of it. I also would think education is something that can get supplemented in other ways as well besides just the school setting. But I certainly think of education as academics but it is also about interpersonal relationships and things like that. I don't look at it purely in terms of how well they can do a Maths exam. My view of education has been broadened whereas before I would have just thought of it as they just go to school.

Another parent also expressed this same need for broadening their concept of education in relation to their child on the autism spectrum:

> The term 'education' means school-based 'education' as well as the assimilation of acceptable social norms and behaviours, as well as mind broadening understandings of those concepts that allows participation in society in a way that could be construed as within the normal range. So that he can make his own way in the world independent of his parents with the best opportunities for happiness and successful relationships with others.

Hence, education is no longer thought of as just the gaining of academic skills in a school setting but it takes on greater import for a child on the autism spectrum where parents seek to educate their child to operate as independently as possible and to target their areas of difficulty especially in the social realm. Parents believe that by increasing the skills and independence of their child on the autism spectrum the whole family's quality of life will also improve as evidenced by the comment of one parent in the study below:

> … but all the extra time and stress and everything that goes into trying to give them (*child on the autism spectrum*) the best education that you possibly can. At the end of the day when they haven't got to the level that is required for them to be an independent person that is a huge impact until the day I die, and a huge impact until the day my kids die. It is a huge impact on them, the more skills that he gains the less he will need to draw from other people who care about him.

Parents also recognize that the education process for their child on the autism spectrum will be much more expensive, intensive, arduous and time consuming as compared to what is needed for other neurotypical children as evidenced by the comments of another of the parents below:

> It is different because the level of effort needed to help our eldest son realize his potential has been much greater than the level of effort required by our other children. Also, our other children have not needed to have the same level of therapy to supplement their mainstream education in order that they realize their greatest potential. I also do not have the same level of anxiety about the future regarding the education of my other children knowing that they will eventually become independent and be able to take over their own educational development. I have no such confidence about my eldest son's ability to take over control of his educational development or other areas of his life.

Another parent in the study also expressed similar sentiments:

> I can't help it but there is a difference. They both need to learn whereas my special needs child needs to survive as well. It is not just a matter of knowing Maths and knowing English and going to university it is learning to survive as well … I think that Adam (*son on the autism spectrum*) has to have much more involvement from me. That is not to say that I will not be involved with my other child but it will not be as intense.

Such understandings leave parents with a sense that their child will be a difficult one to accommodate appropriately in mainstream settings and they approach the task of trying to enrol their child at an appropriate school with trepidation. Unfortunately, as evidenced in the next sub-category *chasing,* they often find that their fears are not without substance when trying to find a place for their child in a formal mainstream schooling context.

In summary, parents broaden (*broadening*) their understandings of 'education' for their child on the autism spectrum. They recognize that the requirements needed to educate their child will need to incorporate both a modified mainstream curriculum and supplementary programs to address the individual profile of their child and prepare them for a mainstream life. Parents expect that the education process will be more intensive, time-consuming and arduous than what is required when educating a neurotypical child. Such understandings increase the pressure on parents to be much more involved in their child's education to maximize their child's life potential to help both the child on the autism spectrum and the rest of their family.

Sub-Category Two: Chasing

At first glance, parents seemingly have a wide range of formal schooling options on offer in WA. These include mainstream public and private schools from kindergarten upwards, with or without special education units/classes, Education Support Centres (separate schools on shared sites with regular schools) and segregated Education Support Schools especially designed for disabled children (on separate sites). Even though parents are sometimes aware that there is Commonwealth legislation (Commonwealth of Australia, 1992; Commonwealth of Australia, 2005) in place to ensure that they have the right to enrol their child on the autism spectrum in their local mainstream school they are often unwilling to place their child in a context where they feel they may be unwanted and not educated appropriately. One parent described the difficulty in this way:

> If the school took no ownership of Kim (*son on the autism spectrum*) or had no desire in supporting his development then his educational demise would be assured. For every difficulty which arose would be conveniently blamed upon Kim with no thought given to the discriminatory education system he was placed within.

Most parents in the study continually chased *(chasing)* an elusive, educational context where their child would be welcomed and have appropriate educational expertise to educate their child over time. Both research (Catholic Association for Special Education Support, 1995; Crosby, 1998; Forlin, 1995, 2004; Forlin et al., 2008; Harrington et al., 2013; Kidd & Kaczmarek, 2010; MacDermott, 2008; McDonald, 2010; McDonald & Lopes, 2012; O'Donoghue & Chalmers, 2000; Roberts, 2013; Shaddock et al., 2007; Victorian Equal Opportunity and Human Rights Commission, 2012; Wills & Jackson, 2000) and the experiences of the parents in the study indicate that parents experience many on-going difficulties accessing and maintaining an appropriate 'inclusive' education for their disabled child in Australian mainstream contexts. Parents in the study most often found that their children on the autism spectrum were viewed as liabilities by mainstream schools because they potentially required extra resources and expertise that the school may not readily or willingly be able to provide.

One parent in the study reported that a primary principal at an exclusive private school indicated that for their child to gain admission the family would be expected to pay privately for a full time aide. This cost was in addition to the already expensive school fees which other parents were also expected to pay. The principal was also reported by the parent to have said the following "inappropriate" comments during her son's enrolment interview:

> But when I had an interview with the primary school principal some very inappropriate things were said, that definitely wasn't the sort of place where I would want him *(son on the autism spectrum)* to go. I was told, when I asked about the level of the boys who attend the unit, one of the boys was one up from a vegetable.

Parents reported that their children were often viewed as potentially placing far more pressure on the staff and other students. Parents often felt like they had to 'go cap in hand' to schools and as one parent put it, "be oh so grateful for actually having somewhere where they would take your children". Research also confirms that teaching staff often believe that a child's type of disability is related to how difficult they will be to teach (Shaddock et al., 2007; Westwood & Graham, 2003). This includes students with emotional/behavioural problems; language and literacy problems, general learning difficulties; autism and intellectual disability who are often regarded by teaching staff as the most challenging to teach (Shaddock et al., 2007; Westwood & Graham, 2003).

Parents were also continually caught off-guard regarding the different enrolment requirements of particular schools. They were also unclear about their child's eligibility for support in different schools. As one parent put it:

> Because again, once you move from one to another *(school)* you don't really know what it is all about until you get thrown in it. I was told in the public school you would get more aide time and more funding but it wasn't the case. You don't know how it all works, you're in this thing where you seem to think that everybody knows what is going on except for you. The only way you know to find out is to ask the right people the right questions because you get thrown around in circles.

When available, parents used the informal network of other parents and trusted professionals to research the quality and requirements of different schools. However, parents indicated that the currency of such information changed rapidly depending upon the philosophy of 'inclusion' adopted by individual administrations and their staff at different points in time. The time-wasting nature of this process often left parents feeling frustrated and angry when their child was already well behind in comparison to the development of their neurotypical peers as exemplified in the comments of this same parent below:

> Yes, and time is wasting and everything. Then you find out it is all too late *(for aide time)*, when your intentions were to get this (*enrolment*) all done before, but it is all that stuffing around with everybody. I would rather be told exactly what I need to do, if you can't help me, who can help me? That is not a lot to ask.

Parents in the study were often left to their own devices to try to navigate the maze of difficulties associated with trying to enrol their child in an appropriate mainstream school. This is contrary to recommendations given in a West Australian report by MacDermott (2008) who investigated the experiences of 92 families who were parenting school-aged children with a suspected or confirmed ASD. The report indicated that the journey for parents who have a child on the autism spectrum should not be undertaken alone. According to the report:

> Families have much to gain from both professional service providers and other more experienced 'ASD parents'. The professionals encountered by parents and their children hold a potential wealth of knowledge, experience and expertise that can be invaluable in assisting families to craft the most beneficial intervention program possible to meet their child's individual needs. Likewise, experienced 'ASD parents' can offer their own unique wealth of practical knowledge about public, private and general community services and systems, as well as the compassion and practical skills that can only come from the daily experience of "walking the walk". Ideally both of these avenues of knowledge and support would inform and enable families, both at the beginning, and throughout their journey (pp. 7-8).

Unfortunately, the parents in this more recent study (McDonald, 2010) did not reliably find easy access to such key sources of information in relation to their child's education and were often left to their own devices to successively find appropriate schooling.

While all of the parents in the study were aware that their child had significant educational difficulties before their foray into seeking mainstream primary enrolment some had not received a formal or accurate diagnosis for their child at that point in time. In some instances, parents were asked to fast track their child's diagnosis to include a particular ASD diagnosis which would potentially gain more support for the school. In one case, the principal of a state-run primary school insisted that the child with a potential ASD be formally assessed before the child began at his school so that the child would be eligible to have an aide. The parent was informed of this very late in the year before the child was due to begin his first year of primary schooling. This placed a great deal of undue pressure on the parent as accurate diagnoses are extremely difficult to gain quickly as previously evidenced in the Sub-Stage Four, *diagnosing*, in the study (McDonald, 2010). The parent explained her experience in the following way:

> … I was suddenly informed that unless he had a diagnosis of autism before he started school he wouldn't get an aide. So we then had to rush around and have him assessed. Which come November, December, was no mean feat because it was quite time consuming.… But I was pretty upset at the time that we had no warning of this and suddenly bang you need it and you don't have it. Obviously something, somewhere went wrong and the fact that we were put in that position.

Parents were also continually in the difficult position of determining how much to reveal about their child's profile before enrolment. While some parents were relatively naïve about the reception they could receive others had already been alerted to the potential discrimination their child may face from their former EI experiences where they had seen specific diagnoses preclude their child from being accepted for enrolment into certain EI programs. Once again, parents were tempted to manipulate the information they had about their child to improve their chances of being accepted, however, this was tempered by their need to gain appropriate help from the educational context by giving accurate information about their child's unusual profile from the start. One parent expressed the internal conflict experienced in the following way:

> I sort of felt like I would be having to make it out as though Bill (*son on the autism spectrum*) was functioning at a level higher than he was for him to get a place there. Not that I was actually told that but I had a feeling they would probably be wanting children who didn't have such a high disability as my son unless I could fill the very big gap. I left there very upset and concerned.

This made the time of enrolment another very stressful period where parents were unsure of the reception they and their child would receive from a particular school. This reception ranged from unwitting acceptance to blatant rejection, with rejection being the more commonplace response from schools.

In one instance, a parent in the study indicated that they had received a letter of acceptance for their child on the autism spectrum from a private primary school of a particular religious denomination only to have the school "back track and say the letter was sent in error". This rejection occurred even though this particular parent had two other daughters already attending this same school.

In a second instance, another set of parents reported that they had their child's name down on an enrolment list at a private school of the same religious denomination since the child had been two years of age. However, when the parents revealed to the school that their child had language difficulties before enrolment they were told to bring the child into the pre-primary for an informal assessment. Once the pre-primary staff had assessed the child, the principal informed the parents that the child could not be accepted for enrolment. The reason given was that the child would need extra assistance in the classroom and under their system the child's diagnosis did not qualify them to be eligible for such assistance. One of the parents described the principal's position in the following manner:

> She (*principal*) explained that the school had no facility for children with special educational needs. Any child with special needs who had been accepted had to receive funding so that an aide could be employed to accommodate that child's learning difficulties. This, she explained, was so that the other children in the classroom were not disadvantaged because of the inclusion of the child with special needs.

Unfortunately, extra assistance in the form of an aide was only available to a child in their system if they could show that the child had an intellectual disability such as that associated with Down syndrome. This was an impossible situation for these parents to solve given their child's profile and made these parents feel angry and regretful they had even disclosed their child's difficulties in the first place.

Even when a child with a potential autism spectrum diagnosis was unwittingly accepted by a school, there was no guarantee that the school would not ask the parent to either remove their child or bridge the gap for support services in their child's schooling context either physically or financially. This is exemplified in the experiences of another parent in the study who was expected to remove her child at certain times of the school day when extra support was not available or become an unpaid aide to her child while they were at school. This is illustrated in the parent's comments below:

> Chris *(son with a potential autism spectrum diagnosis*) first went to (*name of state primary school)* and that was the year that I had Sid (*youngest son*). I got him in and it went relatively easily. I heard a lot of horror stories from other parents about how hard it was to find a school. That must have been the calm before the storm. He did a half a day at school because that was all they could afford with an aide and they didn't want him there without an aide, but prior to me suggesting that - I had to be his aide. So, I had to take Sid down there and I was still breast-feeding him and then be Chris's aide because they didn't have any idea.

This same parent was then asked to remove her child permanently from the school at the end of the first term "because they made it very clear that they were just not able to provide the sort of services that he would need". It took this parent a whole term to find another school willing to take her son because finding a place in the middle of year for such a child was an almost impossible task. This same parent described this difficult and depressing task in the following way:

> The amount of rejections I got after I pulled him out of that primary school. I was so depressed. I kept thinking, "but you have not even met him". In fact, none of them had even seen him or met him. "No, no, no, we can't help you sorry." I went through a huge list that I got from the Education Department of other schools, I was even prepared to go out to *(a distant suburb).* I took him out there and they just didn't want to know about it and pretty much told me so. "We can't help you." Where is the fair, how is that fair?

When this parent finally secured a position at a private school in the middle of the school year it was too late to gain any extra funding to provide an aide for her child. In a desperate response to this situation, the parents agreed to fund an aide for their son even though this put enormous financial pressure on their family who were already funding a supplementary, home-based EI program for their other son. The parent concerned explained it in this way:

> Of course, there was no aide available then, so one of the therapists who used to work with us at home ... she was his aide and I had to fund that. That was the year that we nearly lost our house. We were just out of our minds in debt. We were paying for just about everything that is because he started in the middle of the year.

Parents progressively learned that their child on the autism spectrum was potentially one that schools would rather not have to accommodate, and this included some schools that professed to have a religious mandate to accommodate difference and redress social injustice.

Parents over time, developed a number of strategies, both internal and external, to combat such discrimination. One of the key internal strategies they developed was where parents learned to become relentless and would not give up irrespective of the discrimination they received from different schools. One parent in the study indicated that she and her husband became relentless in their desire to have their child accepted for enrolment at a primary school of a particular religious denomination. They decided to use the strategy of 'going to the top', (which, as previously noted, was one of the strategies used by a parent represented in sub-category two, *school-based*, detailing parents' educational journeys during the early intervention (EI) years). After experiencing many rejections from multiple primary schools of a particular religious denomination, these parents decided to write a lengthy letter directly to the Director of Education of that particular religious body and give her a "moral and ethical dilemma". The parents reiterated their desire that their child be educated both spiritually and academically according to their faith and presented strong social justice/religious arguments as to why their child should be accepted for enrolment.

While individual schools of the same denomination had rejected the child repeatedly because of their inflexible funding and support arrangements the Director was able to circumvent these circumstances by eventually offering a suitable mainstream place. The resulting place was at a school which not only had a special education unit if needed, but also had a principal who was very experienced in and committed to 'inclusive' practice.

A second strategy adopted by parents over time was for them to 'hedge their bets' by enrolling their child very early and in as many different schools as possible to ensure that the greatest choice was available to them when enrolment was imminent. One parent explained this process in the following way:

> Over time, we have found that it is better to enrol your disabled child very early in a large number of good schools so that the best choice can be made at the time when entry to a new school is needed. So many factors change over time, including the ability of the child, which make it impossible to make informed choices so many years before when enrolment of these children is necessary. It is better to have a number of choices than to be forced into one choice because places are so competitive. This way a family can readily assess the administration's commitment to the enrolment much closer to the time of entry.

This strategy assured parents of capturing the best available option in their continual and difficult chase to access best educational 'fit' *(seeking progressive fit)* for their child on the autism spectrum.

A third strategy used to try to combat potential rejection and discrimination after eventual enrolment into a school was for parents to support the supporters within the school. This strategy was achieved by parents volunteering to be involved in the school in many extra-curricular roles on an on-going basis. Some of the parents in the study indicated they undertook key roles in parents associations, school boards, worked in school canteens and the school library, coached school sporting teams and initiated parent-class representative schemes to ensure their child's position in the school was cemented as firmly as possible. This also allowed them to have the best lines of communication open to them with key high profile staff in the administration when difficulties inevitably arose.

A fourth enrolment strategy used by parents was to enrol their child in one of the government-funded autism units prior to formal schooling. Enrolment at the units was officially tied to enrolment at a mainstream school so that appropriate transition could occur between the two schooling environments. A representative of the units explained the reasoning behind this in the following way:

> So we want to try to make it a bit smoother so that we choose the kid, we notify the schools, the kids don't get enrolled with us because we are not a school. They are enrolled in their local school but not attending. So they have an enrolment there but no bums on chairs but that then gives them a foot in the door for the following year. You probably would know that just because you put your name down doesn't mean you are going to get a place and they will give it to the other child, they are not supposed to do that but that does happen.

This created conditions for a smooth transition for the child and their family as explained by the representative of the Units below:

> And what we do, once we have identified the school we go and we send our staff down there. We take pictures of the outside of the school, the classroom, the staff, so that we start doing social stories with the kids before they ever get there. And then, on the first day, because the Mums have taken them there and had play lunch in the playground before school opens and all of that, it is so smooth. We never get kids crying or resisting or any of that, anymore. Before we had done transition to this level it used to be a bit hit and miss. But now, it is much more orderly.

Such successful transitions from EI means that mainstream schools and parents have in-built support for the placement for the child on the autism spectrum and have expertise from the EI team should they need it. The success of such a process builds on itself as further explained by the Autism EI Unit representative below:

> We have got a family who have currently got a little boy in pre-primary with us, so his local school are really happy with him and the second little boy has come through and now is in kindy with us. So they have been through the process, they have seen the transition that we provide and they know they can ring up and get a bunch of COMPIC (*communication system*) if they need it and things like that. That is really positive, two kids in the one school.

Without such creative transition and enrolment initiatives, parents in the study were often left alone to battle their way through an often, hostile maze of mainstream schools and chase down a placement that would not only welcome their child on the autism spectrum but educate them appropriately over time.

To summarize, parents in the study continually chased a place at an accommodating, 'inclusive' mainstream schooling environment because they initially believed that this would give their child on the autism spectrum their best chance to succeed in a mainstream life. Parents found that their child on the autism spectrum was often not welcome for enrolment because of their perceived need for extra resources and the extra pressure they may place on the staff and other students of a school. Parents combated this discrimination with an assortment of strategies that were most often initiated by their own efforts.

Sub-Category Three: Waxing and Waning

When parents finally managed to secure a place in a school for their child on the autism spectrum they often did not realize they were only at the beginning of a long, often arduous, educational journey where they would need to advocate for their child on an on-going basis. This involvement process was one which waxed and waned *(waxing and waning)* according to the success or otherwise of the 'inclusive' practice operating at the school. Two of the parents described the process as follows:

> You have to be there on an on-going basis to oversee, organize, prioritize, monitor, document, you name it – you have to do it, because you know that at any stage of the game you are going to need it. You need to be aware and you need to be in it 24/7, being involved with your child's education on an hourly, daily, weekly, monthly basis as needed. You have to determine it by the skill of the people dealing with your child. Some schools in some years you won't have that much to do with what is going on because you can see they have got a handle on it. Other years you have to be there, all the time, every day.

> … it depends on the teacher you have that year or who is running the program that year. It still does depend a lot on that. You are still having to advocate and push, some years are easier, some years are twice as hard. You do come across to do the extra bit and believe what you do is the best for them. And you get wonderful results and all that sort of stuff happens but it still is a hit and miss affair. I suppose that is the case with other children. It is more important that

> it be more consistent perhaps for our children because they are already behind the eight ball. They have got so much ground to make up and they have all these other things on top of it as well to overcome before they can learn.

According to parents in the study, the degree of success of the placement of the child on the autism spectrum was directly related to the type of 'inclusive' philosophy and practice adopted by the staff of the individual school, with the principal generally taking the lead role in how 'inclusion' translated into action. When staff changed, especially in the ranks of the administration, commitment to a particular form of 'inclusion' could also change rapidly and impact negatively or positively on the 'inclusive' practice operating in the school at that time.

Parents indicated that they involved themselves with the school to a much greater degree than they would normally have had to do when educating a neurotypical child. They negotiated the educational pathway of their child on the autism spectrum by constantly communicating with staff on a regular basis when frequent issues arose. Two parents in the study described the necessity of involvement with the school in the following ways:

> Well, being on the ball with what is happening with him (*son on the autism spectrum*) all of the time I feel it is so necessary. You can't be there for the whole school day watching what they do. There are going to be ups and downs there. But at least by me having a copy of his program, what he did at lunchtime, what he did at sport, reassures me of where I have got him. Seeing some progress reassures me hey this is working for him maybe we are on the right track.

> I will be vigilant about things, keep on top of things and make sure it works, it works, it works.

Most parents realized through their own research *(researching)* that such issues as their child's behaviour, staffing, transitioning, individualized education planning (IEPs), supplementary programs and so on, all needed to be negotiated on a very regular basis with staff. Parents indicated that there was an underlying tension that often operated in mainstream schools between addressing the needs of the child on the autism spectrum and other drivers in the educational context. Parents detailed how they constantly battled to maintain the best educational 'fit' (*seeking progressive fit*) for their child in their mainstream settings. One of the parents commented upon her advocacy role in the following manner:

> I guess I have always also made it clear to anyone involved with Bill (*son on the autism spectrum*) that near enough is not going to be good enough. He deserved to, this is what he needed, this is what he deserves to have. It is not just a matter of, should someone just decide to do something, it has to be whatever is in his best interests and our child deserves this. It is a matter of just having to fight and have a voice. And often you don't really feel like you have got the energy or the extra time to spend. When they are young it is such

> a hard life that you have with them but they're the times when they really need you to be their advocate and be prepared to step up and say that is not going to be good enough, we have to do this. You just have to find that strength and do it for them because they really are quite voiceless. You have to be the sort of person who can be a voice for your child.

Unfortunately, some parents in the study who financially and emotionally were the most at risk were not always in a position to be their child's 'voice' as explained below by one of the parents in the study:

> Because for so long I listened to everything that was told to me. They must know what they are talking about and for a long time I felt really inadequate thinking that this just isn't working. It wasn't until Bob (*son on the autism spectrum*) was in Year 5 that I started to get 'ballsy' and thinking, 'Well no, hang one a sec, I am not going to let you sit here and say that because I don't feel inadequate anymore'. Part of that would have been going through the marriage break up and the hell breaking loose for those two years but yeh, I just started to think 'yeh, I do know my child'.

After previous experiences, parents were often acutely aware of the potential discrimination their child on the autism spectrum may face and this heightened parents' anxiety and fear about the treatment their child may receive in any schooling environment. The following quote illustrates how parents had to overcome such feelings to continue the process of advocacy for their child:

> I think at some points you are much stronger and able to overcome anything and other times it *(the discrimination*) still gets to me and it reduces me to tears. But you have your teary moment and adjust, reassess and then you move on because we do not have an enormous amount of time to sit there and not be proactive because it is not just a matter of reassessing or negotiating … you have to be more so because your child was depending upon you.

Even though parents were aware that such advocacy and involvement was necessary, circumstances determined by an individual's conditional matrix (Strauss & Corbin, 1990) sometimes made it impossible to be as involved as was sometimes needed. One of the most vulnerable parents in the study expressed her regret about this situation:

> When Mark and I were going through our marriage break-up Bob *(son on the autism spectrum*) became very much in the back seat and my whole life fell apart. It was a good three years wasted. So I hold myself accountable for that but there is nothing that I can do so I don't switch myself about it or anything. I regret it. I can't not regret it. But it has just given me more motivational skills to get my shit together so that I can utilize the time that I am seeing with him now.

Therefore, while parents saw the need to advocate on their child's behalf in a mainstream schooling context other life circumstances sometimes interfered with their ability to do so, and this potentially reduced the quality of education their child may receive during this time. This is directly related to the unreliable aspects of the 'inclusive' process in mainstream environments that requires parents to be ever vigilant if they wish to maximize their child's educational potential.

Parents in the study found their child's experience of mainstream education was dependent upon the different understandings of 'inclusive' education that permeated the system. One parent in the study, who had two sons on the autism spectrum, voiced her feelings about this situation in the following way:

> You talk about mainstream and inclusion. They weren't included at (*name of high school*). I guess you have this thought ... you think that is what is going to happen when really that is not really happening. They were pretty segregated anyway.

Because of the varying nature of 'inclusive' practice in schools, parents reported the need for them to be in constant communication with the school. In terms of that communication, parents indicated that the principal was often designated as one of the most important determinants of the success or otherwise of the 'inclusion' of their child on the autism spectrum. The influence of leadership on school culture is also nominated in the research literature as one of the most critical requirements in establishing the beliefs upon which school cultures are founded (Shaddock et al., 2007). One of the parents in the study described the importance of the principal to her son's 'inclusion' in the following way:

> The level of cooperation was amazing and definitely stemmed from the principal who had from the start, made a strong commitment to do whatever it took to maximize our son's development. We felt extremely safe in his hands, as did our son. This helped our whole family feel valued and reduced the level of stress my husband and I constantly felt in relation to our son. This is not to say we did not have challenges with our son's behaviour and social development, we just felt that we were doing all that we could do with the school's help. The school was not another battlefield that had to be faced.

Principals displayed their degree of commitment toward the 'inclusion' of a child on the autism spectrum with their decision-making, from enrolment and beyond, and if that commitment was limited, this would often filter down to determine the type of 'inclusive' practice operating in the school. When difficulties inevitably arose and solutions were sought, the needs of the child on the autism spectrum would often be balanced against other perceived needs of the school at large. Parents reported that some principals could 'tip the balance' in favour of either the child on the autism spectrum or the perceived needs of the school at large. By contrast, other principals understood that by addressing the needs of the child on the autism spectrum, the competency of the teaching staff increased and this allowed the diversity inherent in every mainstream classroom to be more properly understood and accommodated.

As well as principals, parents also indicated that this process of 'tipping the balance' was also evident in the decision-making of other school staff. To exemplify, one of the parents in the study reported that she agreed at an Individualized Education Plan (IEP) meeting to the implementation of an intensive compliance program to combat her child's difficult behaviour. The program was to be overseen and implemented by the mainstream classroom teacher and two separate teaching aides. The program was successful in addressing her child's difficulties in its first year of implementation, but it only occurred for that year because staff commitment to the child on the autism spectrum and 'inclusive' practice changed the following year. This is explained in the parent's comments below:

> Yes, actually he went through quite a good program. In Year Three, after he was diagnosed he had quite an intensive program to teach compliance. He had a teacher aide with him full time and they changed over. There was a morning one and there was an afternoon one because it was one-on-one. He had the charts where he got the sticker, a little dot on the back of the dinosaur if he complied with instructions. After a certain number he got a star, and then after a certain number he got a treat at the end of the day. And then he got a treat at the end of the week and things like that. And that worked quite well so by the end of Year Three he was quite good.

Unfortunately, the following year the balance shifted from accommodating the child on the autism spectrum to supposedly addressing 'other needs' in the educational context and this meant that the program for the child on the autism spectrum did not continue, as described in the parent comment below:

> But then in Year Four, he got a teacher who did not want to have him in the class. And I found that out from a new teacher aide. Everything changed, the teacher changed, the teacher aide changed and the class changed … and the teacher said to the aide, 'You will have to look after Paul (*child on the autism spectrum*) the whole time because I don't want him in this class'. When I found that out, I thought that it was going to be a 'gooood' year for Paul. And it was a tandem teachers' class, one girl was there two days a week and one was there three days a week, and neither of them wanted him in the class. So, they left him to the teacher aide.

Once such decisions were made by staff it was very difficult for the parent to advocate on her child's behalf especially, if there was no extra support forthcoming from the administration. All participants in this study reported experiencing this process of receiving variable support and services depending upon the knowledge, expertise and commitment to 'inclusion' of those dealing with their child's education at different points in time. It served to make parents' worlds very unstable with the constant shifting of support that was often determined by external factors outside of their control. This, in turn, made both the child's and parents' lives far more harrowing as there was no guarantee that once a hard-won solution addressing the specific difficulties of educating their child on the autism spectrum had been found that it would remain in place over time.

To summarize, parents often advocated on behalf of their child on the autism spectrum, in a *waxing and waning* fashion, in a mainstream schooling context to maximize their child's educational progress over time. Parents did this because their child experienced shifting understandings of 'inclusive' education in their mainstream education. Parents therefore, often became their child's 'voice' to ensure student-centred decision making continued to occur for their child over time. The influence of leadership on school culture was also nominated by parents as one of the most critical requirements in establishing the beliefs upon which the 'inclusive' school culture was founded.

Sub-Category Four: Crisis Point

As evidenced in the sub-category three, *waxing and waning,* parents in the study revealed that adverse educational consequences sometimes occurred for their child on the autism spectrum when appropriate 'inclusive' practice was not apparent on a continuous basis. Parents reported that in its worst form this resulted in a *crisis point* being reached, where they would have no option but to remove their child permanently from a school. At least half of the parents in the study reported that they had experienced such a *crisis point*, sometimes repeatedly, in one of two ways. They were either told by the administration to remove their child from a school situation at first temporarily, and then permanently; or they felt compelled to withdraw their child because they were alarmed at the on-going psychological and/or physical harm being experienced by their child in a schooling context continuously lacking in appropriate 'inclusive' practice.

As previously explained in the sub-category, *chasing,* parents often felt duty-bound to continuously seek a school environment that fitted *(seeking progressive fit)* their child's specific educational needs so that their educational development could be maximized. If such a situation was continuously lacking, parents often felt compelled to move their child onto a more productive schooling context where they could trust that their child would be safe and appropriately educated. Unfortunately, finding a new mainstream school which reliably provided such an 'inclusive' context was no easy task as evidenced in the sub-category, *chasing*.

In relation to families reaching a *crisis point*, parents indicated that the behavioural management of their child in a school setting was of paramount importance. Parents stressed that it was essential for staff to have a strong understanding of 'inclusive' practice especially in the area of managing the sometimes-difficult and unusual behaviour of the child on the autism spectrum. This is confirmed by MacDermott (2008) in her study of 92 WA families who were parenting school-aged children with a suspected or confirmed ASD, who indicates that "behaviour management is a focus for most families either on a consistent basis or variably as needs change" (p. 57).

Research by Forlin et al. (2008) regarding how regular WA teachers cope with the 'inclusion' of a child with an intellectual disability in their mainstream classroom reveals that WA teachers find most concerning the behaviour of that child. This is mainly due to their own perceived lack of professional competency to cater adequately for such a child because of insufficient professional development (Forlin et al., 2008).

Other research by Ford (2007) on teacher perceptions of disabled students with significant behavioural challenges also indicates that when such expertise is not available for these types of students serious consequences can sometimes follow:

> ... without effective support, students who exhibit such behaviours may be at risk of (a) being suspended or expelled from school, (b) being transferred to more restrictive or segregated placements, (c) receiving intrusive and punitive interventions, (d) being placed on restrictive medications, and (e) experiencing inadequate, socially isolating and stigmatizing post-school outcomes (p. 110).

The experience of some of the parents in the study confirms that some of these consequences described by Ford (2007) occurred for their child when attending mainstream schooling in WA when expertise was not readily available to deal appropriately with the misunderstood behaviour of their child.

Further to this discussion, it is also important to note the rate of bullying experienced by students on the autism spectrum in mainstream schools that is often a trigger for their difficult behaviour. In a 2007 presentation the Senior Consultant (autism) of the state-run Centre for Inclusive Schooling indicated that the rate of bullying for students on the autism spectrum in mainstream schooling was four times the rate experienced by their peers. She further explained that peer victimization was experienced by over 90% of students on the autism spectrum (Rosendorff, 2007). This is further confirmed in the research literature (Attwood, 2004, 2007; Cappodocia, Weiss & Peplar, 2012; Humphrey & Symes, 2010).

Parents in the study found they were often met with a lack of staff expertise in the areas of both behaviour management and bullying and this eventually led to very poor outcomes for their child on the autism spectrum. To exemplify, one parent in the study expressed the following concern about the lack of appropriate expertise available in one of the schools that her son attended:

> Because there were a cluster of kids being diagnosed (*on the autism spectrum*) at that stage, the diagnosis was there but the knowledge and the experience wasn't. There was good will but there was no knowledge and no experience. And so no-one really knew what to do with these kids.

Unfortunately, when difficulties inevitably arose and appropriate evidence-based interventions did not occur a common process was set in train where parents were called repeatedly to remove their child from the school. This same parent in the study commented about this dysfunctional process by stating:

> He (*son on the autism spectrum*) had to be in charge so he got into a lot of trouble with that. He had an excellent supply of swear words which he would rat-a-tat out in machine gun fashion which all the boys thought was fabulous and so when school got boring it was a matter of pressing Paul's buttons so he would have a swearing tantrum. And this got to be great fun for everyone else. And then I would get rung up and told to come and get him. In Year 5, I was getting more and more phone calls to come and get him. I developed phone phobia at one stage and I wouldn't answer the phone.

This same parent indicated that this dysfunctional process occurred repeatedly at three successive mainstream primary schools that lacked appropriate 'inclusive' expertise when dealing with her son. She kept moving her son to different schools in the hope of gaining greater educational 'fit' (*seeking progressive fit*) through use of more appropriate, evidence-based 'inclusive' practice.

This same parent's variable experience with 'inclusion' was initially exemplified in the previous sub-category, *waxing and waning*, where her son received appropriate 'inclusive' practice one year only to be followed by a lack of 'inclusive' practice the following year. This cycle continually repeated itself until the middle stages of primary school when the mother finally felt that the psychological damage brought on by such a process was far too great for her child. She expressed it as follows:

> And one day I was getting him (*son on the autism spectrum*) ready for school and he said, 'I hate my life I wish I was dead'. And I thought at ten we don't say that. And he shouldn't feel like that at ten. And the warning bells really went off in my head because I have a brother who committed suicide. And we did have depression in the family, we still do. So I just took his shirt off and I said, 'Right you do not go to school anymore. We will think of something different'.

The reaching of this *crisis point* precipitated this mother's decision to withdraw her child from mainstream schooling and to home educate him for most of his remaining formal schooling years with some input from the Schools of Isolated and Distance Education (SIDE).

To further exemplify the reaching of a *crisis point* in some of the families in the study, another parent reported a similar situation occurring when her child attended an education support unit in a private high school mainstream environment. Initially, this parent indicated that the special education staff at the school were skilled in managing the behaviour of her non-verbal son on the autism spectrum and dealt appropriately with his occasional outbursts in the following way:

> … there were different people running the unit then, there were a couple of incidents and I checked through the diary of 2006 and there were two incidents where he had come in contact with an aide and a teacher but it certainly wasn't dealt with in that way. In fact, they told me about it immediately and pretty much said, 'Well you know it is his first time in high school. He was a little anxious, we don't know him well enough to read his body language'. It was

> sort of made out like well this is just a natural progression of what happens from primary school to high school. 'We expect these sort of moments where he is unsettled and unsure and he doesn't know anyone either.' So they were a lot more understanding and accepting of the behaviour and they didn't see him as a threat or, it was just Chris (*child on the autism spectrum*) finding his way in his first year at high school.

Unfortunately, the following year key staff in the education support unit changed. This change gradually eroded the trust that the parent had built up with the staff in the first year of her child's high school education. She was left with a growing sense of unease about what could be happening for her child at school:

> Leaving your children at school and being on edge the whole time is not a nice feeling. That first year in high school I was a little reluctant to let go but I had a feeling of 'Yes, he is in good hands'. You know you feel that then, but after all that and the times that they said, 'Ok he can come back', it was all on their terms. I just ... you are living on edge the whole time ... is he alright, is he alright, is he alright? ... the whole time.

This change in staff and expertise eventually led to the parent being asked to remove her child repeatedly in his second year at the high school when the situation was seemingly untenable for the less experienced staff. The parent expressed reservations to the staff about the wisdom of such a practice as evidenced below:

> So I guess after about the second time when they called me at home to come and pick up Chris (*son on the autism spectrum*) because he had a verbal outburst I brought him home because I am trying to do the right thing by his school. Each time I was told that there are not enough staff, there is not enough this, this is what happened. 'We think he should go home because he is upset'. I might add when I went to pick him up he was fine. The outburst had passed. He got it off his chest and he was calm again. Anyway, by the time I got home I just thought to myself this doesn't seem right to me and I rang and spoke to the teacher-in-charge and said to her, 'I am just curious is this going to be the procedure every time Chris lets off some steam or he has an outburst or something like that?' And she said, 'Yes'. And I expressed that I didn't think it was such a great idea because he is going to quickly learn that if he wants to come home then all that he has got to do is have an outburst or become aggressive.

By the middle of the second year after successive difficult incidents with her son at this high school, the family was told they had to withdraw him permanently from the school. This meant that their other son on the autism spectrum who was also attending the education support unit also had to leave the school. By this stage the parents had lost faith in the school's ability to care and appropriately educate their children. This situation was directly precipitated by a lack of appropriate expertise and 'inclusive' practice operating at the school. This is further confirmed in the parent's description of the staff's inability to provide a functional assessment of her son's behaviour when difficult incidents arose:

> I never did really get how the first event happened anyway. All I was told was that Chris (*son on the autism spectrum*) had bitten someone. They didn't tell me what had happened before-hand. And then when you do get information it is already now in the past so nobody can give you an accurate understanding because nothing is recorded, of course. Just the fact the student bit a teacher. Nothing is recorded so when you are trying to get to the bottom of something and find out how did this happen, was he upset, did you go into … where was he? All these things that I think are important to work out why it happened. They don't really have ... they have their own story but not actually what happened because the aide was not called. She was kept in the background. The people that are supposedly running the unit are telling me what we want to hear because I had numerous meetings with them to try to help them because I am here to support them support my son. I tried different things but, it didn't seem to come across. They kept promising a meeting, all this sort of thing and in the meantime Chris was not allowed to be going to school.

This family were left with a situation where they had to, once again, find schooling to 'fit' *(seeking progressive fit)* not one, but two, of their children on the autism spectrum in the middle of a schooling year. Research into appropriate 'inclusive' practice regarding the key area of behaviour management of children on the autism spectrum indicates that when behavioural difficulties arise a functional assessment of the incident and its context should occur (Myles, 2005).

However, when such understanding of functional behavioural management is continually lacking in mainstream school staff parents find that this then leads to a *crisis point* for their child on the autism spectrum. The child will then often be seen as the problem with little responsibility being taken by the surrounding educational context. This can then lead to either eventual expulsion or removal of the child from the school by the parent when they deem the psychological and/or physical damage to the child is assessed to be too great.

After some desperate searching the parents were eventually able to find a place at a segregated state-run education support school. This was even though these parents had felt initially that mainstreaming was their best solution for their boys on the autism spectrum. In the end, the quality of the educational care and appropriate expertise available was seen by these parents as the more important determinants of a successful education for their boys on the autism spectrum.

Parents in the study found that unless schools were committed, trained and resourced appropriately to provide on-going, ASD specific, 'inclusive' practice, they would not have the collective will, understanding or tools to provide appropriate, evidence-based support for a child on the autism spectrum. This conclusion is borne out in Australian research by Ford (2007) who found that teachers felt they were insufficiently prepared or supported to work successfully with students with significant behavioural challenges and expressed the need for comprehensive, regular, and on-going professional development activities that were aligned with their needs and those of their students.

Unfortunately, parents found that while they were initially desirous of mainstream 'inclusion' for their child on the autism spectrum they eventually qualified that desire with the understanding that there would be on-going, appropriate, evidence-based, ASD specific, 'inclusive' practice operating within that context. Parents indicated that they made educational decisions that would allow both the student on the autism spectrum and their family the best quality of life and mental health possible, and this may or may not involve a mainstream setting. Leading educators (Kavale & Forness, 2000; Warnock, 2005) have also expressed considerable misgivings about 'inclusive' education for students in mainstream settings when the necessary ingredients are missing or inadequate.

Further to this discussion, parents in the study also commented about the increased difficulty of accessing reliable and on-going 'inclusive' practice in a high school setting as compared to that on offer in the earlier years of their child's education. Three parents in the study described the difficulties associated with mainstream high school environments variously below:

> I think because in primary school you have got one teacher, one group of kids that you really get to know throughout the year, don't you? And that could be quite hard for some kids but quite easy for others. But it is more of a family, they are more family orientated, they still have that way of thinking. They protect and they nurture and they help grow, whereas in high school it is every man for himself baby, and it doesn't matter if you have a disability you are thrown out there to cope, and they can't cope, as a lot of kids who have not got disabilities can't cope.

> Unfortunately, the rigidity built into the high school system makes a contextual response to student failure mainly about student deficit. This dynamic effectively negates any pressure being brought to bear on the system which in turn perpetuates the failure of students who do not fit. Unfortunately, students who have specialized learning needs are the first ones to fall by the wayside. Difference is not embraced as a catalyst for effective educational change but is often seen as an extra burden the mainstream system should often not have to address.

> Inclusion was successful to some degree in primary school socially and educationally. Unfortunately, inclusion in the traditional high school model which is dominated by over-confident principals, sometimes lazy teachers and typical unforgiving teenage behaviours create toxic environments where different children are persecuted mercilessly. Smaller, less threatening school environments where thoughtful teachers lead their students in appropriate behaviours would be an appropriate and inclusive environment. It is a pity that economies of scale and traditional attitudes of education will not allow this to become a reality.

This is also borne out in the research on 'inclusion' which indicates that secondary schools experience both external and internal pressures on their use of 'inclusive' practice (Shaddock, 2005; Shaddock et al., 2007). These difficulties are reaffirmed in the comments made by a high school Special Education Coordinator (SEC) nominated by one of the parents in the next sub-category, *finding fit*, as providing exemplary 'inclusive' practice in a high school setting:

> It is very hard to tell some subject teachers at secondary school about that stuff (*appropriate inclusive practice*) because secondary teachers are very curriculum-centred, not child-centred. I think it is easier at primary school because a primary school teacher is very ... she has got her group of kids and she is very child-centred. And you've got a mainstream Science teacher, or whatever they are, there to deliver a curriculum, that's the curriculum and that's it. Even with kids who have no special needs, you are there to listen, bad luck and they are not looking at the individual child as much as the primary school teacher. And that I feel, is the biggest problem, they are not child-centred.

In response to these difficulties, only one of the six families in the study was able to have their child on the autism spectrum successfully mainstreamed in a high school setting for the full five years' duration. The high school where this occurred had an education support unit within the school that regularly provided on-going support to mainstream teachers regarding appropriate inclusive practice for students on the autism spectrum. In relation to the outcomes of the other families in the study, two families, either immediately or eventually, were compelled to place their children into segregated *(segregating)* education support high schools. Another two of the families were also compelled to home educate *(home schooling)* their children on the autism spectrum before or during their mainstream high school years. The remaining family, who had the youngest child on the autism spectrum in the study, indicated at the end of the study that they were also seriously considering the option of placing their child into a segregated education support high school to ensure their child's needs were met.

To recap, parents in the study described how a *crisis point* was reached where they were compelled to permanently remove their child on the autism spectrum from a mainstream school continuously lacking in 'inclusive' practice. They were either asked by the administration to remove their child on the autism spectrum from the school or they felt compelled to withdraw their child because they were alarmed at the on-going psychological and/or physical harm being experienced by their child in a schooling context continuously lacking in appropriate 'inclusive' practice. Parents indicated that without a firm commitment by staff to 'inclusion', appropriate resources and specific evidence-based skills to deal with students on the autism spectrum, the situation rapidly deteriorated to a *crisis point* where the child on the spectrum was seen as the problem with little responsibility being taken by the surrounding educational context.

Sub-Category Five: Finding Fit

While most parents in this study experienced on-going difficulties *seeking, finding,* and *maintaining progressive educational fit* in a mainstream environment for their child on the autism spectrum, these same parents did report some "islands of excellent practice" (Wills & Jackson, 2000, p. 25) operating in both the primary and secondary mainstream educational sector of WA. Several significant elements were designated by parents in the study as important in both the primary and secondary contexts where parents experienced educational *fit* for their child on the autism spectrum.

The paramount element expressed by parents was the unwavering devotion and commitment of all school staff members to the overall development of the child on the autism spectrum, as expressed by two parents in the study below:

> Constants remained though, the unwavering devotion of all staff to Kim's (*son on the autism spectrum*) development even though at times it would have been much easier for them to just attend to those children whose learning behaviours fitted the system more readily.

> Not only in the Education Support Unit ranging from the admin., staff in the office, to the principal and deputies and the lady in the uniform shop, the ladies in the canteen – everyone – they really like Bill (*son on the autism spectrum*) and they really let me know that they really like him. He is a big part of the school and well respected. Everybody knows him but it is in a good way.

This devotion underpinned the school's ownership of the child on the autism spectrum and served to build a fragile trust between the school and the parents that often fostered open communication between them. One of these same parents further commented upon this:

> We, as parents, completely trusted that the school would use all information about Kim *(son on the autism spectrum*) to foster his development and not to excuse it from the responsibility of being inclusive of Kim. This fragile trust had been built up over many years of successive examples of student-centred decision making by the classroom teachers and administration at the school.

This need for parents to trust in the school is borne out in research by Stoner et.al. (2005) who investigated the perspectives of parents who had a child on the autism spectrum and their self-reported roles with education professionals and indicated that:

> The existing research on trust suggests that interpersonal relationships are the primary avenue for building trust (Tschannen-Moran & Hoy, 2000; Tyack & Cuban, 1995) and that trust is built incrementally through personal interactions, encounters and exchanges (Rousseau, Sitkin, Burt, & Camen, 1998). This study's findings support the importance of interpersonal relationships in building trust between parents and education professionals (p. 185).

In relation to this, the parents in the study indicated that when they found *educational fit* they built a relationship over time between the school and themselves that allowed them to feel confident that their child was in the right place to maximize their educational potential and to have their situation supported appropriately.

Secondly, as a precursor to the above element, parents designated as important the type of welcome they received at enrolment time. Parents valued the type of welcome where they (and their child on the autism spectrum) were treated with respect by the administration and were seen, from the beginning, as valuable and equal partners in the education process who had a right to expect an appropriate education for their child. This was in sharp contrast to some receptions parents had received as evidenced in the sub-category *chasing*. The following is a sample of such positive experiences experienced by three different parents in the study:

> He (*the principal*) said that our son (*on the autism spectrum*) would be most welcome to join one of the grade one classes the following year. He explained how he would organize a team approach to help with our son's inclusion. The grade one teacher assigned to my son would be invited to join a meeting scheduled the first week of school where she would hear about our son's learning differences from the outside professionals who were working with him. We, as parents, would also be invited to attend so that we could coordinate the whole process and keep all parties aware of the bigger picture regarding Kim's progress. If needed, the professionals could be consulted by the teacher through us throughout the year if difficulties emerged and alternative strategies were needed to maximize Kim's progress. We could not believe what we were hearing. Finally, a person, better yet a principal, who did not need to be schooled in the ideal and ethos of inclusion of children with special needs.

> But with (*name of high school*) they said that they would like me to come in first because they said they didn't like to talk about the children in front of them. They thought it was disrespectful and not going to be a positive thing for them. And from the first interview they were very welcoming of us they really wanted us there. And then of course, they wanted to meet Bill (*son on the autism spectrum*). We had interviews then with the principal, and the lady who was the coordinator of the education support unit was there and very much letting him know that they wanted us there which was very good and we were offered a place which was a very big relief.

> But when I went to the new school and I was sitting there waiting for her (*the principal*) to make me feel relaxed and 'We will look after you' and she did. She was very honest and very … she told us up front that she had never had children with autism before but she did mention to me about a little boy by the name of (*another child at the school who had learning difficulties*). But, she was just very honest. She wasn't sure how she was going to do this but she could assure me that he was welcome and that he would learn. That is all that I wanted to hear.

Often such a welcoming experience acted as an indicator to parents regarding future dealings with the administration and the type of support that they could expect when difficulties inevitably arose with their child on the autism spectrum.

Thirdly, parents also appreciated being seen as legitimate members of a team where their 'voice', and potentially their child's 'voice', would be heard equally to others. This is exemplified in the dealings which one parent experienced in a state-run primary school where she was invited by the principal to participate in the selection process of her child's aide:

> Yes, and I was totally involved in the interviewing and selection process. I was able to be in the interview stage to go through and describe to them a bit about ABA and direct instruction and try to put it in a game format, how we would help him (*son on the autism spectrum*) to join in and how we would do some academic work.

Given that many parents had spent many years *researching* their child's circumstances, they felt justified in their expectation that they would be included in discussions and decision-making regarding their child's specific educational situation. The importance of this element is further confirmed in research by MacDermott (2008) who investigated the needs of 92 WA families who had school-aged children with a suspected or confirmed ASD and found that there was a "need by families to be heard and for their experiences, expertise and opinions to be accepted as important and equal in the care and development of their children" (p.7). Unfortunately, Australia does not presently have an equivalent US 1997 amendment to the Individuals with Disabilities Education Act (IDEA), which mandates that parents of children with disabilities have the legal right to be involved in all aspects of their children's education. According to Stoner and Angell (2006) IDEA stipulates that:

> parents must be invited to participate on their children's education teams as these teams identify and evaluate children for special education, set educational goals, and make service delivery choices (p. 177).

Research confirms that parents serve a key role in providing effective intervention strategies for children on the autism spectrum (Feinberg & Vacca, 2000; Lord & McGee, 2001). Further to this, MacDermott (2008) states that Western Australian:

> families/carers need to be recognized as having unique and specific information regarding their child's strengths, challenges and learning styles and provided with opportunities to be on-going collaborative partners in designing and implementing intervention/educational programs (p. 9).

A team approach which incorporated relevant expertise regarding the individual profile of the student on the autism spectrum was seen by parents in the study as imperative; with such expertise incorporating the 'voices' of not only the parents but, if possible, the 'voice' of the student on the autism spectrum as well.

A fourth key element that parents in the study found invaluable was an openness and self-awareness of the staff regarding their own knowledge and skill level (or lack thereof) when dealing with and educating a child on the autism spectrum. This then allowed parents and qualified others the opportunity to provide targeted, evidence-based information regarding the idiosyncratic nature of their particular child on the autism spectrum. It also allowed staff to import external expertise to support their interactions with the child on the autism spectrum in order to maximize their student's development. Two parents commented about this process as follows:

> The teacher was quite happy for her (*the aide*) to be just implementing things that we were suggesting from our home program anyway. I think the teachers flounder just like parents do unless they have had a lot of experience. It was lucky for her that we were able to supply her with ideas and programs and everything.
>
> Unlike our pre-primary experience, this teacher was willing to embrace Kim's (*son on the autism spectrum*) learning differences and try to work with them. We started the school year with the help of the speech therapist and clinical psychologist who had both worked with Kim. At the meeting organized by the school, they were able to give valuable input to the classroom teacher at the beginning of the year about Kim's learning needs - including strengths and weaknesses. They were also available to be contacted if needed throughout the year if difficulties arose. This gave the teacher the opportunity to gain support if necessary in areas where she felt she did not have the expertise.

Hence, parents were able to provide external help for the staff to support their efforts to educate their child on the autism spectrum appropriately. This fed into the notion of a team approach that inevitably arose through such a process. Parents reported that Individualized Education Planning (IEPs) meetings were very regularly convened to problem solve and plan when such a relationship was established in order to maximize the individual development of the child on the autism spectrum.

The value of such a dynamic is confirmed in Australian research by Stanley et al. (2005) who reported that "frequent communication between the parents and regular classroom teachers about a student with ASD enables parents and teachers to share their knowledge from their different contexts when designing individualized education programs" (p. 113). This two-way process allowed parents in this study the opportunity to delineate the idiosyncratic nature of their child's ASD, monitor their child's progress and set new educational goals with input from other professionals working with their child. According to parents, this openness also allowed staff members to seek external help from not only parents but from other sources such as their own school-based education support unit (ESU), other school staff, the Autism Association of WA, the Visiting Teacher network through the Centre for Inclusive Schooling within the Department of Education and Training, The Catholic Education Office of WA and other sources of expertise outside of their classroom and school.

However, parents in the study also reported that such 'inclusive' environments did not happen by chance. A fifth key element that parents in the study found invaluable was the existence of at least one key member of the staff, usually the principal, who was committed to 'inclusion' and could muster increasing support from the rest of the staff. One such parent-nominated staff member was a Special Education Coordinator (SEC) of an Education Support Unit (ESU) at a high school of a particular religious denomination who expressed her strategic plan for 'inclusion' in the following way:

> My strategic plan would be that I wanted to change the attitude of the whole culture of the school to be an accepting and welcoming culture. It doesn't matter about the academia. We will get that right eventually and I know that I have to be here for x number of years to get that right because that is not right at the moment. So that was the first thing I was working for and to have the executive on side. All those sorts of things and they take a long time and they take a lot of perseverance, persevere, persevere. And then slowly you have to work on the differentiation of the curriculum, but I think that once you've got an accepting community you can say to them, 'You have to write a totally new program'. They go, 'Ok', whereas if I had said that to them four years ago they would have said, 'Yes, stick it up your ..., I am not doing that'.

The SEC in this case put in train a process of initially establishing unwavering support from all staff at the school, including the executive, to champion the educational rights of students with disabilities. The wisdom of this approach has been previously borne out in West Australian research by Chadbourne (1997) who found that "principals occupied the most powerful position to shape the cultural framework within which the teachers and TA's (*teaching assistants*) worked ..." (p. 58). Similarly, other local research (Department of Education and Training, 2001) investigating service provision for students with disabilities in WA found that the principal was a key stakeholder in developing 'inclusive' schools. Hence, the SEC gained the support of the principal who, in turn, put pressure on the mainstream staff to take ownership of students on the autism spectrum in their educational care. To illustrate, the SEC indicated how the principal routinely sent mainstream staff to the ESU to collaboratively problem-solve the difficulties that arose with students on the autism spectrum, rather than try to get rid of these students from their classes. The SEC explained it in the following way:

> I remember reading this article once about this guy talking about inclusion and he said, 'You always have to work from the top down and the bottom up'. And that is what I believe in, you have to get the executive on side who can ... I have had teachers run to the principal and say, 'I don't want that kid in my room, he is so totally disruptive, and I can't handle that'. And the principal just says, 'Go and talk to (*the SEC*) I don't want to hear it. Figure it out. He is in your class, he is your responsibility, if you can't deal with it....' And that's his way, when people used to go running to him, they have learned not to go running to him.

The SEC outlined a very large number of initiatives that she had implemented to change the culture of the staff, parents and students to enable the school to become as 'inclusive' as possible:

> I have seen other coordinators who have been primary school teachers and they haven't got a handle on what is needed to convert a community, what disability means. And that is what they should be training teachers in, not just the academia. There needs to be a whole thing on disability. The one thing (*you have to do*) ... you have to make the community proud of what they are doing and if you do that you will win them over. It does take more than what you read in these books on inclusion, differentiating curriculum, ABA and all that stuff, it is more than that. It is far more.

The SEC implemented a process that involved placing the child on the autism spectrum in important roles in a public arena so that the school community could witness their increasing value to the school. One important initiative introduced by the SEC was a particular yearly religious mass run by the students from the ESU. This mass initially had only a few people attending it but had since become one of the main events in the school calendar. The students were also involved in other important school events – their art work was entered into art competitions; they provided morning teas for parents and staff; they attended camps with mainstream staff; and became mainstream school prefects. These initiatives were designed to encourage the school community (staff, students and parents) to take ownership of the students with disabilities in their school and see their value in the school community. In particular, they were designed so that the staff would eventually more readily participate in 'inclusion' and be more open to collaboratively and creatively problem solve difficulties in the mainstream classroom with the help of the ESU staff.

The SEC also indicated that the existence of the ESU, especially in a high school environment, allowed 'inclusive' expertise in relation to students on the autism spectrum to be readily available at all times to mainstream staff when it was routinely needed. The SEC commented about this need in the following way:

> It also needs a unit to model how to be with these kids. Having teachers, like our TA's (*teaching assistants*) are great, to model how to speak to them (*disabled students*) and intervene. We have had TA's and myself, support staff, who go out to the mainstream classes to model what to do and to intervene. It is all about intervention at the right time and not too much. To intervene to say, 'This kid is not getting this, you are overloading this kid and he is getting more stressed - back off'. And putting things like visual cues with the teachers, I mean, even having a tick chart for teachers. You are training the teachers as much as the kids.

The SEC nominated this support to other members of the school community, especially the staff, as imperative in the quest to promote on-going, appropriate 'inclusive' practice in the school.

The SEC also indicated that when behavioural difficulties inevitably arose with students on the autism spectrum a high degree of understanding and an evidence-based functional assessment of the student's situation should occur. This is described by the SEC in the extended example below:

> Well, one of our students went through a stage, I think it was Year 8 or Year 9. He would hug girls, not just hug them, tackle them to the ground and lay on top of them and want to rub himself on them. And you have to nip that in the bud. At another school I was talking to the lady there from Special Ed. and she was calling my student 'a deviant' because he was doing this behaviour. I thought he was not a deviant he just didn't understand.
>
> Anyway, we went through a whole lot of talking and social stories and circle concepts and it stopped. What was interesting I used to say to him, 'Feelings are fine, but it is what you do with them, it is like me wanting to go and punch someone's lights out because I am so frustrated with it … I can't do that, it doesn't mean I can't be frustrated'. And he could understand all of that - it was amazing.
>
> We went on camp last year and we had these talks for two years and on and on and on. Anyway, he got a bit attracted to one of the girls on camp and I could see him doing a bit of leaning, doing a bit of groaning. So I pulled him aside and said, 'Now what are we talking about, it's fine that you are attracted to this girl, that is normal, you are fourteen or fifteen and that is normal stuff, it is ok. But instead of doing that (*leaning and groaning*), she doesn't understand that, what she understands is you talking to her and getting to know her as a friend'.
>
> So, at dinner one day, I am sitting opposite, he looked at me and you could see him wanting to lean, he had this beautiful grin on his face and he leaned forward and said, 'So how was your day?' It was kind of like … and then, she knows that I am attracted to this girl but she knows what I am trying to do and that kind of acceptance was just great for him - that I am not going to be berated or called 'a deviant'. Now he does talk to girls and he doesn't do any of that stuff. He doesn't do any of that hugging or wanting to be close to people at all. It is almost like he has grown through that and he has learned that that is not what you do.

Unfortunately, according to the parents in this study this level of 'inclusive' expertise is not reliably available in many mainstream schools in WA, especially at high school level, and as a result the situations described in the sub-categories of *chasing*, *waxing and waning* and *crisis point* often occur. Currently, parents cannot feel confident that their child on the autism spectrum will be reliably welcomed and educated appropriately in mainstream schools in WA. The sub-category of *finding fit* provides some insight into what parents view as vitally necessary in the education of their children on the autism spectrum and presents a preliminary way forward to improve 'inclusivity' in WA schools. It is important to remember that while there may be 'best practice' knowledge available regarding what is needed to produce effective, evidence-based educational practice for students on the autism spectrum (Iovannone et al., 2003; Jones, 2006; Myles & Adreon, 2001; Simpson, 2004, 2005), there still remains the difficulty of trying to gain the commitment of staff to become fully 'inclusive' of students on the autism spectrum. Jordan (2005) makes the valuable point that while "staff need knowledge and skill to understand ASD and the individual child, above all, they need commitment to doing the best for the child" (p. 111).

To recap, parents find educational *fit (seeking progressive fit)* in a mainstream environment where they experience unwavering staff devotion toward the development of the child on the autism spectrum. This commitment to the child is exemplified initially in the type of welcome they and their child receive at enrolment time where parents are seen as equal partners in the education process. Parents also nominate as important the self-awareness shown by the staff regarding their own knowledge and skill level (or lack thereof) when dealing with a child on the autism spectrum. This awareness allows parents and qualified others the opportunity to provide appropriate, evidence-based information to staff regarding the individual educational requirements of the child on the autism spectrum. Parents indicate that at least one key staff member, often the principal, is generally responsible for mustering increasing support for 'inclusive' practice within the school. The existence of an education support unit experienced in inclusive practice often allows other staff access to support at crucial times to ensure the educational welfare of the student on the autism spectrum.

CHAPTER 7

STAGES TWO AND THREE – THE FORMAL SCHOOLING YEARS (SUPPLEMENTING / OPTING OUT)

Three categories of experience emerged when parents tried to access formal schooling for their child on the autism spectrum. The three categories were: category one (*mainstreaming),* category two (*supplementing)* and category three (*opting out)*. Chapter Six detailed and expanded the first category (*mainstreaming).* Chapter Seven now explains the second category (*supplementing)* and the third category *(opting out)* of parent experience during the formal schooling years. From the category of *opting out* two different sub-categories of parental experience emerged, *home schooling* and *segregating*.

Over time, parents in the study chose to supplement *(supplementing*) the formal schooling experience of their child on the autism spectrum with a multitude of interventions to ensure that they maximized the educational progress of their child on the autism spectrum. They often did this because of the unreliable nature of the mainstream schooling experience and the idiosyncratic needs of their child's profile. *Supplementing* is a process that is directly affected by the conditional matrix of the family who has a child on the autism spectrum. At its best, the school is able to work with the family to utilize the supplementary programs within the child's educational program to maximize their development. When a family's resources are limited, *supplementing* is reduced to what is provided through the government system. Families found that such services were often lacking in appropriate individualization, intensity and quality of service provision. Unfortunately, when parents supplement their child's education they undertake yet another responsibility associated with maximizing the educational progress of their child on the autism spectrum and this adds to the already difficult nature of their lives.

When mainstream education is no longer a viable option and a *crisis point* has been reached, parents sometimes choose to opt out (*opting out*) in two ways, *home schooling* and *segregating*. In the first instance, *home schooling* is adopted by parents to create educational 'fit' *(seeking progressive fit)* for their children on the autism spectrum. Parents home educate because they are often concerned about the on-going negative socialization, insufficient academic progress and the failure of regular schools to understand their child's profile or the nature of their disability (Reilly, 2007). However, *home schooling* is only undertaken if the individual circumstances of the family are able to support such a situation. *Home schooling* generally provides a safe, flexible and individualized education program for the child on the autism spectrum but, it also places more responsibility onto the parent-in-charge of the program and often removes their ability to gain external paid work outside of the home. During *home schooling*, parents often use external services and adopt maverick strategies to improvise their own educational programs depending upon the parent's background, experience, confidence, the age of the child and the nature of the educational programs that the child on the autism spectrum may need.

Alternatively, when parents experience a continual lack of 'fit' *(seeking progressive fit)* for their child on the autism spectrum in a mainstream schooling context they may opt to place their child in a segregated *(segregating)* education support school contextually designed for children with disabilities. Parents inculcated in the notion of 'inclusion' often find it hard to reconcile such decisions with their quest to help their child eventually take up their rightful place in the external mainstream world. However, parents gradually accept over time, that they must place their child in an educational environment where they can experience the best educational 'fit' and where their child's and family's mental health will be valued and preserved.

CATEGORY TWO: SUPPLEMENTING

As previously evidenced in the sub-category, *broadening,* parents often see little difference between 'therapy' and 'education' as they both potentially target overall improvement in the development of the child on the autism spectrum and one can reciprocally complement the other. Through experience, evidenced in sub-categories of *chasing*, *waxing and waning* and *crisis point*, parents learn that it is important to provide other supplementary programs to ensure that the child on the autism spectrum has access to a reliable form of education irrespective of their 'fit' with the schooling context occurring at the time. Parents have also become increasingly aware that to maximize their child's educational development they must address the idiosyncratic needs of their child's profile. This means that parents seek to construct an individualized intervention package, sometimes with the help of key professionals and others, which addresses the specific difficulties experienced by their child. As one of the parents in the study put it:

> … there is no single magic bullet. We have had, at times, multiple things on the go. This may not have been the best research-based approach, but we did not feel we had the time to do things any other way.

This quest is tempered by the conditional matrix (Strauss & Corbin, 1990) operating in parents' lives at the time that serves to either reduce or increase their ability to supplement their child's development during their formal schooling years.

According to the parents in the study (McDonald, 2010), s*upplementing* is a process that often extends those therapies begun in the early intervention education years over the formal schooling years, mainstream or otherwise, and includes many different types of interventions, deemed useful by parents in their quest to help their child learn and improve in all areas of development. One parent explained the process of *supplementing* in the following way:

> I guess that is where the therapy programs and extra educational programs come in. You know that they have to be running alongside what they do just in case the school program is not working. It is almost like the secondary stuff that you do on your own is like a safety net and if you crack the jackpot and you have a good educational program at school plus all of the therapies are doing their job too, well you know it is going to be a great year. But, if you have a second rate educational program going on at school you know you have to supplement it. To keep the other situation buoyant and hopefully feed into it what might need to happen if we see that the situation at school is not working because our kids don't have time to waste.

Parents in the study (McDonald, 2010) tried a multitude of therapies and interventions including: speech therapy, occupational therapy, physiotherapy, gluten-free/casein-free diets, Vitamin B12 injections, auditory integration therapy, sensory integration therapy, fluency training, kinesiology, anti-candida regimes, immune-modulating drug therapies, fruit juice supplements, numerous drug regimes, sporting programs, Gymbaroo, drama and music studies, social skills training courses, sibling awareness training, the Kumon method of mathematical and language education (Kumon Australia & New Zealand, 2007) and many more idiosyncratic interventions suggested as useful by both professionals and parents alike. Parents indicated that the results of these therapies were never guaranteed and while one parent may have great success with an intervention there was no guarantee that the same intervention would be useful for another child on the autism spectrum.

Some parents in the study also found that some interventions actually produced harmful effects in their child. For example, one parent in the study had to have her child on the autism spectrum hospitalized after they had an adverse reaction to prescribed drugs. Research (Broadstock, Doughty, & Eggleston, 2007; Kerbeshian, Burd, & Avery, 2001; Posey & McDougle, 2000, 2001) indicates that drug therapy has been used by parents of children on the autism spectrum to treat such disabling symptoms as epilepsy, anxiety, aggression, agitation, hyperactivity, inattention, irritability, repetitive behaviours, self-injury and so on. There has been limited research on investigating the effectiveness of combining drug treatments with behavioural, educational and/or psychosocial therapies (Broadstock et al., 2007; Chalfant, Rapee, & Carroll, 2007). Unfortunately, parents in the study also indicated that there was no guarantee that the results of *supplementing* would always be positive and often the process was a 'hit and miss' affair for their individual children on the autism spectrum.

According to parents, they were often left to their own devices to work out an intervention regime, in a 'trial-and-error' fashion, that would maximize their individual child's development over time. There was often no guarantee that a particular intervention would be successful but parents often felt duty-bound to try different interventions to give their child the best chance of improving as evidenced by the following comments of one parent in the study:

> You never know if you didn't *(try different interventions)* ... Bill's (*son on the autism spectrum)* progress was slow, as I said, until we started the dietary intervention, but you never know with the regression how low he may have got and never got back from if we hadn't been doing what we had been doing. So, that is why it is so hard to gauge (*if a therapy is working*) I think because you don't have that control alongside to know what would have happened otherwise. So, I think you have to, for your own peace of mind, know that you have done everything that you could do even if it helped or not.

Parents in the study indicated that this 'trial-and-error' process took time, financial resources and research *(researching)* to achieve the best results for their child and the process could only be undertaken if the parent's circumstances allowed it to occur. Parents indicated that the process of *supplementing* was yet another, often expensive, task undertaken by parents to ensure their child's educational progress and this added to the already difficult and stressful nature of parents' lives. Parents often sustained *supplementing* by organizing appointments, transporting their child to such appointments, conducting external programs and this reduced their ability to access external work or be available or provide support to other members of their immediate family. This process placed more pressure on family members who had to fund and often implement such interventions. This dynamic also reaffirmed the existing division of duties undertaken by different parents in some families when trying to educate their child on the autism spectrum. That is, some families organised for one parent to be responsible for implementing promising programs, while the other parent took on the bread-winning role by providing the funding for such a process to occur.

Parents further explained that their children on the autism spectrum often had comorbid conditions such as sensory issues, depression, anxiety problems, epilepsy and so on that needed to be investigated and addressed to ensure that maximum educational progress of their child could be achieved. Research has affirmed that the best educational programs for students on the autism spectrum are those that incorporate a variety of objectively verified practices and are designed to address and support the needs of individual students and the professionals and families with whom they are linked (National Research Council, 2001; Olley, 1999; Parsons et al., 2011; Simpson, 2005). However, this situation often places parents in the very demanding circumstance of choosing and sometimes, conducting appropriate and effective educational practices and other interventions regarding their individual child on the autism spectrum. Consequently, there is a long-standing tradition by parents of children on the autism spectrum of choosing educational methods and other intervention strategies that sometimes lack efficacy and proven utility for their individual child (Francis, 2005; Gresham et al., 1999; Heflin & Simpson, 1998; Simpson, 2004, 2005).

At its best, parents in the study found that this process of *supplementing* was fully supported by the school environment where the school and parents worked as a team to ensure that the other interventions were dovetailed into the formal schooling process and used to maximize the child's development. This process was underpinned by a mutual respect and trust between the school, the parents and others whereby details of external programs were shared so that all parties could give feedback to one another and appropriately support the child on the autism spectrum. One of the parents explained this process in the following manner:

> Meanwhile, we continued at home with all the various programs which we knew Kim (*son on the autism spectrum*) still needed so he could progress as quickly as possible. The psychologist visited Kim's classroom in February, May and November of that year. She, once again, provided statistical feedback on the progress of Kim throughout the year in the areas of classroom and playground behaviour. These measures helped to provide feedback to the school and ourselves as to the success or otherwise of strategies adopted in the classroom and playground to help maximize Kim's functional learning and social behaviours. Programs were also implemented at home to support the programs in place at school. My partner and I were completely overwhelmed and delighted by the level of support shown by the school. They had taken complete ownership of Kim and were willing to do everything they could to maximize Kim's potential. The teacher was very willing to implement the suggestions of this (*psychological*) report and subsequent ones and each one confirmed that Kim was rapidly improving in both academic and social areas. The school situation was supported by us in the form of a social skills training course conducted at home. A home therapist (volunteer psychology student) provided an appropriate program which directly supported the skills being targeted at school. Copies of the reports were distributed to the school, to us at home and to the other relevant therapists who could use the information to supplement their own intervention programs. This was especially useful when Kim was experiencing difficulty with the more abstract requirements of the curriculum. Speech therapy could directly target these areas of difficulty by implementing appropriate programs. We, in turn, at home could help to generalize these more difficult concepts. The process became one of fluid communication and problem solving with everyone seemingly on the same side.

As evidenced above, this process of *supplementing* could only occur properly in a school situation exemplified in the sub-category, *finding fit*, where the culture of the school did all in its power to maximize the development of the child on the autism spectrum. It is important to note that these parents were in a financial position to supplement the education of their child on the autism spectrum with private service providers. They were also involved in the type of parent partnership where one parent concentrated on maximizing the development of the child on the autism spectrum while the other parent provided the majority of funds to do so.

The process of *supplementing* the education of a child on the autism spectrum was directly linked to the 'conditional matrix' (Strauss & Corbin, 1990) operating in the lives of the respective families in this study. At the other end of the spectrum to the situation cited above sits one of the more vulnerable single parent families in the study who was financially unable to afford *supplementing* through private means. As evidenced in the category, *settling*, this same parent had to continue to *settle* for what was funded through the state system. In the following comment, this parent expressed the continuing difficulty of her situation:

> As soon as he became school-age, apart from *(government-funded private intervention provider),* if I wanted him to have therapy I had to pay for it privately. So basically, parents who don't have the funds it (*intervention*) comes to a standstill at that time.

This same parent expressed disappointment about the paucity and lack of quality of government-funded intervention services available for her child on the autism spectrum in the following general way:

> And there are a lot of things that are very lacking in Disability Services. I have always thought that they and *(government-funded private intervention provider)* should be called Johnson & Johnson's BandAids because that is all they are a BandAid effect.

She also noted the significant drop in appropriate state-funded intervention services when her child on the autism spectrum began Year One by stating:

> It *(intervention*) only continued up until he hit Year One. If I had kept him in pre-primary for five years I would have been right. There was total inadequacy (*after Year One*), no way can one therapist come out once a week and benefit thirty children, maybe it wasn't thirty then, but there are thirty at (*name of school*) now. But, even if they only had ten, one therapist can't come out.

This parent also remarked about the lack of individualized therapy available to her child at this time. According to this parent, the state-funded therapists conducted her child's program mainly through the other school staff (aides and teachers) and there was little individualized therapy offered. Unfortunately, this meant that the quality of the therapy was potentially affected by the calibre of school staff implementing it as evidenced in the parent's comments below:

> I have written to *(government-funded private intervention provider)* and asked how they treat the individual student and basically the answer that comes back to you is that they work with the teachers and aides who then implement the program over the on-going weeks. If you have got a numbskull of an aide ... (*silence*).

This parent also expressed concern about the lack of consultation between the therapist and herself regarding the intervention program for her child. According to this parent, the process of gaining therapy began with a Family Screening Assessment where the parent was supposed to prioritize the therapy needs of her child before therapy could begin the following year. Unfortunately, because of the lack of services available through the government-funded system, this often translated to a situation where a child received one term of a specific therapy followed by one term of another therapy and so on and that therapy was mainly implemented through the school staff. The parent explained it in this way:

> You don't know what they do, you go to the Family Screening Assessment, then you supposedly prioritize your wants and then they offer you, you never get all the things that you want. They will offer you one term which will be OT (*occupational therapy*), one term will be Speech, I don't remember the last time Bob *(son on the autism spectrum)* had a physiotherapist.

This parent was also very concerned about the lack of communication between herself and the therapists-in-charge of her child's therapy program. She commented that she had never met face-to-face the OT who had been organizing her son's program at his school until some nine months later, as evidenced below:

> Like at the moment, I have just been dealing with the OT and this is a classic example. The OT has been a girl by the name of (*OT's name*) who I had never met. I spoke to her on the phone once. This is since his last family screening in November. Then I get a letter from (*OT's name*) and a phone call to back it up to say that she has a graduate student with her now, (*graduate student's name*) who will be servicing (*school's name*). At this stage I had an appointment at the Independent Living Centre to meet with (*OT's name*) who came along and then introduced me to (*graduate student's name*). I had to laugh, I said, 'Nice to meet you (*OT's name*). I know you have been working with Bob'. It was like tongue-in-cheek because I thought, 'This is ridiculous, it is all pretend'. I can't take it out on them personally because it is the system. It is lip service.

Unfortunately, this parent felt that while there was a semblance of therapy given through the government-funded system in reality it panned out to be a form of 'lip service' because of the paucity and ineffectiveness of the therapy programs given and the lack of consultation with the parents.

In a further example of the futility of the therapy given through the government-subsidized system this same parent described a group therapy session that her son had been involved with in a previous year at his primary school. This after-school group session was conducted by an OT and speech therapist from the same government-funded provider and was organized for all of the children with disabilities in the school irrespective of their type or level of disability. The parent described below the difficulties associated with including her son on the autism spectrum in such a group program in the following way:

> They decided to run a group, the OT and (*name of speech therapist)* - this 'after-school' group. Now we were to all meet down in Special Needs at 3.30pm.

> Well, instantly when you have got children, any child thinks that it is time to go home. The whole thing was bad for me. All of the buses had arrived to pick up and Bob (*son on the autism spectrum*) was fascinated, and Bob was not interested like Jack (*name of another student on the autism spectrum*) sitting at the front having all the kids around reading a story. The story involved going to the fair and there was the ferris wheel, this concept is well beyond Bob. We all had to take food in because they are used to eating at that time. Sean *(another student on the autism spectrum*) wasn't at all happy because he doesn't like everybody in the Unit at the same time that he is in the Unit. And then you had Phil (*another child with a disability*) who wants to help Bob and won't leave him alone and touches him all of the time. I am sitting there thinking, 'This is such a waste of time'. And then they do a task after the story is read relating to the story. And so I am sitting there and thinking and looking at Cathy (*fellow parent of child on the autism spectrum*). At first, I start to think maybe it is me, maybe I am not appreciating what they are trying to do, so I left earlier than everybody else because Bob was just full on and disrupting everything. And then the next week we tried it again. It is not like I did not keep going back. But the next week I thought, 'There is no way that Bob can comprehend this story. I am going to have some time out to watch the buses'. So that became a part of our routine, I just took Bob and we sat happily in front of pre-primary and we watched the buses. Then I would take him back in and if the task was appropriate we would play with the task and in the end, I actually said that I would not be bringing Bob anymore because this is far beyond Bob's skill level. When that happened I just thought this is so inadequate that if this can happen and they can invite us along to this how well have they got to know Bob because this is just far beyond him? I actually said to Cathy (*fellow parent of child on the autism spectrum*), 'You know if this is what they are doing after school in front of me what is happening at school?'

Unfortunately, this parent expressed regret that she was only in a position financially in the latter years of her son's primary school education to bring in some private and individualized *supplementing* to maximize her son's development:

> Unless you can financially provide it there is nothing. And I am only now getting to the stage where I am starting to financially look, which is probably a good thing because maybe Bob is ready for it now. I have got a little bit of money behind me in the bank. I never want to start anything and then you have to stop. The new speech therapist (*private*) that Cathy (*fellow parent of a child on the autism spectrum)* has been going to sounds like she would get to know Bob and would be able to help Bob.

This lack of ability to supplement her child's education appropriately left this single parent with one of the most difficult situations to deal with of all the parents in the study. Presently her adult son on the autism spectrum is non-verbal, self-injurious and has very limited communication skills. This situation exists even though her son has supposedly been given intervention throughout his primary and high school years by government-subsidized therapy providers. The parent explained the difficulties with the process as follows:

> The system at *(name of government-funded private intervention provider)* is that every year I get new therapists. Every year they come in with the best of intentions and they usually give Bob the new kid off the block (*new therapist*). And they are very keen and then they shit themselves on their first meeting with Bob because either they watch him have a full meltdown and bite through his arms or they cop a whack, then it takes them definitely the first semester right up till about August to start to get used to him then I have a term of a little bit (*of appropriate therapy*). Then I get a new therapist all over again the next year.

According to this parent, the government-subsidized process of *supplementing* did not have the quality or intensity of service provision needed to address seriously the major individual difficulties of her child on the autism spectrum. Unfortunately, each year the ineffectual process repeated itself because of the inexperience of the staff dealing with her child. Hence, if parents do not have the financial resources to supplement privately their child's development they will have little chance of maximizing their child's ultimate educational potential as evidenced by the experiences of this parent in the study.

To summarize, parents choose to supplement *(supplementing)* their child's formal schooling with a multitude of interventions to ensure that they maximize the educational progress of their child on the autism spectrum because of the unreliable nature of the formal schooling process and the idiosyncratic needs of their child's profile. *Supplementing* is a process that is directly affected by the individual circumstances of the family who have a child on the autism spectrum. At its best, the school is able to work with the family to utilize the supplementary programs within the child's educational program to maximize their development. When a family's resources are limited, *supplementing* is reduced to what is provided through the government-subsidized system and such services are often lacking in appropriate individualization, intensity and quality of service provision. Unfortunately, when parents supplement their child's education they undertake yet another responsibility associated with maximizing their child's educational progress and this adds to the already difficult and stressful nature of their lives.

CATEGORY THREE: OPTING OUT

In the initial instance, parents in the study experienced the quest of continually *seeking progressive educational fit* for their child on the autism spectrum in a formal mainstream schooling context. However, when such 'fit' was constantly lacking as evidenced in the sub-category of *crisis point*, they were compelled to *opt out* of mainstream schooling by either *home schooling* or placing their child in a segregated education support school (*segregating*). Once again, in these circumstances parents of children on the autism spectrum strategized solutions to meet the individual educational requirements of their child. This *opting out* of mainstream schooling eventually occurred in four of the six families in the study. This '*opting out'* serves to indicate the great degree of difficulty experienced by the majority of families in this study when trying to access reliable and appropriate educational 'fit' for their child on the autism spectrum in a mainstream schooling context. The following two sub-categories of *home-schooling* and *segregating* explain in detail how parents dealt with these situations.

Sub-Category One: Home Schooling

Two families in the study decided to home school *(home schooling)* their children on the autism spectrum after their child's mainstream schooling had reached a *crisis point* as evidenced in the sub-category, *crisis point.* This reaching of a *crisis point* is similarly described in past research investigating how West Australian parents home school their intellectually disabled children where Reilly (2007) indicates that parents choose to home school because they initially reach a "crisis point" in their child's formal schooling (p. 181).

In one family involved in the study (McDonald, 2010), this *crisis point* was reached during the child's primary school years after the child had unsuccessfully attended three state-run primary school mainstream environments. The parent finally intervened at the point where the child on the autism spectrum had expressed suicidal thoughts at the age of ten as evidenced in the sub-category, *crisis point.*

By contrast, the other family's son on the autism spectrum had previously experienced a successful, 'inclusive', private mainstream schooling environment over the duration of his primary school years. Unfortunately, this experience was followed by continuous difficulties in two mainstream high schooling contexts, both private and public. Both mainstream high school environments eventually proved to be untenable for this student who experienced both bullying and a lack of 'inclusive' practice until a *crisis point* was reached. This *crisis point* occurred when this student was physically assaulted on a school bus. The police were subsequently brought into the situation by the parents. Under such circumstances, the parents felt that their son was no longer safe in his mainstream high school environment. The parents also felt that their son had suffered too much emotional trauma attending such a mainstream environment, so they elected to home school their son from that point on.

The experiences of these two families echoes the current research on other West Australian parents who chose to home educate their children with intellectual disabilities including those on the autism spectrum. This research indicates that parents home school because they are concerned about on-going negative socialization (including bullying), insufficient academic progress and a failure by schools to understand their child's academic and social profile or the nature of their disability (Kidd & Kaczmarek, 2010; Reilly, 2004, 2007; Reilly, Chapman, & O'Donoghue, 2002). As evidenced by the parents in this study who eventually chose *home schooling* to educate their child on the autism spectrum, *home schooling* is a viable option only if the family have the resources, financial or otherwise, to support such a situation.

This is consistent with research on *home schooling* of children with disabilities which indicates that parents undertake *home schooling* with limited or no funding and there is often a division of duties where the mother becomes the primary teacher and the father assumes the main breadwinning responsibilities (Ensign, 2000; Reilly, 2004, 2007; Reilly et al., 2002). As will be recalled, this division of duties is already well established in most families who have a child on the autism spectrum when parents have tried to maximize and supplement their child's progress during the EI years and beyond. One of the parents in this sub-category commented about the lack of financial support for *home schooling* parents in the following way:

> If the parents are prepared to home-school for three or four years, or six years as it was for me, they should pay that person to be a home tutor so that you would be getting a wage of some kind because we are saving them a shitload of money in the future by making them independent so that they don't become a drain on welfare as they get older. I think it would help so many parents financially and would help your self-esteem if the government recognized you and said this is your role we can see that you are a home teacher.

The other parent in this sub-category also commented about the on-going financial loss associated with the time that parents take out of the workforce and the implications of this:

> Because it is not the years that you are out (*home schooling*), it is the years that you are not being promoted, it is a range of things that you give up.

Unfortunately, parents who do not have the resources to home educate must continue to undertake the frustrating process detailed in the sub-category of *chasing* in an attempt to *seek, gain* and *maintain progressive fit* for their child on the autism spectrum in the mainstream system. This is especially so when the child on the autism spectrum does not 'fit' the IQ entrance requirements for a segregated education support school. It should be noted that both students who were home educated in the study did not 'fit' the entrance requirements needed for an education support school placement as they had diagnoses of Asperger's Syndrome and high functioning Autistic Disorder and were not deemed to have an accompanying intellectual disability (IQ under 70). To date, there is no education support school in WA that is specifically designed for high functioning students on the autism spectrum at both the primary or high school levels even though such schools are available in others states of Australia.

Through use of the *home schooling* option both families were able to substantially increase the educational 'fit' for their child on the autism spectrum. Parents indicated that individualized education plans could be organised to target their child's specific needs on a one-to-one basis without the need to negotiate a large external mainstream schooling context. Research also confirms that parents who home educate their children with disabilities generally work on a one-to-one basis with their child and eventually, through 'trial and error' individualize instruction according to their child's abilities/interests/social needs and pace of learning (Ensign, 2000; Reilly, 2004, 2007; Reilly et al., 2002).

The parents in this sub-category also indicated that *home schooling* reduced the stress experienced by the student on the autism spectrum substantially. However, *home schooling* also put another layer of responsibility onto the parents and added to the already difficult nature of their lives as evidenced by the comments of one of the mothers below:

> The only problem with it (*home schooling*) is that it is a double-edged sword because then you take it all on and then it is your responsibility and you don't have time for the other parts of your life. And I have found by taking on board everything with regard to Kim (*son on the autism spectrum*) and doing home schooling and all the rest of it I am quite emotionally drained all of the time.

Hence, while *home schooling* reduced stress in some family members, especially the student on the autism spectrum, it also increased the pressure placed on the parent-in-charge of the *home schooling* program.

In relation to reducing this extra pressure, one of the mothers indicated that she enlisted extra support and supplemented her son's *home schooling* program by employing others to help her. She explained this process in the following way:

> I engaged a series of tutors for Paul *(son on the autism spectrum),* that I had to pay for myself. There was no help for that. I had four Uni students, one guy and three girls who I would get to take him out, to come to the home and do little tasks with him, to take him out for social outings, to go bowling, to go on trips. I would tell them what to talk to him about, talk to him about catching the bus, what you had to do, talk about crossing the road, all that sort of thing. Because I would see, especially after my husband left home, that I was going to be a complete cot case if I was going to have to do it all myself.

Both parents-in-charge of the home program also enlisted the support of their mothers to *redress the imbalance* in their lives exacerbated by *home schooling* as evidenced below:

> My mother has been a constant source of help and support to all of our immediate family. Without her, I feel I would have become quite bitter and depressed about how things have turned out for our family. She has always accepted all of the children unconditionally and equally. She comes to my home daily during the working week and helps with the evening meals. She listens to my woes and comments very little. Often this is the best way because

> I often have the solutions within me but I just need time to work them out. Without her, my life would have been much more difficult. I witness friends who also have children on the autism spectrum who are away or estranged from their families and I can see that their situation is so much more difficult than mine. I know that my mother can do little to help with the formal education of my son but her support in other ways is just as important. For without this, I would not have the same level of positive energy to face the challenges which come almost daily with my son's education.

> But, I mean having said I don't get on well with my mother, which I don't, but she was very good with Paul (*son on the autism spectrum*) especially during those years *(home schooling*). I mean, she related to him very well and he would probably go to her place once a fortnight, and spend half a day there and have an overnight stay as well. It is great if you have got a family member.

However, such initiatives were only possible because the resources of the family, financial and otherwise, allowed them to occur. This process of gaining support from others included a range of measures designed to help with a full array of situations from educational to emotional support. These measures lightened the load of the person-in-charge of the *home schooling* program and helped them to sustain their efforts toward the progress of the child on the autism spectrum.

The two families used external home schooling services, researching and adopted maverick strategies to create their own educational programs. This is also borne out in current research on parents who home educate their children with disabilities which indicates that parents receive support for their *home schooling* situation by *researching* and seeking help from external agencies, especially parent *home schooling* networks (Ensign, 2000; Kidd & Kaczmarek, 2010; Reilly, 2004, 2007; Reilly et al., 2002). Both parents in the study who attempted this option had tertiary degrees and felt somewhat empowered to undertake such an option. This empowerment was first evidenced in the sub-category of *improvising* during the early intervention years. One of the parents expressed her reasons for such empowerment in the following way:

> I was just so peed off with dealing with people who were more ignorant than I was. We had very good tertiary educations and that puts us in a very good place to seek out the best information, the best methods. We are not afraid of negotiating bureaucracy and government departments and websites and things like that. I got sick of trying to deal with people who were ignorant, who didn't know what Asperger's was or autism was and that was wigging me out, so I just thought I am just going to do it all myself.

Current research (Reilly, 2007) indicates that parents who home educate their children with intellectual disabilities do so through a process of 'progressive modification'. The three sequential stages involved in this process were identified as: 'the stage of drawing upon readily-available resources', 'the stage of drawing upon support networks in a systematic fashion' and 'the stage of proceeding with confidence on the basis of having a set of principles for establishing a workable pattern of home schooling individualized for each circumstance' (Reilly, 2007). The experience of the parents in this sub-category indicates that while movement through such stages did occur, the former experiences of *improvising* during the early intervention years and *supplementing* during the formal schooling years served to hasten the pace of movement for these parents to the third stage of 'progressive modification'. Parents in this study quickly knew that they would have to tailor their home schooling education program to the individual and idiosyncratic needs of their child on the autism spectrum because of their former educational experiences during the early intervention and the formal schooling years.

In terms of process, the two families in this sub-category indicated how they experienced *home schooling* somewhat differently to one another because of the different ages of their children when they left their mainstream schooling environment. As explained, the first family removed their child when they were still in primary school and this allowed the parent to tailor a specific educational program to target her son's exact needs. The mother indicated that the main advantage of *home schooling* was that she knew her son's strengths and weaknesses well and could organize his education to prepare him for the challenges that he would possibly face in his future adult life. The following comments illustrate how this parent viewed the situation that she faced:

> … and I thought this was very important, that education didn't just mean learning academic things especially for an Asperger's child. It means socialization, learning life skills because that was what was going to set him in good stead for the future so I really concentrated on that.

With this in mind, this parent organized a learning program incorporating not only home-based activities but also community-based activities to prepare her son for the external adult mainstream world. This type of organization is borne out in the research on home schooling of children with disabilities that indicates parents organize the school day flexibly to include not only academic pursuits but also community/social undertakings to improve the socialization and independence of the student with a disability (Ensign, 2000; Reilly, 2004, 2007; Reilly et al., 2002). This mother described how the learning program she devised for her son initially consisted of a morning academic program followed by a more general life/social skills program in the afternoon. The morning academic program was centred on her son's interest areas and his key academic needs as described by her below:

> I just taught him myself, whatever, the basic Science, Maths, English and he was interested in History, Social Studies. And he was interested in the solar system, that was his special interest area. So, anything we could do. I mean he could write little fictional stories about Science Fiction subjects. They were always derivative of things that he had seen on TV.

This parent also recounted how she would often act as her son's scribe and use a computer to combat the difficulties that her son had with writing (dysgraphia). She did this to reduce the anxiety that her son had previously experienced during academic learning times in mainstream education. The afternoons were organized to include such activities as: exercise (walking, riding and swimming), caring for a pet, general self-help skills (cooking, washing, and housework), interacting with the external community (such as visiting the library and shopping).

This interaction with the external community was 'primed' by this parent to ensure that her son's external visits maximized his social skills learning and had the greatest chance to be successful. She did this by initially alerting community members about her son's social differences and indicated ways that they could help her son to become more socially able. She explained the process in the following way:

> We lived within walking distance of the library and that was another afternoon activity because I combined going to the library and getting books out on the topics we were doing and then walking to the library or riding his bike and taking the dog with us. He would either walk or ride his bike and the dog would come. And it was also doing a meeting and greeting at the library. I would prime them up beforehand about who Paul (*son on the autism spectrum*) was and what I was doing and they would also say, 'Hello Paul, how are you today, what books are you looking for?' And, he would have to look at them and shake hands and say, 'Hello' and all the rest of it. I used to make a big thing about that.

Unfortunately, the government Department of Education and Training (DET) did not contact this parent at all during this difficult and isolating time even though her child had stopped attending any formal schooling. The mother did however; eventually make contact herself with the DET Schools of Isolated and Distance Education (SIDE) some time later to ready herself for her son's high school needs, as explained in her comments below:

> … from age 10 to age 16 I was basically in charge of overseeing it (*the home schooling of her child on the autism spectrum*). Whereas from SIDE I got the curriculum, up until then that's when I did (*mother's name*) All Encompassing Education Program. That was the whole thing, the school-work, the proper exercise, eating the right diet. I did heaps of reading on what I should be doing. Think about your child and his needs, what of all these things that you read is going to work for you and your situation as well as the child. What is going to work? And then, you just do that and what works you stick with and what doesn't you discard and try to think of something different.

Hence, this parent specifically tailored her child's education program to 'fit' the individual profile of her son. She once again, used a process of *researching* and 'trial-and-error' to ensure that she maximized her son's progress. As the research confirms she, like other home schooling parents, remained flexible in her approach and targeted her son's specific academic and social needs on a one-to-one basis (Ensign, 2000; Kidd & Kaczmarek, 2010; Reilly, 2004, 2007; Reilly et al., 2002).

This parent also reported that the involvement of SIDE in the process of her son's *home schooling* was eventually also organized around his individual learning needs, interests and comfort level. Like the other parent in this sub-category, her son was eligible to gain the services of SIDE because he had a documented diagnosis of an ASD and it could be proven that mainstream education was no longer a viable option for him. This involvement with SIDE gradually increased over the latter years of primary school in preparation for his high school studies.

Normally, SIDE sends distance education materials to eligible students in remote locations and there is limited face-to-face contact. Communication with teaching staff is done through the telephone, the computer and mail. Students are rarely involved with the day-to-day happenings of the SIDE main school site. However, this parent indicated that SIDE were flexible enough to be able to offer her son the option of visiting their main school site given his close proximity to the school and his learning/ social difficulties. This visiting of the school-site went from one half day a week at the start and built up to two days a week at its peak. In the meantime, work set by SIDE was completed at home. This arrangement allowed her son the ability to become gradually more independent and practise his social skills in a supported, supervised environment. This process was specifically built around the comfort level of her son given his traumatic educational history. The success of this process was dependent upon the open and trusting relationship that was established over time between the staff at SIDE, the parent and student. It is important to note that this is the same type of relationship detailed between staff and parents in successful, 'inclusive' mainstream educational environments as explained in the sub-category, *finding fit*.

According to this parent, the relationship between SIDE and her family was enhanced particularly by a male special needs teacher at SIDE who worked with her son on the autism spectrum on a one-to-one basis. This teacher, who eventually became a trusted mentor, used humour as a way to connect with the student to reduce his anxiety in learning situations. The parent elaborated on this aspect of the relationship below:

> And he (*the teacher*) understood that if you connected with Paul (*son on the autism spectrum*) through humour then you could get Paul to do a lot more than if you laid down the law and said this and this is going to happen. He didn't get his back up. They had this running joke where Paul was the slave and *(teacher*) was the slave driver and what Paul had to slave for that day for the slave driver to be happy.

The establishment of such a relationship allowed both the parent and her son to gradually gain trust in the teacher. The parent and teacher felt encouraged to communicate openly about the student's difficulties and together were able to organize a specific learning program around his educational, emotional needs and interests. This is evidenced in the comments of the parent below:

> *(Teacher's name*) very quickly worked out what Paul's strengths and weaknesses were and also he was cognizant of the fact that Paul's father had recently left home and one of Paul's interests was public transport. He thought it would be good for Paul to increase his independence by coming to SIDE a couple of times a week and to go on the train. And the first time Paul got on the train by himself without me I was standing on the platform at (*name of suburb)* with a mobile phone in my hand and *(teacher's name)* was standing at the platform in Leederville with a mobile in his hand. I said, 'He'll be there in eight minutes'. As soon as he got there *(teacher's name)* rang me and said, 'He's here and we are just walking to SIDE now'. Now he only had to do that twice, wait for Paul at the station and after that Paul said to *(teacher's name),* 'I'm independent enough to walk up to SIDE on my own, you don't need to come and meet me at the station'.

This visiting of SIDE by her son on the autism spectrum also gave this parent some much needed respite because by this time her marriage had broken down and she was trying to home educate her son and parent two other children mainly on her own. The parent recognized the value of this arrangement as indicated below:

> Paul caught the train twice a week, walked up to SIDE crossed at the lights and did lessons with (*teacher's name*), had lunch there and then came home after that. So, that was really good for me because that gave me my break. I was able to have a bit of time to myself and also know that he was in really good hands.

Hence, over time SIDE was able to provide a very successful and flexible educational alternative for this student and respite for the parent as well. The individualized educational program, devised in consultation with the parent, was based around the overall needs and interests of the student, and was implemented in a creative and pragmatic manner by a concerned mentor/teacher. This occurred because of the overall trust that had been built over time between SIDE, the parent and the student. The positive use of mentors in relation to home educating students with disabilities has been previously documented in research by Ensign (2002) who found that mentors often created an informal relationship with the student and used their special interests to engage them in learning.

The other family in this study involved in this sub-category of *home schooling* indicated that they had also experienced a similarly successful relationship with SIDE. It will be recalled that these second set of parents reached their *crisis point* situation later in their child's school career than the previous family. Hence, the parents immediately contacted SIDE in their quest to have their *home schooling* situation supported by them so the least amount of academic disadvantage would accrue for their son in his high school years. According to this parent, the withdrawal from mainstream high-school school and the subsequent association with SIDE resulted in a great reduction in stress for the student on the autism spectrum as evidenced in the mother's comments below:

> In retrospect, putting our son into SIDE has been the very best thing that we could have done for our son. He had an immediate reduction of the high stress that he had lived under daily for most of his high school life.

Similar to the experiences described by the previous family, SIDE showed the same ability to tailor the education process around the needs and interests of the student on the autism spectrum. Their programs were highly organized, individually paced, mainly visual in nature and according to one of the parents in this family, suited her son on the autism spectrum very well:

> The SIDE way of learning has also suited Kim (*son on the autism spectrum*) very well. The SIDE booklets have allowed him to read over sections of his course repeatedly if he needs to do so. He can also ring his teacher on selected days of the week. He knows exactly when all work is due because SIDE prints a yearly timetable indicating due dates for all assignments and tests. He gets on very well with his teachers and does not have to compete with other students for their attention. He also does not have to negotiate difficult adolescent relationships so that he can survive his secondary schooling. We have found that it is a myth that successful high school relationships are a forerunner to successful adult relationships. Our son is much more capable of being accepted in an adult environment than he would ever be in an adolescent environment. This has been borne out in his successful work experience placement at SIDE.

This family also utilized a home schooling network, The Home-Based Learning Network (HBLN), to supplement their son's SIDE education as explained by the mother:

> The *(SIDE)* program was extremely flexible and allowed my son to complete his academic work mainly in the morning. We were then free to go on excursions if we so desired. We linked into the home schooling network that regularly distributed a newsletter and alerted us to group activities organized by other home schoolers. We went along to various excursions with other home schoolers. The other home schoolers were very accepting of our son. Families attended these activities in groups with all different age groups in attendance. The parents were always with the children and monitored their own children's behaviour. The pack mentality that existed at the high schools my son had attended just did not exist. We were free to come and go as we chose to do depending upon the interest level shown by my son. This extremely flexible way of operating was ideal for a student with autism who can often find it difficult to predict how they may respond to a situation.

This experience echoes current research investigating how parents home educate their disabled children in Western Australia at this time. The research indicates that parents often receive moral support from spouses but more practical support in the form of information and contacts from parent *home schooling* networks that increase the parent's confidence to manage the process of *home schooling* (Ensign, 2000; Reilly, 2004, 2007; Reilly et al., 2002).

This parent also indicated that SIDE allowed her son on the autism spectrum access to a wide variety of high school courses so that his educational potential could be maximized. Similar to the experiences of the previous family, this student was also invited to attend SIDE during the week to become more independent, socially able and gain direct feedback for his work from the teaching staff. The parent also commented about the flexibility of SIDE and how the educational profile and interests of this student on the autism spectrum were similarly used by SIDE to develop an appropriate educational program:

> The program is very flexible at SIDE as compared to what is possible at mainstream high school. It suits someone like my son greatly. He has been able to go in to see his teachers on a regular basis because our home is in the next suburb to where SIDE is located. He has also been able to access work experience through the local council library which fulfils the requirements of both the Year 11 and 12 Structured Workplace Learning subjects. So all things considered it has been an excellent educational choice for our son.

While the previous student on the autism spectrum eventually left SIDE at the age of sixteen because of a desire to seek specialized work-based training for students with disabilities at a Technical and Further Education (TAFE) college; this second student on the autism spectrum was able to achieve secondary graduation by completing a modified academic and work-based program at SIDE. Unfortunately, this second student on the autism spectrum had anxiety problems during high-pressure situations and this made it difficult for him to perform well under exam conditions. The parent explained his difficulties in the following way:

> He passed all subjects but found the exams extremely difficult because of the high anxiety he experienced during such times. Fortunately, SIDE and his exam supervisor tried to alleviate some of his anxieties by giving him special conditions. However, even with these special conditions the anxiety he experienced interfered greatly with him performing to his potential. His anxiety interfered with his normally excellent memory and certainly played havoc with his ability to think clearly during the examinations. He was obsessed with the amount of time left and eventually we had to take away any understanding of passing time by removing clocks and watches from his sight. Such are the difficulties associated with having a mind which is difficult to regulate in terms of its ability to hyper-focus on areas of interest or worry.

Hence, the collective decision was made, in consultation with the student on the autism spectrum, to move from an academic course that consisted of mainly tertiary entrance scoring subjects to one that consisted of mainly whole-school assessed subjects that did not have a requirement for external examinations. According to this mother, this set her son on a track to be involved with a particular Structured

Workplace Learning subject in the final years of his SIDE study program. It also allowed him to eventually secure a school-based traineeship at the local library and complete a TAFE Certificate II in Library Studies.

The parents of this student on the autism spectrum and SIDE capitalized on this situation by nominating the student on the autism spectrum for a number of awards regarding his involvement with the school-based traineeship. As previously detailed in the sub-category, *finding fit,* the strategy of positively raising the profile of the student on the autism spectrum was used to increase the student's mainstream acceptance. In this instance, the public profile of the student on the autism spectrum was raised when he eventually won a Council Improved Access Award, a District Vocational Education and Training Award (Special Needs Category) and a National Australian Vocational Student Prize (Open Category) worth $2,000. These awards were given in recognition of outstanding achievement in Vocational Education and Training and allowed the student to be welcomed easily into a mainstream TAFE Multimedia course the following year after his secondary graduation. This student has since successfully completed many TAFE courses: Certificate III in Multimedia, Certificate IV and Diploma in Computer Game Design, an Advanced Diploma in Animation and a Diploma and Advanced Diploma in Engineering (Computer Aided Design). After many stints of work experience this student has also finally gained employment in the area of computer aided design.

To summarize, parents in this sub-category adopted the strategy of *home schooling* to *gain, maintain* and *create progressive educational fit* for their children on the autism spectrum when mainstream 'inclusive' education was no longer a viable option and a *crisis point* has been reached in their mainstream schooling. Parents chose to home educate because they were concerned about on-going negative socialization (including bullying), insufficient academic progress and the failure of schools to understand their child's academic and social profile or the nature of their disability (Reilly, 2007). However, *home schooling* could only be undertaken if the individual circumstances of these families were able to support such a situation. *Home schooling* provided a safe, flexible and individualized education program for their child on the autism spectrum but, it also placed more responsibility onto the parent-in-charge of the program and removed their ability to gain external paid work outside the home. During *home schooling*, parents used external services and adopted maverick strategies to improvise their own educational programs depending upon the parent's background, experience, confidence, the age of the child and the nature of the educational programs that the child on the autism spectrum needed.

Sub-Category Two: Segregating

Alternatively, when parents in the study (McDonald, 2010) experienced a continual lack of 'fit' *(seeking progressive fit)* for their child on the autism spectrum in a formal mainstream schooling context, they opted (*opting out*) to place their child in a segregated education support school (ESS) contextually designed for children with disabilities. Parents inculcated in the social justice concept of 'inclusion' found it hard to reconcile such decisions with their quest to help their child eventually take their rightful place in the external mainstream world. However, these parents gradually accepted over time that they must place their child on the autism spectrum in an educational environment where they experienced the best 'fit' *(seeking progressive fit)* and this included the option of an ESS. Research (Howlin, 1998; Kasari et al., 1999; Moreno et al., 2008) has confirmed that parents of children on the autism spectrum are more likely to endorse schooling where teachers have specialized training and the educational program focuses on the specific needs of students on the autism spectrum. Moreover, parents of children on the autism spectrum in partial or fully segregated settings in mainstream schools have been found to be less satisfied with their child's schooling than their parental counterparts in education support schools (Moreno et al., 2008). In terms of mainstream inclusion of students on the autism spectrum, Moreno et al. (2008) conclude that "it is not the inclusive process itself that parents are concerned with, but the risks of insufficient provision that sometimes accompany it" (p. 172). These are the same conclusions reached by the majority of participants in the study (McDonald 2010) as evidenced by their experiences in the sub-categories of *chasing, waxing and waning, crisis point, home schooling* and now, *segregating.*

Two families in the study (McDonald, 2010) eventually placed their children in education support schools but their trajectories of involvement were different and dependent upon the conditional matrix operating in the parents' lives at the time. As previously indicated, students who have a documented diagnosis of an ASD and have an accompanying intellectual disability (IQ of approximately 70 or below) are generally the only ones eligible for placement in an ESS in Western Australia at this time.

In the first instance, a single parent in one of the families in the study chose specifically to enrol her child in an ESS from the beginning of his high school career. She did this because she felt that this would provide the best educational 'fit' *(seeking progressive fit)* and chance of progress for her son. This parent felt that the former mainstream primary school had reduced expectations of her son and that such expectations would increase if the school population no longer saw her son as 'special'. She explained her decision as follows:

> Because all the kids at school (*mainstream primary school*) know Bob (*son on the autism spectrum*) they don't expect any more out of Bob which is why I think he will do well at (*name of ESS*) because they (*ESS staff*) will expect lots out of him, whereas at (*mainstream primary school*) he is special, whereas at (*name of ESS*) he will not be special.

Unlike the first parent in this sub-category of experience, *segregating,* the parents in the second family did not initially choose to segregate their two sons on the autism spectrum from a mainstream educational environment. As explained in the sub-category of *crisis point,* this family had reached an untenable situation at their sons' previous mainstream high school environment because of a continuing lack of appropriate 'inclusive' practice. This then forced these parents to attempt to find (*chasing*) a suitable educational placement *(seeking progressive fit)* for both boys elsewhere in the middle of a school year. Given the difficulties previously experienced with enrolling their children on the autism spectrum in a mainstream schooling environment elsewhere, evidenced in the sub-category *chasing,* this family eventually decided to pursue the option of attempting to enrol their sons at an ESS instead. At first the mother expressed hesitance at leaving a mainstream schooling environment in the following way:

> I was a little bit hesitant about taking Chris (*eldest son on the autism spectrum*) out of mainstream. You do get set in your way of thinking and you want to make sure that your children are properly prepared for what is waiting out there because it is tough out there and you try to expose them as much as you can to what really goes on out there with kids that are in the mainstream. I remember thinking that wasn't our plan, this was our plan.

However, after both sons had experienced an on-going lack of 'inclusive' practice in their previous high school mainstream setting these parents decided to try the option of an ESS instead. This decision was based upon the recommendations of other parents of children with disabilities who had found a specific ESS school to be exemplary in the level of care shown to both the students and their families.

The experiences of both families who chose the option of an ESS echoed the experiences of parents in the sub-category *finding fit.* Firstly, both families were welcomed into their respective education support schools by an understanding principal, who made them feel that their children would be a welcome addition to the school. In the case of the single parent, she initially visited the school unexpectedly and was immediately taken on a tour of the school by the principal. In contrast to other enrolment experiences had by this parent, this principal seemed un-phased by the parent's description of her child's difficult behaviour. This principal also subsequently enquired about the parent's access to respite given her understanding of the parent's difficult situation. This is evidenced in the recollections of the mother below:

> (*Name of ESS principal*) came out and introduced herself and asked if I had time to look around. So, nothing was too much trouble. As we were walking, she was asking me questions about Bob (*son on the autism spectrum*) and nothing that I said seemed to phase her which would have stopped everybody else in their tracks. I didn't paint a great picture at all. I just thought I am not going to pretend. He had severe behavioural issues as far as self-harming and those sorts of things … Before I left there she'd had enough of a talk with me to ask me what sort of respite that I had.

Similarly the other mother in this sub-category, who had two boys on the autism spectrum and two other children, commented about the very welcoming nature of the

ESS administration. She indicated that the school was not only concerned about the welfare of her boys on the autism spectrum but was also concerned about the welfare of the rest of the family. This is evidenced in the principal's alarm regarding the mother's consideration of the option of placing her sons in two different education support schools because their learning needs were so different. In response to this, the principal suggested that both boys could have their individual educational needs accommodated at the one school to help the mother with the inevitable transport problems that such a decision would create. The mother explained it in the following way:

> When I mentioned to them about Chris (*elder son on the autism spectrum*), I am thinking about this place for him. Their first reaction was, 'Oh gosh, that is going to be a lot of driving for you because one school was in (*suburb name*) and the other is in (*distant suburb name*)'. They asked me why hadn't I thought of sending *Chris* there? I didn't think they had students like *Chris* there. From what I had heard they were more like Jack (younger son on the autism spectrum) who is verbal and quite different. I was getting to the stage where I wasn't sure having them in the same school was such a great idea after all. So they asked to meet *Chris* and they assured me that yes, we have students who are non-verbal. And, you know, with high sensory … you know … they had all that sort of things there. They just said, 'It is up to you but it would certainly save you a lot of time rushing from one place to another. You will have four children in three different schools, consider it.' So I did take Chris there and you know, he seemed to settle and feel comfortable.

These examples illustrate that the principals were not only concerned about the educational welfare of the students on the autism spectrum but were also concerned about the psychological welfare of the parents caring for them. MacDermott's (2008) investigation into 92 WA families who were parenting school-aged children with a suspected or confirmed ASD diagnosis similarly affirmed that:

> the valuing of the family, and its maintenance as an effective and well-functioning entity, cannot be overstated and must be an integral component of any intervention planning … the needs of the family unit, as a whole, must be taken into account when considering policy development and resource planning at both systems and individual levels (p. 9).

It should also be noted that the level of concern displayed for these families by the two ESS principals sits in direct contrast to the treatment one of the families received at their previous mainstream high school where the parents were forced to remove both sons on the autism spectrum in the middle of the school year.

The unwavering devotion and commitment of the staff was also another aspect found in the ESS experience of both parents resembling another element of the *finding fit* sub-category. After the parent with the two boys on the autism spectrum had been at the ESS for some months this parent commented about the staff's level of devotion in the following way:

> They (*ESS*) are well equipped, but the people, there is just no comparison. They just care, they care, they (*the students*) are all treated equally with dignity and respect. Everybody has a voice there. The staff are very dedicated and the teachers are lovely. I have had two really good teachers already. Chris (*elder son on the autism spectrum*) has got a young teacher, she is fabulous, she has really raised the bar for Chris and he is meeting those expectations. He had a couple of incidents when he got there. I think that he didn't really trust anybody anymore. Chris is a very trusting person and he has a big heart and really good nature. And, I think that he got totally rattled with that whole (*previous mainstream high school*) experience. He didn't trust many people and he wasn't as social. He really held back for a long time. They (*previous mainstream high school staff*) must have broken him in places. They (*ESS staff*) knew they had to be patient with him. And they were, that is what they said to me, 'We are not going to push him at first … We just need to build in him that he can trust us and be comfortable with us'.

This parent indicated that the staff knew that they would need to build trust between the student and themselves after his traumatic time at his former mainstream high school placement. This was based upon a keen understanding of his individual psychological needs at the time. Such understanding was underpinned by an open and trusting relationship between the staff and the parents reminiscent of the relationships described by parents in the *finding fit* sub-category.

The other single parent in this sub-category also found that the staff at the ESS seemed very dedicated, positive and skilled in their dealings with the students in their school as explained by this parent below:

> When I went to (*name of school*) and met (*name of principal*) I was really impressed with her. And the way the staff were as I walked around, there didn't seem to be any falseness. I felt that what you saw was what you got. Sometimes a little bit too chirpy, but then I thought that is the way they deal with them through their day. And I felt that they worked as a team. So I was quite happy once I began and when we began transition last year it went quite smoothly.

This parent further explained that when difficulties inevitably arose during her son's first year at the ESS, the school staff were open and responsive in their dealings with her. To illustrate, the parent indicated that her son had received three terms of transition prior to his arrival at his new school. This proceeded very smoothly but only occurred in the afternoons when mainly optional/recreational subjects were done at the ESS. Unfortunately, the transition program did not give her son any experience of the morning academic program undertaken at the ESS. Hence, when her son eventually arrived at the school the following year he was not expecting the accompanying academic morning program. This parent also detailed how her son was initially placed with staff who had never worked with him during transition in his first year at the ESS school. According to this parent, these two aspects served to unsettle her son who did not respond well to change and this made his initial months at the school more difficult than they needed to be. The parent explained these initial difficulties as follows:

> What surprised me was that they did three terms of transition with Bob (*son on the autism spectrum*) last year so they really put the effort in. But, everything was in the afternoon and when Bob got there this year all work schedules were done in the morning, so Bob had only interpreted (*name of school*) as a fun place to go to because he did swimming, Health Ed., in the Gym, sensory diet, bike ride, all the fun things. None of this - we will have to sit at the table and do any work. And no staff that worked with Bob last year worked with Bob this year, not even on day one. There was no one who knew him and no one that he knew.

This parent further explained that in response to her concerns regarding these difficulties the school reduced her son's level of change and were planning to keep him in the same class group next year:

> … but I just felt that he came home very distressed, lots of biting and it would have been just a lack of communication, and he hated all of the transition, going from one room into another area. I don't think he ever really settled into that in the first semester. They changed the whole program for him. He didn't like the senior program at all … (*name of ESS school*) do take on board the needs of the individual student, she (*his teacher at ESS*) realized that Bob really struggled with a lot of things this year and she has already requested to have him in the same class group again next year, because she felt that this is a very settling-in period for all of them going from year seven to year nine.

This example further illustrates another hallmark of 'inclusive' practice deemed valuable by the parents in the *finding fit* sub-category, where staff display openness and self-awareness regarding their own practices and work in combination with the parent to solve any educational difficulties that arise.

This ability of staff at the ESS to be open and self-aware when dealing with the sometimes, difficult behaviour of the student on the autism spectrum was similarly illustrated in the ESS experiences of the other parent of the two boys on the autism spectrum. In direct contrast to this parent's experiences at their previous mainstream high school, this parent indicated that the staff at the ESS regularly conducted a functional assessment (Myles, 2005; Myles & Adreon, 2001) of her son's behaviour when difficulties arose. They did this to understand the situation from her son's point of view and to respond accordingly. Hence, as research into best practice with such students dictates this ESS school was mindful of the fact that:

> Student behaviors do not occur in isolation, nor are they random. They are associated with a reason or cause. Thus, behaviors are a form of communication.

> Functional assessment is a first step in developing effective interventions based on such behavioral messages (Myles & Adreon, 2001, p. 44).

The mother explained the school's response to her son's behaviour by retelling an exemplary incident in the following way:

> There was one incident in the pool where the other students that were there with Chris *(elder son on the autism spectrum)* were quite noisy, quite vocal and a little bit more boisterous and in the swimming pool, because it is an enclosed pool. Things echo, and he is quite sensitive to sound, too much noise. And he apparently grabbed the swimming teacher by the arm and left a bit of a mark on her arm and I heard about it when I picked him up. You know, it's funny, you all of a sudden go into that mode where you have got to be there to negotiate what is going to happen to your child. Because I really thought, 'Great, don't tell me he is going to be sent home now'. You are still in that way of thinking, because that is how you have been treated. And that is the way it is, you are always there trying to smooth things for the child. I rang the principal and I said that I heard about this. I thought she was just going to say to me, 'Yes, maybe it is better if you keep Chris at home tomorrow', or something like that. So you can imagine my absolute shock and surprise when she said to me, 'You know the swimming teacher came and told me about it, so I know about it', and I thought, 'Oh here it comes', bracing myself for it. She said, 'That yes, she thought that it was all her fault because she really doesn't know Chris well enough and it is very noisy in there and she could see that he just can't handle the noise. She felt that she wasn't properly responsive and perhaps what might benefit Chris is maybe some one-on-one lessons, just until he gets used to the group'. I could hear all of that coming out and it wasn't what I was expecting I guess. I said 'Oh', I didn't even know how to respond straight away because I wasn't expecting that response.

As evidenced in the principal's comments in the above example, the teacher involved provided a functional assessment of the situation and hypothesized that the behaviour exhibited by the student on the autism spectrum was a form of communication indicating that he was experiencing an auditory sensory overload in the swimming pool environment. The teacher was mindful of her part in the situation and decided to implement an intervention plan designed to reduce the sensory load on this student by having one-to-one swimming lessons to reduce the noise in that environment. This situation illustrates the openness of the staff to examine their own practices and to understand that a non-verbal student's behaviour is a legitimate form of communication regarding how they are experiencing the world around them.

Another hallmark of best practice nominated by parents in both the sub-categories of *finding fit* and *supplementing* was the ability of the staff at the ESS to imbed supplementary interventions for their child on the autism spectrum within the school educational program. Both parents indicated that supplementary programs being implemented at home were being supported in their ESS classrooms in order to generalize the skills across environments. Research (National Research Council, 2001; Wong, Kasari, Freeman, & Paparella, 2007) has shown that generalizing, or the ability to transfer learning across multiple settings and persons, is a skill that many students on the autism spectrum find difficult.

To illustrate, the single parent in this sub-category found that staff within the ESS classroom supported her efforts with a supplementary speech therapy program. She described their efforts to support her home program in the following way:

> They are still using a schedule for Bob *(son on the autism spectrum)*. What I am doing at home, they just can't do that solely. I am working on very basic results, like I want Bob *(son on the autism spectrum)* to come when I call him, so whilst they are using those words in the classroom he's still following a schedule. He still has a little carry bag that carries his cards, so he is still getting PECS *(Picture Exchange Communication System*), but anything that I do, like I have asked them to use the word 'Open' for everything like 'Open the lunch box, open the fridge door, open the door, open your school bag'. Anything that you get the opportunity to use the word 'Open', please do. They are following it up.

This parent was also intending gaining the ESS's support for a future home-based supplementary toilet training program and was reasonably confident that the staff would help her generalize her son's toileting behaviour over both the home and school environments.

Similarly, the other parent of two boys on the autism spectrum indicated that she was helped by the ESS in her quest to get one of her sons to use an alternative electronic communication device, the MiniMo. This device is designed to allow its users the opportunity for functional social communication rather than just an expression of basic wants and needs. The parent explained that her non-verbal elder son had previously been involved with many different communication systems/ languages (COMPIC, Picture Exchange Communication System [PECS], Auslan) over the years but these were only partially successful for various reasons. The parent explained the benefits of the MiniMo over other communication systems in the following way:

> … well, that (*the MiniMo*) is his bridge to the outside world because not everybody knows sign or understands sign language because he does make himself understood quite clearly through that. But now, he can move further on and he is able to express himself through that (*the MiniMo*). Anybody can understand that.

She asked the school to help generalize the use of the MiniMo across both home and school environments. She explained the ESS's support with the MiniMo in the following terms:

> And it is not all going to rest on my shoulders. It is going to have a bit more support. And they (*the ESS staff*) are so excited about the MiniMo, and that is another thing. They are so excited and they are pushing it, expecting him to use it, wanting him to use it, 'Use your MiniMo Chris'.

This sits in direct contrast to the lack of ability and willingness of the previous mainstream high school environment to attempt to support such intervention initiatives. The parent explained the difference in the following way:

> It was funny because the therapist gave me some forms to record when you use it *(the MiniMo)*. It was funny because I was thinking it but I didn't say it, this is good because if the school (*previous mainstream high school*) is not using it there won't be much recorded on it. And they didn't, they weren't even willing to try. It was too hard.

According to this parent, the previous mainstream high school environment did not have the culture, staff training, commitment or educational program to support the implementing of supplementary interventions appropriately across environments as recommended in ASD best educational practice.

To recap, parents in this sub-category, *segregating*, eventually sought educational fit *(seeking progressive fit)* for their child when they were compelled to remove them from mainstream education and place them in an education support school. The experiences of the parents in this sub-category echo some of the experiences of parents in the *finding fit* sub-category, where parents experienced the process of a genuine welcome into the school followed by an unwavering devotion and commitment from the staff toward the education and welfare of the child on the autism spectrum. Overall, both sets of parents found their experience of segregated schooling to be very positive because they had confidence that the team approach generated between staff and parents would maximize the progress of their child on the autism spectrum.

CHAPTER 8

STAGE FOUR – FRAMING FUTURES

Chapter Eight concludes the development of the theory generated from the central research question 'How do parents deal with the education of their children with an ASD over time?' It explains the fourth stage of the theory (*Framing Futures*) where parents seek to transition *(transitioning)* their children on the autism spectrum from formal schooling to work or study. It also details the process undertaken by these parents to redress the problematic imbalance *(redressing the imbalance)* of attention afforded the child on the autism spectrum continually operating in their families' lives.

In the final years of the formal schooling process, parents' thoughts often turned to *seeking progressive fit* for their child within the oncoming adult world. This influenced educational decisions and sent parents' minds down future planning tracks. Previous experiences, educational and otherwise, indicated to parents that *transitioning* their child on the autism spectrum into the adult world would not be an easy quest. However, parents had gradually learned multiple strategies over time that helped them *seek, gain, maintain* and *create progressive fit* for their child. They had also become acutely aware of the discrimination and difficulties that potentially faced their family and their child into the future. Sub-stage one, *transitioning*, explains the experiences of parents in the study who sought *progressive fit* for their child in both tertiary education and the external working world at the conclusion of the formal schooling process.

With the increasing age of their child on the autism spectrum, some parents' thoughts and actions were no longer as fixated upon maximizing their child's education potential but gradually expanded to incorporate the quality of the other lives within the family. This then started a renewed quest where some parents resolved to continue the process of *seeking progressive fit* for their child on the autism spectrum without such intense involvement from themselves. These parents knew that with their own increasing age they would eventually be unable to personally *seek, find, maintain* and *create progressive fit* for their adult offspring on the autism spectrum over time. Others, internal and external to the family, would need to become increasingly involved to take on this trusted quest on their behalf depending upon the educational progress and independence gained by their child. Some parents in the study realized earlier than others that unless the family could survive intact the chances of maintaining the best quality of life for their child on the autism spectrum over their entire lifetime would be diminished. This knowledge loomed large in their *framing* of the *future* for those parenting a child on the autism

spectrum. Such parental experiences are explained in sub-stage two, *redressing the imbalance.*

SUB-STAGE ONE: TRANSITIONING

In the final years of the secondary formal schooling process, parents' thoughts turned to *seeking progressive fit* for their child in the oncoming adult world. This influenced educational decisions and sent parents' minds down future planning tracks. Parents' thoughts were no longer absorbed in just the gaining of academic and life skills for their child on the autism spectrum but now incorporated a transition toward how these skills would be utilized in the adult world. Research indicates that the difficulties associated with a child's autism can be greatest in adolescence and young adulthood where individuals must negotiate such areas as completing school, finding work, developing a social network, contributing to a household and participating in a community (Kim et al., 2000; Jennes-Coussens et al., 2006; Tantam, 2000). It is during this transition time that these individuals can suffer more seriously from problems of anxiety and depression (Kim et al., 2000).

At the completion of the study, four of the six families still had their children on the autism spectrum at different points in the formal schooling process and had not experienced transition to work or tertiary education. Only two of the families in the study found in the sub-category *home schooling* experienced this type of transition during the study. They did this by seeking and gaining specific Tertiary and Further Education (TAFE) courses for their children, both during and external to their formal secondary schooling. This allowed these parents to secure a targeted work situation for their offspring in the adult world. However, it is important to note that to achieve this both sets of parents had to, once again, be the driving force behind *seeking, gaining maintaining* and *creating fit* for their child on the autism spectrum in the oncoming external adult world.

As previously noted, one of the families in the sub-category of *home schooling* was eventually able to set up a TAFE school-based traineeship in Library Studies (Certificate II) for their son through their Structured Workplace Learning (SWL) course. This occurred during the final years of their son's formal schooling at Schools of Isolated and Distance Education (SIDE). Unfortunately, the parents involved in this situation reported that it was up to the student and their family to secure a work experience placement in a suitable environment for work experience to take place. According to one of the parents in this family, this was no easy matter as students with disabilities are not necessarily welcomed easily into the working world, especially if they are on the autism spectrum.

Research confirms that finding a job placement for individuals on the spectrum is often extremely difficult (Aspect, 2012; Howlin & Moss, 2012;). The parents therefore, contacted their local Autism Association for help with this matter only to be told that support was only available for adults on the autism spectrum who were looking for part-time work (over eight hours) or full-time work, but not work

experience. Research indicates that work experience is considered an essential step for some individuals on the autism spectrum in preparing them for more permanent paid work (Mawhood & Howlin, 1999). The parents also found that there was a significant waiting list for use of such restricted services.

According to the mother in this family, she was, once again, left to her own devices to make successive overtures to their local council to see if a small amount of work experience could be secured for her son. The parents knew that the council had a universal access and equity policy that supported the rights and inclusion of the disabled and were hoping this would allow them a greater chance to gain a work experience placement for their son. The mother recounted how she even became a community member of the council's Universal Access Advisory Group to ensure a firm understanding of the council's policies that could potentially be used to help her son's circumstances. As evidenced in the comments of this parent the initial placement took over a year to secure and had to be handled very carefully to ensure its success:

> Work experience at the (*name of library*) is the closest situation to work that Kim (*son on the autism spectrum*) has experienced. Transition to this was handled very carefully and took much time. The actual placement took over a year to secure. We learned from our high school experiences with Kim that he needed to have more support in certain circumstances than others. So we were cautious about where he should be placed and what he should do when he was there.

As it turned out, the initial work experience placement did not occur where the parents had originally intended. Through a process of open communication and compromise between the involved parties the placement did eventually go ahead but, in a different area of the council than was first intended, as indicated in the parent's comments below:

> The council was hesitant about allowing him to work in an area that we had initially requested. We had requested a placement in their Planning Department with the idea that Kim would be able to gain some experience in the Geographic Information Systems area. This was a possible future study area for Kim. As it turned out, they finally advised us that they could only give Kim a placement in the library but not in the Planning Department. They explained that the Planning Department was quite a busy and sometimes, stressful work environment and may be difficult as a first work experience placement. So Kim ended up in the library which has been a wonderful placement.

According to this parent, to ensure the placement's success it was important that co-workers in the library environment felt supported when difficulties inevitably arose. In this regard, the student on the autism spectrum and the staff at the library were well supported by the parents, the staff at SIDE, and to a lesser degree, an accredited government-subsidized intervention provider as evidenced below:

> He was able to be supported by us, SIDE and (*name of an accredited government-subsidized intervention provider*), to a lesser degree, who oversaw his placement and ensured that if any difficulties arose they could be dealt with appropriately. We found that if the staff felt supported they were much more likely to want to have someone like Kim to work with them. One of the library staff was allocated to be a mentor to Kim during his working time. We decided to keep his working hours quite low initially so that he would not be overwhelmed. Good communication and appropriate levels of support have been the keys to a successful placement for my son.

This mother also provided the head librarian with a copy of a book titled *Developing Talents* (Grandin & Duffy, 2004) to provide autism specific information regarding possible ways to support her son in the workplace. Once again, the strategy of 'supporting the supporters' as detailed earlier in the sub-category of *waxing and waning*, was used by these parents in their quest to secure a successful work experience placement for their son.

After the successful completion of work experience this parent then detailed how her son went on to do a school-based traineeship (Certificate II in Library Studies) through SIDE, TAFE and the council library during the final years of his formal schooling. According to this parent, this was only possible because of the groundwork that had been done during the work experience period. General disability research (Trach & Rusch, 1989; Wehman & Kregel, 1985) and specific ASD research (Hagner & Cooney, 2005, Mawhood & Howlin, 1999; Hurbutt & Chalmers, 2004; Keel, Mesibov, & Woods, 1997) confirms that students with disabilities transition more successfully to work when they receive appropriate support in the form of careful job placement, prior job training, mentoring, advocacy, follow-up monitoring and long-term support to ensure job retention. The parents, the council and SIDE also subsequently raised the profile of the student by nominating him for numerous awards during his traineeship. As will be recalled from the sub-category of *home schooling*, this student eventually won a council, regional and national award for his traineeship work at the library.

On the back of such successful work experiences this same student has since successfully completed a number of media, computer game and engineering mainstream TAFE courses. To enhance her son's chance of success at TAFE, this mother indicated that she contacted the campus Disability Officer for support so that her son would have access to any accommodations if he needed them. With her son's permission, she also disclosed her son's diagnosis and idiosyncratic learning needs to his lecturers and provided contact details if difficulties arose. Her son was also able to supplement his income by gaining some casual work at the library where he had previously worked during this time. It is significant to note that even though the student on the autism spectrum had an inordinate amount of difficulty *seeking, gaining* and *maintaining fit* within a mainstream high school environment (both public and private), he was still able to transition successfully from home education to mainstream employment and a mainstream TAFE environment when the conditions were supported appropriately. This was accomplished with the help of his parents, the council, SIDE and TAFE who provided this student with many successful learning experiences in his secondary and tertiary schooling years. It is also important to register the relentless nature of parental advocacy that was needed over time to ensure that such a situation succeeded for the student on the autism spectrum. Preliminary research into support services for such students in higher education indicates that there are an increasing number of individuals on the autism spectrum entering tertiary education (Aspect, 2012; Smith, 2007). While some limited support is available through student services, it is often generic in nature and not ASD specific or tailored to the individual needs of the student. The research also highlights the need for ASD specific education to help faculty members understand how best to succeed with a student with an ASD (Aspect, 2012; Smith, 2007).

The other parent in the sub-category, *home schooling*, whose son on the autism spectrum also transitioned from SIDE to the external world, similarly had to continue to strategize solutions *(Strategizing Solutions)* on behalf of her son at this time. Her son also took a meandering pathway from SIDE to employment and further study at TAFE. Initially, her son left SIDE at the age of 16. The mother contacted the local Autism Association and was given a place for her son in a segregated work environment with other adults on the autism spectrum. However, her son was not happy in this situation and the parent subsequently investigated enrolling her son in a TAFE course to improve his employability elsewhere. She eventually enrolled him in a TAFE Certificate I Retail Operations Course especially designed for students with disabilities. The students in the course were given the opportunity to learn all of the necessary skills to succeed in such an environment, as evidenced by the comments of the parent concerned:

> They *(the students)* look at the computer spread-sheets and things that are available on the computer. They have got part of the room set up as a little shop with a cash register so they practice the cash register, stacking the shelves, and dealing with customers and telephoning. You have got to take responsibility for making the phone calls if you can't come into work that day. And they practised phone calls.

The parent then tried to enlist some external help to gain work for her son. She contacted a private employment provider specializing in gaining and overseeing work for people with disabilities in order to secure appropriate employment. Unfortunately, the support worker initially assigned to her son advised her and her son to withhold details of his diagnosis so that he would supposedly have a greater chance of being employed. The mother questioned the wisdom of this because she felt that there would need to be understanding and accommodation in the work place and this would not come by withholding information about her son. She explained her thinking in the following way:

> I have found in the past that people are happier when they know what they are dealing with in terms of Asperger's, because not everyone knows what it is, it is a lot more widely known now than it was ten years ago. My understanding is that people are happier when they have got some information about something. It means they can make better decisions.

She therefore decided to forgo this advice and approach a closely situated, large supermarket chain-store herself on behalf of her son, and state his diagnosis and situation up front. Research indicates that generic employment services designed to assist people with disabilities to find work often do not necessarily meet the needs of clients on the autism spectrum (Mawhood & Howlin, 1999). Hence, this parent intuitively bridged the gap herself by using the pre-learned strategies of educating others and advocating on behalf of her son's needs to try to gain employment for him. She fortunately received a very positive response and was told that a small number of other employees at the store also had an ASD diagnosis and were successfully employed there. The mother explained her role in the process of gaining employment for her son in the following way:

> I still think in the end we are the person who knows our child best and it is probably going to be down to us to get them that proper setting which will mean that they are successful in the workplace. I could put him into somewhere or he could be given a job at (name of chain store) but he mightn't succeed if it is not the right setting for him.

With her advocacy, her son was able to be successfully employed at this same work place for over a year before management changed and understanding of her son's unusual profile diminished. The mother indicated that she felt she would be continually involved in the process of *seeking, gaining,* and *maintaining fit* in the mainstream working world for her son over his adult life. When asked about her level of involvement with the overall process she replied in the following way:

> … continually, I think continually at this stage, by helping find a job and helping find it in a place that will suit his ability and then helping the people who employ him make the most of what he can do.

Research confirms the value of providing such a high level of support for individuals on the autism spectrum in relation to them seeking, finding and maintaining employment (Hagner & Cooney, 2005; Hurbutt & Chalmers, 2004; Keel et al., 1997; Mawhood & Howlin, 1999).

The final experiences of these parents during their offsprings' transition period to both work and tertiary study indicate that *seeking, gaining* and *maintaining fit* for their child with an ASD in the adult world may be an on-going quest. The process undertaken by parents in this sub-stage is similar in nature to the quest undertaken during the educational journey. Both sets of parents could not just rely on external services to support their child's transition process to either tertiary study or a suitable work situation. Parents had to, once again, be the driving force behind the successful transition of their children with an ASD from schooling to tertiary study or work in the external adult world.

SUB-STAGE TWO: REDRESSING THE IMBALANCE

With the increasing age of their child on the autism spectrum, some parents in the study indicated that their thoughts and actions were no longer as fixated upon just maximizing their child's educational potential but incorporated a movement to be more cognizant of the quality of all lives being lived within the family. Parents gradually came to the realization that with their own increasing age they would eventually be unable to personally *seek, gain, maintain* and *create progressive fit* over the full lifetime of their child on the autism spectrum. Others, internal and external to the family, would have to be increasingly involved to take on this trusted quest on their behalf depending upon the educational progress and independence gained by their child on the autism spectrum. Some parents in the study realized earlier than others that unless the family could survive intact the chances of maintaining the best quality of life for their child on the autism spectrum over their entire lifetime would be diminished.

In an online study of 1,652 parents of children on the autism spectrum, 80% were found to be extremely or very concerned about the future independence of their children as an adult, as compared to 32% of other typical parents (Harris Interactive, 2008). This knowledge looms large in the framing of the future *(Framing Futures)* for those parenting their children on the autism spectrum. This second sub-stage, *redressing the imbalance,* seeks to explain this parent experience.

As evidenced in the often arduous, educational journeys undertaken by all the parents in this study, the quest of *seeking progressive fit* for their child on the autism spectrum has involved an on-going use of multiple strategies *(Strategizing Solutions)* over time. Parents have used various strategies to increase 'fit' for their child during their respective educational journeys. The use of both problem focused and emotion focused strategies was also borne out by Gray (1994, 2002b, 2006) in Australian longitudinal research that examined how parents of children on the autism spectrum coped over time. General studies on family coping and disability also indicate that success in coping is a long-term process that is linked to a gradual accumulation of skills by family members over time and often a changed perspective on their situation (Berry & Hardman, 1998).

Similarly, parents in this study learned to strategize solutions *(Strategizing Solutions)* continually over time to combat the often relentless, difficulties associated with educating their children on the autism spectrum. The study also revealed that while there was an *increased awareness and confidence* in the parents there was also simultaneously *variable negative feelings* occurring and this tension operated throughout the educational journey. Parents became increasingly aware of the potential discrimination and ignorance that often faced their child on the autism spectrum when trying to gain an appropriate education for them. This on-going tension experienced by parents has been previously revealed in the summary findings of MacDermott (2008) who captured the experiences of 92 West Australian families who were parenting school-aged children with a suspected or confirmed ASD diagnosis:

> Of all the issues that families must address during their child's school-aged years, their relationship with the educational system that their child participates in is of primary importance. Unfortunately, this relationship is frequently characterised by frustration, confusion and conflict, and is described by some families as encountering a "systemic brick wall". Parents routinely feel alienated and excluded from the very environment in which their child spends a majority of each week day. In addition, they feel that their specific and unique knowledge of their child's strengths, needs and challenges are dismissed as unimportant and irrelevant within the school setting. Too often this results in compromised learning for the child; unnecessary conflict and wasted opportunities for collaboration between the parents and the school staff, at the expense of both parties; and increased stress for both the child and their whole family, further adding to the daily challenge of living with ASD (p.84).

Parents learned through a layering of difficult experiences, educational or otherwise, that they must continually advocate on behalf of their child on the autism spectrum in order to combat the potential discrimination and ignorance that they and their child regularly faced in order to maximize the progress of their child. Four of the six parents in the study (McDonald, 2010) outlined in this publication expressed similar sentiments when dealing with the educational journey of their child on the autism spectrum as evidenced below:

> When they are young it is such a hard life that you have with them but they're the times when they really need you to be their advocate and be prepared to step up and say that is not going to be good enough - we have to do this. You just have to find the strength and do it for them because they really are quite voiceless. You have to be the sort of person who can be a voice for your child.
>
> It is a constant battle because you have to keep pushing for it - that is where the battle is. The children fulfil whatever they have to do quite well. It is just getting the powers that be to support you in your need to support your children. That is the energy that I am talking about. You need energy to do that, because it is not going to be handed to you. It has to be gone through different chains of power or whatever they may be. Then you have got to get meetings happening and all this sort of stuff and unless you are behind it they just put you … you have to stress the importance of it and sometimes I do elaborate on the need … why it is so important to me.
>
> If the world was geared to the needs of my son then we would have been able to use a sympathetic and capable system. I do not believe that such a thing exists although there have been some improvements over time. You just have

to develop better options and make changes when things are not progressing the way they need to be for your child. The biggest mistake is not taking action in a situation when your child is at risk or their needs are not being met, physically, emotionally and educationally.

Advocacy is the most important skill that I have to offer my son. Without it, my son's life chances would reduce considerably. Without someone at the helm to negotiate a pathway through life for him he would be reduced to a life dominated by his deficits. With advocacy, he can be given opportunities to enter the world and maximize his development and thereby create a better independent future for himself.

Parents' constant need to advocate often translated into an unrelenting involvement with issues, educational or otherwise, associated with their child on the autism spectrum. However, such a movement, as previously noted in the study, was fraught with a dangerous imbalance with regard to addressing the needs of others in the family, including themselves. Most parents in the study indicated that they had sought psychological and psychiatric support for themselves and others in the family over the course of the life of their child on the autism spectrum. Research indicates that parents, especially mothers, of children on the autism spectrum are more likely to experience serious psychological distress, including depression and anxiety, than parents of children with other developmental disabilities (Bromley et al., 2004; Grayson, 2004; Schieve et al., 2007). This study further indicates the high degree of stress parents often experience when dealing with educational issues associated with their child on the autism spectrum over time.

Some families in the study realized earlier than others that this increased stress and imbalance of attention afforded to the child on the autism spectrum could potentially be damaging to the overall health and longevity of the family unit. One of the mothers in the study decided to redress this life imbalance *(redressing the imbalance)* relatively early in the life of her son on the autism spectrum when another child was subsequently born into the family. She realized, earlier than others in the study, that other family members also had a right to a life that afforded them some quality attention and time. She, therefore, tried to construct a more equitable life for all family members by gradually reducing her own inordinate educational and care commitments in relation to her son on the spectrum by enlisting external support. She explained it in the following way:

I also had to take into account that when Bill *(son on the autism spectrum)* was in Year 4 I had a new-born baby, I also had my other son in Year 1. We still did home programs but I stopped doing as much running around at the end of Bill's third year at primary school simply because life had to get back to normal to some degree. We did take Bill out of school to do additional work at home but also for a while there was a centre in Perth where we took him so we would miss two afternoons a week. So not only in the school day was he

> receiving school time he was also receiving other educational input. But once Jill (*younger sister*) was born and Michael (*younger brother*) started Year 1 we were no longer in a position to be just pulling him out and taking him here, there and everywhere.

This same mother also decided to import regular respite for her family's situation by involving her mother. The grandmother provided frequent weekend respite for her grandson on the autism spectrum so that other family members could have some time to have their own individual wants and needs addressed. The son on the autism spectrum was encouraged by his grandmother to engage in areas of high interest when he was with her. This allowed the other members of the family to redress the on-going imbalance *(redressing the imbalance)* in their lives and gain valuable time and attention for each other and those outside the family. The mother in this family explained how the process of weekend respite worked for her son on the autism spectrum in the following way:

> Well, often we do not have Bill *(son on the autism spectrum)* here on the weekends because over the last twelve months my mum has totally taken Bill's emotional and academic well-being under her wing. She is wanting to put every bit of input she possibly can into him. She is thinking about the fact that he loves transport, what can she do? She often has him sleep on the weekend and they'll visit airports and truck yards. This is what they do every weekend which is just great, and I just wouldn't have the time to do it. Plus, I wouldn't be able to do it with the other two. They wouldn't be happy to just be sitting in the car while we did do it. Bill and I are very lucky that we are in that situation now. It is not the answer to all of our problems but it certainly helps to fill a gap at the moment because Bill tends to get bored on the weekends. He doesn't have friends. Even if I organized to have a friend over he wouldn't necessarily hang around with them or talk to them. His interests are very much based around transport which is not necessarily the same as other kids or other people.

This same mother further explained how this helped decrease the social isolation of the rest of the family and allowed them to gain some valuable attention, time and emotional energy for themselves and each other:

> What it also means is that they (*the other siblings*) can have a friend over to play without the friend asking what is wrong with your brother? Why is your brother doing that? My daughter's little friends who have never probably experienced having a child humming and making funny noises, and asking questions which don't sound like questions other people would ask … having to ask her what is going on. I also sometimes wonder whether some people may not particularly want their little girls over here to sleep over or whatever if my daughter's autistic brother is here. Not that Bill is like that, it is just the whole mystery of autism, I guess. People just do not understand that really

> he would leave them alone more than the average brother. Bill is very much socially aloof and he has no interest in befriending my daughter's friends. He is probably the safest big brother you could have any little child with, but people are scared of the unknown.

Two other families in the study were similarly able to gradually redress the imbalance *(redressing the imbalance)* in their families' lives through the relatively large improvement in skills and independence gradually attained by their children on the autism spectrum throughout the education process. These older children in both families found in the sub-category *home schooling* were able to involve themselves relatively successfully in both tertiary education and mainstream work at the end of their formal schooling. This was due in part to the many years of involvement and intervention undertaken by these parents to maximize the educational progress of their children. These parents were then able to reclaim some time and energy for other family members and themselves at the end of the formal schooling process because of the increased independence and competence of their children on the autism spectrum. In relation to this, one mother has taken up full time study and the other mother has been able to regain some part-time work. One of these mothers indicated how her life had changed in the following way:

> My involvement has changed and the reason is because he *(son on the autism spectrum)* is now in the work force, he does not want to follow any further education and he has got very strong instincts about wanting to be independent. So my overall involvement has declined and I don't have to worry about him ringing me. If things go wrong he is actually able to fix things himself. For example, when he got the bus to work, if the bus doesn't come for some reason or another, as sometimes it might not, you need to stay where you are and ring for a taxi. Now the first time he didn't want to do that and he walked all the way home and rang from here. So I told him why that was a really bad idea. And the second time that it happened he was quite happy to ring a taxi and I gave him a script as to what to say.

However, even these families whose children have seemingly gained the most skill and independence over time still felt the ever-present pressure to ensure that their offspring would cope as independently as possible when they were no longer there to support them in later years. One of the parents expressed the following regarding this ever-present pressure:

> So having him being able to cope independently as an adult is a huge thing especially after my husband left home when Paul *(son on the autism spectrum)* was twelve because being a single parent, I had to be easy in my own mind that he could cope to a certain extent. Now I know it is hard for anyone to cope with being on their own, but to know that he will be able to look after himself physically and get his washing and ironing done and know how to shop and cook are just as important as holding down a job. You can't really hold down

> a job and get yourself dressed and out the door with food. It is all part and parcel of the same thing. Yes, that is what we are still doing. We are now on the life skills, trying to negotiate the banks and making phone calls, shopping for healthy food and cooking.

The study revealed that the educational outcome for each child on the autism spectrum would be different because of the idiosyncratic nature and progress of the condition. Not all families in the study were able to rely on the idea that their children would eventually realize a higher level of independence. One of the families in the study who had two children on the autism spectrum had been struggling for years to gain an acceptable education, level of respite, support and accommodation for their situation within WA. This family eventually decided to *redress the imbalance* in their lives themselves by moving to an Asian country where they have since been able to access a more lucrative work situation for the breadwinner in the family. This has allowed the family to enlist much greater external support for their situation at a much lower cost than would ever occur in Australia. The parents have reported that this move has allowed all family members to have an increase in the time and attention for each other and improved the overall well-being of the whole family unit.

By contrast, the single, most vulnerable parent in the study has been the least able to *redress the imbalance* in her life because of the lack of development attained by her son on the autism spectrum over time and her reduced financial circumstances. As previously noted in the categories *settling* and *supplementing,* this parent was the least able to provide appropriate and timely intervention and advocate on behalf of her son's education because of her family's reduced circumstances. At the conclusion of the study (McDonald, 2010), her son had very limited communication skills, was self-injurious and was still not toilet trained. The majority of respite available to this mother's situation was through the goodwill of family members and friends. She has been reluctant to use external agencies to care for her son because of his severe behavioural difficulties and the cost of such services. Hence, she has been the least able to find an appropriate balance for herself and her immediate family.

Additionally, most parents in the study indicated that their marriages and family relationships were under constant pressure. Two marriages of parents in the study had already broken down over the course of the life of their child on the autism spectrum. Different parents in the study also reported that adult siblings of the child on the autism spectrum had limited or no involvement in the lives of their immediate family. Parents reported that some of these siblings had issues of their own which were unable to be appropriately addressed in a timely fashion because of the imbalance of attention *(redressing the imbalance)* afforded them over time. As one of the parents involved in the study noted:

> If the medical and education systems were vastly improved it would take a huge amount of pressure off the families and then they could get to what they need to get to as early as possible and the child would have the greatest chance of improvement and then the family would have the greatest chance of survival.

MacDermott's (2008) investigation into 92 WA families who were parenting school-aged children with a suspected or confirmed ASD diagnosis similarly affirmed the value of balance in the 'whole family system' when she stated that:

> It is not possible, therefore, to plan effectively to meet the needs of the child with an ASD without also taking into account the needs of their whole family system. This requires both individual and systemic service provider responses that address the information, support, developmental, relationship, educational, respite and financial factors that may operate differentially within each individual family unit (p. 8).

Further to these comments, MacDermott (2008) also recommended that:

> the valuing of the family, and its maintenance as an effective and well-functioning entity, cannot be overstated and must be an integral component of any intervention planning; the needs of the family unit, as a whole, must be taken into account when considering policy development and resource planning at both systems and individual levels (p. 9).

The value of such 'family saving' strategies is borne out in coping research done with parents of disabled children in general, and coping research done with parents of children on the autism spectrum. In a grounded theory study examining how parents cope with their physically and/or intellectually disabled children, it was found that:

> To cope, the family uses its existing resources and strategies. These coping strategies are defined as the active processes and behaviours that the family actually try to employ to help to manage, adapt to or deal with a stressful situation. Coping entails constantly changing cognitive and behavioural efforts to manage specific external and/or internal demands that are appraised as taxing the family's resources (Lazarus & Folkman, 1984; McCubbin & Patterson, 1983; Patterson, 1988) … The aim of familial coping procedures is to maintain or restore the balance between the demands and resources (Patterson, 1988). The family can do this by reducing the number or intensity of the demands applied to it.… It can also strengthen its existing resources … may also involve a cognitive appraisal aiming to alter the meanings applied to the situation (Taanila et al., 2002, p. 74).

Specific research investigating the health and social care needs of family carers supporting adults with an ASD similarly indicates that there is a "need to develop more Autism-friendly options both for short breaks and for long-term alternatives to the family home" and there is a general call "for both an increase in levels of provision and more options for flexibly meeting the needs for respite of the adults with ASD's and their family carers" (Hare, Pratt, Burton, Bromley, & Emerson, 2004, p. 441). Similarly, Howlin (1998) has previously stated that there is:

> a need to ensure that the family's needs in other areas are appropriately addressed. Respite care, on a planned and regular basis, can offer parents the

> rest they often so badly need, provide them with the opportunity to spend time with their other children, and give the child with Autism the chance to spend time away from home (p. 317).

To summarize, as the schooling process progressed there was a movement in the thinking of some parents in the study (McDonald, 2010) from mainly focusing upon maximizing the educational potential of their child on the autism spectrum to one which incorporated the quality of life experienced by all members of the family. Some parents in the study realized earlier than others that unless the family could survive intact the chances of maintaining the best quality of life for their child on the autism spectrum over their entire lifetime would be diminished. These parents were able to redress the imbalance *(redressing the imbalance)* of attention afforded to their child by gradually reducing their involvement and importing external support and respite. Other parents were similarly able to redress the imbalance *(redressing the imbalance)* in their lives by reaping the benefits of their child's increased competence and independence. Still others were limited in their ability to redress the constant imbalance in their lives because of their reduced circumstances and the lack of progress achieved by the child on the autism spectrum. In all circumstances, improved services, both educational and otherwise, were nominated by parents to be imperative to help families maintain a healthy balance for all family members throughout the life journey of their child on the autism spectrum.

CHAPTER 9

CONCLUSION

There are an ever increasing number of families who have a child on the autism spectrum in Australia who need appropriate educational services to maximize the potential of their children (Buckley, 2009, 2012). Research into appropriate educational choices for these children is complicated by the heterogeneity and individual progress of the condition and the accompanying comorbid conditions that may also present along with an autism spectrum diagnosis (Fombonne, 2003; Gillberg & Billstedt, 2000).

It is increasingly evident that there is no single best-suited and universally effective educational method for all children on the autism spectrum over time. Research has found that the best programs are those that incorporate a variety of objectively verified practices and are designed to address and support the needs of individual students and the professionals and families with whom they are linked (National Research Council, 2001; Olley, 1999; Parsons et al., 2011; Simpson, 2005, 2007; Simpson et al., 2003). Research concerning inclusion of students on the autism spectrum in mainstream schooling indicates that some students on the autism spectrum may benefit from fully 'inclusive', partly/fully segregated or home education programs depending upon their individual profile, development and the educational context they must negotiate with or without appropriate support and accommodation (Harrington et al., 2013; Humphrey & Lewis 2008a/b; Humphrey & Symes, 2010; Jordan, 2005; Kidd & Kaczmarek, 2010; MacDermott, 2008; McDonald, 2010; McDonald & Lopes, 2012; Parsons et al., 2011; Parsons & Lewis, 2010; Ravet, 2011; Shaddock, 2003, 2005; Simpson, 2005).

There is a limited amount of comprehensive research investigating educational provision for older students on the autism spectrum (Aspect, 2012; Jenkins, 2005; Knott & Taylor, 2013; Myles, 2005; Myles & Adreon, 2001; Parsons et al., 2011; Shaddock, 2003, 2005; Shaddock et al., 2007; Wolf, Brown & Bork, 2009). Preliminary research into higher education indicates that there are an increasing number of individuals on the autism spectrum entering tertiary education (Aspect, 2012; Smith, 2007; VanBergeijk et al., 2008). While some limited support is available through student services, it is often generic in nature and not autism specific or tailored to the individual needs of the student (Aspect, 2012; Smith, 2007, Wolf, Brown & Bork, 2009) although this situation is gradually improving at some tertiary institutions (Hastwell et al., 2013).

In terms of how parents deal with the situation of educating their child on the autism spectrum, research confirms that parents serve a key role in providing effective educational intervention strategies for their children on the autism spectrum (Feinberg & Vacca, 2000; Kidd & Kaczmarek, 2010; Lord & McGee, 2001; MacDermott, 2008; McDonald, 2010; McDonald & Lopes, 2012; Parsons & Lewis, 2010; Roberts & Prior, 2006). Parents are often a constant in the lives of their children throughout their lifetime and as such have the ability to provide a rich and on-going account of what works best for their child when engaging with education professionals (Ferraro, 2008; MacDermott, 2008; McDonald, 2010; O'Brien & Daggett, 2006).

Unfortunately, many parents have historically been seen as peripheral to their child's education and treatment and in some cases have been viewed as obstacles or even adversaries by teaching professionals (Hardman et al., 1995; MacDermott, 2008; McDonald, 2010; Turnbull & Turnbull, 2001). Parental involvement in the educative process is supported throughout the research literature but engagement with parents is often lacking throughout schooling communities (Ferraro, 2008; Stoner & Angell, 2006). For many years, regular schools in Australia have been encouraged to engage parents in active communication, however, such interactions do not typically occur as state policy directives require (MacDermott, 2008; McDonald 2010; Stanley et al., 2005).

While the field of research investigating the autism spectrum has grown exponentially, our understanding of how parents deal with the elongated education process from a parental perspective is an area somewhat neglected in the research. There has been a call in the research literature to provide alternative research methodologies to answer different questions in regard to education of an individual on the autism spectrum (Horner et al., 2005; Simpson, 2005). The preferred source of such information is at the local level where individuals on the autism spectrum, parents and professionals who possess the most 'authentic' knowledge can be found (Simpson, 2005; Slee, 1996). The study (McDonald, 2010) reported in this publication has attempted in a preliminary way to address this gap in the research by capturing the elongated and complicated social process often undertaken by parents when they deal with education of their child on the autism spectrum over time (McDonald, 2010).

THEORY OVERVIEW

The research aim of the study (McDonald, 2010) was to generate substantive theory about how a small number of WA parents in the Perth metropolitan area dealt with the education of their child on the autism spectrum over time. The central proposition of the theory was that parents move through a series of four stages when they try to deal with the education of their child and in doing so, they continually *seek progressive fit* for their child both within the family and the external context. Parents recognize very early on in their children's lives that the external context is not necessarily welcoming, accommodating or supportive of such different children. In response, parents set about gaining an appropriate education *(seeking progressive fit)* for their child that maximizes their progress, independence and potential. The four stages of the social process were found to be as follows:

1. *Beginning Battle* – the stage where parents struggle to find an appropriate diagnosis.
2. *Waging War* – the stage where parents fight to seek, gain, maintain and create educational fit.
3. *Strategizing Solutions* – the stage where parents strategize solutions to remedy the constant difficulties associated with education.
4. *Framing Futures* – the stage where parents frame futures and begin redressing life imbalance.

The four stages, while sequential, were also found to be indistinct and iterative, whereupon parents could experience two sub-stages at once or revisit a stage depending upon the conditions operating in their lives at the time. The movement between Stages Two (*Waging War)* and Three (*Strategizing Solutions)* had the greatest level of interaction for parents where they continually moved through a series of feedback loops to *strategize solutions* to remedy the often, overwhelming difficulties associated with educating their child. Some of the difficulties experienced by parents gave rise to use of a particular strategy. However, once learned, parents often re-used such strategies to combat other similar difficulties at other times in the educational journey of their child. Parents' direction and speed of movement through the various stages was mediated by the following intervening conditions:

a. the attitude and background of the parents,
b. the level of support and accommodation available,
c. the educational progress of the child over time,
d. the timing and type of engagement with the educational context, and
e. the advancing age of the person on the autism spectrum and their parents.

The study found that as a parent gradually cycled through the stages they were imbued with an *increasing awareness and confidence* regarding how to deal with the individualised education of their child. However, the educational journey also created *variable negative feelings* in these parents as they progressively realised the enormity of the difficulties they often faced trying to *seek, gain, maintain* and *create educational fit* for their child over time. This tension operated throughout the educational journey and its intensity waxed and waned according to the conditions operating in the individual families' lives at the time.

GENERALIZABILITY OF THE THEORY GENERATED

The *theory of seeking progressive fit* does not have generalizability in the traditional 'quantitative' sense, where there is "the possibility of expanding any claims of causality from the group or sample being studied to the population that group represents – that is, that the same effect will be found in another group and/or in other contexts" (Lewin, 2005, p. 216). On this point Charmaz (2000) writes:

> A constructivist grounded theory seeks to define conditional statements that interpret how subjects construct their realities. Nonetheless, these conditional statements do not approach some level of generalizable truth. Rather, they constitute a set of hypotheses and concepts that other researchers can transport to similar research problems and to other substantive fields (p. 524).

IMPLICATIONS OF THE THEORY GENERATED

The theory of *seeking progressive fit* may have implications for the development of further theory in the substantive area of how parents deal with the education of their child on the autism spectrum over time. This is consistent with Strauss and Corbin's (1990) claim that qualitative researchers hope:

> … that their theories will ultimately be related to others within their respective disciplines in a cumulative fashion, and that the theory's implications will have useful application (p. 24).

It is hoped that the theory may stimulate further research to be pursued through a range of other related studies so that a rich understanding and explanation of this research area and interrelated others can continue to occur. Multi-site research across a number of Australian states involving a large number of families who are educating their children on the autism spectrum is urgently needed to more fully investigate the extent of difficulty and nature of the parent experience so that targeted, evidence-based policy and practice can occur and improve the present difficult plight of such families and their children on the autism spectrum.

IMPLICATIONS FOR THE LITERATURE ON HOW PARENTS DEAL WITH THE EDUCATION OF THEIR CHILD ON THE AUTISM SPECTRUM

The theory of *seeking progressive fit* confirms some of the work already done by other researchers in the field who have investigated various aspects of the process of how parents deal with the education of their children on the autism spectrum. In their review of early intervention ASD research, Roberts and Prior (2006) indicate that parents play a critical role in their child's learning and can often drive the decision-making process and take a primary role in delivering early intervention. Roberts and Prior (2006) also indicate that involvement of parents in the education process often leads to improved learning outcomes for the child. Such findings are consistent with the findings of the study (McDonald, 2010) detailed in this publication. The categories of *improvising*, *maximizing, supplementing* and the sub-category of *finding fit* reveal how parents can often become the driving force behind the education process.

Additionally, Ferraro (2008) found that engaging with parents of children on the autism spectrum is an integral component towards the achievement of teacher-parent efficacy in the 'inclusive' classroom. These findings reflect key elements nominated by parents as important regarding exemplary 'inclusive' practice in the *finding fit* sub-category of the mainstream school experience. In this sub-category, parents nominated as important the self-awareness shown by staff regarding their own knowledge and skill level (or lack thereof) when dealing with the child on the autism spectrum. This awareness allowed both parents and qualified others to become a team (community of practice) and provide appropriate, evidence-based information to staff regarding the individual requirements of the student on an on-going basis.

Parent involvement in the educative process is supported throughout the research literature but engagement with parents of children on the autism spectrum is often lacking throughout schooling communities (Ferraro, 2008; MacDermott, 2008; Stoner & Angell, 2006; Stoner et al., 2005; Stanley et al., 2005). Further to this, Stoner and Angell's study (2006) shows that parents often take on a variety of roles when interacting with their child's school and such interactions are mediated by trust. Consistent with the work of these researchers, the theory reported in this publication confirm these findings. Parents in the present study reported an inconsistent, unreliable mainstream schooling context where they had to negotiate and advocate for their child to gain an acceptable educational pathway in order to maximize their progress (McDonald, 2010). Such negotiations occurred in a *waxing and waning* fashion depending upon the quality of the 'inclusive' practice operating and the trust generated in the educational context at the time.

Another study by Stoner et al. (2005) also found that over time parents' trust in recognized experts often reduced while parents' trust in their own instincts was reinforced. This finding is similarly confirmed in the present study where parents indicated that as they gradually cycled through the stages of dealing with the education of their child on the autism spectrum they were imbued with an *increasing awareness and confidence* regarding their child's educational needs. However, the educational journey also created *variable negative feelings* in the parents as they progressively realised the enormity of the difficulties they often faced trying to *seek, gain, maintain* and *create educational fit* for their child over time.

Additionally, while the theory of *seeking progressive fit* focused upon a small number of parents from varied backgrounds situated in metropolitan Perth, WA, who were dealing with the education of their child on the autism spectrum, the study did not concentrate its investigation on the experiences of specific types of parents – especially those from potentially more vulnerable circumstances. Future studies could concentrate their investigation on parents from an English-as-a-second-language background, parents with disabilities, indigenous parents, regional parents or other parents who potentially may have even greater difficulties dealing with the education of their children on the autism spectrum. It would be very valuable to develop a body of research regarding the experiences of such parents. This would potentially indicate the processes involved, expand our understanding of the difficulties of their specific circumstances, and underpin any evidence-based assistance made available to them.

It may also be helpful for future researchers to investigate more comprehensively the different stages of the education process. In particular, parents in this study reported that they often had great difficulty dealing with the education of their child on the autism spectrum in mainstream, high school settings. Four of the six families involved in the study chose to educate their children on the autism spectrum in education settings other than a mainstream, high school setting and this difficulty is also borne out in other disability research (Jenkins, 2005; Shaddock, 2005; Shaddock et al., 2007). It may be worthwhile for researchers to investigate process and generate theory on how parents deal with the education of their child on the autism spectrum under different high school educational contexts over time. This could include an investigation into the processes and practices involved in promising innovations such as the Department of Education (DoE) High School Autism Extension Units presently operating on a trial basis in a small number of mainstream high schools in WA.

Similarly, while some general research (Reilly, 2004, 2007) has been undertaken on how parents deal with the home education of their children with intellectual disabilities, only a small amount of specific research has been undertaken on how Australian parents deal with the *home schooling* of their children on the autism spectrum over time (Kidd & Kaczmarek, 2010; McDonald, 2010; McDonald & Lopes, 2012). Additionally, growing prevalence of students on the autism spectrum entering the adult world indicate there will be an increasing need for research into how parents deal with the tertiary education and working life of their children over time (Aspect, 2012; Howlin & Moss, 2012; Palmer, 2006).

IMPLICATIONS FOR OTHER BODIES OF RESEARCH

While the theory of *seeking progressive fit* has implications for the substantive area in which it is grounded, it may also have relevance for other bodies of theoretical literature. The categories, concepts and processes which comprise the theory may potentially inform the theoretical perspectives in three other areas of the research literature namely, 'inclusive' practice in mainstream education sites, the social impact of parenting a child on the autism spectrum and research investigating how parents cope with their disabled children over time.

'Inclusive' Practice in Mainstream Education Sites

In Western countries, there has been an increasing trend toward the 'inclusion' of students with disabilities in mainstream education sites as part of an international emancipatory movement to include such students in regular classrooms and mainstream life (Shaddock et al., 2007). The efficacy of 'inclusion' for all students on the autism spectrum into mainstream classrooms at all stages of their education has been questioned over time. Research has found that some students on the autism spectrum may benefit from mainstream, partly or fully segregated and home schooling programs depending upon their individual profile, development and the educational context they must negotiate with or without support (Harrington et al., 2013; Humphrey & Lewis 2008a/b; Humphrey & Symes, 2010; Jordan, 2005; Kidd & Kaczmarek, 2010; MacDermott, 2008; McDonald, 2010; McDonald & Lopes, 2012; Parsons et al., 2011; Parsons & Lewis, 2010; Ravet, 2011; Shaddock, 2003, 2005; Simpson, 2005). Mesibov and Shea (1996) who reviewed the outcomes of full inclusion for students on the autism spectrum indicate that these students often benefited less than other students with other types of disabilities. This is evidenced in the different educational trajectories experienced by the families in the study outlined in this publication in the sub-categories of *home schooling* and *segregating* (McDonald, 2010; McDonald & Lopes, 2012).

The theory *of seeking progressive fit* revealed that families made decisions mainly based upon their child's individual, educational, emotional welfare and progress over time. There was a strong call by these parents to have flexibility of choice when choosing an appropriate educational pathway for their child on the autism spectrum. There was also a call by them to ensure that such alternative pathways were supported appropriately. However, this call by parents was accompanied by an equally strong call for there to be an ever growing improvement in the current unreliable nature of 'inclusive' practice in mainstream schools - so that all educational choices would be available to their child on the autism spectrum if and when they should need it. This was especially so for parents who had children on the autism spectrum who had severe sensory dysfunction affecting their learning profile (APA, 2013).

Parents felt strongly that this should remain an on-going and critical quest for researchers and education professionals alike (McDonald, 2010). It may be some time before families can feel confident that reliable inclusivity is available in all mainstream sites. Hence, the research undertaken in this study supports future research designed to continue the quest to improve the 'inclusive' nature of mainstream sites to appropriately accommodate students on the autism spectrum to maximize their educational potential.

The Social Impact of Parenting a Child on the Autism Spectrum

The categories, concepts and processes that comprise the present *theory of seeking progressive fit* may also inform the theoretical perspectives inherent in the research literature regarding the social impact of parenting a child on the autism spectrum. Research confirms that the impact on families who have a child on the autism spectrum can be extremely high where parents are more likely to experience serious psychological distress than parents of children with any other developmental disability (Benson & Karlof, 2009; Bromley et al., 2004; Sanders & Morgan, 1997; Sivberg, 2002). The theory generated in the present study investigating how parents deal with the education of their child on the autism spectrum over time takes a concentrated look at but one of the areas that families must contend with over time – education. This present study indicates that these parents were often constantly under pressure *seeking progressive fit* when trying to maximize the educational potential of their child over time. The general research investigating the social impact of parenting a child on the autism spectrum is inclusive of many areas which parents must constantly negotiate, not just education. Such specific areas need fuller investigation in terms of the processes involved when parents of children with an ASD deal with such areas as spouses, siblings, extended family, work, friendships, finances, external support and so on, because all of these areas potentially impact on the mental health and well-being of such families over time.

How Parents Cope with Their Children with Disabilities Over Time

Related to the research on the social impact of parenting a child on the autism spectrum is general research indicating how parents cope with their children with disabilities over time. A grounded theory study (Taanila et al., 2002) examining how parents cope with their disabled children indicates that families use existing resources and strategies to combat external and internal demands. Coping involves maintaining or restoring the balance between the demands and resources (Patterson, 1988). Other general studies (Berry & Hardman, 1998) also indicate that success in coping is a long-term process that is linked to a gradual accumulation of skills by family members over time and often a changed perspective on their situation.

In terms of specific research investigating how parents cope with their children on the autism spectrum over time, an Australian longitudinal research project found that parents used both problem-focused and emotion-focused coping strategies over a ten-year period (Gray, 1994, 2002b, 2006). Gray's (1994) initial study at the beginning of a ten year period indicated that most parents used a variety of coping strategies with the most common being the use of service agencies, family support, social withdrawal, religion, normalisation, individualism and activism. Gray's (2006) follow-up study conducted some ten years later indicated that parents coping strategies changed from the time of the initial study to include use of more emotion-focused strategies.

The experiences of parents investigated in the study reported in this publication resonate with previous general and specific coping research undertaken. Parents *strategized solutions* to respond to the complex situations they continually faced when dealing with the education of their children on the autism spectrum. They gradually accumulated skills when *seeking progressive educational fit* for their child on the autism spectrum over time. Unfortunately, the parents in the study often found it difficult maintaining a balance between the demands of their circumstances and the resources available to their family during the educational journey. They often felt like they were *Waging* the *War* of their lives trying to maximize the educational potential of their child in a system frequently not geared to 'fit' such children. This would partly explain the high level of stress or *variable negative feelings* experienced by many parents when dealing with the education of their child over time. It is only during the final stage of the theory, *Framing Futures*, where some parents were able to *redress the imbalance* within their family in the hope of improving the quality of life and mental health experienced by all members of the family. This supports the findings of existing research that indicates parents often experience a change in their perspective of the situation over time. In the light of these findings, further research is needed to investigate ways parents can be supported early in the process to decrease demands and increase the resources available to them so that they are able to deal more effectively with the educational journey of their child on the autism spectrum and keep their family intact with good mental health over time.

RECOMMENDATIONS FOR POLICY AND PRACTICE

From the different understandings and explanations derived from research regarding how parents deal with the education of their child on the autism spectrum (Ferraro, 2008; Kidd & Kaczmarek, 2010; MacDermott, 2008; McDonald, 2010; Parsons & Lewis, 2010; Stanley et al., 2005; Stoner & Angell, 2006; Stoner et al., 2005) it is clear that the on-going task undertaken by them is often a difficult and arduous one. At different stages of the educational journey parents have been found to struggle to maximize the individual potential of their child in a system often not geared to 'fit' such children.

The study (McDonald, 2010) reinforces our understanding of the social construction of disability by revealing that it is often the education system which potentially 'disables' such children because it repeatedly fails to 'enable' them to be successful in their education over time (Ainscow, 1993, 1995; Oliver, 1990, 1996; Skidmore, 2004; Slee, 1996). The educational experiences of the families involved in the study (McDonald, 2010) highlight the inability of the WA mainstream education system to presently provide reliable educational 'fit' to such children on the autism spectrum over time.

Research has repeatedly found that students on the autism spectrum may benefit from mainstream, partly or fully segregated and home education programs depending upon their individual profile, development and the educational context they must negotiate with or without support (Jordan, 2005; Mesibov & Shea, 1996; Kidd & Kaczmarek, 2010; MacDermott, 2008; McDonald, 2010; McDonald & Lopes 2012; Shaddock, 2003; Simpson, 1995, 2004, 2005). However, such educational flexibility is presently not readily or reliably on offer to families who have children on the autism spectrum. Research has found that parents of these children are more likely to endorse schooling where teachers have specialized training and the educational program focuses on the specific needs of students on the autism spectrum (Howlin, 1998; Kasari et al., 1999; Moreno et al., 2008) and this type of education should be reliably available in all educational contexts, including mainstream. Unfortunately, as the present study (McDonald, 2010) has highlighted and current Australian research (Kidd & Kaczmarek, 2010; MacDermott, 2008) attests, gaining a best practice, inclusive experience in mainstream education is not yet reliably available to families who have child on the autism spectrum.

The following sections outline specific recommendations for policy and practice designed to address the on-going difficulties experienced by parents when dealing with the education of their children on the autism spectrum over time.

HCWA – Diagnosis

In response to the difficulties associated with educating students on the autism spectrum, some specific support at a national level has been undertaken. From 2008, the Australian Government committed funding to provide a *Helping Children with Autism* (HCWA) support package (AAETC, 2008a, 2008b). This initiative sought to provide an earlier and more accurate diagnosis of children with ASD, increased access to early intervention programs, and further support services for educators and parents/carers of children with an ASD (O'Reilly & Smith, 2008). As evidenced by the findings of the study (McDonald, 2010) and other current research (Ford, 2007; Forlin et al., 2008; Jenkins, 2005; MacDermott, 2008; Takahashi, 2005), it is imperative that such initiatives continue and are refined to support the on-going, difficult lives presently experienced by many parents who must continually *seek progressive fit* when dealing with the education of their children on the autism spectrum over time.

Presently, the federal HCWA package provides funding for diagnosis and development of a treatment plan for children under the age of 13 years. The results of the study (McDonald, 2010) and other recent research (Dissanayake, 2009; Granpeesheh et al., 2009; Prior & Roberts, 2006) continues to indicate that early and accurate diagnosis is imperative to maximize the individual educational potential of children with an ASD. Parents in the current study (McDonald,2010) found that the seeking and gaining of an accurate diagnosis was often an elusive, iterative, expensive and traumatic process, and for some families this process took many years as evidenced in the *Beginning Battle* stage of this research. Since 2007, there has been a 'Two screens by Two years' guideline operating in the USA where very young children are routinely screened for an ASD by their paediatrician twice before they reach two years of age (Duby & Plauche Johnson, 2009).

In relation to this, there has been an urgent call for more accurate, early universal screening of ASDs within Australia (Dissanayake, 2009; Edwards, 2009, September 14). The Australian researcher Dissanayake (2009) has recommended that a developmental surveillance approach be adopted where infants are monitored regularly throughout their first two years for the development of early social attention and communication behaviours by primary health care professionals. A large community-based study using this approach resulted in an 81% ascertainment rate for an ASD (Dissanayake, 2009). The implementation of such a surveillance method would require the education of primary care professionals in identifying the early signs of an ASD. The value of such early identification and its relationship to early intervention cannot be underestimated (Dissanayake, 2009). It is therefore, recommended that HCWA package be expanded to support such a crucial education and surveillance program to ensure parents are able to gain an accurate and timely diagnosis for their children. Such an initiative is especially important for those families who do not have the financial resources to research their own situation or seek a private diagnosis for their children as evidenced in the early intervention category of *settling* in the study (McDonald, 2010) reported in this publication.

HCWA – Supplementing

The HCWA initiative presently provides access to early intervention treatment in the form of a limited amount of services in total per child for children on the autism spectrum under 13 years of age. The study (McDonald, 2010) indicates that parents are often required to *supplement* the education of their child on the autism spectrum over many years with various therapies to ensure their child's maximum progress. According to the experiences of such parents, present-day government-funded therapy services available to their children are grossly inadequate in terms of their intensity and quality of service provision, especially for children with severe needs. It is recommended that such funding be immediately expanded to ensure that when such therapies are needed they can be accessed by parents in a timely fashion in sufficient intensity over as many schooling years as needed, irrespective of the parent's ability to afford them for their child.

Presently there is a National Disability Insurance Scheme being gradually rolled out in selected areas in Australia to provide all Australians with a no-fault insurance scheme for everyone who has, or acquires a significant disability. This would potentially allow parents of children on the autism spectrum to access much-needed therapy services and to gain them in a timely fashion over as many years as they are needed, irrespective of their ability to fund such therapies themselves.

HCWA – Parent and Professional Workshops

The HCWA package is also currently delivering two initiatives through its Positive Partnerships programs. There is professional development for school staff to support school students on the autism spectrum and workshops and information sessions for parents/carers of school students on the autism spectrum. The study (McDonald, 2010) and other research (Crosby, 1998; Ford, 2007; Forlin et al., 2008; Kavale & Forness, 2000; MacDermott, 2008; Shaddock et al., 2007; Ypinazar & Pagliano, 2004) indicates that there can be a fundamental divide between the rhetoric and reality of 'inclusive' practice for children on the autism spectrum in mainstream schooling environments. The experiences of parents in the study (McDonald, 2010) during the formal schooling years indicated that parents were frequently *chasing* a placement for their child in an often, unwelcome mainstream system. They had to continually negotiate an acceptable educational pathway in a *waxing and waning* fashion to ensure 'inclusivity' reliably occurred for their child over time. Parents were also continually *supplementing* their child's education because of the unreliable nature of the inclusive education process and the idiosyncratic needs of their child. Some families also experienced a *crisis point* in their child's mainstream schooling where the parents were compelled to remove their child because of a continual lack of appropriate 'inclusive' practice and the deteriorating mental health of their family. This led to a situation where parents opted to either *home school* or *segregate* their child from the mainstream as evidenced in the sub-categories of *home schooling* and *segregating*. These parental experiences reflect current research that indicates that while disabled students may have increased rights regarding access and enrolment in regular schools, issues have now arisen regarding the quality and outcomes of the education they receive in such environments (Cologon, 2013; Ford, 2007; Forlin et al., 2008; Harrington et al., 2013; Roberts, 2013; Shaddock et al., 2007; Ypinazar & Pagliano, 2004).

This is especially so in relation to the experiences of students on the autism spectrum in some Australian schools (Harrington et al., 2013; MacDermott, 2008; McDonald, 2010; McDonald & Lopes, 2012; Kidd & Kaczmarek, 2010; Roberts, 2013; Shaddock, 2005). Hence, it is highly recommended that the HCWA education programs for both education professionals and parents/carers be a continuing initiative with refinement incorporating current critical needs. This study and other research indicates that the areas of bullying (Attwood, 2004, 2007; Cappodocia et al., 2012; Heinrichs, 2003; Little, 2002; Olweus, 1993; Rosendorff, 2007, Symes & Humphrey, 2010) and the functional treatment of problem behaviour (Ford, 2007; Forlin et al., 2008; Myles, 2005; Myles & Adreon, 2001) in mainstream contexts are current areas of high concern for parents, school staff and students on the autism spectrum, and should therefore, receive priority in the HCWA education programs.

The workshops should also provide information regarding all the different education options available to parents when dealing with the education of their child on the autism spectrum over time as evidenced in the categories of *mainstreaming* and *opting out* (sub-categories of *home schooling* and *segregating)*. This instruction should be provided by exemplary practitioners (including parents) in their fields to allow parents to make informed choices regarding the educational options available to their family and child over time. Parents should have the right of self-determination in this regard for they are in the best position to make such decisions for their families. This information is especially critical when families hit a series of *crisis points* during their mainstream education and need to make informed decisions about maintaining the mental health and well-being of their families especially in relation to their child on the autism spectrum (McDonald, 2010). Mainstream education should be seen as but one of the options available to parents when educating their children on the autism spectrum. It is also highly recommended that families be regularly consulted in relation to their on-going educational needs to keep the HCWA workshops highly relevant and ensure their effectiveness is maximized.

HCWA – Discrimination

Another area that deserves comment is the legislation that underpins the inclusion of the disabled in mainstream educational environments. As explained in the context chapter of this publication, 'inclusion' has been supported at the federal level within Australia by the enactment of both the *Disability Discrimination Act* (DDA) (Commonwealth of Australia, 1992) and the *Disability Standards for Education* (Commonwealth of Australia, 2005).

The study, especially in the sub-categories of *chasing, waxing and waning* and *crisis point* (McDonald, 2010; McDonald & Lopes 2012), and other research (Ford, 2007; Forlin et al., 2008; Kidd & Kaczmarek, 2010; MacDermott, 2008; Shaddock et al., 2007) illustrate the on-going difficulties experienced by some parents of children with disabilities in relation to their child's 'inclusion' in mainstream contexts. The parents in the study (McDonald, 2010) often lacked knowledge regarding their rights under the DDA and the Education Standards. As explained in the sub-category, *chasing,* parents of these children were often unwilling to enrol their child into a school where they felt unwelcome because they feared the on-going negative treatment that their vulnerable child and their family may receive over time. As evidenced in the sub-category, *waxing and waning,* parents indicated that their children were often at the mercy of slippery notions of 'inclusive' practice that sometimes permeated mainstream contexts that could change rapidly at any time. Sometimes, as exemplified in the sub-category *crisis point,* a specific time would be reached where a parent would be compelled to remove their child permanently from a school because of a continual lack of appropriate 'inclusive' practice occurring in that mainstream environment. To combat such potential discrimination, parents should be supported to understand the relevant legislation to a point where they can determine if discrimination has occurred in relation to their child.

As explained, the legislation does not prevent discrimination from taking place but rather deals with it after the discrimination has occurred. The onus of proving discrimination rests with the complainant initially and once it has been established that discrimination has occurred the onus moves to the respondent who may seek to prove that the discrimination can be excused through limited defence under the Acts (Guthrie & Waldeck, 2008). This present process is one that most parents of a child on the autism spectrum would potentially find very daunting and onerous given their fragile mental health and the ongoing difficulties inherent in their lives. Research confirms the difficulties associated with use of the legislation by the disabled and their advocates (Newell, 1995, 2005).

It is therefore recommended that through the Parent and Professional workshops, parents be given a very clear and concise understanding of their child's rights under the legislation and the process needed to make a complaint under the Acts (See Appendix 2; Guthrie & Waldeck, 2008). This would encourage parents to alert schools regarding their responsibilities and also allow them to make an informed decision regarding the worth of pursuing a complaint of discrimination on behalf of their child. In particular, the Education Standards now provide some specific guidance on the issue of 'reasonable adjustment' (Guthrie & Waldeck, 2008). This issue can be a constant source of contention in some mainstream educational environments as evidenced in the experiences of the families in the study (McDonald, 2010) outlined in this publication. Otherwise, Australian parents of children on the autism spectrum will remain at the mercy of the policy and practices of individual education providers who may or may not comply with the present legislation. This knowledge is especially important for parents who have the least amount of resources available to them and cannot choose or afford alternative means (*home schooling*) when educating their child on the autism spectrum.

Autism Advisors

Presently, the HCWA initiative provides some direct support to parents through a national program of Autism Advisors. These advisors provide parents of children on the autism spectrum with advice regarding the most appropriate early intervention services and their funding. These services represent only a beginning in terms of providing specific, professional, on-going educational support to parents who have pre-school and school-aged children on the autism spectrum. Parents in the study (McDonald, 2010) indicated that there is no one agency that presently operates with all current information in a centralized location that is available to families. This is especially so once their child is school-aged when all services become more decentralized and parents need to become effective case managers for their children – a task that not every parent has the skills or resources to accomplish. The study (McDonald, 2010) has shown that parents must be far more involved with the education of their child on the autism spectrum than with a neurotypical child to ensure that their child's educational potential is maximized. Parent's ability to do this is often compromised by the nature of the individual circumstances experienced by them. Research indicates that a parent's general journey with their child on the autism spectrum is fraught with many difficult times (Benson & Karlof, 2009; Gray, 2002b; McDonald, 2010; MacDermott, 2008; Singer, 2006; Tehee et al., 2009). Families can sometimes experience overwhelming episodes when dealing with their child's education over time (Kidd & Kaczmarek, 2010; MacDermott, 2008; McDonald, 2010; McDonald & Lopes, 2012). Traumatic *crisis points* can occur for some families during the educational journey of their child, and immediate, accurate information and support at these times is crucial to ensure the mental well-being of these parents and their families to ensure drastic consequences do not occur (Lamont, 2004, June 1).

This support is especially needed during key transition periods and throughout the high school years where stress for such families can be at their highest (Gray, 2002b). The research (Benson & Karlof, 2009; Ewart, 2002; Hastings & Brown, 2002; McDonald, 2010; MacDermott, 2008) indicates that appropriate, targeted informal and formal support can improve the outcomes for many of these families.

Hence, it is highly recommended that the role of Autism Advisors be available to parents throughout the educational journey of their children on the autism spectrum. These advisors would then be able to develop strong and cohesive connections with all of the various agencies, government departments, referral services, local councils, local area coordinators and other service providers and potentially provide pro-active support especially for 'at-risk' families who have limited informal and formal support available to them.

Tertiary Education

According to the findings of the study (McDonald, 2010) and other research (Aspect, 2012; Camarena & Sarigiani, 2009; Smith, 2007; VanBergeijk et al., 2008) tertiary education is potentially another area of importance to some families who have children on the spectrum. The experiences of the parents in the study (McDonald, 2010) during their child's transition (*transitioning*) to both work and tertiary study indicate that *seeking, gaining, maintaining* and *creating fit* for their child on the autism spectrum in the adult world was another on-going quest for these parents. Parents could not just rely on external services to support their child's transition process to either tertiary study or a suitable work situation. Parents had to, once again, be the driving force behind the successful transition of their children from schooling to tertiary study or work in the external adult world. To date, there has been limited investigation into the tertiary education of students on the autism spectrum. Preliminary research (Aspect, 2012; Chown & Beavan, 2012; Hastwell, Harding, Martin & Baron-Cohen, 2013; Smith, 2007) into support services for students with an ASD in higher education indicates that there are an increasing number of individuals with an ASD entering tertiary education. While tertiary institutions provide some limited support through student services, it is often generic in nature and not tailored to the individual needs of the student (Aspect, 2012; Smith, 2007) however this situation is slowing changing (Hastwell et al., 2013).

It is therefore, recommended that there be specific instruction on autism tertiary education issues to help faculty members understand how best to succeed with such students. Support services at tertiary level should also be expanded to allow effective individualised support into potential areas of difficulty for such students including such areas as communication, social and independent living skills and executive functioning (VanBergeijk et al., 2008).

Related to this discussion of tertiary education is the area of preparation of pre-service teachers. Parents in the study (McDonald, 2010) indicated in the *mainstreaming* sub-categories of *chasing, waxing and waning* and *crisis point*, that they were often required to advocate on their child's behalf in often unwelcome, unreliable, mainstream environments to ensure the educational potential of their child was maximized. Other research similarly indicates that there is often a difference between the rhetoric and reality of 'inclusive' practice in mainstream schooling environments (Cologon, 2013; Crosby, 1998; Ford, 2007; Forlin et al., 2008; Kavale & Forness,

2000; MacDermott, 2008; McDonald, 2010; Shaddock et al., 2007; Ypinazar & Pagliano, 2004). Research has found that parents of students on the autism spectrum identify appropriate teacher training as the single, most enabling factor in providing for their children in a mainstream setting (Jindal-Snape, Douglas, Topping, Kerr, & Smith, 2005). Given that students on the autism spectrum are much more likely to be bullied and rejected by their peers (Symes & Humphrey, 2010) it stands to reason that teachers should have appropriate training to successfully include such students in mainstream settings (Leach & Duffy, 2009). Furthermore, strategies used can vary with the age of the student, the classroom setting and specific student being included (Hess, Morrier, Heflin, & Ivey, 2008). Research has shown that appropriate training can result in increased teacher awareness of autism issues (Leblanc, Richardson, & Burns, 2009) along with a significant improvement in the classroom behaviour of students on the autism spectrum and reduced teacher stress (Probst & Leppert, 2008). Unfortunately, not all education faculties in the tertiary sector register the crucial need to offer such courses in their pre-service programs; even though such instruction has widespread application for the increasingly diverse student population now apparent in current mainstream classrooms (Cologon, 2013; Shaddock et al., 2007).

Home Schooling

The findings in the study reported in this publication (McDonald, 2010) in the sub-category, *home schooling,* echo the current research by Reilly (2002, 2004, 2007) on how West Australian parents deal with the home schooling of their children with intellectual disabilities. In line with some of the recommendations for improvement in practice made by Reilly (2007), it is similarly recommended that there be improvement in the support and funding of *home schooling* practice for parents in relation to the *home schooling* of their children on the autism spectrum.

Parents in the study (McDonald, 2010) found that there was very limited support, especially at the beginning of the process when dealing with the *home schooling* of their child on the autism spectrum. During *home schooling* these parents eventually used formal and informal, external home schooling services and adopted maverick strategies to improvise their own educational programs depending upon the parent's background, experience, confidence, the age of the child and the nature of the educational programs that their child may need. As suggested by Reilly (2007), there is a critical need for support and guidance regarding such areas as *home schooling* structures, teaching techniques, content and resources. Therefore, it is similarly recommended that there be a government-funded home schooling consultant with links to local *home schooling* organizations to help support parents at such crucial times.

The existence of such a consultant would be especially valuable at the beginning of the process of *home schooling* when parents have often experienced a traumatic *crisis point* in their child's schooling that precipitated their decision to home school their child as evidenced in the sub-category *home schooling* of this study

(McDonald, 2010; McDonald & Lopes, 2012) and other studies (Reilly, 2007; Kidd & Kaczmarek, 2010). It would also be helpful for the home schooling consultant to have some background in disability, especially in relation to the education of children on the autism spectrum, to support parents appropriately over the course of their child's *home schooling* (Schetter & Lighthall, 2009).

Reilly (2007) also recommends that *home schooling* parents be funded to support them in the process of educating their child with an intellectual disability. Similarly, parents in the study (McDonald, 2010) and other recent research (Kidd & Kaczmarek, 2010) has found that parents were often unable to gain external work and home school their child/ren on the autism spectrum at the same time and this caused financial and emotional strain within the family. Both government and non-government schools are currently funded to educate students in WA but there is limited provision to pay parents who choose to, or are compelled by circumstance, to home school their child, even though New Zealand currently provides precedent and funds their *home schooling* parents (Reilly, 2007). *Home schooling* parents must presently absorb nearly all costs associated with educating their child on the autism spectrum, unless they can access the services of the Schools of Isolated and Distance Education (SIDE) (McDonald, 2010; McDonald & Lopes, 2012). However, parents' knowledge regarding the existence of and eligibility for SIDE is presently ad hoc given the absence of a funded *home schooling* consultant. Additionally, the entry requirements for use of SIDE services as experienced by parents in the study (McDonald, 2010) was found to be stringent and unwelcoming. It is therefore, highly recommended that home schooling parents be funded appropriately to educate their children on the autism spectrum, especially if the WA government is unable to provide an appropriate way to educate such children and this responsibility falls to them.

CONCLUSION

In a speech given at the opening of the 2009 Asia Pacific Autism Conference, in Sydney, The Hon. Bill Shorten MP, (former Parliamentary Secretary for Federal Disabilities and Children's Services, presently Parliamentary Leader of the Federal Opposition) admitted:

> I am embarrassed at the struggle that families in Australia have to do to find doctors, therapists and teachers with experience, or indeed even with empathy, for what it means to be autistic or to care for someone with autism (The Hon Bill Shorten MP, 2009).

He also stated that he saw:

> … the life experience of a parent of a child with autism, and indeed the life of a person with autism as a series of collisions where the system that should be supporting the parents, in fact, fails and betrays them time and time again (The Hon Bill Shorten MP, 2009).

These words accurately echo the experiences of the brave, and often, fragile parents who participated in the study (McDonald, 2010) reported in this publication and give an insight into how they deal with the education of their child on the autism spectrum over time.

The Hon. Bill Shorten MP also acknowledged that, "there are major fundamental problems with the way the support system works for ASDs in Australia" (The Hon Bill Shorten MP, 2009). Given such 'understanding' of the situation faced by parents, it remains to be seen whether such words will be followed appropriately by government policy and further funding, both state and federal, to increase the help and support available to such embattled families. For we, like The Hon Bill Shorten MP, continue to desperately ask:

> Why can't we have a system in this country that upon diagnosis a child with any developmental delay and their parents will be provided with a case manager to help them navigate the system? Why cannot we, we are a rich and generous nation …our nation is rich enough to afford equal treatment for the families and people with ASDs. We as a nation, should be able to arrive at a point where we cannot only provide the case manager, for that individualized support, but people can have the expectation that their child will receive early intervention services, they will be able to go to a primary school, they will be able to go to a secondary school depending upon their needs, their desires and their directions. They will be able to live in supported accommodation or not depending upon the severity of their ASD. They will be able to have the opportunity to participate, not just at work, but socially and culturally. I see no reason why the presence of an impairment should remain to be the defining feature of an individual's life. This country is capable of coming up with solutions that provide genuine equity (The Hon Bill Shorten MP, 2009).

Only time will tell whether successive governments will be part of the solution or be part of the problematic system that often "fails and betrays" parents and their children with an ASD "time and time again" (The Hon Bill Shorten MP, 2009). For the HCWA package is only a beginning, there is still much work to be done – just ask the parents who have a child on the autism spectrum. For their voices are often silenced in the discourse concerning the education of their own children on the autism spectrum.

APPENDIX 1

2012 SUBMISSION TO THE WEST AUSTRALIAN PARLIAMENTARY EDUCATION AND HEALTH STANDING COMMITTEE

The following is an edited copy of a 2012 Submission that was made to the West Australian Parliamentary Education and Health Standing Committee addressing: An Inquiry into Improving Educational Outcomes for Western Australians of all Ages. The submission was made on behalf of and in conjunction with the Northern Suburbs Autism Mum's Support Group (representing approximately 80 WA families who have children on the autism spectrum) and the Home Based Learning Network (representing approximately 1000 WA families presently home educating their children).

Inquiry Term of Reference

Factors Influencing Positive or Negative Childhood Development from Birth to Year 12.

Submitted by

Name: Dr Jasmine McDonald BA DipEd MSpEd(Hons) PhD
Position: Honorary Research Fellow, University of WA, Graduate School of Education

Underlying Problem

Presently in Western Australia (WA), parents of children with an Autism Spectrum Disorder (ASD) persistently struggle to gain for their child:

- a timely, accurate diagnosis.
- timely, evidence-based, affordable early intervention at appropriate intensity.
- a reliable inclusive education based on best practice principles in mainstream schooling sites that maximizes their educational potential (especially in high school contexts).
- appropriate support and direction when compelled to home educate their child.
- a separate school for their children with an ASD who do not have an accompanying intellectual disability (IQ 70 or under).

The WA government has been made aware of these ongoing difficulties for families and their children with an ASD since the late 1990s (Crosby, 1998) and subsequently by other recently conducted WA research (MacDermott, 2008; McDonald, 2010). However, little has changed for these families as evidenced by the parent testimonies circa May 2012 submitted by the Northern Suburbs Autism Mums' Group, Perth (Appendix 1A).

Issues Arising

Prevalence rates for all forms of Autism Spectrum Disorders (ASDs) worldwide have risen dramatically since the mid-1960s. One in 88 U.S. children has an ASD, according to a new report from the Centers for Disease Control and Prevention, representing a 23 percent increase in prevalence from the previous autism report, released in 2009, which estimated that autism affected one in 110 children (Chan, 2012). The report showed the condition is nearly five times higher among boys than girls, (Chan, 2012). One recent Australian report similarly indicates that more than 1% of Australian school-age children have a confirmed diagnosis of Autistic Disorder or Asperger's Disorder (Buckley, 2009). As a consequence, there is an ever increasing need in Western Australia to understand how to best educate such students so that their potential and independence in life can be maximized.

It is commonly agreed that students with an ASD experience a triad of impairments involving idiosyncratic difficulties with communication, socialization and stereotyped behaviour (American Psychiatric Association 2000; AAETC, 2008). Beyond the triad of impairments there are often more cognitive characteristics to consider and these involve deficits in theory of mind skills, difficulties with executive function, weak central coherence, sensory processing and motor functioning problems (AAETC, 2008). Such students may also have a number of relative cognitive strengths in the areas of rote memory, visual spatial abilities, compartmentalized learning, preference for routine and rules, intense interests and being logical (AAETC 2008). Research indicates these students have potential for good educational outcomes when they have access to timely, appropriate best practice early intervention (Granpeesheh et al., 2009) and their difficulties are accommodated and their relative strengths utilized with appropriate use of evidence-based ASD educational teaching and learning practice (Frederickson et al., 2010; Laluvein, 2010; Garguilo & Metcalf, 2010; Leach & Duffy, 2009).

International, Australian and West Australian research continues to indicate that early and accurate diagnosis is imperative to maximize the individual educational potential of children with an ASD so that they may access appropriate evidence-based early intervention at the earliest time (Dissanayake, 2009; Granpeesheh et al., 2009; MacDermott, 2008; McDonald, 2010; Roberts & Prior, 2006). Parents in WA have found over many years that gaining an accurate diagnosis of an ASD for their child is often a very expensive, protracted and traumatic process where waiting lists are common, and for some families this process can take many months or years (Appendix 1A; MacDermott, 2008; McDonald, 2010). Since 2007, there has been a 'Two screens by Two years' guideline operating in the USA where very young children are routinely screened for an ASD by their paediatrician twice before they reach two years of age (Duby & Plauche Johnson, 2009). In relation to this, there has been an ongoing call for early universal screening of ASDs within Australia (Dissanayake, 2009). A recent large Australian community-based study using a surveillance approach by child health nurses resulted in an 81% ascertainment for an ASD (Dissanayake, 2009). If such a program were to be implemented universally within WA through the recently expanded child health nurse network (Keast, 2012), it would guarantee that children could be diagnosed at the earliest possible time ensuring that they would have the best chance to access timely evidence-based early intervention. Alternatively, this screening process could occur in conjunction with the new federal Healthy Kids Check program targeting three year olds to be managed by GPs from July 1 (AAP, 2012).

Additionally, parents in WA routinely find it difficult to access and afford appropriate intensive, best practice early intervention (EI) in a timely manner for their child with an ASD (MacDermott, 2008; McDonald, 2010). Financial support for one of the most efficacious EIs based on long-term research (Roberts & Prior, 2006) is presently still greatly under-funded. The federal Helping Children With Autism (HCWA) initiative currently provides all children aged six and under who are diagnosed with an ASD and are not yet school-aged with funding of up to $12,000 (up to $6,000 per financial year) to assist with the financial cost of accessing EI services. This figure falls far short of providing appropriate funding for the intensity of EI recommended by a federal government review which investigated current research regarding the most efficacious models of EI for children with an ASD (Roberts & Prior, 2006). The review recommended that best practice EI consisted of a model based on Applied Behaviour Analysis / Discrete Trial Training (ABA/DTT) methods. It also recommended that the EI "be extensive and intensive" and be conducted for a "a minimum of 20 hours a week over two or more years" as early as possible in order for young children to make major gains (Roberts & Prior, 2006, p. 3). Government funding for this model is still greatly inadequate and does not cover the recommended intensity of intervention needed in best practice models. Most families continue to struggle to find up to $60,000 per year (Eccleston, 2005), even with the HCWA package, to cover the intensive therapy needed to conduct this best practice model (Roberts & Prior, 2006). All families who have a child with an ASD need easy access to the most efficacious EI at the recommended intensity at the earliest time possible at a reasonable cost.

Over the past two decades there has been an increasing development of inclusive practice regarding appropriate accommodation of students with an ASD in mainstream schooling sites (Frederickson et al., 2010; Garguilo & Metcalf, 2010; Leach & Duffy, 2009). This has been in response to powerful moral, social justice and political arguments that have for some time asserted that positive attitudes towards individuals with disabilities are developed when children with disabilities and their typically developing peers interact at school and these attitudes are sustained in adult life (Oliver 1990, 1996; Oliver & Barnes, 2010; Slee, 2011). However, recent international, Australian and WA research has shown that students with intellectual and cognitive disabilities, including those with an ASD, often cannot access reliable and consistent mainstream inclusive practice that maximizes their progress over time (Ford, 2007; Forlin et al., 2008; Humphrey & Lewis, 2008a, 2008b; Humphrey & Symes, 2010; MacDermott, 2008; McDonald, 2010; Shaddock, 2005; Shaddock, Smyth King & Giorcelli, 2007). Concerns have been raised about the lack of appropriate, individualized attention and support available, the high attrition rates and the inordinate degree of bullying experienced by students with an ASD in mainstream settings (Humphrey & Lewis, 2008b; Humphrey & Symes, 2010; Lynch & Irvine, 2009; MacDermott, 2008; McDonald, 2010). Additionally, such students often experience social isolation, anxiety and sensory difficulties in mainstream settings where their need for routine and predictability is often at odds with the chaotic, noisy happenings of mainstream school life, especially at the high school level (Humphrey & Lewis, 2008a; Symes & Humphrey, 2010).

In response to these ongoing difficulties, a growing number of parents in WA have been compelled to home educate their children with an ASD (Appendix 1B; Kidd and Kaczmarek, 2010; McDonald, 2010). Other families have been compelled to withdraw their child with an ASD from mainstream schools and place them into segregated schooling sites specifically designed for children with disabilities to ensure that an appropriate education is gained and to protect the overall well-being of the family (McDonald, 2010). Unfortunately, WA families can only choose to home school their child with an ASD if their family circumstances can support such a decision because there is presently limited government funding or appropriate formal expertise provided (Appendix 1B; Kidd and Kaczmarek, 2010; McDonald, 2010). Additionally, families routinely find the entry requirements particularly stringent when they try to gain the support of the Schools of Isolated and Distance Education (SIDE) to guide the home education of their child with an ASD even though such support has been shown to be beneficial to both the child and their family (McDonald, 2010). To complicate matters further, the option of placing a child with an ASD into a segregated school site in WA is only available to families who have a child with an ASD who also has an accompanying intellectual disability (IQ of approximately 70 or below). Parents who have a child with an ASD without an intellectual disability (such as those with Asperger's Disorder or High Functioning Autistic Disorder) are currently not eligible for enrolment at segregated school sites (McDonald, 2010).

As attested by recent WA research (Kidd and Kaczmarek, 2010; MacDermott, 2008; McDonald, 2010) and the very recent parent testimonies provided (Appendix 1A), many families who have a child with an ASD are under constant pressure because of the unreliability of the inclusive experience in mainstream Western Australian schools and the lack of support for other educational pathways (Kidd and Kaczmarek, 2010; MacDermott, 2008; McDonald, 2010). There is an urgent need for greater understanding, support and application of best practice teaching and learning principles of children with an ASD in mainstream schools especially at the high school level (MacDermott, 2008; McDonald, 2010). There is a critical call for much greater educational choice for families who have a child with an ASD, with appropriate support for the different pathways (ASD specific segregated school sites and home schooling) that parents may feel is appropriate for their child at different points in their educational process (Kidd and Kaczmarek, 2010; McDonald, 2010).

Without improvements to diagnosis, early intervention, the inclusive nature of mainstream schools and appropriate support for alternative educational pathways (home schooling and ASD segregated school sites), families who have a child with an ASD will continually be at increased risk of serious mental health issues and family breakdown (Hartley et al., 2010). Current research indicates that parents of children with an ASD are potentially at greater risk for mental health problems than any other parent group who have a child with a disability (Benson and Karloff, 2009; Tehee, Honan and Hevey, 2009). If the present government is serious about helping these families and their children with an ASD they should immediately take steps to adopt the following recommendations.

Recommendations

1. Routine screening for an ASD to occur on or before a child turns 3 to be conducted by WA Child Health Nurses and local GPs during regular developmental checks.
2. Timely access (three months or less) to an affordable ASD diagnostic process in both the government and private system to ensure best practice early intervention can occur at the earliest time.
3. Timely access (three months or less) to affordable evidence-based early intervention in the recommended intensity of best practice models.
4. Provision of specific educational funding organised as an entitlement for students with an ASD irrespective of sector to help cover the costs of meeting their educational needs as suggested in the recent federal Review of Funding for Schooling (Gonski et al., 2011, pp.183-185).
5. Improved access to reliable ASD inclusive education in mainstream schooling sites (both public and private) where educators are given appropriate pre-service and in-service training, allocated time to differentiate the curriculum, and access to ongoing ASD expertise and support for the child with an ASD.
6. Expansion of the Secondary Autism Extension Program with appropriate independent reviews conducted to ensure best practice education is occurring for these students in mainstream secondary school sites.
7. Expansion of the services of the Department of Education's (DoE) Centre for Inclusive Schooling (CIS) Autism Education Service (AES) team to allow parents to directly request their involvement in their child's education (both public and private) without having to seek permission from the class teacher and the school's administration.
8. Establishment of Home Schooling Consultants (Diversity) who would provide best practice guidance regarding home schooling of children with special needs and access to appropriate support networks, curriculum materials and

professional development. Relaxed entry into Schools of Isolated and Distance Education for those families who choose to use this service.

9. Redistribution of per capita education funds (presently allocated to students at formal schooling sites) to home schooling parents of children with an ASD given that many parents are often compelled to home school because of the failure of the mainstream education system to appropriately educate their children.
10. Establishment of a state government funded K-12 school especially designed for students with an Asperger's Disorder and high functioning Autistic Disorder where students would be able to have their idiosyncratic profiles understood and accommodated by appropriately trained staff using best practice teaching and learning principles for students with an ASD.

Criteria for Evaluating Solutions

1. Regular feedback from parent groups representing families who have child with an ASD in relation to diagnosis, early intervention and schooling issues.
2. Regular funded research (both quantitative and qualitative) to monitor the effectiveness of ASD interventions and initiatives.

REFERENCES

AAP (2012, June 10). *Govt stands by child mental health tests*. Thewest.com.au. http://au.news.yahoo.com/thewest/a/-/breaking/13916737/govt-stands-by-child-mental-health-tests/

American Psychiatric Association. (2000). *Diagnostic and Statistical Manual of Mental Disorders, Fourth Edition, Text Revision (DSM IV TR)*. Washington, DC: Author.

Attwood, T. (2007). *The Complete Guide to Asperger's Syndrome*. London: Jessica Kingsley.

Australian Autism Education and Training Consortium (AAETC). (2008). *Positive Partnerships: supporting school-aged students on the Autism spectrum. Professional development for teachers and other school staff.* Forestville, NSW: Autism Spectrum Australia (Aspect).

Benson, P., & Karlof, K. (2009). Anger, stress proliferation, and depressed mood among parents of children with ASD: A longitudinal replication. *Journal of Autism and Developmental Disorders, 39*, 350–362.

Buckley, B. (2009). *Relating Autism spectrum prevalence and government policy*. Paper presented at the Asia Pacific Autism Conference 2009, Sydney, Australia.

Chan, A. (2012, March 29). Autism Prevalence: Study Shows 1 in 88 Kids has the Condition. *The Huffington Post*. http://www.huffingtonpost.com/2012/03/29/autism-prevalence-rate-kids-united-states_n_1387886.html

Crosby, I. (1998). *Models of Educational Service Provision for Students with Autism Spectrum Disorder within Government Mainstream Schooling*. Perth, WA: Department of Education and Training.

Dissanayake, C. (2009). *Promoting the early identification of infants and toddlers with an Autism Spectrum Disorder.* Paper presented at the Asia Pacific Autism Conference 2009, Sydney, Australia.

Duby, J., & Plauche Johnson, C. (2009). Universal Screening of Autism Spectrum Disorders: A Snapshot within the Big Picture. *Pediatric Annals, 38*(1), 36–42.

Eccleston, R. (2005, Oct 8–9). *A World of their Own*. The Australian, pp. 26–30.

Gonski, D., Boston, K., Greiner, K., Lawrence, C., Scales, B., & Tannock, P. (2011). *Review of Funding for Schooling: Final Report*. Canberra: Department of Education, Employment and Workplace Relations.

Ford, J. (2007). Educational Supports for Students with Disabilities and Significant Behavioural Challenges: Teacher Perceptions. *Australasian Journal of Special Education, 31*(2), 109–127.

Forlin, C., Keen, M., & Barrett, E. (2008). The Concerns of Mainstream Teachers: Coping with Inclusivity in an Australian Context. *International Journal of Disability, Development and Education, 55*(3), 251–264.

Frederickson, N., Jones, A. P., & Lang, J. (2010). Inclusive provision options for pupils on the autistic spectrum. *Journal of Research in Special Educational Needs, 10*, 63–73.

Gargiulo, R. M., & Metcalf, D. (2010). *Teaching In Today's Inclusive Classrooms: A Universal Design for Learning Approach.* USA: Wadsworth Cengage Learning

Granpeesheh, D., Dixon, D. R., Tarbox, J., Kaplan, A. M., & Wilke, A. E. (2009). Effects of Age and Treatment Intensity on Behavioral Intervention Outcomes for Children with Autism Spectrum Disorders. *Research in Autism Spectrum Disorders, 3*(4), 1014–1022.

Hartley, Sigan L., Barker, Erin T., Seltzer, Marsha Mailick., Floyd, Frank., Greenberg, Jan., Orsmond, Gael., & Bolt, Daniel. (2010) The relative risk and timing of divorce in families of children with an autism spectrum disorder. *Journal of Family Psychology, 24*(4), 449–457.

Heinrichs, R. (2003). *Perfect Targets: Asperger Syndrome and Bullying; Practical Solutions for Surviving the Social World.* Kansas: Autism Asperger Publishing.

Humphrey, N., & Lewis. S. (2008a). 'Make me normal'. The views and experiences of pupils on the autistic spectrum in mainstream secondary schools. *Autism, 12*, 23–46.

Humphrey, N., & Lewis. S. (2008b). What does "inclusion" mean for pupils on the autistic spectrum in mainstream secondary schools? *Journal of Research in Special Education Needs, 8*, 132–140.

Humphrey, N., & Symes, W. (2010). Perceptions of social support and experience of bullying among pupils with autistic spectrum disorders in mainstream secondary schools. *European Journal of Special Needs Education, 25* (1), 77–91.

Kidd, T., & Kaczmarek, E. (2010). The experiences of mothers home educating their children with autism spectrum disorder. *Issues in Educational Research, 20*(3), 257–275.

Keast, K. (2012, May 24). *More Child Health Nurses Earmarked for WA. Nursing Careers Allied Health.* http://www.ncah.com.au/news-events/more-child-health-nurses-earmarked-for-wa/1217/

Laluvein, J. (2010). School inclusion and the 'community of practice'. *International Journal of Inclusive Education, 14*(1): 35–48.

Leach, D., & Duffy, M. L. (2009). Supporting students with autism spectrum disorders in inclusive settings. *Intervention in School and Clinic, 45*, 31–37.

Lynch, S. L., & Irvine, A. N. (2009). Inclusive education and best practice for children with Autism spectrum disorder: an integrated approach. *International Journal of Inclusive Education, 13*(8), 845–859.

MacDermott, S. (2008). *Can you Help Us to Help You? Autism School-age Family Needs Report.* Perth: A Joint project by The State Child Development Centre, the Autism Association of Western Australia & Therapy Focus Inc.

McDonald, J. (2010). *Seeking Progressive Fit: A constructivist grounded theory and autoethnographic study investigating how parents deal with the education of their child with an Autism Spectrum Disorder (ASD) over time.* Unpublished Doctor of Philosophy Thesis: The University of Western Australia, Perth.

Oliver, M. (1990). *The Politics of Disablement.* Basingstoke: Macmillan.

Oliver, M. (1996). *Understanding Disability.* Basingstoke: Macmillan.

Oliver, M., & Barnes, C. (2010) Disability Studies, disabled people and the struggle for inclusion. *British Journal of Sociology of Education, 31*(5), 547–560.

Roberts, J., & Prior, M. (2006). *A Review of the Research to Identify the Most Effective Models of Practice in Early Intervention for Children with Autism Spectrum Disorders.* Canberra: Australian Government Department of Health and Ageing.

Shaddock, A. (2005). Students with Autism in High Schools: A challenge for Inclusive Practice. In C. Newell & T. R. Parmenter (Eds.), *Disability in Education: Context, Curriculum and Culture* (College Year Book 2005) (pp. 22–36). Deakin West: Australian College of Educators.

Shaddock, A., Smyth King, B., & Giorcelli, L. (2007). *Project to Improve the Learning Outcomes of Students with Disabilities in the Early, Middle and Post Compusory Years of Schooling.* Barton, ACT: Department of Education, Employment and Workplace Relations.

Slee, R. (2011). *The Irregular School: Exclusion, Schooling and Inclusive Education.* London: Routledge.

Tehee, E., Honan, R., & Hevey, D. (2009). Factors Contributing to Stress in Parents of Individuals with Autistic Spectrum Disorders. *Journal of Applied Research in Intellectual Disabilities, 22,* 34–42.

APPENDIX 1A

NORTHERN SUBURBS AUTISM MUMS' GROUP, PERTH, WA
SUBMISSION TO THE EDUCATION AND HEATH STANDING COMMITTEE
PARENT COMMENTS (CIRCA) MAY 2012

Please consider our challenging, highly stressful daily lives, the brick walls we have all repeatedly faced and the enormous frustrations of dealing with an education system that preaches "inclusion" into mainstream and then practices discrimination, ignorance and total incompetence when managing our children's education and welfare. It's time for things to CHANGE!

> "...public duty demands and requires that what is right should not only be made known, but made prevalent"

Family 1

We spent five long and stressful years banging our heads against the walls of our local public primary school. As our child with ASD is also our oldest child, we had no experience of the school system, or DET system, or District Offices role, and assumed that Principals, Teachers and EA's are trained and experienced in dealing with, supporting and educating children with special needs. (After all, isn't inclusive school in mainstream schools their very policy?)

How very, very wrong we were.....

Kindy - The teacher tells us our child is showing "signs of autism" (was yet to be diagnosed over two years later). The Principal told us "not to bother applying for Schools Plus because you'll never get it" (we subsequently got funding which changed regularly but ranged from 0.2 to 0.9 FTE). NB That same Principal is now at another public primary school where one of the mums from our group has her child - they have had ongoing extremely negative interactions with the same person, and we have subsequently decided to lodge a joint complaint to DET regarding her unacceptable treatment of children with disabilities and their families.

PP - The next teacher told us she needs a full time EA to "be able to deal with" our child because she "doesn't listen" and "isn't like the other kids" and "doesn't do what she's told". New Principal at the school applies for funding, which is rejected by Schools Plus due to lack of diagnosis. Constantly called in after school by teacher listing all the things our child wouldn't "listen to" to make her life easier. No solutions or support offered by teacher or school, just continual complaints to us.

Year 1 - We finally reached the top of the waiting list for an autism assessment (after 15 months wait in the private system, the public system would have taken a further 9 months)and our child was diagnosed with autism by Paediatrician/Speech Therapist/Clinical Psychologist. Teacher says to a co-worker when discussing our child - in front of us - "anyone can buy a diagnosis these days if you have enough money". We found this deeply offensive and upsetting as well as totally inaccurate. When we offered to bring in Psych or OT to provide PD on autism, teacher says "all I need to know is how do you discipline her?". Last term of year 1 we are allocated 0.2 FTE EA time based on Schools Plus Assessment of our application. Unhappy with this outcome, we advised Schools Plus we had made appointment to see Elizabeth Constable our local MP, also the Education Minister. The following day after advising them of this (the appointment hadn't yet occurred) they increased EA funding time to 0.9 with no explanation.

Year 2 - Schools Plus funding of 0.9 FTE time used to employ an EA already employed at the school who was "floating" ie the child she had been allocated to had left the school (no surprise to us). This person was not recruited to work with our child, it was just that her FTE time of 0.9 matched our child's funding of 0.9. This recruitment did not use appropriate methods and was highly inappropriate for our child. The EA's totally and completely inappropriate, invasive and overly emotional and highly unsuitable manner dramatically increased our child's anxiety levels, resulting in previously unrequired visits to Clinical Psychologist and Child Psychiatrist, medication for anxiety, frequent school refusal, constant nail-biting, ongoing bed wetting, and a range of other anxiety related behaviours - all of which are ongoing to this day 3.5 years later. We met with the Principal at least 6 times to express concern at the lack of suitability of this person to work with our child. No action was taken other than frequent and endless meeting without any resolution or support or change. The EA time was cut to 0.7 then 0.5 by Schools Plus again without explanation. This Principal was removed by the DET the following year for incompetence. During this same year, the Deputy Principal, herself the parent of a child with autism spectrum disorder, stated in one of the many ineffective team meetings (re our child's inability to use standard student toilets and preference for the universal accessible toilet for a range of psychological issues) "your child is not disabled and does not need to use the disabled toilets". This was said approximately 2 minutes before the meeting was drawn to a close because "no DOTT time was available for the teacher to be at the meeting". We expressed our strong concern regarding this statement however in hindsight we should have taken this further with the Human Rights Commission or Equal Opportunity Commission. Parents of autistic children are battling to get through each day and night, without having to take on these sorts of antagonistic battles.

Year 3 - finally a teacher who listened and tried her very best to help support and educate our child. The Principal (who was to be removed by the DET shortly afterwards for a range of other competence issues) did not support this teacher or her extra efforts, told her "not to meet with the parents without a witness present" - as a result she stopped communicating with us for a number of months until we approached her - she broke down and cried, saying she so wanted things to go back to how they were before, she loved working with our child and appreciated our contribution and involvement (we provided textbooks, articles, private OT visits to the school, paid for her to attend a PD course etc). She told us that he had said that they were "worried about getting a Ministerial" and that it's best to "stay away from" us. She supported a change of EA and finally when an interim Principal was placed in the school, on her **first** day in the role (after discussions with the teacher and ourselves) the EA was replaced and things improved significantly. However the Principal who was effective, dynamic, experienced in working with special needs and who could have brought about great change - was transferred to another school. Another interim Principal and then he was recruited permanently. So far 5 Principals over 5 years. The last before this permanent Principal, who was there for the least time, did the most good and was then removed before she could do everything necessary to change the school. What kind of a system are they running one has to ask?

In the latter half of year 3 our child was in an altercation with another child. The school was aware of this and did nothing to prevent or assist the situation. We had repeatedly told them she requires supervision and support by an EA during lunch and recess breaks (when the incident occurred) as this is the most stressful time for a child with a lack of social understanding. The other child continued to taunt, tease and then ignore my child for the remainder of the year. She dreaded going to school after what had been a fantastic first term. Her anxiety snowballed, requiring further intervention. Getting to school each day became a major challenge.

Finally after 5 years of stress, frustration, and both of us developing our own anxiety disorders (now requiring medication and treatment), we agreed reluctantly to remove her from school and home school her. I had to give up my own business which was rewarding both professionally and financially. This has placed even greater strain on our family in so many ways. Our child is now going to a private school part-time (as she is psychiatrically unfit to attend full time due to severe and ongoing anxiety) where we pay exorbitant fees and have to fund the EA ourselves - this further increases our stress.

We feel deeply let down by the Department of Education, whose website states is " ...committed to inclusive schooling and the provision of effective classroom programs that value the diversity of students". Never has a **falser** word been spoken (with apologies to the original author). Excuse our cynicism, but as it appears that the DET and school involved has not familiarized itself with the implementation of its own principles of inclusive education - based on our 5 years experience and our discussions with over 50 families with children with ASDs - we reproduce them here from the DET website for your reference:

What are the Principles of Inclusive Education?

1. All students have the right to enrol, access and participate in schooling which **meets their individual needs.**
2. All levels of the **system value diversity** and operate within an inclusive framework.

3. A range of **effective and appropriate adjustments** is provided to ensure access, participation and achievement.
4. Adjustments are provided on a **needs basis and are equitably resourced.**
5. The system supports the development of pedagogy to **meet individual student needs.**
6. The range of coordinated **programs and services provided are flexible** and delivered **according to student needs**.
7. Services are provided and supported by **collaborative** models and partnerships.

The enormous gap between these Principles and reality is, to be honest, laughable. Urgent changes are required within DET to even begin to address these principles. An autism specific school - such as those run successfully in NSW, Vic, Tas and other states around the country and overseas in USA ,UK and Singapore amongst others - is ***desperately needed*** in Western Australia. Specifically trained teachers and EA's, appropriate environments and resources, a school where our children can be safe, happy and learn. Most parents (of children with ASD) don't want their child mainstreamed in a weak and unsupported, uncoordinated attempt to "normalise" their child and their child's life (and neither do teachers have adequate time or skill to meet their needs) - all we want is for our children to learn, have friends and fun, and be happy.

Unfortunately we do not feel able to sign this document as too many people will be identifiable as a result including our own child. We would like to complete this submission with the following words from Edmund Burke:

"Evil prevails when good men do nothing"

Family 2

3rd May 2012

Dear Sir / Madam

I am writing this statement to support some wonderful women I have met along the way who are now continuing the fight for change as I can no longer find the energy time or resource to do so.

I have two children on the Autism spectrum both high functioning one also has co morbid anxiety disorder clinical depression and one has Crohn's disease.

I suspect the reason for my cynicism is four State primary schools, SIDE, one State high school and a private high school education support unit between year 2 and year 8 for my son and one private primary school one catholic primary school and one catholic high school for my daughter from kindy to year 5

Endless meetings with principal's teacher's sometimes on a daily basis meetings with the department of inclusive schooling, telephone conversations ,and sadly a necessary and successful complaint to the human rights commission relating to the disability discrimination act resulting in a formal apology from the Director General and an undertaking to support my son for the rest of his school life!!

All of these meetings and assurances failed to help. As a result we now Home School with no support from the Department of Education other than a yearly visit from the home school moderator

Home schooling is not perfect the issues are still the same it is hard work for all of us, I have had to give up my career, the stress and anxiety it causes myself my husband our relationship and of course the autism does not go away

But what does happen is that my children feel safe, they feel that they are listened to, they are no longer bullied and their anxiety is less

They are able to get the socialisation with other homeschoolers that they never got in school because I am able to better manage their expectations and that of people we meet. We can talk openly to other families about our needs and we get the understanding we do not get in school

I heard many times (particularly for my son),

"But he must do it our way we must consider the other children he must learn to do it our way" all nicely packaged under the umbrella of inclusive schooling

I no longer have to beg for aide time I just do it myself. I spent so much time trying to get help and believe I ultimately neglected my children. This way they have my attention whereas when they were in school they had no ones attention

I am no longer made to feel like I am a bad parent I no longer have condescending people ask me if I have tried a parenting course or a "star" chart to reward good behaviour!

We regularly heard from schools that we needed to "change" my children into what they perceive are NORMAL CHILDREN instead of accepting their unique gifts. I seriously doubt if they ever once asked my child for their opinion

My children now get invited to activities (not a lot given their problems with social skills) but at least they now occur

My daughter was invited to only one birthday party in all the years at school and my son was never invited!

There is no "inclusive" school policy amongst homeschoolers because we don't need one because we are accepted for who we are.

Both my children are at a level educationally that was never possible in school, in fact recent testing suggests that my daughter is gifted and my son is certainly at university level in some areas. There are gaps in their performance due to their ASD but we are now able to celebrate their achievements not focus on failings.

No matter how high a grade my daughter achieved (which was usually top in class for all subjects except English) we were always pulled up over her deficit in English where quite honestly anyone who knows anything about her disability should know this is typically one area that a child on the autistic spectrum will not do so well!!

The tutors and teachers and parents who home school take the time to listen to our needs and work with us to help our children achieve. They are never too busy and I haven't met anyone yet who is not willing to try to change things to help

We have met many nice people in the system and certainly some very horrible people along the way, and they have all been unable to cope in a classroom situation, because I believe the support they are given from the Education Department does not equate to the needs of individual children with Autism. This is because they refuse to offer support that is meaningful to an individual and they only provide what they believe in which is a "one style fits all" and as anyone who truly understands children on the autistic spectrum knows whilst the behaviours of the autistic spectrum student are similar the triggers are different for everyone because it is, after all, "spectrum". In short, what works for one will not necessarily work for the other.

I believe the training given to educational support assistants is not sufficient to give them the skills to deal with this condition and puts enormous stress on themselves, the child and the family. The same goes for the teacher and it is grossly unfair to expect the staff in the classroom to cope with this and all the other children. What is needed is schools specific to our children particularly high functioning autism.

I believe the State and Federal governments need to address this issue as soon as possible before more children and their families are damaged. My son will probably never ever recover fully from the trauma of school and that saddens me greatly.

Inclusive schooling is a wonderful ideal but its current practice does not seem to work for many children because the levels of anxiety they feel when left unsupervised in playgrounds with their peers is unhealthy. The curriculum modifications in class are inadequate and it is also unfair to expect a teacher to be able to teach and accommodate so many different learning styles

We need our own School our own teachers we need very small classes with individual support for those that need it

My son cannot work in large groups and needs one on one support and can only really work in his areas of special interest. In reality this will never change and we need to stop trying to make our children NORMAL and acknowledge WHAT IS NORMAL FOR THEM. We are lucky our brains are flexible, theirs are not! WHAT IS WEIRD IS WE HAVE THE FLEXIBLE BRAIN BUT WE REFUSE TO CHANGE OUR THINKING SO I AM SO NOT SURE WHO HAS THE PROBLEM HERE!!!

WHAT WE NEED ARE TEACHERS AND SUPPORT STAFF PROPERLY TRAINED TO DEAL WITH HIGH FUNCTIONING AUTISTIC PEOPLE, PEOPLE WITH A PASSION FOR TEACHING AND A WILLINGNESS TO WORK WITH THE FAMILIES OF THESE CHILDREN.JUST BECAUSE AN EXPERT IN AUTISM SAYS ONE THING DOES NOT MEAN WE AS PARENTS ARE NOT RIGHT!!

There are so many more things I could say but this letter is so long already which I think is testament to the enormous problems we have with education and there are so many more things our family has to deal with and this is only one part of our life

Thank you on behalf of my family

Family 3

As a teacher for almost 20 years I can understand teachers not having the expertise in the area of disability. I don't even remember if it was mentioned when I was at uni. I believe the supports need to come from the school systems such as the school administration, Ed Dept, Catholic Ed Office etc. Often it is pretty overwhelming to have a student with extra needs in a classroom when you don't have the skills/ training to help them. I've experienced this personally.

On the other hand I know I've been guilty of having an attitude that "I know what is best because I've been to uni". Being on the other side of the fence ie as a parent has given me a whole new perspective and I can see how working together as a team will help towards achieving the best possible outcome the child, family and the class.

Family 4

This is exactly why I home school my children. How on earth can anyone leave their child with confidence in the school system as it is now. I fought this battle for over 6 years and have been homeschooling now for 5 years and seems nothing has changed!!!

As for socialization we have so much more there are so many homeschoolers out there for various reasons we have no worries about meeting people - the bonus is if we don't feel like seeing any one we don't have to and no one questions my parenting skills or my Childs behavior. Not sure what I would add to attending as I will probably never ever send my children to school (having sent them to numerous schools already). There doesn't seem any point they are much happier being home schooled and for me their comfort and happiness far out weighs any academic qualification.

Family 5

Teachers are not trained or supported by their Principals to be inclusive. They have to keep fighting the DET system to get help and support. What hope do our children have?

Family 6

It is a sad fact that our schooling system is a constant hit and miss affair with regard to inclusive practice for our children with an ASD. This message came through loud and clear with my own family's experiences trying to educate my son over the past 20+ years. That is why I decided to do some research in the area. To look at how parents deal with this situation over time, I investigated a number of different WA families whose children had various diagnoses across the autism spectrum at different points in the education process.

All of these families endured a very unreliable educational pathway for their children with an ASD. After all the families began their educational journeys in mainstream settings, two families ended up home schooling their children, another two placed their children into segregated school sites and of the last two, only one family was able to educate their child in mainstream settings to Year 12. The final family had a child with an ASD who was still in mainstream primary school at the end of the study. However, they were looking at a segregated school site as a possible option for high school.

While there is appropriate legislation supposedly in place to ensure our children's rights to an inclusive education, all the parents in the study indicated it was very often up to them to ensure their children's educational rights were observed time and time again. This is not to say that the parents did not experience some examples of excellent inclusive practice, especially at the primary school level, however, it was the inconsistency that was the major difficulty. When teachers or administration changed so did the nature of inclusivity on offer in the classroom. This was especially apparent in the high school context, where change can occur on a very frequent basis.

Family 7

But from every 10 mums I talk to, I hear 9.5 tales of woe about our kids and schooling. Please tell me I'm wrong, but what happens in our schools is an absolute outrage and a denial of our children's rights as human beings.

We settle for whatever little help we get. We might get someone to shadow our kids in the playground, but where are the social skills programs, educating our children in best practice methods etc? How good do the schools make you feel as a parent. Are we a "team" working for the best outcomes for our children? Why should we, exhausted, have to do Masters' in education level research to find out how best to deal with our children in an educational setting? Why do we ALL seem to be – correct me if I am wrong – struggling so hard with the schools our kids go to?

Family 8

We had 5 years of enormous stress dealing with the local public primary school, fighting for EA time, for curriculum differentiation, for the Autism Education Team to come and visit, for visual aids and IT assistance, fighting fighting, fighting for everything. Aren't we tired and stressed and frustrated enough just living with a child with autism? Feels like they are punishing us for having a child with a disability. We might be stressed but it's our kids who are really being punished, not being cared for, not being educated adequately, ruining their self-esteem and confidence, what are we thinking? This is supposed to be a developed country, a leader in education - what a joke.

Family 9

I do not quite know where to start when it comes to the service we have received from the Education Dept. I think our children our doubly disadvantaged as a high percentage do not have an intellectual disability so they have to fit into a system which is definitely not designed with them in mind and not enough is done to support them through.

Listening to 2 parents - both have children with special needs both are teachers - whilst waiting for X to finish his horse riding lesson. I mentioned that I had tried to get X into the school in which one of them is teaching. Both teach in a mainstream school. Here are the comments they made:

Children with disabilities should be in a special school. These children should be with teachers that want to teach them. Special Education Unit/centres have teachers whose passion is to teach these children. Mainstream teachers are not trained to work with children with disabilities and it is not their interest. Children do not receive the support they need- special ed schools/units have lots of support. Putting children with disabilities in mainstream is segregation not integration. These children just wander without friends. You see these children go on errands finding them jobs to do - this is not teaching them.

I did state have you tried to get a child into a special education school that does not have an intellectual disability - practically impossible - the children whom do manage to get in there are constantly forced out back into mainstream.

The journey with education has not been a good one for us. X is now in his 3rd primary school through the lack of understanding of autism and support he needs. The discrimination I got from the 1st primary school was so bad my LAC (local area coordinator from DSC) advised me to get an independent advocate as the discrimination we experienced was beyond her capacity of a government worker.

I have continued to battle – Yes, he still needs visuals/timetables/schedules when he going into yr 4 . Yes, a sports day is different to a sports lesson. Complete misunderstanding of his sensory needs which is interpreted as poor behaviour.

The complete inability for teachers to work outside their normal routine – so what if we get to school a couple of minutes after the morning siren. It is because he is avoiding the morning chaos. Yes, this is out of the morning routine but it allows him to transition a whole lot better. They would rather him get into on time and completely stressed so they can check that he has read his home reader. I have had therapists going into schools continuously modelling strategies which are not supported by the principal as they do not fit into whole school policy. (in other words using positive behaviour strategies)

I have moved X to a new school this year and so far it is the best school in the terms of I do not have to chase them to arrange case conferences or to get help to access help from school age services/Visiting teachers. They do come to me when activities out of normal structure as to what assistance they can do to help support him.

Yet they still have total control of how his aide time is used which is for the use of the classroom and to the detriment of X and the intensity of the support he needs. Such as X really needs one on one to help him with his learning. This is not possible as he has to share the aide with another child. Instead of doubling up to 2 aides in the classroom it is used for 1 aide to be there fulltime. Which means that the aide cannot leave the class to support X- such as when he has a meltdown. Or let X have intensive one on one on the areas of learning he needs as it would mean taking X out of the class thus leaving class without an aide for the other child. So X has to sit through Japanese which he hates then the teacher talks about how he is so far behind in English, spelling, reading and comprehension. It is totally beyond me that the school have full control of how the aide time is used and can be used for whatever reason they see fit.

His work station is placed outside of the classroom as he may get too noisy for the other children or too noisy for him. Yet they have been advised by me and the therapists involved that his seating position in class is far too visually distracting for him (full view of the class) but refuse to move him. I could continue but I better not. I am still waiting for his quiet chill out area to be set up.

My conclusion is that X would benefit greatly from being home schooled. Unfortunately I have not managed to work out how to do this as I have to work. I am unable to give up work as my household needs 2 wages to pay the bills.

Family 10

Our stories are of the same theme, but are so different. And in my experience you may start off feeling great but with the constant changes in personnel and curriculum and attitudes, life can go to "hell in a handbasket" very quickly!!!

Family 11

The main points are that every teacher I have come across are overwhelmed. They are given no/very little training and expected to get on with it. Just as they are getting to have some understanding of my child - painful process to this point - the school year is practically over and he has to start all over again with another teacher for the next school year. This has a great negative impact upon his learning.

Family 12

This is our story….

As an early childhood teacher, I was deeply concerned about my son's development from a very young age. Prior to his 2nd birthday I ignored the professional advice from his paediatrician and Child Health Nurse to "wait and see", and independently sought help from a private occupational therapist. Quickly following on from the occupational therapist, we enlisted the aid of a private speech therapist and a developmental paediatrician, for which even going private there was still a six month wait list. Over time, he was diagnosed with verbal, motor and oral dyspraxia (at age 3), followed by Global Developmental Delay (at age 3 1/2) and then Autism (at age 4 ½). At the age he is now (6 ¼) he is currently being educated within the government system at a special education school, and continues to receive both privately funded and FaHCSIA funded therapy. His current school is superb, however the journey from my initial concerns (when he was 9 months old) to now (a total of 5 ½ years) has been one of sheer anger and frustration, with healthy portions of devastation, depression, sorrow, and pain thrown into the at the endless road blocks, knock backs, wait lists, and complete lack of services available to children with developmental issues, including Autism.

We began enlisting services from the private sector because, although we were a 'high priority' there was still up to a 12 month wait list to receive services from the Child Development Centre. Nine months later, we received a six week block with a combined OT and Speech therapist for 1hr/week. There was no assessment of our son or any parent questionnaire, we just got therapy. The limited therapy that we did receive therefore was **NOT** tailored to satisfy the needs of our son, and it also appeared that the therapists did not know what to do with him. I also felt like I was treated by the system as a bad parent and that my son had problems because of the lack of stimulation I provided. The six week block ended and I was told I would receive another block of therapy after 5 – 6 weeks. Several months past with no contact from the Child Development Centre, and no Government funded therapy (although we still had our son seeing private therapists during this time) and five months later I received a letter saying that my son was on a wait list for a review. I queried this letter, as I was originally told by the Child Development Centre that our son was a "high priority", and was told that because we could afford private health cover, he was no longer considered a priority. I was in total shock as I didn't think that being able to afford private health cover discriminated against my son receiving the help he needed.

I wrote a letter to the Executive Director of Child and Adolescence Health Services which went ignored, and it was too distressing for me to take the matter further. I felt that instead of pursuing my son's issues, it was much easier to simply 'get him out of the system' rather than attempt to continue to support him. I felt very alone and at a complete loss as to what to do, and unfortunately I did not pursue the issue. Things may have turned out differently if I had, our son may have ended up at his current school a lot sooner and he would have had the benefit of those additional years in an environment that identifies supports and tailors the education / therapy program to satisfy his needs. This failure of the government system led us on a long, frustrating and winding journey trying to find the support our son needed.

We continued to search for what services were out there. We attended the Language Development Centre Playgroup (which we waited 9 months to get into), we attended the Telethon Speech and Hearing Playgroup (a 6 month wait list), and we attended Ngala coffee mornings, in a bid to find a 'place' that could help our son. The Anglican School where we had initially enrolled our son informed us that they would not be able to support his developmental needs (at least they were upfront and honest about it).

Our journey, alone, then led us to the belief that he may qualify for the Language Development Centre as at this stage he hadn't been diagnosed with Autism or Global Developmental Delay. Our hopes were restored, but eventually they were crushed when his application was rejected. We were also then informed by the psychologist at the Telethon Speech and Hearing Centre that he would not be suitable for their Kindy program either, however she had managed to get him a spot at the Sunshine Room, a program at UWA attached to the Psychology Department – at least that was something and we weren't left in the lurch.

The Sunshine Room however was only for Kindy aged children, and come the following year we would need to find a "permanent" school for our son. We had hit another roadblock with our son's schooling and were forced to renegotiate the ever winding and twisting road of our son's developmental issues to try and identify an educational institution, private or public – it didn't matter, that would cater for his needs, where could we send him?. By this stage we were getting quite desperate and feeling that there just wasn't a place out there for him. The worst of it all is that we were on this journey alone; there was no assistance or useful advice from the various Organisations or Government Departments.

I knew mainstream school was not the answer for him, and assistance for him would be minimal and inadequate, but that's where we ended up and unfortunately I was right. His level of care was basic (I received many complaints from his teacher about the time it took with his 'toileting' and the difficulties in consoling him, their answer was to call to come and collect him and take him home- this was a frequent occurrence). His learning was minimal and his teaching program was developed, instructed and assessed by the teacher assistant with no input at all from his class teacher. There was no involvement from outside sources, such as the Centre for Inclusive Schooling (even after I had queried it, the response being "on no, we don't want to get them involved." There were no meetings what so ever prior to him starting school, or throughout the school year, with myself or with any of his therapists.

I would receive comments from staff like "you know when k's done a poo, he's surrounded by flies", followed by laughter; or parents would tell me how 'cute' it was that K was 'digging' in the sandpit and singing (this was stimming and little attempt was made to interact with him, he was just left, as he 'appeared' occupied). At the time I would laugh these comments off as a coping mechanism, however they were quite hurtful, this was my son that they were talking about. Their strategy for dealing with him was to phone me when it all got 'too much' to go and pick him up, and complain to me about how much of their time he was taking. Unfortunately this occurred often. He also continued at the Sunshine Room for 2 half days/week, but while the staff/student ratio was sufficient they too did not know how to best cater for my son. To my disbelief, there was no assistance at the Sunshine Room from psychologists; even 4th year supervised students as I was lead to believe and as there had been in the past.

After the Autism diagnosis (which I had to fight tooth and nail for, but thankfully I had a wonderful Paediatrician) I placed my son in a Private Catholic School for a trial period which had a special education unit attached to it. For a good part of third term, and all of forth term this was my son's timetable in his Kindy year:

Monday am:	Sunshine Room
Monday pm:	ABA Therapy
Tuesday am:	Special Ed unit at Catholic School
Tuesday pm:	Sunshine Room
Wednesday am:	Alternate speech/OT
Wednesday pm:	Mainstream School
Thursday am:	Special Ed unit at Catholic School
Thursday pm:	ABA Therapy
Friday am & pm:	Mainstream School

At some stage during this time something happened and what little progression he had completely stopped and regression set in. It took 20 months to regain what had been lost (including language, toileting, skills such as drawing circles & riding a bike). Seizures were ruled out and the only explanation for this regression was stress. During this regression, therapy was pursued with little results.

At the end of my son's Kindy year, I pulled him out of the mainstream government system as the level of support, the program and resources were completely inadequate. At the beginning of Pre-Primary he began his schooling at the Catholic School in the Special Education Unit, as well as half a day/week at the Autism Association. While care and concern was there and they never gave up on him, unfortunately my son did not cope with the structure of their day – Special Education in the morning and mainstream in the afternoon (where he would often go to extra curriculum classes) on top of therapy and attending the Autism Association.

It was only through discussions with other parents who also had children with Autism that I found out about a couple of other options. Firstly I contacted Beckenham Primary School as they run an ABA program for children with Autism. I was told that they only take high functioning Autism and that this program would not be suitable for my son – at least they were honest. That led me to my final option – a Special Education School that takes children with low functioning Autism (which I previously was not aware of). The decision was agonising and heart breaking, but we were left with no choice. Thankfully it has been the best place for him and he has flourished ever since. He is happy, he is learning, he no longer has melt downs, and I no longer have to pick him up from school because they can't deal with him.

Trying to explain our journey is very difficult in such few words, and with time, the hardest days are difficult to recall (perhaps an inbuilt mechanism to save us from going mad!) What I do remember, very clearly was how easy it was for people to give up on us, and more importantly our son. The tears along our journey far out way the laughter, and the road blocks and round-a-bouts were endless, not to mention the thousands and thousands of dollars we spent on private therapy. If it wasn't for my persistence and determination and constant searching for where our son would be best placed within the education system we would not be in such a wonderful place now. Thankfully, we only spent one year in the mainstream sector, I hate to think what kind of a situation we would be in now had we have persevered there.

In summary, our journey would have been far less stressful, and less complicated (not to mention much, much cheaper) had the Child Development Centre supported our son. We could have been at the Special Education School right from the start, his diagnosis could have been discovered at a much earlier age and perhaps we would not have endured the heartache of seeing him regress (and the endless EEG/s and MRI and neurology appointments at PMH).

Obviously, money (and lots of it) is needed to put these support systems in place. It felt like we were 'kicked out' of the Child Development Centre because of lack of funding and resources and they clearly needed to 'cull' their wait list. The integration theory in mainstream schools is wonderful, but perhaps we need to seriously ensure that intervention is occurring at the same time or perhaps even before we consider integration.

It baffles me as to why in the UK families receive 15 hours of intensive intervention per week and in America they receive 20 hours per week with an ASD diagnosis, yet in Australia (the supposed lucky country) our funding (both state and federal) equates to a mere 5 and a half hours per week. It all comes down to money, and how important our country perceives the needs of our children to be. As research clearly indicates, the level of support our children with Autism and other developmental delays requires is between 25 and 40 hours/week. I'm sure if my son was correctly managed, the concerns I had voiced were listened to, and my son's developmental issues were not merely 'left' for me to deal with, we would not have endured the roller coaster ride we did in trying to support and find the best school and intervention services for our son.

APPENDIX 1B

20 May 2012
Premier
Hon. Colin James Barnett MLA
Suite 12,
589 Stirling Highway
Cottesloe WA 6011

Dear Premier,

HBLN (Home Based Learning Network) as the peak body, supporting close to a 1000 home educators in Western Australia, has seen an escalation in the number of families with Special Needs children seeking support and services from our organisation over the last 12 months. As a result of this we have now adjusted our membership applications to reflect this as this vulnerable section of society is the fastest growing population within the local home education community here in Western Australia.

These families find themselves home educating, usually utterly exhausted from the rigours and demands of a school system that was simply unable to meet their needs, and from the daily challenges thrown at them by the constant needs of their Special Needs child/ren.

On behalf of these families', HBLN (Home Based Learning Network) is advocating for a more supportive environment within DETWA. Currently the educational support offered these families stops at the yearly moderators visit leaving families to struggle with compliance of academic requirements that are often at odds with the child's actual needs and abilities. The pressures of living with a Special Needs child/ren while finding their own resources with no outside funding for their home education program further drains the energy, passion and strength of these courageous families, families that are already under enormous financial, emotional and mental stress.

HBLN is concerned for their welfare, especially the mental health of the primary carer and educator; therefore we ask that the following supports be implemented to greatly aid in the delivery of quality of life, learning and lifestyle, to enable families to achieve better learning and living outcomes:

1. That the families of special needs children are able to access the current Special Needs Curriculum resources that support the modification and adaptations of the curriculum that schools currently have access too, and later the National Special Needs Curriculum, as this will better reflect the educational needs of these children enabling both the families and their moderators to realize these children's abilities in their learning journey.

2. That the position of "Home Educator Special Needs Assistant" be established under the current Centre for Inclusive Schooling. Where families needing educational support can access guidance and information via phone or email support; the person filling this position would need both a solid foundation in special needs education and an understanding of the various methodologies used in the home based community to enable best practice models and processes per the children's needs and development.
3. We would ask that a chaplain/counsellor position be appointed to support these families, especially the mental health of the primary educator and carer who often feels isolated and unsupported. We see this role as a support for the parents, rather than for the children.
4. That Professional Development days are offered to families as the ones responsible for their children's learning. We ask that these days be offered gratis and with care services provided for their children. We see the care being provided for via different avenues, namely through University programs e.g. UWA 'Thriving or Uni-Gym programs; Hiring community minded services and venues such as "Beachside" or Autism West to provide a safe environment for the children during these sessions with HBLN to provide funding for families to pay for care.

HBLN is committed to providing support and service to the home based community, however as a grassroots organisation with no outside funding there are limits as to what we can provide. Though the home educating community is comprised of many people willing to share their time and expertise free of charge, the influx of new families struggling with the challenges of a Special Needs child needing assistance on a daily basis is overwhelming and there is only so much our families are able to do to help one another while still meeting their own family's needs.

HBLN are therefore seeking an appointment to discuss further this government's willingness to assist meeting the needs of these families who are currently saving the state $100,000 of dollars each year in support services and school funding.

Yours Sincerely
Hayley Ayers-Findlay
President HBLN

www.hbln.org.au
Post Office Box 1893, Midland W.A. 6936

HBLN
Learning for Life

APPENDIX 2

The following form is reproduced from the Australian Human Rights Commission website: https://www.humanrights.gov.au/sites/default/files/content/complaints_information/pdf/WEB_Complaints_under_DDA.pdf

Australian Human Rights Commission

Complaints under the Disability Discrimination Act

What is the Disability Discrimination Act?

The *Disability Discrimination Act 1992* (Cth) (the DDA) makes it against the law to treat you unfairly because of your disability.

You are also covered if you had a disability in the past, may develop a disability in the future or if people think you have a disability.

People who are relatives, friends and carers of people with a disability are also protected by the DDA.

When can this law be used?

You can use the DDA to get fair treatment in many areas of public life such as in:

- **Employment** – getting a job, terms and conditions of a job, training, promotion, being dismissed.
- **Education** – enrolling or studying in a course at a private or public school, college or university.
- **Accommodation** – renting or buying a house or unit.
- **Getting or using services** – such as banking and insurance services, services provided by government departments, transport or telecommunication services, professional services like those provided by lawyers, doctors or tradespeople, services provided by restaurants, shops or entertainment venues.
- **Accessing public places** – such as parks, government offices, restaurants, hotels or shopping centres.

You can also use the DDA if you are harassed because of your disability.

What is disability discrimination?

Disability discrimination happens when a person with a disability is treated less favourably than a person without the disability in the same or similar circumstances. For example, it would be 'direct disability discrimination' if a nightclub or restaurant refused a person entry because they are blind and have a guide dog.

Discrimination also happens when there is a rule or policy that is the same for everyone but has an unfair effect on people with a particular disability. This is called 'indirect discrimination'. For example, it may be indirect discrimination if the only way to enter a public building is by a set of stairs because people with disabilities who use wheelchairs would be unable to enter the building.

Exceptions

Like other anti-discrimination laws, the DDA says that in some circumstances treating someone differently because of their disability won't be against the law. This is known as an exception or exemption.

For example, the DDA says it may not be against the law to refuse to employ a person with a disability, if because of their disability they cannot perform the inherent requirements of a job. However, the DDA also says that employers must consider how the person with a disability could be provided with reasonable adjustments to help them do the job. An adjustment is reasonable if it does not impose 'unjustifiable hardship' on the employer.

Unjustifiable hardship also applies to other situations. For example, it may not be against the law to only provide entrance to a building by a set of stairs if the owner of the building can show that it would cause unjustifiable hardship to modify the building to provide wheelchair access.

What can I do if I experience discrimination?

You may want to deal with the situation yourself by raising it directly with the person or people involved.

If this does not resolve the situation, or you do not feel comfortable doing this, you can make a complaint to the Australian Human Rights Commission. You can also have someone such as a solicitor, advocate or trade union make a complaint on your behalf.

It does not cost anything to make a complaint to the Commission.

Your complaint needs to be put in writing. The Commission has a complaint form that you can fill in and post or fax to us or you can lodge a complaint online at our website. If you are not able to put your complaint in writing, we can help you with this.

The complaint should say what happened, when and where it happened and who was involved.

A complaint can be made in any language. If you need a translator or interpreter, the Commission can arrange this for you.

What will happen with my complaint?

When the Commission receives a complaint about something that is covered by the DDA, the President of the Commission can investigate the complaint and try to resolve it by conciliation. The Commission is not a court and cannot determine that discrimination has happened. The Commission's role is to get both sides of the story and help those involved resolve the complaint.

Commission staff may contact you to get further information about your complaint.

Generally, the Commission will tell the person or organisation the complaint is against (the respondent) about your complaint and give them a copy of the complaint. The Commission may ask the respondent for specific information or a detailed response to your complaint.

Where appropriate, the Commission will invite you to participate in conciliation. Conciliation is an informal process that allows you and the respondent to talk about the issues and try to find a way to resolve the complaint.

If your complaint is not resolved or it is discontinued for another reason, you can take your complaint to the Federal Court of Australia or the Federal Magistrates Court.

Where can I get more information?

The Australian Human Rights Commission's contact details are:

Telephone
Complaint Info line: 1300 656 419 (local call)
TTY: 1800 620 241 (toll free)
Fax: (02) 9284 9611

Post
Australian Human Rights Commission
GPO Box 5218
Sydney NSW 2001

Online
Email: complaintsinfo@humanrights.gov.au
Website: www.humanrights.gov.au

You can make a complaint online by going to
www.humanrights.gov.au/complaints_information/online_form/index.html.

If you are deaf or have a hearing impairment the Commission can arrange for an Auslan interpreter if this is needed. You can also communicate with us by TTY by calling 1800 620 241.

If you are blind or have a vision impairment, the Commission can provide information in alternative formats on request.

If you are thinking about making a complaint, you might also want to consider obtaining legal advice or contacting your trade union. There are community legal services that can provide free advice about discrimination and harassment. Contact details for your closest community legal centre can be found at www.naclc.org.au/directory.

Disability discrimination legal services
There are also legal services which provide free specialist advice about disability discrimination. Contact details for your nearest Disability Discrimination Legal Centre can also be found at www.naclc.org.au/directory.

Disclaimer

The information on this fact sheet is only intended as a guide.
It is not a substitute for legal advice.

APPENDIX 3

The following is an extract regarding West Australian Education Services from a recently produced Autism Parent Handbook by fellow parent, Heidi Brandis. The full publication can be accessed from www.autismwest.org.au or autismparentshandbook@gmail.com.

EDUCATION

There are three main options in Perth – government, private school or home schooling.

1. WA GOVERNMENT PUBLIC SCHOOLS – DEPARTMENT OF EDUCATION (DET)

   Early Intervention Units

   Contact Principal of Autism Education: (08) 9426 7110
   DET runs 11 Education Support Centres in WA offering intensive behavioural intervention programs for Kindergarten and Pre-Primary children with Autism.

   Accelerated Learning Centres

   DET centres operate in Heathridge and Beckenham Primary Schools (Kindy/Pre-Primary) providing a two-year intensive intervention based on ABA principles (12 hours per week).

   Secondary Autism Extension Program

   DET has four high-school Autism Extension Programs for years 8–10, located at Ashdale Secondary College, Ocean Reef High School, Canning Vale College and South Fremantle Senior High School, catering for students with high functioning Autism, incorporating life skills and community access programs in curriculum. There are currently no specific autism education programs for years one to seven or years 11 and 12 in Western Australia.

   Education Support Centres/Units

   DET runs a number of Education Support Centres and Units, both attached to mainstream schools and independent units. Contact your local DET District Office to find out if your local schools have an education support service.

Schools Plus

Website: det.wa.edu.au/schoolsplus/detcms/portal
Deals with funding applications for an education assistant (EA) to work in the classroom with your child. This application is done through your child's school. The Principal/Deputy at your school will need to submit an application if the teacher requires support to facilitate your child's education. This can be a lengthy process but well worth it to get necessary support for your child at school. Amount of funding and subsequent EA time depends on the quality of application. This decision can be appealed.

School of Special Educational Needs: Disability (SSEND)

Address: Statewide Services Centre
33 Giles Avenue, Padbury, WA 6025
Tel: (08) 9402 6100
Email: SSEND.Enquiries@education.wa.edu.au
Website: det.wa.edu.au/ssen
The Autism Education Service (AES) provides specialist services to networks and school communities for students with an ASD, whose educational needs and self-regulation skills require specialist support. An Autism Education Service Officer can visit the school, provide resources and support to teacher and school. A visiting teacher will come first and then may request the Autism Team visit.

2. PRIVATE and INDEPENDENT SCHOOLS

Association of Independent Schools (AISWA)

Address: PO Box 1817, Osborne Park, WA 6916
Tel: (08) 9441 1600
Email: reception@ais.wa.edu.au
Website: www.ais.wa.edu.au
AISWA oversees all non-Catholic private and independent schools in WA. AISWA employs two Inclusive Education Consultants to support independent school students with a disability. Limited funding may be available to support your child at school. Parents need to discuss supports for their child at school directly with the school principal.

Catholic Education Office (CEOWA)

Address: 50 Ruislip Street, Leederville, WA 6007
Tel: (08) 6380 5200
Email: swd@ceo.wa.edu.au
Website: internet.ceo.wa.edu.au Search word 'Disabilities'.

Students may receive assistance through a range of options including: Access to learning support teachers; small group or individual instruction, teacher assistant support. A number of Catholic schools have an Education Support Centre where students may receive additional support with specialist staff. Catholic Education Support Centres are an integral part of the school where students are enrolled in the school in the same way as students without disability. Depending on needs and abilities, some students may work primarily in the centre, while others will spend the majority or the whole of their time in regular classes with varying levels of support.

Non-Government Schools Psychology Service (NGSPS)

Address: Care of: Catholic Education Office,
50 Ruislip Street, Leederville WA 6007
Tel: (08) 6380 5256
Website: www.ais.wa.edu.au/non-government-school-psychology-service/
Funded by the State Government through the Department of Education Services (DES). All registered non-government schools throughout WA are eligible for access to services provided by the NGSPS. The NGSPS has a reference group consisting of representatives from CEOWA and AISWA. Services include: Assistance to staff within schools with either broad-based or individually directed programs or interventions; individual needs-based interventions in relation to educational or psychological needs; centralised and school-based training in evidence and best-practice-based intervention programs; broad based, system level school interventions to address educational, behavioural or social and emotional needs; crisis management planning and response; individual needs-based interventions in relation to educational or psychological needs.

3. HOME EDUCATION

Department of Education (DET)

Website: www.det.wa.edu.au/homeeducation/detcms/portal
Approval to educate children at home is required from the WA Department of Education. For requirements and resources contact your nearest district education office and ask for Home Education Moderator. Addresses and telephone numbers are on their website.

School of Isolated and Distance Education (SIDE)

Tel: (08) 9242 6300
Address: 164-194 Oxford Street, Leederville, WA 6007
Email: info@side.wa.edu.au
Website: www.side.wa.edu.au

The Schools of Isolated and Distance Education is the centre of distance and on-line learning within DET. The Leederville campus of SIDE provides education for students in years 8-12 who, for various reasons, cannot attend classes in a regular school.

Home Based Learning Network

Website: www.hbln.org.au
For those considering home education, start with HBLN. They can get you started and offer a range of activities, discounts, newsletters, and other services. HBLN is a volunteer, not-for-profit organization, dedicated to supporting all home-based learners based in WA.

Southlands Christian College

Tel: (08) 6818 6000
Email: southlands@acc.edu.au
Website: southlands.accde.edu.au
Distance education program which can be purchased for home education, either online or as a hardcopy.

Swan Christian College – online high school learning

Tel: (08) 9374 8300
Address: 381-401 Great Northern Highway Middle Swan, WA 6056
Email: swanjuniorschool@scea.wa.edu.au or swanseniorschool@scea.wa.edu.au
Website: www.swan.wa.edu.au/swan-online
Aims to provide a caring learning environment in which students are educated, encouraged and equipped to be people of passion and integrity.

Khan Academy

Website: www.khanacademy.org
Free educational videos on huge range of topics.

Home Education Australia

Website: www.hea.edu.au
Aims to encourage and promote the practice of home educating in Australia and to provide members with benefits which would be difficult to obtain by individuals or smaller groups.

Perth Homeschoolers Program

Website: www.perthhomeschoolers.com
Online Perth home schoolers' community.

Perth Too Cool for School Home School

Group on Facebook: www.facebook.com/groups/329600967141215/

4. TERTIARY EDUCATION

Curtin Specialist Mentoring Program (CSMP)

Curtin University has recently introduced a pilot peer-to-peer mentoring program for tertiary students on the autism spectrum. The program is to be replicated and evaluated at the University of Western Australia in 2015. The mentoring module will eventually be available Australia wide through the Autism Cooperative Research Centre (CRC) website (http://www.autismcrc.com.au/).
Enquiries: Dr. Jasmine McDonald (Jasmine.Mcdonald@curtin.edu.au), and Theresa Kidd (theresa.kidd@postgrad.curtin.edu.au).

REFERENCES

Adreon, D., & Stella, J. (2001). Transition to middle and high school: Increasing the success of students with Asperger syndrome. *Intervention in School and Clinic, 36*, 266–271.

Ainscow, M. (1993). Teacher education as a strategy for developing inclusive schools. In R. Slee (Ed.), *Is there a desk with my name on it? The politics of integration* (pp. 201–217). London: The Falmer Press.

Ainscow, M. (1995). Education for all: Making it happen. *Support for Learning, 10*(2), 147–157.

Ainscow, M., Booth, T., & Dyson A. (2006). Inclusion and the standards agenda: Negotiating policy pressures in England. *International Journal of Inclusive Education, 10*(4–5), 295–308.

Allen, K. A., Bowles, T. V., & Weber, L. L. (2013). Mothers' and fathers' stress associated with parenting a child with autism spectrum disorder. *Autism Insights, 5*, 1–11.

American Psychiatric Association. (1980). *Diagnostic and statistical manual of mental disorders, Third Edition, (DSM-III)*. Washington, DC: American Psychiatric Association.

American Psychiatric Association. (1994). *Diagnostic and statistical manual of mental disorders, Fourth Edition (DSM-IV)*. Washington, DC: American Psychiatric Association.

American Psychiatric Association. (2000). *Diagnostic and statistical manual of mental disorders, Fourth Edition, Text Revision (DSM IV TR)*. Washington, DC: American Psychiatric Association.

American Psychiatric Association. (2013a). *Autism spectrum disorder.* Retrieved June 2, 2013 from http://www.dsm5.org/Documents/Autism%20Spectrum%20Disorder%20Fact%20Sheet.pdf

American Psychiatric Association. (2013b). *Diagnostic and statistical manual of mental disorders, Fifth Edition, (DSM 5)*. Washington, DC: American Psychiatric Association.

Andrews, R., Elkins, J., Berry, P., & Burge, J. (1979). *A survey of special education in Australia.* Queensland: University of Queensland: Fred and Eleanor Schonell Educational Research Centre.

Anderson, S. R., Dipietero, E. K., Edwards, G. L., & Christian, W. P. (1987). Intensive home-based early intervention with autistic children. *Education and Treatment of Children, 10*, 352–366.

Arora, T. (2006). Elective home education and special education needs. *Journal of Research in Special Education Needs, 6*, 55–66.

Arthur, N. (1998). The effects of stress, depression and anxiety on post secondary students' coping strategies. *Journal of College Student Development, 39*(1), 11–22.

Ashman, A., & Elkins, J. (2005). *Educating children with diverse abilities* (2nd ed.). French's Forest: Pearson Education Australia.

Asperger, H. (1991/1944). Autistic psychopathy in childhood. In U. Frith (Ed.), *Autism and Asperger syndrome* (pp. 37–92). Cambridge: Cambridge University Press.

Attwood, T. (1998). *Asperger's syndrome: A guide for parents and professionals.* London: Jessica Kingsley.

Attwood, T. (2004). Strategies to reduce the bullying of young children with Asperger syndrome. *Australian Journal of Early Childhood, 29*(3), 15–23.

Attwood, T. (2007). *The complete guide to Asperger's syndrome*. London: Jessica Kingsley.

Australian Advisory Board on Autism Spectrum Disorders. (2011, November). *National Call to Action.* Retrieved from www.autismadvisoryboard.org.au

Australian Autism Education and Training Consortium (AAETC). (2008a). *Positive partnerships: Supporting school-aged students on the autism spectrum. Professional development for teachers and other school staff.* Forestville, NSW: Autism Spectrum Australia (Aspect).

Australian Autism Education and Training Consortium (AAETC). (2008b). *Positive partnerships: Supporting school-aged students on the autism spectrum. Workshops and information sessions for parents/carers.* Forestville, NSW: Autism Spectrum Australia (Aspect).

Australian Autism Education and Training Consortium (AAETC). (2009, December). Update. *Positive Partnerships Newsletter*. Retrieved from AAETC @Autismspectrum.org.au

Australian Government. (2014, May) *Budget 2014-2015.* Retrieved May 25, 2014 from http://www.budget.gov.au/2014-15/content/bp1/html/bp1_bst1-01.htm

REFERENCES

Autism Spectrum Australia (Aspect). (2012). *We belong: Investigating the experiences, aspirations and needs of adults with Asperger's disorder and high functioning autism.* Sydney: Autism Spectrum Australia.

Australian Curriculum, Assessment and Reporting Authority (ACARA). (2013). *Student diversity and the Australian curriculum: Advice for principals, schools and teachers.* Sydney: Australian Curriculum, Assessment and Reporting Authority.

Autism Management Group. (2005). *Minutes of 23 February, 2005 Meeting.* Perth: WA Department of Education and Training.

Autism Speaks. (2008, October). *A look at state laws forcing autism coverage.* Retrieved October 19, 2008 from www.Autismspeaks.org

Autism Spectrum Australia (Aspect). (2012). *We Belong: Investigating the experiences, aspirations and needs of adults with Asperger's disorder and high functioning autism.* Forestville, NSW: Autism Spectrum Australia.

Bailey, A., Palferman, S., Heavey, L., & Le Couteur, A. (1998). Autism: The phenotype in relatives. *Journal of Autism and Developmental Disorders, 28*(5), 369–392.

Baird, G., Cass, H., & Slonims, V. (2003). Diagnosis of autism. *British Medical Journal, 327*, 488–493.

Ball, S. (1994). *Education reform: A critical and post-structural approach.* Buckingham: Open University Press.

Banks, M. (2005). *Autism management program. 2005 parliamentary estimates hearings.* Perth: Department of Education and Training.

Barnes, C. (1996). Theories of disability and the origins of oppression of disabled people in western society. In L. Barton (Ed.), *Disability and society: Emerging issues and insights* (pp. 42–50). London: Longman.

Baron-Cohen S., Bolton, P., Wheelwright, S., Scahill, V., Short, L., Meade, G., & Smith, A. (1998). Autism occurs more often in families of physicists, engineers, and mathematicians. *Autism, 2*, 296–301.

Barratt-Peacock, J. (1997). *The why and how of Australian home education.* Yankalilla, SA: Learning Books.

Beazley, K. (1984). *Report of the committee of inquiry into education in Western Australia.* Perth: Ministry of Education.

Benson, P., & Karlof, K. (2009). Anger, stress proliferation, and depressed mood among parents of children with ASD: A longitudinal replication. *Journal of Autism and Developmental Disorders, 39*, 350–362.

Berry, J. O., & Hardman, M. L. (1998). *Lifespan perspectives on the family and disability.* Boston: Allyn & Bacon.

Bettelheim, B. (1967). *The empty fortress: Infantile autism and the birth of the self.* New York, NY: Free Press.

Bibby, P., Eikeseth, S., Martin, N. T., Mudford, O. C., & Reeves, D. (2002). Progress and outcomes for children with autism receiving parent-managed intensive interventions. *Research in Developmental Disabilities, 23*, 81–104.

Bickers, C. (2014, July 20). At last – a level field for all schools. *Sunday Times*, p.13.

Birnbrauer, J. S., & Leach, D. J. (1993). The Murdoch early intervention program after two years. *Behaviour Change, 10*, 63–74.

Blok, H. (2004). Performance in home-schooling, An argument against compulsory schooling in the Netherlands. *International Review of Education, 50*, 39–52.

Booth, T., Ainscow, M., Black-Hawkins, K., Vaughan, M., & Shaw, L. (2000). *Index for inclusion: Developing learning and participation in schools.* Manchester: Centre for Studies on Inclusive Education: Centre for Educational Needs, University of Manchester.

Briskman, J., & Happe, F. (2001). Exploring the cognitive phenotype of autism: Weak "Central Coherence" in parents and siblings of children with autism: II. Real-life skills and preferences. *Journal of Child Psychology and Psychiatry, 42*(3), 309–316.

Broadstock, M., Doughty, C., & Eggleston, M. (2007). Systematic review of the effectiveness of pharmacological treatments for adolescents and adults with autism spectrum disorder. *Autism, 11*(4), 335–348.

Bromley, J., Hare, D. J., Davidson, K., & Emerson, E. (2004). Mothers supporting children with autistic spectrum disorders. *Autism, 8*(4), 409–423.
Buckley, B. (2009). *Relating autism spectrum prevalence and government policy.* Paper presented at the Asia Pacific Autism Conference 2009, Sydney, Australia.
Buckley, B. (2012). *Interpreting data on autism spectrum disorders from Australian government sources.* Paper presented at Australian Society for Autism Research 2012, Sydney, Australia.
Camarena, P. M., & Sarigiani, P. A. (2009). Postsecondary educational aspirations of high-functioning adolescents with autism spectrum disorders and their parents. *Focus on Autism and Other Developmental Disabilities, 24*(2), 115–128.
Cantwell, D. P., & Baker, D. L. (1977). Families of autistic and dysphasic children. II. Mothers' speech to the children. *Jounal of Autism and Childhood Schizophrenia, 7*, 313–327.
Cantwell, D. P., Baker, D. L., & Rutter, M. (1979). Families of autistic and dysphasic children. I. Family life and interaction patterns. *Archives of General Psychiatry, 36*(6), 682–687.
Cantwell, D. P., & Baker, L. (1984). Research concerning families of children with autism. In E. Schopler & G. Mesibov (Eds.), *The effects of autism on the family* (pp. 41–63). New York, NY: Plenum Press.
Cappodocia, M., Weiss J., & Peplar, D. (2012). Bullying experiences among children and youth with autism spectrum disorders. *Journal of Autism and Developmental Disorders, 42*(2), 266–277.
Carrick Institute for Learning and Teaching in Higher Education. (2006, December 4). *Creating accessible teaching and support.* Retrieved December 4, 2006 from http://www.adcet.edu.au
Castelli, F., Frith, C., Happe, F., & Frith, U. (2002). Autism, Asperger syndrome and brain mechanisms for the attribution of mental states to animated shapes. *Brain, 125*, 1839–1849.
Catholic Association for Special Education Support. (1995). *Invitation To The Banquet* (Report on the Survey of the Educational Needs of Catholic Children with Disabilities/Special Needs). Perth, WA: Catholic Association for Special Education Support.
Chadbourne, R. (1997). *Including children with intellectual disabilities in regular schools: A review of the Western Australian project.* Perth, W.A: Joint Management Committee of the Inclusion Pilot Project.
Chalfant, A. M., Rapee, R., & Carroll, L. (2007). Treating anxiety disorders in children with high-functioning autism spectrum disorders: A controlled trial. *Journal of Autism and Developmental Disorders, 37*(10), 213–231.
Chalmers, R. (1998). *How teachers manage their work in 'inclusive' classrooms* (Unpublished doctor of philosophy thesis). University of Western Australia, Perth.
Charman, T., Taylor, E., Drew, A., Cockerill, H., Brown, J., & Baird, G. (2005). Outcome at 7 years of children diagnosed with autism at age 2: Predictive validity of assessments conducted at 2 and 3 years of age and pattern of symptom change over time. *Journal of Child Psychology and Psychiatry, 46*(5), 500–513.
Charmaz, K. (2000). Grounded theory: Objectivist and constructivist methods. In N. K. Denzin & Y. S. Lincoln (Eds.), *Handbook of qualitative research* (2nd ed., pp. 509–535). Thousand Oaks, CA: Sage.
Charmaz, K. (2006). *Constructing grounded theory: A practical guide through qualitative analysis.* Thousand Oaks, CA: Sage.
Chown, N., & Bevan, N. (2012). Intellectually capable but socially excluded? A review of the literature and research on students with autism in further education. *Journal of Further and Higher Education, 36*(4), 477–493.
Clifford, S. M., & Dissanayake, C. (2008). The early development of joint attention in infants with Autistic disorder using home video observations and parental interview. *Journal of Autism and Developmental Disorders, 38*, 791–805.
Cologon, K. (2013). *Inclusion in education: Towards equality for students with disability.* Sydney: Children and Families Research Centre, Institute of Early Childhood, Macquarie University.
Commonwealth of Australia. (1992). *Disability discrimination act.* Canberra: Australian Printing Service.
Commonwealth of Australia. (2005). *Disability standards for education.* Melbourne: Federal Government of Australia.
Commonwealth of Australia. (2006). *Disability discrimination act (No.SLI 2006 No. 50).* Canberra: Attorney General's Department.

Coo, H., Ouellette-Kuntz, H., Lloyd, J. E., Kasmara, L., Holden, J., & Lewis, M. (2008). Trends in autism prevalence: Diagnostic substitution revisited. *Journal of Autism and Developmental Disorders, 38*(6), 1036–1046.

Cooper, J. (2003). From exclusion to inclusion: Some lessons from abroad. In S. Powell (Ed.), *Special teaching in higher education: Successful strategies for access and inclusion* (pp. 19–36). London: Kogan Page Ltd.

Courchesne, E. (2004). Brain development in autism: Early overgrowth followed by premature arrest of growth. *Mental Retardation and Developmental disabilities Research Review, 10*(2), 106–111.

Cox, A., Rutter, M., Newman, S., & Bartak, L. (1975). A comparative study of infantile autism and specific developmental receptive language disorder: II. Parental characteristics. *British Journal of Psychiatry, 126*, 146–159.

Crosby, I. (1998). *Models of educational service provision for students with autism spectrum disorder within government mainstream schooling.* Perth, WA: Department of Education and Training.

Cummings, L. (2006, October 14). Coroner criticises failures. *The Daily Telegraph*, p. 7.

Dawson, G., & Osterling, J. (1997). Early intervention in autism. In M. J. Guralnick (Ed.), *The effectiveness of early intervention* (pp. 307–326). Baltimore: Brookes Publishing.

Dempsey, I., Foreman, P., & Jenkinson, J. (2002). Educational enrolment of students with a disability in New South Wales and Victoria. *International Journal of Disability, Development and Education, 49*(1), 31–46.

DeMeyer, M. K. (1979). *Parents and children in autism.* Washington, DC: V.H. Winston & Sons.

Department of Education and Training. (2004). *Pathways to the future: A report of the review of educational services for students with disabilities in government schools: A summary.* East Perth: Department of Education and Training.

Department of Education and Training. (2006, December 15). *Schools Plus Handbook.* Retrieved from www.schoolsplus.det.wa.edu.au

Department of Education, Employment and Workplace Relations. (2012). *Report on the Review of the Disability Standards for Education 2005.* Canberra, DEEWR.

Department of Education, Employment and Workplace Relations (DEEWR). (2013). *Fact Sheet 10: DSM-5 and autism spectrum disorder.* Retrieved from the Autism Training Positive Partnerships website: http://www.autismtraining.com.au/orionfiles/upload/public/files/Fact%20Sheet%2010_DSM-5_July2013.pdf

Deppeler, J., & Harvey, D. (2004). Validating the British index for inclusion for the Australian context: Stage one. *International Journal of Inclusive Education, 8*(2), 155–184.

Dissanayake, C. (2009). *Promoting the early identification of infants and toddlers with an autism spectrum disorder.* Paper presented at the Asia Pacific Autism Conference 2009, Sydney, Australia.

Donovan, M. (2008, May 20). Research tool can detect autism at 9 months of age. *EurekAlert*. Retrieved from www.eurekalert.org

Dor-Shav, N. K., & Horowitz, Z. (1984). Intelligence and personality variables of parents of autistic children. *The Journal of Genetic Psychology, 144*, 39–50.

Duby, J., & Plauche Johnson, C. (2009). Universal screening of autism spectrum disorders: A snapshot within the big picture. *Pediatric Annals, 38*(1), 36–42.

Duffey, J. G. (2002). Home schooling children with special needs: A descriptive study. *Home School Researcher, 15*(2), 1–13.

Dunlap, G., Robbins, F. R., & Darrow, M. (1994). Parents' reports of their children's challenging behaviors: Results of a statewide survey. *Mental retardation, 32*, 206–212.

Duvall, S. F., Delquadri J. C., Ward D. L., & Greenwood C. R. (1997). An exploratory study of home school instructional environments and their effects on the basic skills of students with learning disabilities. *Education and Treatment of Children, 20*, 150–172.

Eccleston, R. (2005, October 8–9). A World of their Own. *The Australian*, 26–30.

Education Department of Western Australia. (1993). *Social justice in education: Policy and guidelines for the education of students with disabilities.* Perth: Ministry of Education.

Education Department of Western Australia. (1998). *Making the difference: Students at educational risk.* Perth: Education Department of Western Australia.

Education Department of Western Australia. (1999). *School education act, 1999*. Division 3 (s.73); Division 4 (S86 and 87); Division 5: Author.

Edwards, V. (2009, September 14). Study by Flinders University detects signs of autism in first weeks. *The Australian*. Retrieved from http://search.news.com.au/

Eisenmajer, R., Prior, M., Leekham, S., Wing, L., Gould, J., Welham, M., & Ong, B. (1996). Comparison of clinical symptoms in Autism and Asperger's disorder. *Journal of the American Academy of Child and Adolescent Psychiatry, 35*, 1523–1531.

Eldar, E., Talmor, R., & Wolf-Zukerman, T. (2010). Successes and difficulties in the individual inclusion of children with autism spectrum disorder (ASD) in the eyes of their coordinators. *International Journal of Inclusive Education, 14*(1), 97–114.

Ellis, C. (2009). *Revision: Autoethnographic reflections on life and work*. Walnut Creek, CA: Alta Mira.

Ensign, J. (2000). Defying the stereotypes of special education: Home school students. *Peabody Journal of Education, 75*(1–2), 147–158.

Ewart, K. H. (2002). *Parents' experience of having a child with autism* (Unpublished doctor of philosophy thesis). California School of Professional Psychology, Fresno, CA.

Feinberg, E., & Vacca, J. (2000). The drama and trauma of creating policies on autism: Critical issues to consider in the new millenium. *Focus on Autism and Other Developmental Disabilities, 15*, 130–138.

Ferraro, C. A. (2008). *A study of factors contributing toward parental efficacy of the cognitive, behavioral, and social development of autistic children* (Unpublished Doctor of Philosophy in Educational Leadership thesis). TUI University: Cypress, CA.

Fombonne, E. (2003). Epidemiological surveys of autism and other pervasive developmental disorders: An update. *Journal of Autism and Developmental Disorders, 33*(4), 365–382.

Fombonne, E. (2009). *Autism and PDDs: Current rates and trends over time in prevalence*. Paper presented at the Asia Pacific Autism Conference 09, Sydney, Australia.

Fombonne, E., Zakarian, R., Bennett, A., Meng, L., & McLean-Heywood, D. (2006). Pervasive developmental disorders in Montreal, Quebec Canada: Prevalence and links with immunizations. *Pediatrics, 118*(1), e139–e150.

Ford, J. (2007). Educational supports for students with disabilities and significant behavioural challenges: Teacher perceptions. *Australasian Journal of Special Education, 31*(2), 109–127.

Forlin, C. (1995). *Concerns and beliefs about inclusive education: Appraisal of stress and coping* (Unpublished doctor of philosophy thesis). University of Western Australia, Perth

Forlin, C. (2004). Promoting inclusivity in Western Australian schools. *International Journal of Inclusive Education, 8*(2), 185–202.

Forlin, C. (2005). Sustaining inclusive practices in primary school communities. In C. Newell (Ed.), *Disability in education: Context, curriculum and culture* (pp. 13–21). Australia: Australian College of Educators.

Forlin, P. R., & Forlin, C. (1998). The constitutional and legislative framework for inclusive education in Australia. *Australian Journal of Education, 42*, 204–217.

Forlin, C., Keen, M., & Barrett, E. (2008). The concerns of mainstream teachers: Coping with inclusivity in an Australian context. *International Journal of Disability, Development and Education, 55*(3), 251–264.

Francis, K. (2005). Autism interventions: A critical update. *Developmental Medicine and Child Neurology, 47*(7), 493–499.

Frederickson, N., Jones, A. P., & Lang. J. (2010). Inclusive provision options for pupils on the autistic spectrum. *Journal of Research in Special Educational Needs, 10*, 63–73.

Frith, U. (1989). *Autism: Explaining the enigma*. Oxford, UK: Blackwell.

Fuchs, D., & Fuchs, L. S. (1994). Inclusive schools movement and the radicalisation of special education reform. *Exceptional Children, 60*(4), 294–309.

Fulcher, G. (1993). Schools and contests: A reframing of effective schools debate? In R. Slee (Ed.), *Is there a desk with my name on it? The politics of integration* (pp. 125–138). London: The Falmer Press.

Gargiulo, R. M., & Metcalf, D. (2013). *Teaching in today's inclusive classrooms: A universal design for learning approach*. Belmont, CA: Cengage Learning.

Gibbs, V. Aldridge, F., Chandler, F., Witzlsperger, E., & Smith, K. (2012). Brief report: An exploratory study comparing diagnostic outcomes for autism spectrum disorders under DSM-IV-TR with the proposed DSM-five revision. *Journal of Autism and Developmental Disorders, 42*, 1750–1756.

Gillberg, C., & Billstedt, E. (2000). Autism and Asperger syndrome: Coexistence with other clinical disorders. *Acta Psychiatrica Scandinavica, 102*(5), 321–330.

Glasson, E., Bolton, H., Chauvel, P., Cohen, D., Cook, H., Dixon, G.,. . . Wray, J. (2006) . *WA Register for autism spectrum disorders–2004 Report.* Perth, Western Australia.

Goldfarb, N., Levy, D., & Meyers, D. (1972). The mother speaks to her schizophrenic child: Language in childhood schizophrenia. *Psychiatry, 35*, 217–226.

Goldfarb, W., Goldfarb, N., & Scholl, M. (1966). The speech of mothers of schizophrenic children. *American Journal of Psychiatry, 122*, 1220–1227.

Grandin, T., & Duffy, K. (2004). *Developing talents: Careers for individuals with Asperger syndrome and High-Functioning Autism.* Shawnee Mission, KS: Autism Asperger Publishing Co.

Granpeesheh, D., Dixon, D. R., Tarbox, J., Kaplan, A. M., & Wilke, A. E. (2009). Effects of age and treatment intensity on behavioral intervention outcomes for children with autism spectrum disorders. *Research in Autism Spectrum Disorders, 3*(4), 1014–1022.

Gray, D. E. (1993). Perceptions of stigma: The parents of autistic children. *Sociology of Health & Illness, 15*(1), 102–120.

Gray, D. E. (1994). Coping with autism: Stresses and strategies. *Sociology of Health & Illness, 16*(3), 275–300.

Gray, D. E. (1998). *Autism and the family.* Springfield, IL: Charles C. Thomas.

Gray, D. E. (2002a). 'Everybody just freezes. Everybody is just embarrassed': Felt and enacted stigma among parents of children with high functioning autism. *Sociology of Health & Illness, 24*(6), 734–749.

Gray, D. E. (2002b). Ten years on: A longitudinal study of families of children with autism. *Journal of Intellectual & Developmental Disability, 27*(3), 215–222.

Gray, D. E. (2006). Coping over time: The parents of children with autism. *Journal of Intellectual Disability Research, 50*(12), 970–976.

Gray, D. E., & Holden, W. J. (1992). Psychosocial well-being among the caregivers of children with autism. *Australia and New Zealand Journal of Developmental Disabilities, 18*, 83–93.

Grayson, J. (2004). *The maternal experience of caring for an adult with autism.* Dissertation Abstracts International. Vol. 64 (9-B), 4678, US: University Microfilms International.

Green, G. (1996). Early behavioural intervention for autism: What does the research tell us? In C. Maurice (Ed.), *Behavioural intervention for young children with autism* (pp. 29–44). Austin, TX: Pro-Ed.

Gresham, F., Beebe-Frankenberger, M., & MacMillan, D. (1999). A selective review of treatments for children with autism: Description and methodological considerations. *School Psychology Review, 28*(4), 559–575.

Guthrie, R., & Waldeck, E. (2008). Disability standards and inclusiveness in education: A review of the Australian landscape. *International Journal of Discrimination and the Law, 9*, 133–162.

Hagner, D., & Cooney, B. F. (2005). "I Do That for Everybody": Supervising employees with autism. *Focus on Autism and Other Developmental Disabilities, 20*(2), 91–97.

Happe, F. (2009). *Is it time to give up on a single explanation for the autistic triad?* Paper presented at the Asia Pacific Autism Conference 2009, Sydney, Australia.

Happe, F., Ehlers, S., Fletcher, P., Frith, U., Johansson, M., Gillberg, C., . . . Frith, C. (1996). "Theory of mind" in the brain: Evidence from a PET scan study of Asperger syndrome. *Neuroreport, 8*, 197–201.

Hardman, M. L., Drew, C. J., & Egan, M. W. (1995). *Human exceptionality: Society, school and family.* Needham Heights, MA: Allyn & Bacon.

Hare, D. J., Pratt, C., Burton, M., Bromley, J., & Emerson, E. (2004). The health and social care needs of family carers supporting adults with autistic spectrum disorders. *Autism, 8*, 425–444.

Harrington, C., Foster, M., Rodger, S., & Asburner, J. (2013). *The educational trajectories of students with ASD: Mainstream school experiences over time.* Paper presented at the Asia Pacific Autism Conference 2013, Adelaide, Australia.

Harris Interactive. (2008, December 5). *Easter seals' living with autism study.* Retrieved from http://www.actforAutism.org

Harrison, J. E., & Bolton, P. F. (1997). Annotation: Tuberous Sclerosis. *Journal of Child Psychology and Psychiatry, 38*, 603–614.

Hartley, S. L., Barker, E. T., Seltzer, M. M., Floyd, F., Greenberg, J., Orsmond, G., & Bolt, D. (2010). The relative risk and timing of divorce in families of children with an autism spectrum disorder. *Journal of Family Psychology, 24*(4), 449–457.

Hastings, R. (2008). Stress in parents of children with autism. In E. McGregor, M. Nunez, D. Cebula, & J. Gomez (Eds.), *An integrated view from neuroscience, clinical, and intervention research* (pp. 303–324). London: Blackwell.

Hastings, R., & Brown, T. (2002). Behaviour problems of children with autism, parental self-efficacy, and mental health. *American Journal of Mental Retardation, 107*, 222–232.

Hastwell, J., Harding, J., Baron Cohen, S., & Martin, N. (2012). Giving Cambridge University students with Asperger syndrome a voice. A qualitative, interview-based study towards developing a model of best practice for students with Asperger syndrome/Autism in higher education. *Good Autism Practice (GAP), 13*(1), 56–63.

Hastwell, J., Harding, J., Martin, N., & Baron-Cohen, S. (2013, June). *Asperger syndrome student project, 2009–12: Final project report.* Retrieved from University of Cambridge, Disability Resource Centre website: http://www.admin.cam.ac.uk/univ/disability/asperger/project.html

Heflin, J., & Simpson, R. L. (1998). Interventions for children and youth with autism: Prudent choices in a world of exaggerated claims and empty promises. Part II: Legal policy analysis and recommendations for selecting interventions and treatments. *Focus on autism and other devlopmental disabilities, 13*(4), 212–220.

Heinrichs, R. (2003). *Perfect targets: Asperger syndrome and bullying: Practical solutions for surviving the social world.* Shawnee Mission, KS: Autism Asperger Publishing.

Henry, S., & Myles, B. S. (2007). *The comprehensive autism planning system (CAPS) for individuals with Asperger syndrome, autism and related disabilities: Integrating best practices throughout the Student's Day.* Shawnee Mission, KS: Autism Asperger Publishing Co.

Herbert, M., Ziegler, D., Makris, N., Filipek, P., Kemper, T., Normandin, J., . . . Caviness, V. (2004). Localization of white matter volume increase in autism and developmental language disorder. *Annals of Neurology, 55*, 530–540.

Herbert, M., Ziegler, D., Deutsch, C. K., O'Brien, L., Kennedy, D., Filpek, P., . . . Caviness, V. (2005). Brain asymmetries in autism and developmental language disorder: A nested whole-brain analysis. *Brain, 128*(1), 213–226.

Hess, K., Morrier, M., Heflin, L., & Ivey, M. (2008). Autism treatment survey: Services received by children with autism spectrum disorders in public school classrooms. *Journal of Autism and Developmental Disorders, 38*(5), 961–971.

Higgins, D. J., Bailey, S. R., & Pearce, J. C. (2005). Factors associated with functioning style and coping strategies of families with a child with an autism spectrum disorder. *Autism, 9*(2), 125–137.

Horner, R. H., Carr, E., Halle, J., McGee, G., Odom, S., & Wolery, M. (2005). The use of single-subject research to identify evidence-based practice in special education. *Exceptional Children, 71*(2), 165–179.

Howlin, P. (1997). Prognosis in autism: Do specialist treatments affect long-term outcomes? *European Child & Adolescent Psychiatry, 6*, 55–72.

Howlin, P. (1998). Practitioner review: Psychological and educational treatments for autism. *Journal of Child Psychology and Psychiatry, 39*(3), 307–322.

Howlin, P. (2009). *Outcome for adults with autism spectrum disorders.* Paper presented at the Asia Pacific Autism Conference 09, Sydney, Australia.

Howlin, P., & Asgharian, A. (1999). The diagnosis of autism and Asperger syndrome: Findings from a survey of 770 families. *Developmental Medicine and Child Neurology, 41*, 834–839.

Howlin, P., Cantwell, D. P., Marchant, R., Berger, M., & Rutter, M. (1973). Analyzing mothers' speech to young autistic children: A methodological study. *Journal of Abnormal Child Psychology, 1*, 317–339.

Howlin, P., & Moore, A. (1997). Diagnosis of autism: A survey of over 1200 patients in the UK. *Autism, 1*, 135–162.

Howlin, P., & Moss, P. (2012). Adults with autism spectrum disorders. *The Canadian Journal of Psychiatry, 57*(5), 275–283.

Howlin, P., & Rutter, M. (1987). *Treatment of autistic children*. Chichester, U.K: Wiley.

Howard, H. S., Sparkman, C. R., Cohen, G. C., Green, G., & Stanislaw, H. (2005). A comparison of intensive behavior analytic and eclectic treatments for young children with autism. *Research in Developmental Disabilities, 26*, 359–383.

Humphrey, N., & Lewis, S. (2008a). 'Make me normal'. The views and experiences of pupils on the autistic spectrum in mainstream secondary schools. *Autism, 12*, 23–46.

Humphrey, N., & Lewis, S. (2008b). What does "inclusion" mean for pupils on the autistic spectrum in mainstream secondary schools? *Journal of Research in Special Education Needs*, 8, 132–140.

Humphrey, N., & Symes W. (2010). Perceptions of social support and experience of bullying among pupils with autistic spectrum disorders in mainstream secondary schools. *European Journal of Special Needs Education, 25*(1), 77–91.

Hurbutt, K., & Chalmers, L. (2004). Employment and adults with Asperger syndrome. *Focus on Autism and Other Developmental Disabilities, 19*(4), 215–223.

Institute of Medicine - Committee on Immunization Safety. (2004). *Immunization safety review: Vaccines and autism, "Executive Summary"*. Washington, DC: National Acacemies Press.

Iovannone, R., Dunlap, G., Huber, H., & Kincaid, D. (2003). Effective educational practices for students with autism spectrum disorders. *Focus on Autism and Other Developmental Disabilities, 18*(3), 150–165.

Itard, J. M. G. (1962). *The wild boy of Aveyron*. New York, NY: Appleton Century Crofts. (Original work published 1801).

Jamain, S., Betaneur, C., Giros, B., Leboyer, M., & Bourgeron, T. (2003). Genetics of autism: From genome scans to candidate genes. *Medecine Sciences. (Paris), 19*(11), 1081–1090.

James, R., Baldwin, G., Coates, H., Krause, K., & McInnis, C. (2004). *Analysis of equity groups in higher education 1991–2002*. Canberra: Commonwealth of Australia. Department of Education, Science and Training.

Jenkins, H. (2002). *A choice for all: West Australian independent schools' responses to students with disabilities and learning difficulties*. Perth, Western Australia: Association of Independent Schools of Western Australia.

Jenkins, H. (2005). *Building inclusive secondary schools: Barriers and facilitators in the West Australian context*. Perth, WA: Curtin University of Technology.

Jenkinson, J. (2001). *Special education: A matter of choice* (1st ed., Vol. 46). Melbourne: ACER.

Jennes-Coussens, M., Magill-Evans, J., & Koning, C. (2006). The quality of life of young men with Asperger syndrome: A brief report. *Autism, 10*, 403–414.

Jindal-Snape, D., Douglas, W., Topping, K. J., Kerr, C., & Smith, E. F. (2005). Effective education for children with autism spectrum disorder: Perceptions of parents and professionals. *International Journal of Special Education, 20*(1), 77–87.

Johnson, E., & Hastings, R. (2002). Facilitating factors and barriers to the implementation of intensive home-based behavioural intervention for young children with autism. *Child Care Health and Development, 28*(2), 123–129.

Jones, G. (2006). Department of education and skills/Department of health good practice guidance on the education of children with autism spectrum disorder. *Child: Care, Health & Development, 32*(5), 543–552.

Jordan, R. (2004). Meeting the needs of children with autistic spectrum disorders in the early years. *Australian Journal of Early Childhood, 29*, 1–7.

Jordan, R. (2005). Managing autism and Asperger's syndrome in current educational provision. *Pediatric Rehabilitation, 8*(2), 104–112.

Jones, M., & Basser Marks, L. (1999). Disability, rights and law in Australia. In M. Jones & L. Basser Marks (Eds.), *Disability, diversability and legal change* (Vol. 56, pp. 189–208). The Hague: Kluwer Law International.

Just, M., Cherkassky, V., Keller, T., & Minshew, J. (2004). Cortical activation and synchronization during sentence comprehension in high-functioning autism: Evidence of underconnectivity. *Brain, 127*(8), 1811–1821.

Kanner, L. (1943). *Autistic disturbance of affective contact*. Retrieved from http://www.aspires-relationships.com/articles autistic disturbances of affective contact.htm

Kanner, L. (1973). Early infantile autism, 1943–1955. In L. Kanner (Ed.), *Child psychosis: Initial studies and new insights* (pp. 91–101). Washington, DC: Winston.

Kasari, C., Freeman, F. N., Bauminger, N., & Marvin, C. A. (1999). Parental perspectives on inclusion: Effects of autism and Down syndrome. *Journal of Autism and Developmental Disorders, 29*(4), 297–305.

Kavale, K. A., & Forness, S. R. (2000). History, rhetoric and reality: Analysis of the inclusion debate. *Remedial and Special Education, 21*, 279–313.

Keel, J. H., Mesibov, G., & Woods, A. V. (1997). TEACCH supported employment programme. *Journal of Autism and Developmental Disorders, 27*, 3–10.

Kemper, T., & Bauman, M. (1993). The contribution of neuropathologic studies to the understanding of autism. *Neurologic Clinics, 11*, 175–187.

Kerbeshian, J., Burd, L., & Avery, K. (2001). Pharmacotherapy of autism: A review and clinical approach. *Journal of Developmental & Physical Disabilities, 13*, 199–228.

Kidd, T., & Kaczmarek, E. (2010). The experiences of mothers home educating their children with autism spectrum disorder. *Issues in Educational Research, 20*(3), 257–275.

Kim, J. A., Szatmari, P., Bryson, S. E., Streiner, D. L., & Wilson, F. J. (2000). The prevalence of anxiety and mood problems among children with autism and Asperger syndrome. *Autism, 4*(2), 117–132.

King, G., Zwaigenbaum, L., King, S., Baxter, D., Rosenbaum, P., & Bates, A. (2005). A qualitative investigation of changes in the belief systems of families of children with autism and Down syndrome. *Child: Care, Health & Development, 32*(3), 353–369.

Kirby, D. (2005). *Evidence of harm: Mercury in vaccines and the autism epidemic: A medical controversy.* New York, NY: St Martin's Press.

Konstantareas, M. M., & Homatidis, S. (1988). Stress and differential parental involvement in families of autistic and learning disabled children. In E. D. Hibbs (Ed.), *Children and families: Studies in prevention and intervention* (pp. 321–336). Madison, WI: International Universities Press.

Knott, F., & Taylor, A. (2013). Life at university with Asperger syndrome: A comparison of student and staff perspectives. *International Journal of Inclusive Education, 18*(4), 411–426. doi: 10.1080/13603116.2013.781236

Kohler, F. (1999). Examining the services received by young children with autism and their families: A survey of parent responses. *Focus on Autism and Other Developmental Disorders, 14*, 150–158.

Koshino, H., Carpenter, P., Minshew, N., Cherkassky, V., Keller, T., & Just, M. (2005). Functional connectivity in an fMRI working memory task in high-functioning autism. *Neuroimage, 24*, 810–821.

Kumon Australia & New Zealand. (2007). *The Kumon method.* Retrieved May 5, 2009 from http://www.kumon.com.au/programmes

Lake, J., & Billingsley, B. (2000). An analysis of factors that contribute to parent-school conflict in special education. *Remedial & Special Education, 21*, 240–252.

Lamont, L. (2004, June 1). When love is not enough. *Sydney Morning Herald.* Retrieved from http://www.smh.com.au/articles/2004/05/31/1085855494917. html

Larkey, S. (2005). *Making it a success: Practical strategies and worksheets for teaching students with autism spectrum disorder.* London: Jessica Kingsley Publishers.

Laluvein, J. (2010). School inclusion and the 'community of practice'. *International Journal of Inclusive Education, 14*(1), 35–48.

Lawson, W. (2009). *The changing face of autism spectrum.* Paper presented at the Autism: The Whole Child AISWA Conference, Fremantle, WA.

Lazarus, R. S., & Folkman, S. (1984). *Stress, appraisal and coping.* New York, NY: Springer Publishing Company.

Leblanc, L., Richardson, W., & Burns, K. A., (2009). Autism spectrum disorder and the inclusive classroom. teacher education and special education. *The Journal of the Teacher Education Division of the Council for Exceptional Children, 32*(2), 166–179.

Le Couteur, A., Bailey, A., Goode, S., Pickles, A., Roberson, S., & Gottesman, I. (1996). A broader phenotype of autism: The clinical spectrum in twins. *Journal of Child Psychology and Psychiatry, 37*(7), 785–801.

Leach, D., & Duffey, M. L. (2009). Supporting students with autism spectrum disorders in inclusive settings. *Intervention in School and Clinic, 45*, 31–37.

Leighton, D. J. (1969). Casework with the parents of autistic children. *British Journal of Psychiatric Social Work, 10*, 17–21.

Lewin, C. (2005). Elementary quantitative methods. In B. Somekh & C. Lewin (Eds.), *Research methods in the social sciences* (pp. 215–225). London: Sage.

Lewis, A. (2009). *Autism services directory 2009*. Perth: Therapy Focus Inc.

Lindsay, K. (2004). 'Asking for the moon'? A critical assessment of Australian disability discrimination laws in promoting inclusion for students with disabilities. *International Journal of Inclusive Education, 8*(4), 373–390.

Little, L. (2002). Middle-Class mothers' perceptions of peer and sibling victimization among children with Asperger syndrome and non-verbal learning disorders. *Issues in Comprehensive Pediatric Nursing, 25*, 43–57.

Lord, C., & McGee, J. P. (2001). *Educating children with autism*. Washington, DC: National Academy Press.

Lord, C., Risi, S., DiLavore, P., Shulman, C., Turm, A., & Pickles, A. (2006). Autism from 2 to 9 years of age. *Archives of General Psychiatry, 63*(6), 649–701.

Lovaas, O. I. (1987). Behavioural treatment and normal educational and intellectual functioning in young autistic children. *Journal of Consulting and Clinical Psychology, 55*, 3–9.

Lovaas, O. I. (2003). *Teaching individuals with developmental delays*. Austin, TX: Pro-ed.

Luna, B., Minshew, N., Garver, K., Lazar, N., Thulborn, K., Eddy, W., & Sweeney, J. (2002). Neocortical system abnormalities in autism: An fMRI study of spatial working memory. *Neurology, 59*, 834–840.

Lynch, S. L., & Irvine, A. N. (2009). Inclusive education and best practice for children with autism spectrum disorder: An integrated approach. *International Journal of Inclusive Education, 13*(8), 845–859.

MacDermott, S. (2008). *Can you help us to help you? Autism school-age family needs report*. Perth: A Joint project by The State Child Development Centre, the Autism Association of Western Australia & Therapy Focus Inc.

MacDermott, S., Williams, K., Ridley, G., Glasson, E., & Wray, J. (2007). *The prevalence of autism in Australia. Can it be established from existing data? A report for the Australian Advisory Board on autism spectrum disorders.* Retrieved Feb 22, 2008 from www.Autismaus.com.au

Madsen, K., Lauritsen, M., Pedersen, C., Thorsen, P., Plesner, A., Anderson, H., & Mortensen, P. (2003). Thimerosal and the occurrence of autism: Negative ecological evidence from Danish population-based data. *Pediatrics, 112*(3), 604–606.

Madsen, K., Vestergaard, M., Schendel, D., Wohlfahrt, J., Thorsen, P., Schendel, D., . . . Olsen, J. (2002). A population based study of measles, mumps and rubella vaccination and autism. *New England Journal of Medicine, 347*, 1477–1482.

Magiati, I., Charman, T., & Howlin, P. (2007). A two-year prospective follow-up study of community-based early intensive behavioural intervention and specialist nursery provision for children with autism spectrum disorders. *Journal of Child Psychology and Psychiatry, 48*(8), 803–812.

Mandell, D., Novak, M., & Zubritsky, C. (2005). Factors associated with the age of diagnosis among children with autism spectrum disorders. *Pediatrics, 116*(6), 1480–1486.

Mandell, D. S., Ittenback, R. F., Levy, S. E., & Pinto-Martin, J. A. (2007). Disparities in diagnoses received prior to a diagnosis of autism spectrum disorder. *Journal of Autism and Developmental Disorders, 37*, 1795–1802.

Marcus, L., Kunce, L. J., & Schopler, E. (1997). Working with families. In D. J. Cohen & F. R. Volkmar (Eds.), *Handbook of autism and development disorders* (pp. 631–649). New York, NY: John Wiley & Sons.

Marcus, L. M., Garfinkle, A., & Wolery, M. (2001). Issues in early diagnosis and intervention with young children with autism. In E. Schloper, C. Yirmiya, C. Shulman, & L. M. Marcus (Eds.), *The research basis for autism intervention* (pp. 171–185). New York, NY: Kluwer Academic.

Marshall, V., & Long, B. C. (2010). Coping processes as revealed in the stories of mothers of children with autism. *Qualitative Health Research, 20*(1), 105–116.

Marks, S. U., Shaw-Hegwer, J., Schrader, C., Longaker, C., Peters, I., Powers, F., & Levine, M. (2003). Instructional management tips for teachers of students with autism spectrum disorder (ASD). *Teaching Exceptional Children, 35*, 50–55.

Matson, J. L., Hattier, M. A., & Williams, L. W. (2012). How does relaxing the algorithm for autism affect DSM-V prevalence rates? *Journal of Autism and Developmental Disorders, 42*, 1549–1556.

Maurice, C. (1993). *Let me hear your voice: A family's triumph over autism*. New York, NY: Ballantine Books.

Maurice, C., Green, G., & Luce, S. (1996). *Behavioural intervention for young children with autism*. Texas, TX: Pro-ed.

Mawhood, L., & Howlin, P. (1999). The outcome of a supported employment scheme for high-functioning adults with autism or Asperger syndrome. *Autism, 3*, 229–254.

McCarthy, J. (2009). *Mother warriors: A nation of parents healing autism against all odds*. New York, NY: Penguin Group.

McCubbin, H. I., & Patterson, J. M. (1983). The family stress process: The double ABCX model of adjustment and adaptation. In H. I. McCubbin, M. B. Sussman, & J. M. Patterson (Eds.), *Social stress and the family: Advances and developments in family stress theory and research* (pp. 7–37). New York, NY: The Haworth Press.

McDonald, J. (2010). *Seeking progressive fit: A constructivist grounded theory and autoethnographic study investigating how parents deal with the education of their child with an autism spectrum disorder (ASD) over time* (Unpublished Doctor of Philosophy Thesis). The University of Western Australia, Perth.

McDonald, J., & Lopes, E. (2012). How parents home educate their children with an autism spectrum disorder with the support of the schools of isolated and distance education. *International Journal of Inclusive Education, 18*(1), 1–17. doi:10.1080/13603116.2012.751634

McEachin, J. J., Smith, T., & Lovaas, O. I. (1993). Long-term outcome for children with autism who received early intensive behavioural interventions. *American Journal of Mental Retardation, 97*, 359–372.

McPartland, J. C., Reichow, B., & Volkmar, F. R. (2012). Sensitivity and specificity of proposed DSM-5 diagnostic criteria for autism spectrum disorder. *Journal of the American Academy of Child and Adolescent Psychiatry, 51*(4), 368–382.

Medlin, R. G. (2000). Homeschooling and the question of socialization. *Peabody Journal of Education, 75*(1–2), 107–123.

Mesibov, G. (1993). Treatment outcome is encouraging. *American Journal on Mental Retardation, 97*(4), 379–380.

Mesibov, G., & Shea, V. (1996). Full inclusion and students with autism. *Journal of Autism and Developmental Disorders, 26*(3), 337–346.

Ministry of Health. (2008). *New Zealand autism spectrum disorder guideline*. Wellington: Ministries of Health and Education.

Moreno, J., Aguilera, A., & Saldana, D. (2008). Do Spanish parents prefer special schools for their children with autism. *Education and Training in Developmental Disabilities, 43*(2), 162–173.

Morewood, G. D., Humphrey, N., & Symes, W. (2011). Mainstreaming autism: Making it work. *GAP, 12*(2), 62–68.

Moses, K. (1987). *The impact of a child's disability: The parent's struggle*. Evanston, IL: Ways Magazine.

Mudford, O. C., Martin, N. T., Eikeseth, S., & Bibby, P. (2001). Parent-managed behavioural treatment for preschool children with autism: Some characteristics of UK programs. *Research in Developmental Disabilities, 22*, 173–182.

Myles, B. S. (2005). *Children and youth with Asperger syndrome*. California, CA: Corwin Press.

Myles, B. S., & Adreon, D. (2001). *Asperger syndrome and adolescence. Practical solutions for school success*. Kansas, KS: AAPC.

Myles, B. S., Swanson, T. C., Holverstott, J., & Duncan, M. (2007). *Autism spectrum disorders: A handbook for parents and professionals*. Westport, CT: Praeger Publishers.

National Research Council. (2001). *Educating children with autism*. Washington, DC: National Academy Press.

National Autistic Soceity. (2014). *Autism act 2009*. Retrieved April 19, 2014 from http://www.autism.org.uk/working-with/autism-strategy/the-autism-strategy-an-overview/autism-act-2009.aspx

Newell, C. (1995). Consumer reflections on the disability discrimination act. *Australian Disability Review, 2*, 60–65.

Newell, C. (2005). From other to us: When ethics and law meet education. In C. Newell & T. R. Parmenter (Eds.), *Disability in education: Context, curriculum and culture* (pp. 54–59) Canberra: Australian College of Educators.

Niehart, M. (2011, July–August). *Helping Gifted Children with autism spectrum disorders Succeed.* Publication of papers from the *11th Asia Pacific Conference on Giftedness,* Asia Pacific Federation of the World Council for Gifted and Talented Children, Sydney.

Nieiminen-von Wendt T., Metsahonkala, I., Kulomaki, T., Aalto, S., Autti T., Vanhala, R., & Wendt, L. (2003). Changes in cerebral blood flow in Asperger syndrome during theory of mind tasks presented by the auditory route. *European Child & Adolescent Psychiatry, 12*, 178–189.

Nixon, S. (2008, September 10). Early insights into autism hold promise of better lives. *The Sydney Morning Herald*, p. 7.

Noterdaeme, M., Amorosa, H., Mildenberger, K., Sitter, S., & Minow, F. (2001). Evaluation of attentional problems in children with autism and children with specific language disorder. *European Child & Adolescent Psychiatry, 10*(1), 58–66.

Nussbaum, M. (2009). The capabilities of people with cognitive disabilities. *Metaphilosophy, 40(*3–4), 331–351.

O'Brien, M., & Daggett, J. A. (2006). *Beyond the autism diagnosis: A professional's guide to helping families.* Baltimore, MD: Paul H. Brookes Publishing Co.

O'Donoghue, T. A. (1998). The education of children with intellectual disabilities in Western Australia: An historical perspective. *Journal of Educational Administration and History, 30*(1), 1–16.

O'Donoghue, T. A., & Chalmers, R. (2000). How teachers manage their work in inclusive classrooms. *Teaching and Teacher Education, 16*, 889–904.

O'Hanlon, M., & Firestone, B. (2007, November 14). Beyond early diagnosis of autism. *Washington Times*. Retrieved from http://nl.newsbank.com/nl-search/we/Archives

Ohta, M., Nagai, Y., Hara, H., & Sasaki, M. (1987). Parental perception of behavioural symptoms in Japanese autistic children. *Journal of Autism and Developmental Disorders, 17*(4), 549–563.

Oliver, M. (1990).*The politics of disablement.* Basingstoke: Macmillan.

Oliver, M. (1996). *Understanding disability*. Basingstoke: Macmillan.

Oliver, M., & Barnes, C. (2010). Disability studies, disabled people and the struggle for inclusion. *British Journal of Sociology of Education, 31*(5), 547–560.

Olley, G. (1999). Curriculum for students with autism. *School Psychology Review, 28*(4), 595–607.

Olweus, D. (1993). *Bullying at school.* Oxford: Blackwell Publishers.

O'Reilly, B., & Smith, S. (2008). *Australian autism handbook.* Edgecliff, NSW: Jane Curry Publishing.

Painter, S. (2009, August 3). Autism centre to help children communicate. *The West Australian*, pp. 1, 5.

Palm Consulting Group. (2005). *National autism forum.* Canberra: Parliament House.

Palmer, A. (2006). *Realizing the college dream with autism or Asperger syndrome: A parent's guide to student success.*Philadelphia, PA: Jessica Kingsley Publishers.

Parner, E.T., Thorsen, P., Dixon, G., de Klerk, N., Leonard, H., Nassar, N., . . . Glasson, E.J. (2011). A comparison of autism prevalence trends in Denmark and Western Australia. *Journal of Autism and Developmental Disorders, 41*(12), 1601–1608. doi: 10.1007/s10803-011-1186-0

Parsons, S., Guldberg, K., MacLeod, A., Jones, G., Prunty, A., & Balfe, T. (2011). International review of the evidence on best practice in educational provision for children on the autism spectrum. *European Journal of Special Needs Education, 26*(1), 47–63.

Parsons, S., & Lewis. A. (2010). The home-education of children with special needs or disabilities in the UK: Views of parents from an online survey. *International Journal of Inclusive Education, 14*(1), 67–86.

Patterson, J. M. (1988). Families experiencing stress. I. The family adjustment and adaptation response model. II. Applying the FAAR model to health-related issues for intervention and research. *Family Systems Medicine, 6*(2), 202–237.

Patwell, M., & Herzog, A. (2000). Bridging the gap: A disability services perspective on transition. *Disability Studies Quarterly, 20*(4).

Pearce, M., & Forlin, C. (2005). Challenges and potential solutions for enabling inclusion in secondary schools. *Australasian Journal of Special Education, 29*, 93–105.

Perryman, H. P. (2005). Parental reaction to the disabled child: Implications for family courts. *Family Court Review, 43*(4), 596–606.

Pierce, K., Muller, R., Ambrose, J., Allen, G., & Courchesne, E. (2001). Face processing occurs outside the fusiform "face area" in autism: Evidence from functional MRI. *Brain, 124*, 2059–2073.

Posey, D. J., & McDougle, C. (2000). The pharmacotherapy of target symptoms associated with autistic disorder and other pervasive developmental disorders. *Harvard Review of Psychiatry, 8*, 45–63.

Powell, S. (2003). *Special teaching in higher education: Successful strategies for access and inclusion.* Herndon, VA: Stylus Publishing LLC.

Powers, M. D. (1989). Children with autism and their families. In M. D. Powers (Ed.), *Children with autism: A parent's guide* (pp. 105–139). Bethesda, MD: Woodbine House.

Prior, M., & Roberts, J. (2006). *Early intervention for children with autism spectrum disorders: Guidelines for best practice*. Australian Government Department of Health and Ageing, Australia.

Prior, M., & Roberts J. (2012). *Early intervention for children with autism spectrum disorders: Guidelines for good practice*. Retrieved from Helping Children with Autism (HCWA) website: http://www.dss.gov.au/our-responsibilities/disability-and-carers/program-services/for-people-with-disability/helping-children-with-autism

Probst, P., & Leppert, T. (2008). Brief report: Outcomes of a teacher training program for autism spectrum disorders. *Journal of Autism and Development Disorders, 38*(9), 1791–1796.

Ravet, J. (2011). Inclusive/exclusive? Contradictory perspectives on autism and inclusion: The case for an integrative position. *International Journal of Inclusive Education, 15*(6), 667–682.

Ray, B. D. (1997). *Strengths of their own: Home schoolers across America: Academic achievement, family characteristics, and longitudinal traits.* Salem, OR: National Home Education Research Institute.

Reilly, L. (2004). *How Western Australian parents manage the home schooling of their children with disabilities.* Paper presented at the Australian Association for Research in Education, AARE 2004 International Education Research Conference.

Reilly, L. (2007). *Progressive modification: How parents deal with home schooling their children with intellectual disabilities* (Unpublished Doctor of Philosophy Thesis). University of Western Australia, Perth.

Reilly, L., Chapman, A., & O'Donoghue, T. A. (2002). Home schooling of children with disabilities. *Queensland Journal of Educational Research, 18*, 38–61.

Ring, H., Baron-Cohen, S., Wheelwright, S., Williams, S., Brammer, M., Andrew, C., & Bullmore, E. (1999). Cerebral correlates of preserved cognitive skills in autism: A functional MRI study of embedded figures task performance. *Brain, 122*, 1305–1315.

Robbins, F. R., Dunlap, G., & Plienis, A. J. (1991). Family characteristics, family training and the progress of young children with autism. *Journal of Early Intervention, 15*, 173–184.

Roberts, J. (2004). *A review of the research to identify the most effective models of best practice in the management of children with autism spectrum disorders.* Sydney: Centre for Developmental Disability Studies.

Roberts, J. (2013). *An inclusive whole school capacity building approach.* Paper presented at the Asia Pacific Autism Conference 2013, Adelaide, Australia.

Roberts, J., & Prior, M. (2006). *A review of the research to identify the most effective models of practice in early intervention for children with autism spectrum disorders.* Canberra: Australian Government Department of Health and Ageing.

Rogers, S. (1998). Empirically supported comprehensive treatments for young children with autism. *Journal of Clinical and Child Psychology, 27*, 168–179.

Rose, L., Dunlap, G., & Kincaid, D. (2003). Effective educational practices for students with autism spectrum disorders. *Focus on Autism and Other Developmental Disabilities, 18*, 150–168.

Rosendorff, S. (2007). *Autism spectrum disorder: The secondary school perspective* (Powerpoint Presentation). Perth: Centre for Inclusive Schooling, Department of Education and Training.

Rutter, M. (2005a). Aetiology of autism: Findings and questions. *Journal of Intellectual Disability Research, 49*, 231–238.

Rutter, M. (2005b). Genetic influences and autism. In F. Volkmar (Ed.), *Handbook of autism* (3rd ed.). New York, NY: John Wiley.

Rutter, M. (2005c). Incidence of autism spectrum disorders: Changes over time and their meaning. *Acta Paediatrica, 94*(2), 2–15.
Ryan, S., & Cole, K. R. (2009). From advocate to activist? Mapping the experiences of mothers of children on the autism spectrum. *Journal of Applied Research in Intellectual Disabilities, 22*, 43–53.
Sallows, G. O., & Graupner, T. D. (2005). Intensive behavioural treatment for children with autism: Four-year outcome and predictors. *American Journal of Mental Retardation, 110*(6), 417–438.
Sanders, J. L., & Morgan, S. B. (1997). Family stress and adjustment as perceived by caregivers of children with autism or Down syndrome: Implications for intervention. *Child and Family Behaviour Therapy, 19*(4), 15–32.
Sasson, N. J. (2006). The development of face processing in autism. *Journal of Autism and Developmental Disorders, 36*, 381–394.
Schafer, L. (2006, June 13) . National Program Launched to Combat Divorce Rates in autism Community. *Schafer Autism Report.* Retrieved from schafer@spry net.com
Scheeren, A. M., & Stauder, J. E. A. (2008). Broader autism phenotype in parents of autistic children: Reality or myth? *Journal of Autism and Developmental Disorders, 38*, 276–287.
Schieve, L. A., Blumberg, S. J., Rice, C., Visser, S. N., & Boyle, C. (2007). The relationship between autism and parenting stress. *Pediatrics, 119*, S114–S121.
Schopler, E. (1971). Parents of psychotic children as scapegoats. *Journal of Contemporary Psychotherapy, 4*(4), 17–22.
Schopler, E. (1994). Neurobiologic correlates in the classification and study of autism. In S. H. Broman & J. Grafman (Eds.), *A typical cognitive deficits in developmental disorders: Implications for brain function* (pp. 87–100). Hillsdale, NJ: Erlbaum.
Schopler, E., & Mesibov, G. (1984). Professional attitudes towards parents: A forty year progress report. In E. Schopler & G. Mesibov (Eds.), *The effects of autism on the family* (pp. 3–17). New York, NY: Plenum Press.
Schopler, E., & Mesibov, G. (1986). Introduction to social behavior in autism. In E. Schopler & G. Mesibov (Eds.), *Social behavior in autism* (pp. 1–14). New York, NY: Plenum Press.
Schreibman, L. (1988). Autism: A historical perspective. In L. Schreibman (Ed.), *Autism* (pp. 11–13). Newbury Park, CA: Sage.
Schetter, P., & Lighthall, K. (2009). *Homeschooling the child with autism: Answers to the top questions parents and professionals ask.* San Francisco, CA: Jossey-Bass (A Wiley Imprint).
Seligman, M., & Darling, R. B. (1997). *Ordinary families, special children.* New York, NY: Guildford.
Shaddock, A. (2003). *High functioning students with autism in high school.* An issues paper for the NSW Department of Education's Autism working party.
Shaddock, A. (2005). Students with autism in high schools: A challenge for inclusive practice. In C. Newell & T. R. Parmenter (Eds.), *Disability in education: Context, curriculum and culture (College Year Book 2005)* (pp. 22–36). Deakin West: Australian College of Educators.
Shaddock, A., Smyth King, B., & Giorcelli, L. (2007). *Project to improve the learning outcomes of students with disabilities in the early, middle and post compusory years of schooling.* Barton, ACT: Department of Education, Employment and Workplace Relations.
Sharpe, D. L., & Baker, D. L. (2007). Financial issues associated with having a child with autism. *Journal of Family and Economic Issues, 28*, 247–264
Shean, R. (1993). *Report of the state government taskforce: The education of students with disabilities and specific learning difficulties.* Western Australia: Ministry of Education.
Sheinkopf, S. J., & Siegal, B. (1998). Home-based behavioural treatment of young children with autism. *Journal of Autism and Developmental Disorders, 28*(1), 15–22.
Shore, S. M., & Rastelli, L. G. (2006). *Understanding autism for dummies.* NJ: Wiley Publishing.
Simpson, R. L. (1995). Individualized education programs for students with autism: Including the parents in the process. *Focus on Autistic Behavior, 10*(4), 11–16.
Simpson, R. L. (2004). Finding effective intervention and personnel preparation practices for students with autism spectrum disorders. *Exceptional Children, 70*(2), 135–144.
Simpson, R. L. (2005). Evidence-Based practices and students with autism spectrum disorders. *Focus on Autism and Other Devlopmental Disabilities, 20*(3), 140–150.

Simpson, R. L. (2007). Notes from the field: Effective practices for students with autism spectrum disorders. *The Journal for Vocational Special Needs Education, 29*(2), 33–35.

Simpson, R. L., & LaCava, P. (2007). Autism spectrum disorders. In *The sage encyclopedia of educational psychology* (March 6, 2009 ed.). Retrieved from http://www.ereference.com/research/Article

Simpson, R. L., LaCava, P., & Graner, P. (2004). The no child left behind act (NCLB): Challenges and implications for educators. *Intervention in School and Clinic, 40*(20), 67–75.

Simpson, R. L., de Boer-Ott, S. R., & Smith-Myles, B. (2003). Inclusion of learners with autism spectrum disorders in general education settings. *Topics in Language Disorders, 23*(2), 116–133.

Sivberg, B. (2002). Family system and coping behaviours. *Autism, 6*(4), 397–409.

Singer, G. (2006). Meta-analysis of comparative studies of depression in mothers of children with and without developmental disabilities. *American Journal of Mental Retardation, 111*, 155–169.

Skidmore, D. (2004). *Inclusion: The dynamics of school development.* Buckingham: Open University Press.

Slee, R. (1996). Inclusive schooling in Australia? Not Yet! *Cambridge Journal of Education, 26*(1), 19–32.

Slee, R. (2011). *The irregular school: Exclusion, schooling and inclusive education.* London: Routledge.

Smith, C. P. (2007). Support services for students with Asperger's syndrome in higher education. *College Student Journal, 41*(3), 515–531.

Smith, L. E., Seltzer, M. M., Tager-Flusberg, H., Greenberg, J. S., & Carter, A. S. (2008). A comparative analysis of well-being and coping among mothers of toddlers and mothers of adolescents with ASD. *Journal of Autism and Developmental Disorders, 38*, 876–889.

Smith, S., English, R., & Vasek, D. (2002). Student and parent involvement in the transition process for college freshmen with learning disabilities. *College Student Journal, 36*(4), 491–503.

Smith, T. (1993). Autism. In T. R. Giles (Ed.), *Handbook of effective psychotherapy* (pp. 107–133). New York, NY: Plenum.

Smith, T. (1996). Are other treatments effective? In C. Maurice, G. Green, & S. Luce (Eds.), *Behavioural interventions for young children with autism* (pp. 45–59). Austin, TX: pro-ed.

Smith, T., Groen, A. D., & Wynn, J. W. (2000). Randomized trial of intensive early intervention for children with pervasive developmental disorder. *American Journal of Mental Retardation, 105*(4), 269–285.

Smith, T., & Lovaas, O. I. (1998). Intensive and early behavioural intervention with autism: The UCLA young autism project. *Infants and Young Children, 10*(3), 67–78.

Smith, T., Wynn, J., & Lovaas, O. I. (1996). *Outcome in adulthood.* Paper presented at the Early Intervention Conference, Los Angeles, CA.

Sonne, T. (2009a). *Autism as competitive advantage in business markets.* Paper presented at the Asia Pacific Autism Conference 2009, Sydney, Australia.

Sonne, T. (2009b). *Employing people with an ASD.* Paper presented at the Asia Pacific Autism Conference 2009, Sydney, Australia.

Stanley, A., Beamish, W., & Bryer, F. (2005). Communication between home and school of children with autistic spectrum disorder in primary schools. In B. Bartlett, F. Bryer & D. Roebuck (Eds.), *Stimulating the "action" as participants in participatory research* (pp. 113–122). Griffith, NSW: School of Cognition, Language and Special Education, Griffith University.

Stehli, A. (1991). *The sound of a miracle.* New York, NY: Doubleday.

Stehr-Green, P., Tull, P., Stellfield, M., Mortenson, P., & Simpson, D. (2003). Autism and thimerosal-containing vaccines: Lack of consistent evidence for an association. *American Journal of Preventative Medicine, 25*(2), 101–106.

Stoner, J. B., & Angell, M. E. (2006). Parent perspectives on role engagement: An investigation of parents of children with ASD and their self-reported roles with education professionals. *Focus on Autism and Other Developmental Disabilities, 21*(3), 177–189.

Stoner, J. B., Angell, M. E., House, J. J., & Bock S. J. (2007). Transitions: Perspectives from parents of young children with autism spectrum disorder (ASD). *Journal of Developmental and Physical Disabilities*, 19, 23–39.

Stoner, J. B., Bock, S. J., Thompson, J. R., Angell, M. E., Heyl, B., & Crowley, E. P. (2005). Welcome to our world: Parent perspectives of interactions between parents of young children with ASD and educational professionals. *Focus on Autism and Other Developmental Disabilities, 20*, 39–51.

Strauss, A., & Corbin, J. (1990). *Basics of qualitative research: Grounded theory procedures and techniques.* Newbury Park, CA: Sage.

Strauss, A., & Corbin, J. (1994). Grounded theory methodology: an overview. In N. K. Denzin & Y. S. Lincoln (Eds.), *Handbook of qualitative research* (pp. 273–285). Thousand Oaks, CA: Sage.

Strauss, A., & Corbin, J. (1998). *Basics of qualitative research: Grounded theory procedures and techniques* (2nd ed.). Thousand Oaks, California: Sage Publications.

Symes, W., & Humphrey, N. (2010). Peer-group indicators of social inclusion among pupils with autistic spectrum disorders (ASD) in mainstream secondary schools: A comparative study. *School Psychology International, 30*(4), 478–494.

Synergies Economic Consulting Pty Ltd. (2007, December 11). *Economic costs of autism spectrum disorder. 1–141.* Retrieved from http://aeiou.org.au/blog

Taanila, A., Syrjala, L., Kokkonen, J., & Jarvelin, M. R. (2002). Coping of parents with physically and/or intellectually disabled children. *Child: Care, Health & Development, 28*(1), 73–86.

Takahashi, K. E. (2005). *Needs of families of adolescents with a diagnosis of autism spectrum disorder* (Unpublished Master of Applied Psychology Thesis). Murdoch University, Perth.

Tantam, D. (2000). Psychological disorder in adolescents and adults with Asperger syndrome. *Autism, 4*(1), 47–62.

Taylor, B., Miller, E., Farrington, C., Petroppoulos, M., Favout-Mayaud, I., Li, J., & Waight, P. A. (1999). autism and measles, mumps, and rubella vaccine: No epidemiological evidence for a causal association. *Lancet, 353*, 2026–2029.

Tehee, E., Honan, R., & Hevey, D. (2009). Factors contributing to stress in parents of individuals with Autistic Spectrum Disorders. *Journal of Applied Research in Intellectual Disabilities, 22*, 34–42.

The Hon Bill Shorten, MP. (2009). *Official Opening Asia Pacific Autism Conference 2009.* Sydney: Autism Spectrum Australia (Aspect), Australian Advisory Board on Autism Spectrum Disorders.

Therapy Focus. (2012). *Autism services directory.* Perth: Therapy Focus.

Thomas, A. (1998). *Educating children at home.* London:Cassell.

Toner, M. E. (2009). *Students diagnosed with AD/HD and their first year at university: A theory of developing empowerment* (Unpublished Doctor of Philosophy Thesis). University of Western Australia, Perth.

Trach, J. R., & Rusch, F. R. (1989). Supported employment program evaluation: Evaluating degree of implementation and selected outcomes. *American Journal of Mental Retardation, 94*, 134–140.

Trudgeon, C., & Carr, D. (2007). The impacts of home-based early behavioural intervention programmes on families of children with autism. *Journal of Applied Research in Intellectual Disabilities, 20*, 285–296.

Tullemans, A., & Larkey, S. (2005) . *The essential guide to successful secondary school: A guide for teachers and families of students with ASD.*

Tullemans, A., & Larkey, S. (2005) . *Teacher assistants' big red book of ideas for supporting students with ASD.* Redcliffe, Queensland: Secondary School Solutions.

Turnbull, A. P., & Turnbull, H. R. (2001). *Families, professionals, and exceptionality: Collaborating for empowerment* (4th ed.). Colombus, OH: Merrill Prentice Hall.

Uditsky, B. (1993). From integration to inclusion: The Canadian experience. In R. Slee (Ed.), *Is there a desk with my name on it? The politics of integration.* (pp. 79–92). London: Falmer Press.

University of California. (2009, December 9). New gene linked to autism risk, especially in boys. *ScienceDaily.* Retrieved from http://www.sciencedaily.com/releases/2009/05/090519172155.htm

Valentine, K., Rajkovic, M., Dinning, B., & Thompson, D. (2010). *Post-Diagnosis support for children with autism spectrum disorder, their families and carers. (Occasional Paper No. 35 for Department of Families, Housing, Community Services and Indigenous Affairs, Australian Government).* Sydney, NSW: Social Policy Research Centre, University of NSW.

VanBergeijk, E., Klin, A., & Volkmar, F. (2008). Supporting more able students on the autism spectrum: College and beyond. *Journal of Autism and Developmental Disorders, 38*, 1359–1370.

VanBergeijk, E., & Shrayermman, O. (2005). Asperger syndrome: An enigma for social work. *Journal of Human Behavior in the Social Environment, 2*(1), 23–27.

Victorian Equal Opportunity and Human Rights Commission. (2012). *Held back: The experiences of students with disabilities in Victorian Schools.* Melbourne, Victorian Equal Opportunity and Human Rights Commission.

Wade, J. (2003). Students with Schizophrenia in higher education. In S. Powell (Ed.), *Special teaching in higher education: Successful strategies for access and inclusion* (pp. 185–213). London: Kogan Page Ltd.

Wakefield, A. J., Murch, S. H., Anthony, A., Linnell, J., Casson, D. M., Malik, M., Berelowitz, M., . . . Walker-Smith, J. A. (1998). Ileal-lymphoid-nodular hyperplasia, non-specific colitis, and pervasive developmental disorder in children. (Early Report). *The Lancet, 351*, 637–641.

Waldeck, E., & Guthrie, R. (2004). *Disability discrimination in education and the defence of unjustifiable hardship.* Perth: Curtin Business School, Curtin University of Technology.

Warnock, M. (2005). *Impact. Special educational needs: A new look.* Great Britain: Philsophy of Education Society of Great Britain.

Wehman, P., & Kregel, J. (1985). A supported work approach to competitive employment for individuals with moderate and severe handicaps. *The Journal of The Association for Persons with Severe Handicaps, 10*, 3–11.

Westby, C. (2000). Who are adults with learning disabilities and what do we do about them? *Topics in Language Disorders, 21*(1), 1–14.

Westwood, P. S., & Graham, L. (2003). Inclusion of students with special needs: Benefits and obstacles perceived by teachers in New South Wales and South Australia. *Australia Journal of Learning Disabilities, 8*, 3–15.

Wills, D., & Jackson, R. J. (2000). Inclusive education in Western Australia. The UNESCO education for all 2000 assessment. *Interaction, 14*(2–3), 24–29.

Wing, L. (1976). *Early childhood autism: Clinical, educational and social aspects (2nd ed.).* Oxford, NY: Pergamon.

Wing, L. (1981). Asperger's syndrome: A clinical account. *Psychological Medicine, 11*, 115–130.

Wing, L. (1988). The continuum of autistic characteristics. In E. Schloper & G. Mesibov (Eds.), *Diagnosis and assessment in autism* (pp. 91–110). New York, NY: Plenum.

Wing, L. (1996). *The autistic spectrum.* London: Constable.

Wing, L. (2007). Children with autistic spectrum disorders. In R. Cigman (Ed.), *Included or excluded? The challenge of mainstream for some SEN children* (pp. 23–33). London: Routledge.

Wing, L., & Gould, J. (1979). Severe impairments of social interaction and associated abnormalities in children: Epidemiology and classification. *Journal of Autism and Developmental Disorders, 9*(1), 11–29.

Wolf, L. (2001). College students with AD/HD and other hidden disabilities: Outcomes and interventions. *Annals New York Academy of Sciences, 931*, 385–395.

Wolf, L., Thierfeld Brown, J., & Kukiela Bork, G. (2009). *Students with Asperger syndrome: A guide for college personnel.* Shawnee Mission, KS: Autism Asperger Publishing Co.

Wolff, S., Naraan, S., & Moyes, B. (1988). Personality characteristics of parents of autistic children: A controlled study. *Journal of Child Psychology and Psychiatry, 29*(2), 143–153.

Wong, C. S., Kasari, C., Freeman, S., & Paparella, T. (2007). The acquisition and generalization of joint attention and symbolic play skills in young children with autism. *Research & Practice for Persons with Severe Disabilities, 32*(2), 101–109.

Yell, M., Katsiyannis, A., Drasgow, E., & Herbst, M. (2003). Developing legally correct and educationally appropriate programs for students with autism spectrum disorders. *Focus on Autism and Other Developmental Disabilities, 18*(3), 182–191.

Ypinazar, V., & Pagliano, P. (2004). Seeking inclusive education: Disrupting boundaries of 'special' and 'regular' education. *International Journal of Inclusive Education, 8*(4), 423–442.

INDEX

CPSIA information can be obtained at www.ICGtesting.com
Printed in the USA
BVOW06s0857150615

404381BV00004B/19/P

9 789462 097803